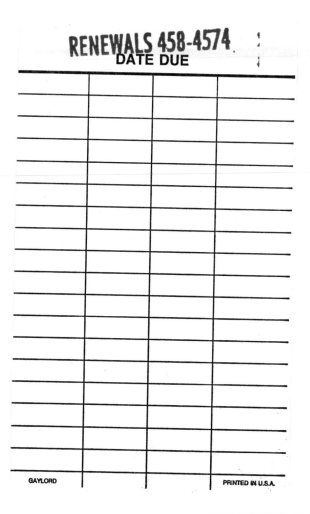

UNU WORLD INSTITUTE FOR DEVELOPMENT ECONOMICS RESEARCH (UNU-WIDER)

was established by the United Nations University as its first
research and training centre and started work in Helsinki, Finland,
in 1985. The purpose of the Institute is to undertake applied research
and policy analysis on structural changes affecting the developing
and transitional economies, to provide a forum for the advocacy of
policies leading to robust, equitable, and environmentally sustainable
growth, and to promote capacity strengthening and training in
the field of economic and social policy-making. Its work is
carried out by staff researchers and visiting scholars in
Helsinki and through networks of collaborating
scholars and institutions around the world.

UNU World Institute for Development Economics Research (UNU-WIDER)
Katajanokanlaituri 6B, FIN-00160 Helsinki, Finland

New Sources of Development Finance

Edited by
A. B. ATKINSON

*A study prepared by the World Institute for Development Economics
Research of the United Nations University (UNU-WIDER)*

OXFORD
UNIVERSITY PRESS

OXFORD

UNIVERSITY PRESS

Great Clarendon Street, Oxford OX2 6DP

Oxford University Press is a department of the University of Oxford.
It furthers the University's objective of excellence in research, scholarship,
and education by publishing worldwide in

Oxford New York

Auckland Bangkok Buenos Aires Cape Town Chennai
Dar es Salaam Delhi Hong Kong Istanbul Karachi Kolkata
Kuala Lumpur Madrid Melbourne Mexico City Mumbai Nairobi
São Paulo Shanghai Taipei Tokyo Toronto

Oxford is a registered trade mark of Oxford University Press
in the UK and in certain other countries

Published in the United States
by Oxford University Press Inc., New York

© United Nations University
World Institute for Development
Economics Research (UNU-WIDER) 2005

British Library Cataloguing in Publication Data

Data available

Library of Congress Cataloging in Publication Data

Data available

ISBN 0–19–927855–5 (hbk.)
ISBN 0–19–927856–3 (pbk.)

1 3 5 7 9 10 8 6 4 2

Typeset by Newgen Imaging Systems (P) Ltd., Chennai, India
Printed in Great Britain
on acid-free paper by
Biddles Ltd., King's Lynn, Norfolk

Preface

Two powerful and divergent forces grip the world at present. On the one hand, the effectiveness of international organizations has been called into question. The role and functioning of the UN are debated. Some nations exhibit frustration with multilateral cooperation, resorting to unilateral action. Solutions are sought in regional groupings rather than in worldwide coordination. On the other hand, the recognition is being cemented that a global economy requires global institutions. International organizations are viewed by many as the key to the free movement of goods, services, and capital. We have seen the adoption of ambitious development targets in the form of the Millennium Development Goals (MDGs). Donor countries have pledged increases in official development assistance.

The tension between these two forces pervades discussion of resources for world development. On the one hand, there is talk of 'donor fatigue', and official development assistance (ODA) has stood still for many years. The amendment to the IMF's Articles approved by the board of governors in 1997 allowing a special allocation of Special Drawing Rights (SDRs) remains unratified. Proposals for any form of global taxation meet immediate opposition from powerful elements in the US Congress. On the other hand, there is widespread appreciation of the need for new resource flows to allow the MDGs to be achieved. There are interesting proposals for new sources of revenue such as a global lottery or the International Finance Facility (IFF). Individuals continue to support development charities. US billionaires are personally funding development and world health activities.

The direction taken at this juncture will depend largely on political events and political decisions. But sober economic analysis has an important role to play. This book reports the work of a project on 'Innovative Sources of Development Finance' undertaken at the request of the UN. As a result of the Five Year Review of the World Summit for Social Development, the UN General Assembly adopted a resolution calling for 'a rigorous analysis of the advantages, disadvantages and other implications of proposals for developing new and innovative sources of funding, both public and private, for dedication to social development and poverty eradication programmes'. As the UN Secretary-General observed, there has been a great deal of innovation in private financial markets, but less in the sphere of public finances. The UN Department of Economic and Social Affairs (DESA) in turn requested the World Institute for Development Economics Research of the United Nations University (UNU–WIDER) in Helsinki to commission the study of Innovative Sources.

The execution of this project has involved many people. First, as coordinator of the project, I should like to thank most warmly the other members of the project team, who in addition to the authors of chapters in the book included Ilene Grabel of the University of Denver. They have not only written individual chapters but also contributed significantly to the development of the overall analysis. The introductory Chapters 1 and 2, and the concluding Chapter 12, owe a great deal to their ideas, and in a number of places I have used material that they have drafted. The project meeting in May 2003, and extensive e-mail exchange, have helped considerably in trying to achieve a book that, we hope, is both balanced in its views and integrated in its contents.

The work of the project group has benefited much from the comments of external commentators. An earlier version of Chapter 2 was presented at the World Bank ABCDE Meeting in Paris in May 2003, where most helpful comments were made by the discussants, Adrian Wood, chief economist at the Department for International Development, and P.-B. Spahn of the University of Frankfurt, and by conference participants. An overall perspective of the report was presented at an open meeting of the project in Helsinki in September 2003, attended by some 100 people. We are most grateful for their comments to members of the panel: Ahmed Ndyeshobola of the African, Caribbean, and Pacific Group of States, Teresa Ter-Minassian, director of the Fiscal Affairs Department of the IMF, and Adrian Wood. Individual chapters were presented at the conference 'Sharing Global Prosperity' at UNU-WIDER on 6–7 September 2003. The comments of conference participants were most valuable, as were those of the Oxford University Press referees. There are therefore many people who have contributed. We should, however, single out Anthony Clunies-Ross of the University of Strathclyde, Inge Kaul of UNDP, and Adrian Wood, whose work and comments have had a significant impact on the structure of the report. However, neither they nor any of those thanked should be held in any way responsible for the views expressed.

UN-DESA and UNU-WIDER initiated the project and provided crucial support. We are grateful to Ian Kinniburgh of the Development Policy Analysis Division, UN-DESA, for his active encouragement. At WIDER, Tony Addison has not only managed the project with a disarmingly light touch but also contributed the chapter on the global lottery. Liisa Roponen has been unfailingly helpful and cheerful as project secretary, ensuring that all ran smoothly, and Adam Swallow most efficiently steered the manuscript through the publication process.

UNU-WIDER gratefully acknowledges the support to the project from the United Nations Department of Economic and Social Affairs (UN-DESA). UNU-WIDER also acknowledges the financial contributions to the 2002–2003 research programme by the governments of Denmark (Royal Ministry of Foreign Affairs), Finland (Ministry for Foreign Affairs), Norway (Royal Ministry of Foreign Affairs), Sweden (Swedish International Development Cooperation Agency–Sida), and the United Kingdom (Department for International Development).

Tony Atkinson
May 2004

Foreword

Mobilizing additional finance to meet the challenges of the Millennium Development Goals (MDGs) is now an urgent priority. Increased inflows of both private and public money are needed in order for the world's poorest countries to invest in the basic services and infrastructure necessary to meet the MDG targets for human development, and to improve livelihoods and employment for poor people. Developing countries themselves are mobilizing resources to meet the MDG targets by 2015, but they will fall short of the targets without additional external flows. The consensus adopted by the United Nations International Conference on Financing for Development conference in Monterrey, Mexico, in March 2002 noted the meagre level of official and private capital flows to most developing countries. Official development assistance, although on the rise since Monterrey, still falls far short of the level necessary to meet the MDGs, and private flows to the poorer countries are small: Africa's share of the flow of global foreign direct investment is only 3 per cent.

As a result of the Five-year Review of the World Summit for Social Development, the United Nations General Assembly in September 2000 called for the mobilization of new and additional resources for social development and for 'a rigorous analysis of advantages, disadvantages and other implications of proposals for developing new and innovative sources of funding'. The present book contains the results of the study carried out by UNU-WIDER, under the direction of Sir Anthony Atkinson on behalf of the United Nations Department of Economic and Social Affairs.

The book examines a range of innovative sources of finance. The best known of the ideas under consideration is the tax on currency transactions, widely known as the 'Tobin tax'. Well known also is the proposal for a carbon tax levied on fuel use. Both of these have many advocates, but they are also controversial. Rigorous economic analysis is therefore necessary. In particular, it is important to separate the argument for these taxes as corrective mechanisms (reducing currency speculation and carbon emissions) from the revenue raising function. The concern in this book is with revenue, which may mean that low rates of taxation may be sufficient to make a major new contribution.

Taxes are only one of the possible new sources. The book examines proposals for a development-focused allocation of Special Drawing Rights (SDRs), and the International Finance Facility (IFF) proposed by the UK's Chancellor of the Exchequer. The terms of reference of the UNU-WIDER study asked the authors to consider the potential for private funding. The study therefore considers the financing associated with remittances by emigrants, and private philanthropy. It considers the scope for a global lottery or a global premium bond.

The book brings new thinking to bear on these very important global questions. The intellectual perspective that marks the book from others in the field is that the authors bring to bear the tools of modern public economics, more commonly applied to national problems of finance. The book argues that this can provide new insights. We can learn from the analysis of fiscal federalism within nation states. We can learn from the analysis of the ear-marking of taxes and from the literature on political economy.

The findings of this book will be of considerable interest to the development community, including not only national governments, the UN, and bilateral and multi-lateral agencies but also civil society. The ultimate aim is to help break the present impasse in external finance for developing countries, and we believe that this study will make an important contribution to the debate.

José Antonio Ocampo
Under-Secretary General
Department for Economic & Social Affairs
United Nations

Tony Shorrocks
Director
World Institute for Development Economics Research
United Nations University

New York and Helsinki, May 2004

Contents

List of Boxes   xi
List of Figures   xii
List of Tables   xiii
List of Acronyms and Abbreviations   xiv
List of Contributors   xvi

1. Innovative Sources to Meet A Global Challenge   1
   Anthony B. Atkinson

2. Over-Arching Issues   17
   Anthony B. Atkinson

3. Environmental Taxation and Revenue for Development   33
   Agnar Sandmo

4. Revenue Potential of the Tobin Tax for Development Finance:
   A Critical Appraisal   58
   Machiko Nissanke

5. A Development-Focused Allocation of the Special Drawing Rights   90
   Ernest Aryeetey

6. The International Finance Facility Proposal   110
   George Mavrotas

7. Private Donations for International Development   132
   John Micklewright and Anna Wright

8. A Global Lottery and a Global Premium Bond   156
   Tony Addison and Abdur R. Chowdhury

9. Remittances by Emigrants: Issues and Evidence   177
   Andrés Solimano

10. Global Public Economics   200
    James A. Mirrlees

11. National Taxation, Fiscal Federalism and Global Taxation   210
     Robin Boadway

12. The Way Forward   238
     Anthony B. Atkinson

Index   247

List of Boxes

Box 1.1. Summary of MDGs   2
Box 1.2. Innovative sources of development funding considered   5

List of Figures

2.1. Net addition to development resources or alternative source 18
2.2. Fiscal architecture: national taxation 21
2.3. Fiscal architecture in global setting 22
4.1. Foreign exchange market turnover at constant April 2001 exchange rates by market segment 74
4.2. Foreign exchange market turnover by counterparty as per cent of total reported turnover 75
5.1. SDR flows 93
5.2. Proposed SDR flows 100
6.1. Overview of the IFF 113
6.2. Stylized representation of donor commitments 115
6.3. IFF inflows (income) and outflows (disbursements) 116
6.4. IFF debt profile during the life of the Facility 116
6.5. Illustrative example of IFF income and disbursement patterns—phased streams 117
7.1. UNICEF national committee contribution and national income, 2001 144
7.2. UNICEF national committee contribution and official ODA, 2001 144
9.1. Long-term resource flows to developing countries, 1991–2001 182
9.2. Top twenty developing-country recipients of workers' remittances, 2001 183
9.3. Top twenty developing-country recipients of workers' remittances, 2001 184
9.4. Top twenty country sources of remittance payments, 2001 184

List of Tables

4.1. Global foreign exchange market turnover   73
4.2. Reported foreign exchange market turnover by counterparty   74
4.3. Currency distribution of reported foreign exchange market turnover   76
4.4. Reported foreign exchange market turnover   77
4.5. Geographical distribution of reported foreign exchange market   78
4.6. Foreign exchange trading, world trade and global official reserves   79
4.7. CTT revenue estimate applied to 2001 foreign exchange trade volumes   84
5.1. Worldwide non-gold reserves, 1970–2000   94
7.1. Examples of UK charities   136
8.1. World lottery sales by region, 1996–2001   157
8.2. Regions with online gambling   163
9.1. Remittances received by region, 1980–2002   179
9.2. Remittances received by country groups, 1995–2001   180
9.3. Remittances received by developing countries, 1996–2002   181
9.4. Resource flows to developing countries, 1991–2002   182
9.5. Sources of remittances: countries and transfer agents   192
9.6. Average costs of sending money to selected non-Latin American countries 193
9.7. Charges by type of operators for sending a remittance of US$200 to
      selected countries   193
9.8. Average charges for sending a remittance of US$200 from the United
      States to Latin America   194
9.9. Cost of remittances from the United States to the Andean Countries   194
12.1. New sources of development funding: summary of conclusions   240

List of Acronyms and Abbreviations

BIS	Bank for International Settlements
CMI	Crisis Management Initiative (NGO, Finland)
CLS	Continuous Linked Settlement Bank
CTT	currency transaction tax
DAC	OECD's Development Assistance Committee
DFID	Department for International Development
EMS	European Monetary System
ENRD	exchange-rate normalization duty
ERM	exchange rate mechanism
FAO	Food and Agriculture Organization
FXE	foreign currency exchange
GNI	gross national income
HIPC	heavily indebted poor country
HTAs	home town associations
IBRD	International Bank for Reconstruction and Development
ICT	information and communications technology
IATA	International Air Transport Association
IDA	International Development Association
IFF	International Finance Facility
ILO	International Labour Office
IMF	International Monetary Fund
LDCs	least developed countries
MCA	Millennium Challenge Account
MDGs	Millennium Development Goals
MTOs	money transfer operators
NEPAD	New Partnership for African Development
NGOs	non-governmental organizations
NFB	net fiscal benefit
NPV	net present value
ODA	official development assistance
OECD	Organization for Economic Cooperation and Development
PVP	payment versus payment settlement
RTGS	real time gross settlement systems
SDRs	Special Drawing Rights
STT	security transaction tax
UNDP	United Nations Development Programme
UNFPA	United Nations Population Fund

UNICEF	United Nations Children's Fund
UNCTAD	United Nations Conference on Trade and Development
WLA	World Lottery Association
WFP	World Food Programme
WHO	World Health Organization

List of Contributors

Tony Addison is Deputy Director of UNU-WIDER.

Ernest Aryeetey is Professor at the Institute of Statistical, Social, and Economic Research, University of Ghana.

Sir Anthony B. Atkinson is Warden of Nuffield College, Oxford.

Robin Boadway is Professor of Economics at Queen's University, Kingston, Canada.

Abdur B. Chowdhury is Director of the Economic Analysis Division at the United Nations Economic Commission for Europe (ECE) in Geneva.

George Mavrotas is Research Fellow and Project Director at UNU-WIDER.

John Micklewright is Professor of Social Statistics and Policy Analysis at the University of Southampton and was previously Head of Research at UNICEF Innocenti Research Centre, Florence.

Sir James Mirrlees is Professor of Political Economy at the University of Cambridge and Winner of the Nobel Prize in Economics in 1996.

Machiko Nissanke is Professor of Economics at the School of Oriental and African Studies, London.

Agnar Sandmo is Professor of Economics at the Norwegian School of Economics, Bergen.

Andrés Solimano is Regional Advisor, United Nations Economic Commission for Latin America and the Caribbean.

Anna Wright is a freelance researcher, who has worked for UNICEF.

1

Innovative Sources to Meet A Global Challenge

ANTHONY B. ATKINSON

1.1. INTRODUCTION

At the Millennium Summit in September 2000, the states of the UN affirmed their continued commitment to sustained development and the eradication of poverty. They set out a vision of a global partnership for development, directed at the achievement of specific targets. Specifically, the world's leaders signed up to the Millennium Development Goals (MDGs) summarized in Box 1.1. The concrete goals include the halving by 2015 of the proportion of people living in extreme poverty, the proportion hungry, and the proportion lacking access to safe drinking water. The goals include the achievement of universal primary education and gender equality in education, the achievement by 2015 of a three-fourths decline in maternal mortality and a two-thirds decline in mortality among children under five. They include halting and reversing the spread of HIV/AIDS and providing special assistance to AIDS orphans, while improving the lives of 100 million slum dwellers.

Since the declaration of the MDGs, a number of attempts have been made to estimate the financing requirements. In the case of Africa, achieving the MDGs implies an increase in the *per capita* consumption of over half of its population in order to reach a minimum of US$1 per day. To achieve that level of consumption, it is reckoned that African and other low-income countries must, on the average, grow at 8 per cent per annum for the period. UNCTAD (United Nations Conference on Trade and Development) (2000) judged it unlikely that the poor nations could find the resources to finance such growth from the traditional sources, that is, domestic savings (both private and public) and foreign savings (existing levels of official development assistance (ODA) and private capital flows). This made it essential to identify sources of additional financing, while boosting the capacity to generate further resources from the traditional sources and improving the effectiveness with which financing is employed.

At a global level, taking all the above considerations into account, the Report of the Panel chaired by President Zedillo (UN 2001) estimated conservatively that an additional US$50 billion would be required annually to achieve the international development goals. The Panel argued that there was a strong case for international financing of global public goods, and identified the goods that fell in that category as

Box 1.1. *Summary of MDGs*

Goal 1 Eradicate extreme poverty and hunger	• Halve, between 1990 and 2015, the proportion of people whose income is less than US$1 a day • Halve, between 1990 and 2015, the proportion of people who suffer from hunger
Goal 2 Achieve universal primary education	• Ensure that by 2015 all children will be able to complete a full course of primary schooling
Goal 3 Promote gender equality and empower women	• Eliminate gender disparity in all levels of education by 2015
Goal 4 Reduce child mortality	• Reduce by two-thirds, between 1990 and 2015, the under-5 mortality rate
Goal 5 Improve maternal health	• Reduce by three-quarters, between 1990 and 2015, the maternal mortality ratio
Goal 6 Combat HIV/AIDS, malaria and other diseases	• Have halted by 2015 and begun to reverse the spread of HIV/AIDS • Have halted by 2015 and begun to reverse the spread of malaria and other major diseases
Goal 7 Ensure environmental sustainability	• Integrate principles of sustainable development into country policies and reverse the loss of environmental resources • Halve, by 2015, the proportion of people without sustainable access to safe drinking water • Have achieved, by 2020, a significant improvement in the lives of at least 100 million slum dwellers
Goal 8 Develop a global partnership for development	• Develop the world trading and financial system • Address the special needs of the least developed and landlocked and small island countries • Deal comprehensively with the debt problems of developing countries

peacekeeping; the prevention of contagious diseases; research into tropical medicines, vaccines, and agricultural crops; the prevention of chlorofluorocarbon emissions, the limitation of carbon emissions, and the preservation of biodiversity. Thus, in addition to the financing needs of individual poor nations, there is also the need to finance global public goods in achieving those goals. The provision of global public goods is covered in depth by Kaul *et al.* (1999) and Kaul *et al.* (2003). The UK government (HM Treasury and Department for International Development 2003: para 1.11) estimated that to achieve primary schooling for all it needs some US$10 billion more each year; that to reduce infant and maternal mortality requires an extra US$12 billion a year, and that halving world poverty requires an investment of up to US$20 billion a year.

All such figures are estimates, and involve matters of judgement. More detailed calculations are being made, disaggregated by individual countries. But it seems reasonable for present purposes to take a figure of additional US$50 billion as being required annually to achieve the international development goals. This is the 'ballpark' figure used in what follows. The aim of the analysis that follows is to investigate ways in which such additional resources can be financed. Our focus is on flows of resources from high-income to developing countries. In so concentrating, we are not denying the importance of resources channelled into development by developing countries themselves; nor are we seeking to under-play the potentially significant contribution of middle-income countries to development funding.

The first major delimitation of our field is therefore that our spotlight is on the *role of rich countries*. The second delimitation is that our primary concern is with the funding side, not with the spending side. As is discussed below, the two cannot be fully separated. Use of resources may affect their availability. The two sides may be interdependent in that more effective use of funds may stimulate additional supply. But our ultimate objective in this book is to analyse possible *sources of funds*.

1.1.1. *Official Development Assistance*

An important vehicle for financing development is ODA. The need for an additional US$50 billion per year must be seen against the current level of ODA, which was US$57 billion in 2002. Of this total, a half was provided by the European Union and its members, and a quarter was provided by the United States. As is well known, ODA stagnated in the 1990s. As a proportion of the gross national income of donor countries, ODA has fallen from 0.33 per cent in the mid-1980s to 0.23 per cent in 2002 (figures published by the OECD—Organization for Economic Cooperation and Development—Development Assistance Committee (DAC) for net official development assistance from DAC countries to developing countries and multilateral organizations). Few countries reach the UN target of 0.7 per cent of GNP for official assistance.

The Zedillo Report for the UN concluded, 'the inescapable bottom line is that much more funding is needed for official development assistance' (UN 2001: 10). 'Meeting the International Development Goals alone would require almost double the current ODA total of more than US$50 billion per year' (UN 2001: 16). At the Monterrey Conference on Financing for Development in March 2002, donor countries recognized that they needed to set more ambitious targets for ODA. The EU prior to Monterrey had committed itself to raising its ODA to 0.39 per cent of gross national income, from the then figure of 0.33 per cent. Three countries have given firm dates to reach the UN 0.7 per cent target: Belgium, France and Ireland. The US government announced that it was increasing its core development assistance by US$5 billion annually, these increased funds being placed in a 'new millennium challenge account' (MCA). The new account is distributed to developing countries showing a strong commitment to 'good governance, health and education, and sound economic policies'. (The MCA is discussed in Chapter 6.)

Viewed in relation to previous aid achievements and aspirations, the US$50 billion increase seems quite feasible. As noted by the World Bank, 'a return by donors to their early-1990s average aid ratio of 0.33 per cent of GNP would provide an extra US$20 billion' (2001: 89). If the average could be raised to 0.5 per cent, then the US$50 billion additional ODA would have been realized. The search for alternative sources would become redundant. The ballpark target is less ambitious than asking all G7 countries to reach the UN target of 0.7 per cent of GNP for official assistance. Nor is an increase of ODA by existing donors the only route by which ODA could be increased. The world distribution of income is changing. At present the DAC countries of the OECD account for over 95 per cent of worldwide ODA disbursements, but the future funding of development should take account of the growth of middle-income countries, which can be expected to come into the equation.

The funding of the MDGs could be achieved solely by increasing ODA. At the same time, it would require a step change from the present, going considerably beyond what has so far been promised. Increasing public spending on development assistance is not an easy political option. The widening of the circle of aid donors is going to take time. Time is, however, of the essence. For this reason alone, it is necessary to consider new sources.

1.2. NEW DEVELOPMENT FINANCE: INNOVATIVE SOURCES

The gap between current ODA and the amounts required to meet the MDGs is a major reason for looking at alternative sources of development funding. These are the subject of this book. In the chapters that follow, we examine a number of ways in which new funding can be generated. The purpose of the project is not to *devise* new schemes of funding, of which there is already a bewildering variety. (Although some novel ideas, such as the global premium bond, have emerged as part of our work.) Rather our main aim is to consider some of the best known, examining their design and implications.

Specifically, we are considering (see Box 1.2):

— Global environmental taxes (carbon-use tax);
— Tax on currency flows ('Tobin tax');
— Creation of new Special Drawing Rights (SDRs);
— International Finance Facility (IFF);
— Increased private donations for development;
— Global lottery and global premium bond;
— Increased remittances from emigrants.

Box 1.2. *Innovative sources of development funding considered*

Source	
Global environmental taxes	Tax on goods generating environmental externalities, with specific reference to a tax on use of hydrocarbon fuels according to their carbon content. See Pearce (1991), Poterba (1991), and Cooper (1998).
Currency transactions tax ('Tobin tax')	Tax on foreign currency transactions, collected on a national or a market basis, covering a range of transactions to be defined (spot, forward, future, swaps, and other derivatives). See Haq *et al.* (1996), Spahn (1996), Mendez (1997), Patomäki and Denys (2002).
Creation of new Special Drawing Rights (SDRs)	Creation of SDRs for development purposes, with donor countries making their SDR allocation available to fund development. See Soros (2002).
International Finance Facility (IFF)	Long-term, but conditional, funding guaranteed to the poorest countries by the donor countries. Long-term pledges of a flow of annual payments to the IFF would leverage additional money from the international capital markets. See HM Treasury and Department for International Development (2003).
Increased private donations for development	Charitable donations by private individuals and firms. Measures to encourage private funding of development: tax incentives, global funds, corporate giving, and the Internet.
Global lottery or global premium bond	Global lottery operated through national state-operated and state-licensed lotteries, with proceeds shared between national participants and an independent foundation established in conjunction with UN. See Ahde *et al.* (2002). Global premium bond, parallel to national bonds with lottery prizes.
Increased remittances from emigrants	Logistics (reducing cost of remittances), financial institutions (encouraging repatriation) and citizenship rather than residence basis for taxation. See Bhagwati and Hamada (1982), Mirrlees (1982), Bhagwati and Wilson (1989), and Solimano (2001).

A number of these sources have already been extensively discussed in the literature, and we owe a considerable debt to earlier writing. Citations are given in Box 1.2, but we should make specific reference here to the paper prepared by Clunies-Ross (1999) for the Preparatory Committee for the Special Session of the General Assembly in the Year 2000, to the Technical Note prepared by the Department of Economic and Social

Affairs (UN 2002) for the Monterrey Conference, and to the paper prepared for the ILO Commission on the Social Dimensions of Globalization by Clunies-Ross (2003).

It will be evident that our coverage is far from exhaustive. There are a number of other global taxes that have been advanced. These include a 'brain drain' tax, an international air transport tax, taxation of ocean fishing, taxation of arms exports, a 'bit tax', and a luxury goods tax. Each of these warrants examination. We are not arguing that the global taxes investigated here are superior to those not covered. Rather we have taken two of the most widely discussed—the Tobin tax and environmental taxes—as exemplars of the potential for global taxation. If we conclude that they can serve the purpose of raising the necessary US$50 billion, this does not mean that these two taxbases should be adopted in preference to others. Alternatives certainly need to be explored. And if we conclude that the two taxes cannot, singly or jointly, serve the purpose, then the other taxes will certainly have to come into play. In this sense, the project is part of an evolving debate.

The innovative sources considered in this book are not confined to taxation. Two of the proposals are close to ODA. The proposal for a new round of SDRs involves the high-income countries in making these available for development purposes. The UK government proposal for an IFF in effect involves a pre-commitment of future ODA in a way that allows leveraging on the capital market. The remaining three schemes involve a degree of voluntary choice by individuals. The choices range from a voluntary transfer, as where people give their small change to UNICEF or make regular payments to Oxfam, to buying tickets in a global lottery, where the transfer of profits to development purposes is only a subsidiary motive. It includes proposals to increase the remittances sent home by workers abroad, which, if channelled into development purposes, can increase the flow of resources available for development. Again, however, it should be stressed that the coverage of non-fiscal measures is not exhaustive. We do not, for example, cover measures to raise capital funds in developed countries or measures to leverage the funds arising from trade.

1.2.1. *Classification of Proposals*

The seven proposals may be classified in different ways. They differ in the extent to which they represent a *radical departure*. The encouragement of private donations, or of emigrants' remittances, may lead to significant changes in scale, but the activities are not new. There would be no major changes in the rules of the game. More radical is the special SDR allocation by the IMF, which is novel to the extent that donor countries would make their share available for development purposes. The IFF works through ODA but would involve a new international treaty. In organizational terms, it would be a significant change; and the extent of pre-commitment would be unprecedented. Both of these proposals represent new uses of existing instruments. The most radical are the global taxes and the global lottery/premium bond. These would be fundamental departures.

The proposals can be classified according to the *lead actors*. The SDR allocation has the IMF at centre stage, with national governments having to ratify the IMF proposals.

The introduction of global taxes requires national governments to agree to act multi-laterally, via a new or existing international organization. This may require universal agreement, or may only require a subset of major countries to agree. In Chapter 2, we explore some of the possibilities opened up by allowing for 'flexible geometry', where countries may or may not participate. The key actors may be national organiza-tions. The global lottery requires the collaboration of national lotteries. The key actors may be individuals. Increased private donations and remittances will only happen if individuals (or enterprises) decide to increase their contributions to development.

Although the use of funds is not our primary focus, the *intermediation mechanism* is a valuable way of classifying the different proposals. In some cases, the source and use are closely aligned. The destination of increased remittances is largely under the control of the individual making the transfer. A worker in California sending money to India may decide to finance her parents' consumption or to fund the construction of a village school. Charitable contributions by the citizens of rich countries are likely to flow via non-governmental organizations (NGOs), allowing the individuals to decide on their relative preferences for disaster relief or water development or agricultural improvement or medical care. In these cases, it is likely that the amount given will depend on the choice of uses. A good example has been debt for nature swaps, where environmental NGOs like the Worldwide Fund for Nature have cancelled developing-country debt in exchange for agreed conservation projects. Donors will doubtless appreciate that funds are fungible, and recipients may offer commitment devices that increase confidence that the funds are indeed ring-fenced. The governmental sources, on the other hand, are likely to disburse funds through existing bilateral or multilateral delivery channels. These may tie aid to particular uses or to the adoption of particular policies. Much of the literature is sceptical about conditionality (e.g., see Kanbur 2000), but this does not mean that conditionality cannot affect the willingness of donors to make transfers. Here it is useful to separate the *perceived* effectiveness and the *actual* effectiveness of the funds. The actual impact of a transfer may differ from that intended because of misadministration or because funds are fungible, but as long as it remains credible that there is a link between the transfer and the stated purpose, then donors may continue to provide funding.

1.3. ORIGINS OF THE PROPOSALS

In this book, we consider the range of innovative proposals described above. We seek to evaluate them according to a variety of criteria, and these criteria are explained below. First, however, it is important to consider the political origins of the proposals. Why are alternatives being sought to ODA? What is the basis of support for different proposals? What is the political context? The proposals considered in this book were not developed in a laboratory; they emerged from a political debate about global policy. They are a product of summit meetings and of street demonstrations. Understanding their origins and political context helps us in turn understand the form of the proposals and their likely impact. It helps us predict their chance of being put into effect.

If we start with global environmental taxes, then these have been championed on the grounds that they yield a 'double dividend'. Such an argument has been made at the national level for corrective taxes on environmental external diseconomies (the damage done to the environment). A tax on the consumption of goods, such as hydrocarbon fuels, which harm the environment has a positive allocational effect, switching spending away from polluting goods towards those causing less or no environmental damage. In contrast to the usual case with taxes, such switching behaviour is desirable. So we have *both* the revenue *and* the environmental gain. This is discussed further in Chapters 2 and 3, but for the present the important point is that the tax proposal is designed with *two* purposes in mind. Revenue is only one objective. Indeed, if we succeed through the Kyoto Agreement and other means in reducing the use of polluting fuels, then the resources available for development will be reduced.

The Tobin tax is another clear example of such a double dividend argument. Indeed, the second purpose historically came first. James Tobin first put forward the idea for a currency transactions tax to enhance the efficacy of macroeconomic policy. The subtitle of the book on *The Tobin Tax*, edited by Haq *et al.* (1996) was 'Coping with Financial Volatility'. The potential of the currency transactions tax as a generator of revenue was suggested 'as a by-product of the proposed tax, not as its principal purpose' (Tobin 1996: x). This ancestry explains the differences in rates proposed by different authors. As is made clear in Chapter 4, a rate of tax of 1 or 2 basis points may be considered too little sand to restrain the wheels of international finance but may generate revenue sufficient to make a significant difference to development funding.

Ideas and policies have their time. Tobin (1996) reflected somewhat ruefully on the fact that his 1978 proposal 'did not make much of a ripple. In fact, one might say that it sank like a rock' (1996: x). A quarter of a century later, it features on many political agendas. In considering the different proposals here, we have to bear in mind their timing and dynamics. The adoption of the MDGs represents a moral commitment from which governments will find it hard to withdraw. The poverty target is not a line in the sand that will be gone with the next tide. This in turn means that the search for revenue has acquired greater salience. Governments may reject particular proposals. They may block multilateral action. But they cannot totally evade the question of alternatives. As 2015 approaches, pressure will increase for results to be registered.

Just as policy goals have a degree of durability, so too policies themselves have a high degree of persistence. This applies particularly to those reached after lengthy inter-country negotiation, as is witnessed by the experience of the European Union. The introduction of a global tax would not be easily reversed, if only because some of the revenue would be necessary to finance the collection machinery. A global lottery might be dismantled, but this would be a significant political reverse. In the case of the IFF, there will be a succession of funding rounds, but the key feature of the proposal is to pre-commit future flows of assistance. Future governments will not be able to go back on the promises made today.

Proposals for new sources also find their origins in a search for alternatives to ODA. Here it is helpful to distinguish three types of motive for seeking an alternative to

increased ODA. The first is to reduce government spending. Many OECD governments are under pressure to reduce government deficits. In the case of the euro zone
countries, these pressures are institutionalized in the form of the Stability and Growth
Pact. The reactions of countries in this position will depend on the form of these
constraints. For example, the attractiveness of the IFF may depend on how the future
commitments appear in the government budget. The second concern is with the level
of taxation, which would need to rise to finance increased ODA. In this case, the
alternatives may not offer a solution. A globally administered Tobin tax may not enter
the government budget of a particular country, but it may contribute to the perceived
burden of doing business in that country. The profitability of London or Frankfurt
as financial centres, for example, might be reduced. Third, governments may be concerned with 'donor fatigue' among their electorate. This would inhibit government
participation in the devising of new sources, as well as discouraging increased ODA.
Given the possible importance of such 'fatigue', it is significant that the OECD study
by McDonnell *et al.* (2003) reports that 'public support in OECD DAC-member
countries for helping poor countries has remained consistently high for almost two
decades: there is no aid fatigue' (2003: summary). They caution that concern remains
about effectiveness, and that public understanding of poverty and development issues
remains low. This is a further role for the present book: to contribute to public debate.

1.4. POLITICAL ECONOMY

This book is largely about the economics of new sources of finance for development,
but we need also to consider the political economy of new sources. The political
economy is important for at least three reasons. The first is that, as we have just seen,
politics influences the shape of the proposals. In the next chapter, we ask a number
of questions about the design of the proposals, and the answers reflect the political
context. Are the proceeds of a Tobin tax, for example, to be seen as a net addition
to the flow of resources or as an alternative to ODA? What is the fiscal architecture:
would global taxation be collected by national governments? The second reason for
examining the political economy is that it affects the economic consequences of the
new sources. The reaction of individuals and businesses to global taxes is influenced by
the degree to which the taxpayers accept the purposes for which the taxes are levied.
Avoidance and evasion are higher where the tax is regarded as unjustified. In a global
context, the economic impact of taxes and other measures depends on the actions
of national governments. The third reason is that the feasibility of new sources of
development finance is ultimately a political issue. Political acceptability should not be
a consideration that influences our economic analysis of given proposals, but it may
influence the choice of proposals to study.

The behaviour of the state, and its interactions with citizens, has long been an
important part of the subject matter of public economics. Analysis of public policy
has to take account of the process by which policy is made. We are, for example,
starting from a position where donor countries make significant transfers via ODA
and where the citizens of those countries make private donations. The co-existence

of public and private transfers means that either the government is not providing aid of the quantity and/or type that its electorate prefers or that there are differences of views among voters. Citizens cannot spend less than their government chooses but they can add private transfers to official aid. How, in such a context, can we interpret the impact of the adoption of the MDGs? Have donor governments moved closer to the level of ODA that their voters preferred? In that case, we might expect the expansion of public transfers to be partially offset by a scaling back of private donations. Have governments sought to bring about a shift in public opinion in favour of increased support for development? In this case, we may even see an increased flow of private donations. In the same way, we can ask how the innovative financing proposals would enter into this equation. Are these new ideas a means to reduce the perceived costs of development finance? Are the new institutions a vehicle for shifting national political balances?

In evidence to the World Commission on the Social Dimensions of Globalization, Clunies-Ross (2003) suggests that there are four factors that may reduce the political cost of development funding. The first is where the revenue sources are *not highly visible*. The global lottery may be an example, where participants are largely focused on the possibility of winning. The second is the time required for *legislation and negotiation*. Piloting a bill for a global tax through parliament may have a high political cost, whereas measures to encourage private donations can be achieved without new laws. The third is described by Clunies-Ross as the *'two birds' test:* 'the collection of revenue is itself linked to the achievement of some widely desired end, such as a recognized global public good, so that two birds can be killed with one stone' (2003: 5). Finally, from a national perspective, the cost is reduced when the effort is worldwide, and there are *no freeriders*. Thus it may be feasible for the European Union, for example, to introduce a currency transactions tax without the participation of the United States, but this may run into political objections. Voters in the European Union may object to the Tobin tax not being levied in the country of its inventor.

It should be emphasized that these considerations are positive statements about political feasibility, not judgements about intrinsic desirability. Indeed, their desirability can be questioned. Low visibility is not a property that would commend itself in an open civil society. Legislation is a proper activity of democratic governments. A country's policymakers should form their own judgements independently. There is a strong normative element to political economy. Moreover, extension to a global stage raises new normative issues. As is increasingly evident from public debate, there is questioning of the status of international organizations that are only indirectly accountable. If, as we consider in this book, global taxes are to be introduced, then how are the taxpayers to be represented? If tax revenue accrues to the UN or to international agencies, there will be heightened pressure for democratic accountability. Falk (2002) has considered how the UN could develop a people's assembly. The political structure may therefore itself be influenced by the introduction of new sources of development finance. Just as at a national level, political structures may evolve in response to fiscal developments.

For these reasons, we do not allow considerations of political feasibility to dictate the scope of our analysis of innovative sources. We cannot ignore the political context but one of the key roles of economic analysis is to spell out the menu of options. If a politician asks which sandwiches are available, we should not leave the vegetarian option off the list simply because we know that he comes from a cattle ranching state. As put by Boadway, it is 'inconsistent to rule out on a priori grounds options that are normatively superior simply on the basis of a perception that the policy process itself will choose not to adopt them' (2002: 55). This does not mean that our analysis of the consequences of a particular policy option should ignore the political context, for the reasons given at the start of this section, but that we should not give it primacy.

Statements about political feasibility are, of course, predicated on a view about the working of the political process. Consider, for instance, the proposition that the double dividend argument strengthens the case for certain global taxes: the 'two birds' test. This argument is related to the classic model of 'logrolling' where two politicians agree to support each other's pet projects. However, the logrolling model assumes a particular distribution of benefits and losses from the projects, the former being concentrated and the latter diffuse (Drazen 2000: 330). But the reverse may be true: the costs may be largely borne by a small interest group, and the benefits widely dispersed. To be more concrete, opening up two fronts also invites attack from both directions, particularly if the two objectives require taxes at very different levels. In several of the proposals considered here, the tax required for allocational reasons is likely to be considerably higher than that needed to add significantly to development funding. The Tobin tax can make a major contribution to raising revenue at a much lower rate than that suggested as needed to stabilize exchange rates. (Taking this argument to the limit, we may note that a carbon tax that reduced emissions to zero would be an environmental success but a revenue failure.) The double dividend case risks attracting the hostility of opponents of the exchange stabilizing level of taxation, who would not necessarily oppose the much lower rate envisaged here. What is required is an analysis of the coalitions likely to form in support or opposition of different proposals.

In what follows, our primary focus is on the economic impact of the different proposals and on evaluation according to a set of economic criteria described in the next section. But we have to take account of the political context, and recognize that our analysis is itself part of the political process.

1.5. CRITERIA FOR EVALUATION

The different proposals are here evaluated, in broad terms, according to the total, and the distribution, of benefits and costs to the citizens of the world. Our analysis is an application of global public economics (Chapter 10). The benefit is seen principally in terms of securing funds for development, and the first question is whether the innovative sources, singly or in conjunction, can raise in a guaranteed way the annual flow of US$50 billion judged necessary to achieve the MDGs by 2015. How far is it feasible to ensure a stable flow of substantial additional revenue from the proposed source?

'Funds for development' in turn raises the question of the relation between dollars collected and development achieved. The meaning of 'development' is one of considerable subtlety, to which we cannot do justice here. The aim of the increased funding is to ensure a *lasting* rise in living standards *broadly interpreted*. 'Broadly interpreted' is very much the spirit of the MDGs. The halving of extreme poverty is linked with improved education and health, the empowerment of women, and environmental sustainability. 'Lasting' means that the targets are to be reached in 2015 and then sustained. The emphasis is on long-term investment to raise living standards. This means that we have to ask how the use of funds differs across the different sources. Are private donations more or less likely to contribute to investment than ODA? How far do emigrants' remittances finance consumption rather than investment? Of course, current consumption is of value. In that case, however, a continuing transfer is necessary.

Our primary focus is on the cost side, in that we are concerned with the economic impact of the new sources and with the distribution of the burden. The impact may not be immediately obvious. A new global tax will affect economic activity by households and by enterprises. The reactions of those taxed may allow them to shift the burden onto their customers or onto their workers or onto their shareholders. The reactions may generate additional costs or may have positive economic outcomes. New sources will affect—either negatively or positively—the efficiency of the working of the world economy.

Who bears the cost is essential from the standpoint of assessing the justice or otherwise of the proposed measures, and this too is a complex matter. To begin with, public debate tends to think in terms of redistribution from rich to poor countries. But a number of the proposed measures could potentially impose costs on people outside rich countries. The Tobin tax would reduce the net sum received by the families of migrant workers. A global lottery could attract customers from all round the world. Nor is the world neatly divided. We have already drawn attention to the potential role of middle-income countries. Even if the impact is confined to rich countries, we have to worry about the distribution of the burden within those countries. An annual flow of an extra US$50 billion is only a fifth of 1 per cent of the GNP of donor countries, but there is no reason to suppose that the cost would be shared proportionately. We need to ask how far it is the poor in rich countries that would bear the burden.

1.6. GUIDE TO THE CONTENTS OF THE BOOK

The rest of the book contains three general chapters (Chapters 2, 10 and 11), seven chapters (Chapters 3–9) considering separately the different innovative schemes analysed here, and a concluding chapter (Chapter 12).

We believe that there are merits in setting different proposals alongside each other. Such a joint analysis helps the reader assess their relative strengths and weaknesses. We hope also that our book makes a contribution in terms of the methods of analysis. This is the main function of Chapter 2 and Chapters 10–11, which approach the question in a theoretical way, rather than examining individual proposals for sources of funding. They may appear rather abstract to some readers, but there is considerable value in standing back and asking hypothetical questions—such as (Chapter 11) what would happen if there were a central world taxing authority? It may suggest new ways of viewing the problem. What is reality today was often hypothetical in the past. These theoretical chapters deal with over-arching issues, and this is the title of Chapter 2. Its aim is to set out a number of the common questions that arise in considering sources of new revenue for development finance. These concern the precise specification of the proposal, its relation with ODA, and the administrative architecture.

The taxation of externalities is the subject of the first of the chapters examining potential sources: Chapter 3 on environmental taxation. Much of the literature relates to taxes as instruments of national environmental policy, and their role in relation to economic development has been less discussed. The chapter begins therefore by preparing the ground, setting out the welfare economics of environmental taxation in a national context, including a detailed account of the double dividend issue. This provides the basis for an analysis of global environmental taxation, with specific reference to the carbon tax. The second major proposal for global taxation considered here is that for a currency transactions tax: the celebrated Tobin tax. As already noted, Tobin first put forward the idea for a currency transactions tax as a means of combating financial volatility. The potential of the currency transactions tax as a generator of revenue was suggested as a by-product. Here, Chapter 4 focuses on the by-product: the Tobin tax as a source of revenue for development. It examines the technical feasibility and the revenue potential from this source.

There has long been a campaign for the issue of development-focused SDRs by the IMF. The original purpose of SDRs was to increase international liquidity, but Chapter 5 concentrates on the potential role of SDR creation in providing funds for development finance. Calls have been made for developed countries to re-allocate their share of the SDR issue to developing countries. The chapter describes the historical development of SDRs and the recent proposals. It examines the arguments for and against development-oriented SDRs, and the institutional mechanisms necessary for their creation.

A starting point for this study was the observation that innovation in the sphere of public finances has not kept up with innovation in private financial markets. Making use of the latter to enhance the effectiveness of ODA is the essence of the recent proposal for the IFF, which is the subject of Chapter 6. Taking the proposal by the UK government as a case study, the chapter describes the possibility of a limited duration substantial increase in ODA where the value is enhanced by pre-commitment, allowing leverage by borrowing on the international capital markets. It sets out the institutional machinery proposed, and assesses the potential advantages and disadvantages.

Chapter 7 asks how far charitable donations by private individuals and firms can contribute to funding the Millennium Development Goals. What are the prospects for increasing donations for development, whether from small-scale donors, the super-rich, or the corporate sector? Charitable giving in rich countries is very substantial: in the US more than 1.5 per cent of national income. People give large amounts of free time. Development, however, commands only a small share. The chapter analyses the under-researched question as to how people determine the objects of their giving, drawing on other subjects, notably marketing. It asks why people give to support the UN agencies, notably United Nations Childrens Fund (UNICEF), and whether private donations are crowded-out by governmental contributions or by ODA. It examines measures to encourage private funding of development: tax incentives, Global funds, corporate giving, and the Internet.

A relatively new idea for new development funding is that of a global lottery, which has received attention particularly on account of the recent proposal by the Crisis Management Initiative. World sales of gaming products are large and growing. Chapter 8 considers the prospects for tapping this market for the purposes of development finance by means of a global lottery and—a new idea—a global premium bond (a loan instrument where the interest takes the form of a lottery prize, the capital being repayable on request). The chapter investigates the feasibility of these mechanisms and their potential as revenue sources for development. It assesses their strengths and weaknesses, including both economic and ethical issues.

Remittances from migrants are a growing force, and Chapter 9 considers the role that they can play in financing development. To an important extent, they finance consumption. As Chapter 11 notes, they are an international mechanism of social protection based on private transfers. They can also contribute to financing investment, providing community infrastructure (such as schools) and funds for the financing of new enterprises. The chapter considers the motives for making such remittances, and the problems of measuring their extent. Remittances are channelled through a variety of financial entities, ranging from the formal to the highly informal. The chapter considers policies to reduce the cost of remittances and to enhance their development potential.

One purpose of our study is to bring to bear the accumulated knowledge in the field of national public finance, and more generally public economics. It is for this reason that, in thinking how the subject can be taken forward, we have included Chapter 10 on global public finance and Chapter 11 on the lessons from the fiscal federalism literature. The former considers the lessons from optimal tax design when applied at a global level. The latter chapter highlights some of the similarities and some of the differences between fiscal institutions in federations and those that might apply in a global setting. It draws a number of conclusions about sources of new revenues for development, dealing specifically with taxes on nations, taxes on global externalities, and taxes on internationally mobile taxbases.

Chapter 12, which is the final chapter, summarizes the key points to emerge and considers the way forward.

REFERENCES

Ahde, M., A. Pentikäinen, and J.-M. Seppänen (2002). *Global Lottery*. Helsinki: Crisis Management Initiative.

Bhagwati, J. N. and K. Hamada (1982). 'Tax Policy in the Presence of Emigration'. *Journal of Public Economics*, 18(3): 291–317.

—— and J. D. Wilson (1989). *Income Taxation and International Mobility*. Cambridge, MA: MIT Press.

Boadway, R. (2002). 'The Role of Public Choice Considerations in Normative Public Economics', in S. L. Winer and H. Shibata (eds), *The Role of Political Economy in the Theory and Practice of Public Finance*. Cheltenham, UK: Edward Elgar, 47–68.

Clunies-Ross, A. (1999). 'Sustaining Revenue for Social Purposes in the Face of Globalization', in *Experts Discuss Some Critical Social Development Issues*. New York: United Nations Department of Economic and Social Affairs.

—— (2003). 'Resources for Social Development.' Paper prepared for the World Commission on the Social Dimensions of Globalization.

Cooper, R. (1998). 'Toward a Real Global Warming Treaty (The Case for a Carbon Tax)'. *Foreign Affairs*, 77(2): 66–79.

Drazen, A. (2000). *Political Economy*. Princeton: Princeton University Press.

Falk, R. (2002). 'The United Nations System: Prospects for Renewal', in D. Nayyar (ed.), *Governing Globalization: Issues and Institutions*. UNU-WIDER Studies in Development Economics. Oxford: Oxford University Press.

ul Haq, M., I. Kaul, and I. Grunberg (eds) (1996). *The Tobin Tax*. Oxford: Oxford University Press.

HM Treasury and Department for International Development (2003). *International Finance Facility*. London: HM Treasury.

Kanbur, R. (2000). 'Aid, Conditionality and Debt in Africa', in F. Tarp (ed.), *Foreign Aid and Development*. London: Routledge.

Kaul, I., I. Grunberg, and M. A. Stern (eds) (1999). *Global Public Goods*. New York: Oxford University Press.

——, P. Conceição, K. Le Goulven, and R. U. Mendoza (eds) (2003). *Providing Global Public Goods*. New York: Oxford University Press.

McDonnell, I., H.-B. S. Lecomte, and L. Wegimont (2003). 'Public Opinion Research, Global Education and Development Co-operation Reform: In Search of a Virtuous Circle'. Discussion Paper No 10. Paris: OECD Development Centre.

Mendez, R. P. (1997). 'Financing the United Nations and the International Public Sector: Problems and Reform'. *Global Governance*, 3: 283–310.

Mirrlees, J. A. (1982). 'Migration and Optimal Income Taxes'. *Journal of Public Economics*, 18 (3): 319–41.

Patomäki, H. and L. A. Denys (2002). *Draft Treaty on Global Currency Transactions Tax*. Nottingham: Network Institute for Global Democratization.

Pearce, D. (1991). 'The Role of Carbon Taxes in Adjusting to Global Warming'. *Economic Journal*, 101(407): 938–48.

Poterba, J. M. (1991). 'Tax Policy to Combat Global Warming: On Designing a Carbon Tax', in R. Dornbusch and J. M. Poterba (eds), *Global Warming: Economic Policy Responses*. Cambridge, MA: MIT Press.

Solimano, A. (2001). 'International Migration and the Global Economic Order: An Overview'. *World Bank Working Paper* No. 2720. Washington, DC: World Bank.

Soros, G. (2002). *On Globalization*. Oxford: Public Affairs Ltd.

Spahn, P. B. (1996). 'The Tobin Tax and Exchange Rate Stability'. *Finance and Development*, June: 24–7.

Tobin, J. (1996). 'Prologue', in M. ul Haq, I. Kaul, and I. Grunberg (eds), *The Tobin Tax*. Oxford: Oxford University Press.

UN (2001). *Report of the High-Level Panel on Financing for Development* (chair Ernesto Zedillo). New York: United Nations.
—— (2002). *Financing for Development*. New York: United Nations.
UNCTAD (2000). *Capital Flows and Growth in Africa*. Geneva: UNCTAD.
World Bank (2001). *Global Development Finance*. Washington, DC: World Bank.

2

Over-Arching Issues

ANTHONY B. ATKINSON

2.1. INTRODUCTION

Proposals for new sources of development finance are considered in detail in the chapters that follow. Each of them raises a number of distinct issues, which are properly discussed in the individual chapters. But there are also over-arching issues. What is the role of new sources in relation to existing official development assistance (ODA)? Should we be seeking new sources that generate a double dividend? Can the key elements of a proposal be achieved by another route? It is with these general concerns that the present chapter deals. Its aim is to set out a number of the common questions that arise in considering sources of new revenue for development finance.

One purpose of our study is to bring to bear on *global public finance* the accumulated knowledge in the field of national public finance, and more generally public economics. This process is two-way. Public economics has increasingly had an international dimension, as evidenced by the founding in the early 1990s of the journal *International Tax and Public Finance*. There has been a close link between public economics and development planning. However, changes in the world economy mean that a global perspective has to be built in from the start. For both national governments and for individual households and firms, we need to analyse public policy taking account of the inter-relations between countries. As was observed by Mendez, 'a critical element lacking in the fields of finance and international relations is a theory and system of international public finance' (1992: 11).

The application of the public economics approach leads one to ask a number of key questions. Those considered here are set out in the titles of Sections 2.2–2.6. The aim is not to provide definitive answers, but to clarify the questions being asked and to suggest possible answers that are not immediately apparent. To illustrate the issues, I refer at different points to the seven schemes studied in this book. There is of course a risk that by considering together such disparate measures we may be confounding the issues. The different instruments raise different concerns. However, one of the key lessons of modern public economics is that it is often valuable—indeed necessary—to consider within a common framework different forms of government policy. The first two questions concern the specification of the proposals; the remaining three questions involve the economic impact of the proposals. In each case, precision requires a degree of economic reasoning, but every attempt has been made to render this accessible. Bearing in mind the dictum of Stephen Hawking that each equation halves the number of readers, there are no equations.

2.2. WHAT IS THE ROLE OF NEW SOURCES?

The first question we need to address is the relation between new sources of development finance and an expansion of ODA. Are these to be seen as alternatives? As we have seen in Chapter 1, many proponents of new sources view them as a way of achieving an increased flow of development resources without recourse to increased ODA. Other people see this as a reason for opposing the exploration of new sources: Tobin taxes or other new schemes would, on this view, weaken the resolve of rich countries to meet the UN ODA target. Alternatively, the new sources would 'crowd out' other forms of finance. The new global lottery may generate new revenue but reduce the receipts of existing lotteries that have been used to fund development projects. According to this school of thought, the new sources should be a *net addition* to the flows of ODA.

In this book, both kinds of argument are treated, and it is important to distinguish between the case where the new sources are a net addition to the total of development resources and the case where they are a substitute for ODA. Figure 2.1 seeks to clarify the issue. We are agreed that additional resources are required to meet the development targets. This involves moving from the starting point O in Fig. 2.1. This could be achieved by increased ODA, moving from O to B horizontally in Fig. 2.1. Alternatively, it could be achieved by exploiting new sources, which is the move from O to A vertically in Fig. 2.1. In both cases, we have a package of increased resource flows and increased development spending. On the other hand, proponents, or opponents, of new sources

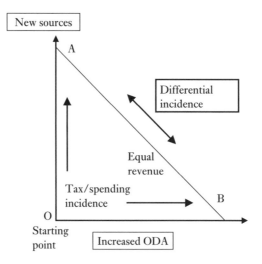

Figure 2.1. *Net addition to development resources or alternative source*

may *contrast* them with increased ODA. They may say that, holding the total transfer constant, the position A is better or worse than the position B.

The importance of distinguishing between the two types of movement illustrated in Fig. 2.1 is a key lesson from the public finance literature. The incidence of taxation depends on what else is being varied at the same time. As Musgrave set out in his classic *Theory of Public Finance* (1959), one possibility is 'tax/expenditure incidence', where revenue is increased and spending goes up by the same amount. As shown in Fig. 2.1, the introduction of new sources involves moving vertically. ODA remains unchanged and the benefit from the additional revenue is seen in the contribution to development goals. In this case, we have to consider the effectiveness of aid in achieving these goals and the absorptive capacity of the recipient countries. Alternatively, we can move along a line holding development-spending constant, while varying the sources of funding. In Musgrave's terminology, this is 'differential tax incidence': the differential implications of different means of securing a given flow of resources. For example, if a global Tobin tax raises new revenue, and this is used to reduce the need for additional ODA, then it allows domestic taxation to be lower. The case for the new tax then turns on the differential impact of the two kinds of taxation—and their relative political appeal.

The distinction between two different types of incidence is drawn from the taxation literature, but similar questions arise with other proposals for new sources. Consider the global lottery discussed in Chapter 8. Opponents criticize this proposal on the grounds that the burden falls predominantly on poorer people in rich countries and on poor countries, whereas the cost of ODA financed through income taxation is borne by the better off. This distributional analysis relates to a differential analysis of substituting a global lottery for increased ODA (moving from B to A in Fig. 2.1). In contrast, a global lottery as an addition to existing funding may have quite different implications. The transfer from rich countries may be distributionally progressive in world terms, and the redistribution within the rest of the world may favour development. We may think differently about a lottery that moves us from O to A than about one which moves us from B to A. The International Finance Facility (IFF), discussed in Chapter 6, involves an increase in ODA but of limited duration, timed to achieve the Millennium Development Goals (MDGs) by 2015, and donors making a pre-commitment, so that the promises can be 'banked'. We can consider the proposal either as a net addition to existing ODA (moving from O to A) or compare it with the alternative of a steady annual flow of 'un-precommitted' ODA of the same present value (comparing A and B).

2.2.1. *Conclusion*

When considering innovative sources, we need to be clear whether they are seen as a complement to expanding ODA or as an alternative. In the former situation, the case has to be made in terms of enhanced funding for development; in the latter situation, the case is being made that the innovative sources are a better way of funding a given development effort.

2.3. WHAT FISCAL ARCHITECTURE?

New sources of development finance potentially involve a number of actors. In some cases, private individuals acting alone, like Ted Turner, or the person putting coins in the United Nations Children's Fund (UNICEF) Change for Good envelope, can make the key decision. In many cases, national governments are involved. They can simply involve a country acting unilaterally. A single country could provide matching funds for private funding of development by its citizens. A government could decide that a fraction of the proceeds from its state lottery is to be allocated to development aid. A country acting unilaterally could decide to allow emigrants' remittances as a deductible item against its national income tax. But in most cases, it is envisaged that there would be a multilateral agreement. Indeed, in the case of the creation of new Special Drawing Rights (SDRs), the constitution of the International Monetary Fund (IMF) requires a super-majority (85 per cent) of members to ratify the agreement before it can be put into effect. Where the source involves multilateral action, then two questions arise under the general heading of 'architecture'. In discussing this, I am presupposing that the participating countries have agreed on the form and scale of the action to be undertaken. What we are considering is the shape of the necessary institutions. (The political economy of countries acting together has already been considered in Chapter 1.)

2.3.1. *Flexible Geometry*

The first question is: Does the success and effectiveness of any particular proposal depend on complete adhesion of all countries or all donor countries? The natural instinct of many people is to assume that there is an inherent freerider problem and that there has to be general, if not universal, agreement. In the present climate, with multilateralism under question, this presumption provides grounds for pessimism about the chances of making progress.

On the other hand, suppose that we start from the position that universal agreement may be impossible and examine the implications of going ahead with a subset of countries. The United States has so far prevented the creation by the IMF of SDRs, and in this case, no action seems possible. But it does not follow that other measures are also blocked. With the other six proposals, it would be possible, at least theoretically, for progress to be made even without the agreement of all major countries. Here we can learn from the internal experience of the European Union. The European Union has in the past faced situations where one member state chose to 'opt out' of collective decisions. In these circumstances, flexibility in the resulting institutions has allowed the majority to respect the opting-out decision but still make progress towards the majority objectives. Partial adhesion has had costs. For instance, a member state opting-out of social protection may (or may not) enjoy a competitive advantage, exporting unemployment to the rest of the Union. These costs have to be placed in the balance. But the issue becomes one of balance, rather than of an absolute block on action.

We have to ask therefore in the case of each proposal whether we can in fact have a 'flexible geometry', where it is viable to go ahead with a subset of countries? The likely answer to this question varies from one proposal to another. The costs of incomplete coverage depend on the nature of the source of funding. Failure of countries to participate in the International Finance Facility (IFF) means that the scale of the operation is reduced, but the proposal is not undermined. The same applies to the global lottery, or the global premium bond; indeed insofar as these schemes offer a new product (see Chapter 8), those not participating may lose out. With global taxation, the free-riding problems become potentially more significant. Significant opting-out from a global carbon tax may erode the taxbase, as producers relocate to non-participating countries, and expose participating countries to intense lobbying from domestic interests. With a currency transactions tax, ease of relocation of financial activity depends on how extensive is the taxing jurisdiction. The larger the jurisdiction, the less elastic the response, and hence the greater the revenue potential.

2.3.2. *Fiscal Architecture*

The second question concerns the institutional arrangements under which multilateral action takes place. Where countries are acting in concert, then the organizational structure is important, as is illustrated in this section by reference to global taxation. A flow chart for national taxation is shown schematically in Fig. 2.2. National governments determine the rates of taxation and the taxbase. Individual taxpayers pay the taxes to the government, which both enforces payment and is in turn accountable to the electorate. Many taxes involve intermediary agents. The individual taxpayer, for example, pays the aircraft departure tax to the airline, which then accounts for the revenue to the government. Employers collect payroll taxes. Retailers or wholesalers collect excise taxes.

One evidently cannot apply exactly the same process to global taxation (Fig. 2.3). We have both global institutions and national governments, and it is the latter which have to agree to the taxes being levied and which are accountable to their electorates. It could indeed be that the global tax is treated as simply a glorified domestic tax, with the revenue being forwarded by national governments to a global spending body (the

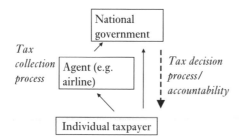

Figure 2.2. *Fiscal architecture: national taxation*

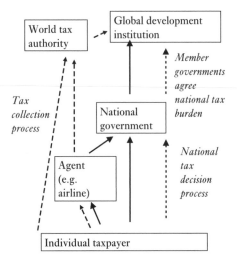

Figure 2.3. *Fiscal architecture in global setting*

heavy lines in Fig. 2.3). But there are more possibilities, as shown by the dashed and dotted lines. If there were an international air transport tax determined at the global level, then the airline could transfer the money, not to the national government, but to a global tax authority, in which case the new source of finance would bring a new actor into play. The dashed lines in Fig. 2.3 show this. Whether or not such a world tax authority is envisaged is one of the questions that have to be considered. (This may be different from an international tax organization, see Tanzi 1999.) The feasibility of creating such a tax authority depends on the universe of taxpayers. In the case of airlines, there is already an international organization (IATA—International Air Transport Association) and the international air travel tax could be collected by this body. A world tax authority could not deal with taxes paid by individual households, but one could envisage it operating a tax levied on multinational corporations, which would have to be registered where their cross-border activity exceeded a certain amount (just as there is an exemption level for VAT registration in national systems). In the literature on the corporation tax, one of the arguments for such a taxbase is that the status of incorporation confers benefits on organizations adopting this legal form. It is normally agreed that this does not justify present levels of corporate income taxation, but a more modest rate of global corporation tax could be seen as a form of benefit taxation for engaging in cross-border economic activity.

Moving in the opposite direction from the introduction of a world tax authority is the case shown by dotted lines in Fig. 2.3, where national governments retain not only control over the administration of the tax process but also discretion over the tax rates. In this case, participating governments would agree on their national tax liability but retain freedom to decide how the revenue is to be raised. This would in effect be applying the principle of subsidiarity adopted by the European Union.

To give a concrete illustration, suppose that the participating governments agree that each country should pay a tax related to national carbon emissions. This determines the amount that each participating country has to pay, but the national government would remain free to raise the revenue in whatever manner it thought fit. The national government might consider, for example, that a tax on air journeys was unfair on those living in remote rural areas, and choose for domestic reasons a different taxbase. We would then have a two-tier structure, with the national tax obligation requirement being agreed multilaterally, but the tax implementation being chosen locally. Countries with more emissions would pay more total tax, but this would not necessarily mean higher fuel taxes. Income tax or a broad-based VAT could be raised instead. One reason why, under the subsidiarity architecture, a national government may choose a different taxbase is that it faces political opposition to a particular form of taxation. The fuel tax protests of 2000 in Europe provide a good illustration.

2.3.3. *Fiscal Federalism*

The United States and other federal states, such as Canada and Australia, came into existence by a voluntary adhesion of previously sovereign states. The formation of the United States of America represented a pooling of sovereignty, just as the acceptance of a global responsibility for development involves some limitation on the freedom of action of national governments. This leads us to ask what lessons we can learn from the extensive literature on fiscal federalism, and this is the subject of Chapter 11. The reader may object that fiscal federations involve a degree of symmetry among participants that invalidates the application to the global context, where it is the inherent asymmetry in the world that generates the very problem with which we are concerned. But many of the federations that came into existence involved participating states that were unequal to a significant—if not the same—extent. Much of the debate about federal finance is concerned with the treatment of unequals: the design of equalization formulae.

2.3.4. *Conclusions*

Proposals for new forms of development funding raise important issues of institutional shape. In designing the architecture of global fiscal system, there is considerable scope for choice and it should not be assumed that all depends on universal support by donor countries. As the references to 'flexible geometry' and to 'subsidiarity' illustrate, we can learn usefully about the range of alternatives from the experience of supranational groupings such as the European Union. The parallel with the public finances of federal states seems worth exploring.

2.4. LEAKY BUCKET OR DOUBLE DIVIDEND?

As Arthur Okun expressed it in his book *Equality and Efficiency* (1975), transfers are made using a leaky bucket. To raise US$10 billion for new development purposes may cost more than US$10 billion. Put another way, the marginal cost of US$1 extra public funds for development may be more than US$1, because taxes and other interventions distort economic decisions. 'The cake gets smaller as we seek to share it out.' On the other hand, there are arguments, usually put under the banner of 'double dividend', that there may be efficiency gains, so that the amount in the bucket is actually increased. And the literature on the marginal cost of public funds has shown that there are circumstances when the marginal cost of US$1 extra funds is less than US$1 (see Atkinson and Stern 1974; Fullerton 1991; Sandmo 1998). In this section, I consider these two different perspectives.

Why are buckets leaky? The first source of leakage is the cost of administration. Currency transactors may pay $X billion in tax but $(X−A) billion is the net revenue, where A is the cost of operating the tax collection and enforcement agencies. It may, for this reason, be preferable to raise an existing tax, such as income tax, rather than to institute new taxes with all the fixed costs of administration. The second source of leakage is that a new revenue source may *crowd out* other sources of development funding. One of the lessons of public finance is that in calculating the change in revenue resulting from an increase in one tax, one has to take account of the possible impact on the revenue from other taxes. A good example would be an international tourist tax (not considered in this study). As Clunies-Ross (1999) points out, tourism is an important source of government revenue for a number of poor countries. To the extent that visiting tourists have less to spend after they have paid the tourist tax, these countries will be receiving less sales tax on the purchases made by tourists and would have to be compensated before the tax yields net additional revenue. Similarly, the introduction of a global lottery will affect national budgets. Part of the customer base will be drawn from existing national state lotteries, reducing their revenue. Part will be drawn from spending on private gambling subject to national taxes, so that fiscal revenue will fall.

But these are not the only potential leakages. Most taxes have an impact on the decisions of taxpayers apart from the pure effect of reducing their incomes. An income tax may cause people to work less hard, or it may cause them to work harder to maintain their level of expenditure. In the conventional public finance format, there is a deadweight loss, or excess burden associated with taxation. The currency transactions tax causes people to avoid activities that attract the tax. They will, for example, be inhibited from switching their investment portfolio away from domestic securities towards those denominated in other currencies. This has an efficiency cost, since they are not allocating their investments according to the return at the margin. In the case of the income tax, the choice between income and leisure is distorted (this applies whether the tax causes the person to work more or to work less). Moreover, there is a presumption that the distortionary cost increases with the tax rate. The distortion is much more significant with a transactions tax rate of 20 basis points (0.2 per cent) than for one with a rate of 2 basis points (0.02 per cent). This may be an argument for seeking a new taxbase, rather than increasing existing taxes such as income tax. If one adds to an already high tax, then the efficiency loss is larger.

Adjustments in behaviour, in turn, may induce market reactions. If a tax on carbon use is passed on in higher consumer prices, then demand will shift away from goods that are intensive in their direct or indirect use of fuels. This will make worse off those people who cannot shift easily from working in those industries, as well as those whose budgets are particularly weighted towards those goods. The ultimate incidence of the tax may be rather different from its initial incidence. In order to establish this, we need to follow through the full general equilibrium effects, allowing for market clearing. There may be effects on prices, as discussed in Section 2.4.

2.4.1. *A Double Dividend?*

The standard analysis of tax incidence is indeed based on examining a world of perfectly competitive, perfectly functioning markets. In such a 'first-best' context, government intervention—whatever its distributional advantages—has an efficiency cost. In the currency transactions tax example, if it were not for the tax the market would be efficient. The economies of the world are not, however, well characterized by perfectly competitive, perfectly functioning markets, and one of the major contributions of modern public economics has been to explore the implications of market failure. This has led to arguments that taxes may serve a corrective function: that the excess burden may become a benefit. The classic example is a corrective tax on environmental external diseconomies. A tax on the consumption of goods that harm the environment has a positive allocational effect, switching spending away from polluting goods towards those causing less or no environmental damage. In these circumstances, switching behaviour is desirable. Moreover, if the revenue is used to reduce other taxes that have a negative allocational effect, we have a 'double dividend' (for overviews, see Goulder 1995; Sandmo 2000).

The double dividend can arise in the present case in two ways. If the new source is seen as an alternative to ODA, then it can both make its own efficiency contribution *and* allow a reduction in the taxes presently used to finance ODA. This is a good example of the differential incidence argument in operation. Taxing air transport will not only reduce the environmental damage of tourism but also allow the income tax to be reduced, so making staying in the office financially more attractive at the margin. Taxing carbon may allow payroll taxes to be reduced, leading to a fall in unemployment. There is an 'employment dividend' as well as an 'environmental dividend'. The second possibility is that the new source is a net addition to development resources. In this case, the double dividend consists of the reduced environmental damage *and* the benefit from achieving the development goals.

2.4.2. *Questioning the Double Dividend Argument*

The double dividend idea appeals to the imagination. However, one has to ask why, if a new revenue source can generate a positive sum outcome, have national governments not already adopted such a policy? Why do Organization for Economic Cooperation and Development (OECD) countries not operate lotteries to raise funds to finance their ODA? If a carbon use tax would reduce external diseconomies, why is this not already reflected in domestic taxes? If governments could reduce unemployment by a switch in taxation, why have they not already done so? To this central question, there are several responses. Here I consider two. First, in a dynamic world there may well be unexploited opportunities. Second, it may be that the dividend is global rather than national.

In a dynamic world, new opportunities are always arising and reaction speeds are not instantaneous. It takes time for new policy needs to become apparent and for governments to react. A good example is provided in the present context by the issue of remittances. The arrival of immigrant workers in a city creates a demand for money transfer services. If entry into this industry is slow, then a few firms, able to extract monopoly rents, may dominate it in the early stages. Government policy to encourage competition in the sector can increase the proportion of the transfer that arrives in the destination country. In this case, competition policy may combine with development policy to yield a positive sum outcome.

2.4.3. *A Global Double Dividend?*

National governments may not impose corrective taxes because the benefits accrue disproportionately outside their boundaries. The switch from general taxation to carbon use taxation may be positive sum globally but negative sum nationally. The revenue calculations of governments take account only of receipts and payments to the national treasury. The impact of spillovers from one state to another is a staple of fiscal federalism. Under certain circumstances, local governments may under-supply public goods that benefit people living outside their borders; and they may over-tax where taxpayers come from outside. There are fiscal externalities. In the present case, there is a possible under-supply of fiscal correction to external diseconomies because the costs spill over to others. It could be said that we have externalities squared: there is a possible under-supply of fiscal correction to external diseconomies because there are externalities in these very costs.

How is this potential argument for additional environmental taxation affected by the fiscal architecture? We are presupposing that the tax is indeed levied on individuals and firms in the form of a carbon levy (or other environmental taxbase). Suppose, however, that we have subsidiarity, where the burden on national governments is determined by their carbon emissions, but the national governments are free to decide how to raise the revenue. As noted above, they may for political or other reasons choose another taxbase. It is still, however, the case that the government faces a financial incentive to reduce its emissions by other policies, such as auctioning emission permits or regulation.

2.4.4. *Conclusion*

The calculation of the leakage, or extra dividend, is a complex matter. Depending on the circumstances, it may strengthen or weaken the case for new sources as opposed to existing taxes. The framework needs to be broadened to recognize the departures of real-world economies from the textbook world of perfectly competitive, perfectly clearing markets with full information. These departures may mean that there is a double dividend, where new taxes have a beneficial impact on resource allocation.

Moreover, the double dividend may be global in character, not taken fully into account in national decisionmaking.

2.5. IS THERE A TRANSFER PROBLEM?

Economists worry about the effect of policy changes on market prices. A substantial resource transfer between countries may lead to changes in the prices of different goods—those exported and imported, and those not traded—that have implications for recipient and donor countries. These price changes may undermine, or re-enforce, the benefits from the original transfer.

Keynes (1929) addressed this problem after the First World War, when he was concerned with the impact of reparations being paid by Germany. He identified the 'transfer problem' that a country making a transfer might suffer an additional loss through a shift in demand against their products, causing the terms of trade to turn against them. The 'terms of trade' refer to the price of a country's exports divided by the price of its imports. If the terms of trade worsen, then a country has to export more units to get the same number of units of imports. Applied to transfers for development, this would mean that the recipient countries could enjoy a further benefit from improved terms of trade, if demand switches towards the products they produce. As clarified by Ohlin (1929) and subsequent writers (see Bhagwati and Srinivasan 1983: Lecture 12; Brakman and van Marrewijk 1998: chapter 2), international trade theory shows that the direction of the terms-of-trade effect depends on the relative marginal propensities to consume in the donor and recipient countries (how much out of an additional US$1 of income is spent on home and on imported goods) and the magnitude depends on the price elasticities.

It may be tempting to dismiss the terms-of-trade effects as of only footnote importance. However, international trade economists take them seriously. Referring to the inflows of loans to the United States in the early 1980s, Krugman and Obstfeld say 'the transfer effect was a major contributor to the large temporary improvement in the US terms of trade' (1994: 102). According to them, US residents spend about 80 cents of a dollar of additional income on US goods, whereas foreign residents spend only 10 cents. What then is the relevance of the transfer problem in the present context? First, it should be noted that, as far as the impact on recipient countries is concerned, the issue is only relevant when new sources of funding are a net addition. (When considering the differential effect of new sources versus increased ODA, the total size of the transfer is assumed constant.) The transfer problem arises when we contemplate increasing the scale of transfers. In that case, we have to consider the use made of the funds. Here the balance between investment and consumption may be significant. If the transfer is largely used to fund investment, then the pattern of demand may shift towards manufactured capital goods exported by the donor countries. (This is of course one of the possible functions of the practice of tying aid.) Account has also to be taken of the intertemporal impact. If there is a process of catch up over time, then the production possibilities of developing countries will come to resemble more closely those of rich countries, and the terms-of-trade effects will become smaller. If the pattern of transfers is brought forward, as with the IFF, then the terms-of-trade effect may be accentuated relative to a smoother time path. This may not outweigh the advantage of earlier disbursement, but needs to be put into the balance.

The transfer problem also potentially affects the donor countries, and this may be the case even when the total transfer is held constant. If we consider the differential effect of new sources and increased ODA, then they may impact on different income groups. In her analysis of the transfer problem, Chichilnisky (1980) distinguished two income groups in the donor country, and identified circumstances in which the recipient country only gained if the poorer group in the donor country were made worse off. Reduced international inequality was achieved at the expense of increased within-country inequality. Put differently, this is another example of the possibility that, when we allow for the changes in market-clearing prices, the ultimate incidence of a new source of funding may differ from the initial incidence.

2.5.1. *Absorption and the 'Dutch Disease'*

For a small developing country, with no specific natural resources, it may appear fanciful to suppose that its receipt of increased aid could affect the world prices for the goods it exports and imports. As commonly assumed in economic analysis, many countries are 'small', facing fixed world prices. If they wish to import new investment goods, then there is an unlimited supply on the world market. In this sense, there is no problem of 'absorbing' the increased flow of funds.

The position is, however, different once we allow for non-traded goods or services, the prices of which reflect domestic supply and demand (see Corden and Neary 1982). To the extent that the transfer increases demand for the non-traded good, its price tends to rise. There is a real appreciation, in that domestic goods/services become more expensive relative to the goods traded on the world market. This can cause the movement of labour out of the sectors producing traded goods. This movement is in the reverse direction from that required for development and worsens the foreign balance. As is noted in Chapters 6 and 9, domestic policy has to take account of the possible impact on domestic demand and inflation. As with the transfer problem, the issue potentially applies to all proposals for increased transfers of aid.

2.5.2. *Stimulus to World Economy*

The treatment by Keynes of the transfer problem was 'notable . . . for the classical, or pre-Keynesian, way he analysed the problem, concentrating on relative price movements' (Skidelsky 1992: 309). The existence of involuntary unemployment and excess capacity can, however, change the conclusions, in that the responses may be purely in terms of expanded output, not price changes. One of the arguments for the creation of Special Drawing Rights (SDRs) is indeed that they would provide a macroeconomic stimulus to the world economy. This depends on the extent to which the transfers of SDR allocations from rich to poor countries lead the latter to increase spending. Clark and Polak (2002) argue that a regular allocation will not lead to a rise in spending, most countries adding to their reserves (which in itself has a development benefit), but this may not apply where there are substantial transfers of SDRs to poor countries.

Macroeconomic stimulus is another form of potential double dividend. Again, we have to explain why this cannot already be achieved. The macroeconomic literature has extensively discussed the problem of international policy coordination failure. The existence of failure does not mean that policy coordination necessarily leads to efficiency gains, but it is possible that there may be a global positive sum outcome to a creation of additional liquidity. Global spillovers apply at the macroeconomic as well as the microeconomic level. More concretely, those European governments seeking a way to re-stimulate their economies should be particularly aware of the potential mutual benefit. Increased flows of resources for development, generating additional world demand, may allow Europe to escape the constraints of its macro-policymaking.

2.5.3. *Conclusions*

Consideration of the effect of new sources of finance takes us into the working of the international economy. Substantial transfers may lead to changes in the terms of trade with implications for both recipient and donor countries. They may affect the relative prices of traded and non-traded goods, causing domestic inflation. Even holding the level of transfers constant, different sources of funding and different timing of the flows may have different effects on demand patterns. Once we allow for involuntary unemployment and excess capacity, there may be a global double dividend through stimulus to the world economy. Such a macroeconomic bonus would benefit both developing and developed countries.

2.6. EQUIVALENT MEASURES?

Policy tools may look different but have equivalent effects. International trade theory and public finance have demonstrated a number of important equivalences. A government can set a tariff on the import of a commodity, or it can set a quota and auction the import permits. If the quota is set at the level of imports generated by the tariff, then in a competitive economy the impact is the same, including the revenue to the government. An income tax with an exemption of all savings is equivalent to a uniform value-added tax (see Atkinson and Stiglitz 1980). Such equivalences operate at the level of the impact on individuals and firms. It is, of course, quite possible that individuals and firms perceive them differently (an example is given below) and that their economic consequences are different. Moreover, the political attractiveness may be quite different. Recasting a proposal in an equivalent form may convert it from an election-loser to a vote-winner.

In the present context, consideration of such equivalences may allow one to see existing proposals in a new light or the creation of new ideas. Pursuing the parallel with tariffs and quotas, we can see for instance that there is a potential equivalence between a global carbon tax, considered in Chapter 3, and the auction of tradeable permits (see Pearson 2000; Sandmo 2000). Attention has focused on the global carbon tax, but another possibility is to auction permits, to produce the same level of revenue, and, in a world of certainty and perfect competition, the same level of pollution. There are reasons why in reality the two approaches may differ, but we need to ask, when considering the global carbon tax proposal, whether it is clearly superior to the alternative of auctioning permits.

A second example is provided by the discussion of the global lottery in Chapter 8. The authors come up with the novel alternative proposal of a global premium bond, which is a government bond where the capital is maintained (in money terms) but the interest takes the form of lottery prizes. Experience in the United Kingdom suggests that this appeals to a different market, with the middle- and upper-income groups participating whereas they do not play the national lottery. Yet, the premium bond is financially equivalent as a transaction to placing money in a regular savings bank and drawing out the interest each month to buy lottery tickets. There are, of course, differences in the prize structure and level, and in the tax treatment, but we need to ask what lies behind the differences in reaction.

The third example concerns the IFF. Understanding this imaginative proposal is aided by considering whether or not it is equivalent to a particular time path of ODA. As noted earlier, it involves bringing forward the disbursement of funds, but it goes beyond a variation in the time shape in that donors are precommitted. We have therefore to ask how far the guarantee of funding by donor countries increases the net value of ODA. How much net additional resources are generated by the certainty of underwritten flows rather than annual allocations by donor governments?

2.6.1. *Conclusions*

Consideration of the equivalence of different policy instruments is a good discipline and a source of new ideas. For each proposal, we have to consider how far there are equivalent ways of achieving the same objectives.

2.7. CONCLUSION: CONTRIBUTION TO THE POLICY DEBATE

The answers given to the questions posed in this chapter have been given in the conclusions to each section. I hope that they will help provide the reader with a framework to assess the contributions of the different proposals analysed in the next seven chapters. Here I end with a reflection on the role of economic analysis in the policy debate. As discussed in Chapter 1, the proposals for new sources of development funding have to be seen in a political context. They have been put forward in the light of political objectives and perceived constraints. This does not imply that economic analysis should accept these objectives uncritically or that it should be bound by these constraints (see Boadway 2002). But economic analysis has a role to play in elucidating the implications of proposals for the achievement of the professed objectives, and in identifying the costs of political constraints. We might, for example, conclude that the constraint that the taxbase be chosen by national governments, weakens the contribution of a carbon tax to environmental goals and hence reduces the double dividend. We might, for example, conclude that the objectives of the global lottery are better served by designing a prize structure that does not compete with that of national lotteries. Analysis of this type is intended to contribute to the public debate.

REFERENCES

Atkinson, A. B. and N. H. Stern (1974). 'Pigou, Taxation and Public Goods'. *Review of Economic Studies*, 41(1): 119–28.

—— and J. E. Stiglitz (1980). *Lectures on Public Economics*. New York: McGraw-Hill.

Bhagwati, J. N. and T. N. Srinivasan (1983). *Lectures on International Trade*. Cambridge, MA: MIT Press.

Boadway, R. (2002). 'The Role of Public Choice Considerations in Normative Public Economics', in S. L. Winer and H. Shibata (eds), *The Role of Political Economy in the Theory and Practice of Public Finance*. Cheltenham, UK: Edward Elgar, 47–68.

Brakman, S. and C. van Marrewijk (1998). *The Economics of International Transfers*. Cambridge: Cambridge University Press.

Chichilnisky, G. (1980). 'Basic Goods, the Effects of Commodity Transfers and the International Economic Order'. *Journal of Development Economics*, 7(4): 505–19.

Clark, P. B. and J. J. Polak (2002). 'International Liquidity and the Role of the SDR in the International Monetary System'. *IMF Working Paper* WP/02/217. Washington, DC: IMF.

Clunies-Ross, A. (1999). 'Sustaining Revenue for Social Purposes in the Face of Globaliza- tion', *Experts Discuss Some Critical Social Development Issues*. New York: UN Department of Economic and Social Affairs.

Corden, W. M. and J. P. Neary (1982) 'Booming Sector and De-Industrialization in a Small Open Economy'. *Economic Journal*, 92: 825–48.

Fullerton, D. (1991). 'Reconciling Recent Estimates of the Marginal Welfare Cost of Taxation'. *American Economic Review*, 81(1): 302–8.

Goulder, L. H. (1995). 'Environmental Taxation and the Double Dividend: A Reader's Guide'. *International Tax and Public Finance*, 2(x): 157–83.

Krugman, P. R. and M. Obstfeld (1994). *International Economics*, 3rd edition. New York: Harper Collins.

Keynes, J. M. (1929). 'The German Transfer Problem'. *Economic Journal*, 39: 1–17.

Mendez, R. P. (1992). *International Public Finance*. Oxford: Oxford University Press.

Musgrave, R. A. (1959). *Theory of Public Finance*. New York: McGraw-Hill.

Ohlin, B. (1929). 'The Reparation Problem: A Discussion'. *Economic Journal*, 39: 172–83.

Okun, A. M. (1975). *Equality and Efficiency*. Washington, DC: Brookings Institution.

Pearson, C. S. (2000). *Economics and the Global Environment*. Cambridge: Cambridge University Press.

Sandmo, A. (1998). 'Redistribution and the Marginal Cost of Public Funds'. *Journal of Public Economics*, 70(3): 365–82.

Sandmo, A. (2000). *The Public Economics of the Environment.* Oxford: Oxford University Press.

Skidelsky, R. (1992). *John Maynard Keynes: The Economist as Saviour 1920–1937.* London: Macmillan.

Tanzi, V. (1999). 'Is There a Need for a World Tax Organization?', in A. Razin and E. Sadka (eds), *The Economics of Globalization.* New York: Cambridge University Press.

3

Environmental Taxation and Revenue for Development

AGNAR SANDMO

3.1. INTRODUCTION

This chapter considers the possible role of environmental taxes for economic development. This role is quite complex and has not so far been widely discussed in the literature. It is therefore useful to start with a review of the basic economic insights in the field of environmental taxation in order to prepare the ground for the application of the theory to problems of economic development and the global environment.

Section 3.2 below starts with a review of the welfare economics of environmental taxation in a single closed economy; analytical details are provided in Appendix A. Section 3.3 discusses alternatives to taxes as instruments of environmental policy, considering both fixed and transferable quotas. Section 3.4 is a review of the double dividend issue, which has received much attention in recent literature, while Section 3.5 considers the extent to which distributional concerns should be reflected in the design of environmental policy. Since much of the literature in this area relates to the economies of industrialized countries, Section 3.6 takes up some special problems in its application to developing economies. Section 3.7 extends the analysis from the single country to the case of global externalities where each individual country is affected by the environmental pollution of all other countries; a formal analysis in the context of a two-country model is in Appendix B. The political economy of global environmental taxes is considered in Section 3.8, which also compares alternative tax designs with regard to the equity-efficiency tradeoff. After a brief discussion of some practical problems of tax collection in Section 3.9, Section 3.10 evaluates the revenue potential of such taxes with special reference to the carbon tax. Some concluding remarks are collected in the final section of the chapter.

This chapter has been prepared for the UNU–WIDER project on Innovative Sources for Development Finance. I am indebted to the project participants, especially Tony Atkinson and Robin Boadway, for their comments on an earlier version, and to Ottar Mæstad and David Wildasin for helpful suggestions.

3.2. THE GENERAL THEORY OF ENVIRONMENTAL TAXATION

A basic economic insight is that a competitive economy, under ideal conditions, will generate a socially efficient or Pareto optimal allocation of private goods, meaning that it is not possible to reallocate resources in such a way that everyone becomes better off.

In partial equilibrium terminology, an efficient allocation of private goods is achieved when, first, the marginal cost of producing a commodity is the same for all producers; this requirement is what is known as *production efficiency*. Second, the marginal willingness to pay for the commodity—the marginal benefit—should be the same for all consumers, ensuring *consumption efficiency*. Third, the marginal cost of production should equal the marginal willingness to pay; this final requirement ensures overall *Pareto optimality*. In an ideal competitive environment, optimizing behaviour by firms and consumers will ensure that marginal costs and marginal benefits will be equated to the equilibrium prices for all goods. Thus, a competitive equilibrium is a Pareto optimum, and there is no waste of resources.

One element of the 'ideal conditions' requirement is the absence of external effects. Originally introduced by Alfred Marshall, the externality concept was further developed by Arthur C. Pigou (1920), who also pioneered the application of the theory to environmental problems in the modern sense. In recent decades, the increasing awareness of the environmental damage caused by modern societies has greatly increased the importance of externality theory as a tool for applied policy analysis.[1]

Environmental externalities may be both positive and negative, but we focus here on the latter case. Externalities may arise both on the production and consumption side of the economy. A famous type of production externalities is the category known as 'the tragedy of the commons' (Hardin 1968). If there is common ownership of land, each owner has an incentive to let his cattle graze more than is rational from the viewpoint of the group of owners as a whole. A more modern example is where a manufacturing plant releases emissions into air, soil, or water so as to affect negatively the production possibilities or costs of firms in the tourism or fishing industries. This case can be seen as another example of the tragedy of the commons, since the natural recipients can be defined as commons in a more general sense.[2] A central example of consumption externalities is traffic congestion, which arises from the fact that no individual car owner has an incentive to take account of the additional cost imposed on other drivers by his own car use. Thus, externalities may be generated by actions both by producers and consumers, and they may also affect both producers and consumers. A common element of the examples is that the agents who generate the externalities increase the costs or reduce the benefits of other agents. The competitive price mechanism fails to

---

[1] It is interesting to note that as late as 1957, George Stigler wrote that after Marshall, it was left for Pigou 'to elaborate, and exaggerate, the importance of this source of disharmonies' (1957). With the increasing awareness of environmental problems over the last few decades, few would now argue that Pigou was guilty of any exaggeration.

[2] In addition to its effect on production possibilities, this type of emission also has negative consequences for consumers through health effects and the degradation of natural beauty.

equate marginal social costs and marginal social benefits. Another unifying perspective on these examples is that negative externalities from the consumption or production of private goods reduce the availability of *public goods* like clean air, clean water, or uncongested roads.

It is far from obvious that, having identified potential cases of market failure, economists should proceed to recommend government action for their resolution. In a commons type of situation in which there is a relatively small number of agents, each one of them will have an incentive to negotiate a contract with the other affected parties in order to arrive at an efficient solution; this is the argument developed in the influential paper by Coase (1960). However, as the number of affected agents becomes large, individual incentives to enter into costly negotiations become very weak. A natural outcome in such cases is that the responsibility to arrive at a socially efficient solution comes to rest on some political authority, be it local, national, or even global. Even in the context of a large number of agents, however, attempts by the government to improve on the market outcome may not be successful; there are policy failures as well as market failures. Policy recommendations should take into account whether or not government is *in fact* likely to improve on the performance of an imperfect market.

The inefficiency generated by environmental externalities arises because individual agents do not take account of the effects of their own actions on the welfare of others. Levying a tax on the action in question that reflects the social impact of these harmful effects, leads agents to act *as if* they take the effects into account. The optimal environmental tax internalizes the externality and restores the efficiency of the market mechanism.

How high should optimal environmental taxes be? There are two issues here, one concerning the theoretical principles behind the determination of the taxes and one that concerns the empirical implementation of these principles.

The theoretical principles can briefly be described as follows: If the damage takes the form of deterioration of an environmental public good, the tax should reflect the marginal loss of that deterioration to society as a whole, and that marginal value is the sum of the losses suffered by all agents affected by the externality. In the perfect world of first-best welfare economics, these corrective or Pigouvian taxes are the only indirect taxes that are consistent with an efficient market equilibrium. Any further revenue to finance public expenditure or redistribute incomes should be raised by individualized lumpsum taxes.[3] When, more realistically, distortionary taxes have to be used for revenue purposes, a Pigouvian element should be included in the second-best optimal taxes for the commodities that generate the externalities. In both cases, one sees the operation of the *principle of targeting*; the tax incentive aims to affect the decisions that directly influence the externality and to be as neutral as possible with respect to other decisions.[4]

---

[3] A simple model of the first-best case is set out in Appendix A.

[4] The principles of second-best environmental taxation were discussed in Sandmo (1975); see also Sandmo (2000: chapter 5).

How should one estimate the marginal social loss or damage? Obviously, an estimate that is built up from information about the losses suffered by thousands or millions of individuals is not practicable, and simpler methods have to be employed. The value of the ideal theoretical measure of marginal social damage is mainly to guide one's thoughts in the selection of a practical estimation procedure. Empirical analyses of environmental taxes typically start with some target reduction in the amount of emissions and then ask what level of taxes (or other instruments) is required to achieve the target. For this procedure to be optimal, one must assume that the target reduction has been chosen as a result of a cost–benefit analysis of the benefits and costs of the reduction in emissions.

Although the use of taxes is not the only alternative for policy implementation, they have a number of advantages from an efficiency point of view. Consider the case where the externality is generated through the activities of a large number of individual firms, and where the government's aim is to reduce the aggregate level of these activities. To reduce the activity in question imposes a cost on each individual polluter, and in the interests of production efficiency one would like the total cost of achieving the reduction to be as small as possible. Assuming that the marginal cost is increasing, this is achieved when all polluters have the same marginal cost of pollution reduction, which will be the case when they all face the same tax. If the polluters are consumers instead of firms, the argument has to be modified in terms of expenditure rather than cost, and the effect of the tax is to achieve consumption efficiency rather than production efficiency, but the basic economic insight is the same: the environmental tax can achieve the desired reduction of the activity in question at minimal sacrifice to society as a whole.

3.3. ALTERNATIVES TO TAXES

The main alternative to taxes is the use of quantitative regulations or quotas. In principle, it is clear that if one wishes to achieve a given reduction of the level of some harmful activity, this can in fact be done either by taxes or quotas, and various versions of a quota system have been widely used in practice. In judging the efficiency aspects of quota systems, one has to distinguish between fixed and transferable quotas.

In principle, any quota system presumes that a quota can be levied on each individual polluter. With a fixed quota, the polluter must limit his emissions to the quota that has been allocated to him; if he exceeds it, he is liable to punishment. The environment can be regarded as a public good that is being 'produced' by the actions of a large number of individual polluters; a reduction of emissions produces more environmental quality. Since efficiency in production implies that the marginal cost of production should be the same for all producers, quotas should be tight for polluters with a low marginal cost of reducing pollution and liberal for high-cost polluters. Imposing individual quotas on polluters according to this principle raises enormous informational problems if the number of polluters is large. In practice, therefore, some simpler rule—like basing quotas on past emissions—has to be found, and this is likely to violate the requirement of production efficiency.[5]

An alternative to the fixed quota system is to make quotas transferable between polluters. Someone who finds that it is extremely costly to meet the demands of the quota may buy additional units of quota from another polluter whose cost of reducing emissions is relatively low. Suppose that there is a large number of polluters, and consequently a large volume of quota units being traded. One could then imagine a competitive equilibrium in quotas, where all polluters buy or sell quota units at a uniform price so that the demand for quotas equals the supply. Cost minimization on the part of polluters implies that they will reduce pollution to the point where the marginal cost of reducing pollution is equal to the price of a unit of quota. But this means that the marginal cost of reducing pollution will be the same for all polluters, so that production efficiency is obtained under the system of transferable quotas, just as with a tax on emissions.

In fact, the equivalence between the two systems can be pushed even further. The optimal Pigouvian tax rate on emissions will result in some overall level of pollution. Suppose that one starts with the optimal level of emissions and issues quotas in exactly this amount. Then the equilibrium unit price of quotas will be exactly equal to the Pigouvian tax rate. If initial ownership of the quotas rests with the government, it could sell quotas to private polluters—either through some type of quota exchange system or by auction—and collect the same amount in sales revenue as it would otherwise collect in taxes. Thus, in terms of both production efficiency and in their implications for government revenue, environmental taxes and transferable quotas are equivalent.

In choosing between the two systems, one must rely on considerations that have not been included in the present discussion, and an obvious item that has been left aside is the cost of administration. This includes, first, the cost of the necessary bureaucracy in setting up the systems and running their daily operations. Second, it would include the resources necessary to control environmental tax evasion and quota violations. The relative costs of taxes versus quotas are likely to be specific to the particular type of environmental pollution being considered, so that it is difficult to draw a general conclusion concerning the relative costs of running a tax or quota system. Another consideration that might be important for social and political acceptance has to do with the perceived morality of the two systems. It is not unusual to hear it being said that the government should not be allowed to earn money on socially harmful activities. This viewpoint is based on a complete misunderstanding of the role of incentives, and in any case, it is an argument against *both* taxes and transferable quotas.[6] A more subtle point is that under the tax system, polluters pay for the harmful activities that they have in fact undertaken, whereas under the quota system they buy themselves the right

---

[5] In Sandmo (2002), I consider the extent to which the expected fine for quota violations can play the same role as an environmental tax in achieving production efficiency, and show that this will be true only in very special cases.

[6] In fact, it could also be seen as an argument against fixed quotas, since these, to be effective, must obviously specify punishments for quota violations. If punishment takes the form of fines, the government will be getting revenue from pollution activities in this case also.

to carry out these activities in the future, and the latter case may possibly be seen as morally more objectionable than the former.

We conclude that a system of transferable quotas is an alternative to the use of environmental taxes that have many of the same properties. If wisely used, it leads individual economic agents to modify their behaviour in a way that causes the market system to function efficiently, even in the presence of external effects. Keeping this result in mind, we now revert to the case of environmental taxes. Are there other gains or 'social dividends' from the use of environmental taxes? So far, we have neglected the possible benefit of the tax revenue that accrues to the government. Could this revenue generate additional dividends for society?

3.4. THE DOUBLE DIVIDEND ISSUE

The introduction of environmental taxes creates a new source of tax revenue for the government. Because this happens without any efficiency loss to the economy—at least not in the ideal version of the tax system—the revenue can be seen as a pure transfer between the private and public sector, just like the individualized lumpsum taxes familiar from welfare economics. However, a number of researchers have pointed out that this new source of revenue may in fact create a social gain for the economy over and above its effect on the environment, so it has become customary to speak of 'the double dividend'. The second dividend has been defined in several different ways, but it may be useful to distinguish between three kinds.

First, if one assumes that the level of public expenditure is to be held constant during the process of introducing environmental taxes, this implies that other taxes will have to play a smaller role in the economy, leading to a reduction of other indirect and direct taxes. The reduced role of distortionary taxes in the economy will diminish the overall efficiency loss from taxation, so that this tax efficiency dividend is in addition to the environmental dividend. This is the most fundamental notion of the double dividend.

Second, however, one may question the rationale of assuming constant tax revenue. If the tax system as a whole becomes more efficient, it may not be rational to hold the level of public expenditure constant. An optimal level of public expenditure should satisfy the condition that the marginal value of the expenditure should be equal to its marginal social cost. The latter has two components: there is the direct resource cost of factor use, and in addition there is the efficiency cost of the taxes used to withdraw the resources from the private sector. With the introduction of environmental taxes, the tax system as a whole becomes more efficient and the efficiency cost goes down. This may justify higher public expenditure, and the justification is obviously stronger, the less efficient the tax system was at the time of introduction of environmental taxes.

Third, much attention has been given to the possibility that a 'green' tax reform might lead to a reduction of unemployment. The idea behind this possibility is that wages, for a variety of possible reasons, are in fact set above the level required for full employment, with actual employment being determined from the demand side of the labour market. An increase of environmental or 'green' taxation in combination with a reduction of the payroll tax would lower labour cost to employers, increase the demand for labour and consequently reduce unemployment (assuming a constant supply of labour).

All the three candidates for the second dividend have been subjected to intensive theoretical research; for recent surveys see Goulder (1995), Bovenberg (1999), and Schöb (2003). The research has demonstrated that any of the three versions of the double dividend hypothesis are indeed possible outcomes of a green tax reform, but that a positive second dividend is by no means assured. Here we can only touch on the reasons for these ambiguities. In the case of the tax efficiency dividend, whether or not it is realized depends on which distortionary taxes are being cut. Suppose, for example, that the tax system discourages labour, but that the proposal for a green tax reform does not involve the reduction of taxes on labour; instead, it is proposed to cut taxes on consumer goods that are in fact complementary with leisure. It is easy to see that this reform could exacerbate the distortion of the labour-leisure choice and increase the overall efficiency loss from the tax system. This could also increase the marginal cost of public funds and thus jeopardize the public expenditure dividend. In the case of the employment dividend, a complicating issue is the incidence effect of the tax changes. It seems unrealistic to believe that a trade union will not try to capture some of the benefits from a reduction of the payroll tax in the form of higher gross wages; in addition, it might demand compensation for the increase of indirect taxes. The result is that there is no guarantee that employment costs will fall and that employment will go up.

To conclude this brief review of the double dividend arguments, there are no guarantees that a green tax reform will also involve a secondary dividend in terms of a more efficient tax system, a lower social cost of public expenditure or a decrease of unemployment. However, this should not be construed to mean that a secondary dividend is not possible. What the literature does point out is that the secondary gain depends on the precise nature of the reform, that is, on all the components of the proposed tax reform. If the reform is carried out with careful attention to the interaction between taxes and markets, it has the potential to result in a double dividend. Finally, it should be stressed that the empirical magnitude of the dividends will depend not on the magnitudes of the tax rates as such, but on their effects on quantities, as reflected in the elasticities of demand and supply.

3.5. DISTRIBUTIONAL CONCERNS

One important objection to the introduction of environmental taxes focuses on the distributional effects. A greater role for environmental taxes means, it is argued, more emphasis on indirect taxes, and consequently a diminished role for the tax system in the redistribution of income. A green tax reform may improve efficiency, but it does so at the cost of redistributing income from the poor to the rich. This is particularly important in the case of energy taxes. Expenditure on energy, particularly for heating and cooking, weighs more heavily in low-income budgets, so that higher energy prices redistribute income in disfavour of the poor. There are several reasons why this view is too simplified, and one needs to consider more carefully exactly how such a reform is carried out.

If one imagines, in line with the first of the three double dividend hypotheses, that an increase of environmental taxation is combined with cuts in the direct taxation of income and wealth, it is a reasonable assumption that the substitution of indirect for direct taxes will involve more inequality of after-tax income. But there is no particular reason why the tax cuts should be carried out with a complete disregard for their distributional impact. A society that cares both about efficiency and equity could let any adverse distributional effects of a green tax reform be compensated by changes in the degree of progressivity of the combined system of direct taxation and income transfers, or it could substitute green taxes for other indirect taxes that have a less egalitarian profile. Some economists would go as far as to argue that environmental taxes should be set with sole regard for their main function, which is to internalize environmental externalities, while there are other policy instruments which are better suited for redistribution of income.

How convincing this argument is obviously depends on how effective the other instruments are in terms of achieving redistributive goals. If a country has a progressive tax system of direct taxation, a well-developed system of social assistance and social security as well as a system of differentiated regional transfers, the distributional argument against environmental taxes is weak. The less the degree to which these assumptions are satisfied, the more important it becomes to strike a balance between efficiency and equity considerations in the design of environmental taxes.[7]

However, there is also a need to take a wider view. Suppose that an environmental tax is levied on a consumer good, which has harmful environmental effects. This has two distinct effects on the welfare of the consumer. On the one hand, he or she suffers a loss of real income, since the price of one of the goods that he consumes has gone up. On the other hand, the tax increases the quality of the environment, which is a gain. In judging the overall distributional impact of the tax, one has to take account of both effects. Even if the consumption of this good were proportional to income so that a price increase had no effects on the distribution of real incomes, the tax increase could still benefit the poor, provided that the environmental impact of the tax were such as to benefit them in particular. Of course the reverse effect is also a possibility; the main point is that both effects have to be taken into account in a serious study of the distributional effects of environmental taxes.[8]

3.6. APPLICATION TO DEVELOPING COUNTRIES

The theory of environmental externalities has been developed mainly with a view towards application in industrialized countries. Nevertheless, when one reads the literature on environmental taxation, one may easily get the impression that its policy conclusions make a claim to almost universal validity. There are hardly any explicit

[7] Dinan and Rogers (2002) analyse the related problem of the distributional effects of a system of tradable carbon quotas in the United States. It turns out that the impact of the system across five income groups is crucially dependent on the assumption that they make about offsetting changes in the tax system.

[8] A further complication in the study of distributional effects of energy taxes is that energy is not only a consumption good but also a factor of production. Higher energy prices will lead to higher prices of consumption goods that are produced by energy-intensive technologies, and a full study of tax incidence would have to take account of these general equilibrium effects.

discussions of the institutional framework in which the policies are assumed to work, and one has to look behind the formal apparatus in order to discover that there are in fact some implicit assumptions that should make one cautious about applying the conclusions to countries at a different stage of development. An example of such an assumption is that markets work in a way that can at least roughly be described as perfect competition. Another is that the statutory taxes are at least roughly equal to effective taxes, that is, there is no major problem of avoidance or evasion. Last but not least, it is assumed that a policy of environmental taxation can, to a large extent, be designed without much regard for its distributional impact. The reason for this view is the one mentioned above, viz. that any adverse distributional effects can be neutralized by means of compensating changes in direct taxation. None of these assumptions are completely realistic in industrial countries either, but in the context of developing countries they are much more likely to be seriously misleading. In particular, the assumption that environmental tax design can be completely isolated from redistributive aspects becomes very doubtful in countries where direct taxes are of little importance because of problems with taxpayer literacy and inadequate resources for tax administration.

Another area where the theory of environmental taxation perhaps needs a different emphasis is in the nature of the externalities caused by environmental pollution. In industrialized countries, the emphasis has been on the environment as a public consumption good. But as Dasgupta (2001) and others have pointed out, environmental pollution and resource depletion in developing countries are likely to have major effects on the productive economic base of society and so have more direct material consequences for the standard of living of poor people. In fact, environmental degradation not only worsens the material conditions under which poor people live, it also causes poverty through the incentive mechanisms that exist in subsistence agriculture. One example of such a mechanism is where the need to provide cheap fuel for heating and cooking leads poor farmers to cut down the trees on their soil. This may start or speed up a process of soil erosion, which makes the conditions for farming worse than they were before. This perspective on the link between the environment and the standard of living is a different one from that which we find in some of the literature, where environmental goods tend to be regarded as luxury consumption goods, something that one can afford once the more important consumer needs have been satisfied.

3.7. GLOBAL EXTERNALITIES

Many types of environmental externalities are transnational; harmful emissions in one country are carried by land, sea, or air to cause damage in other countries. In some cases, like the emission of greenhouse gases that contribute to global warming, all countries are both polluters and victims of pollution. A direct application of standard insights should lead one to recommend taxes on polluters in order that they may internalize the damages that they cause. But there are some difficulties with this solution in an international setting.

The most obvious complication is that there exists at present no international authority to impose taxes and collect revenue. In a single country, the government that makes decisions about tax rates can also provide the resources for tax administration and enforcement. People, who are opposed to a new tax in their own country because they stand to lose by it, will nevertheless be forced to pay it. But in the international community of nations, with a proposal to impose a uniform tax on CO_2 emissions, for example, each nation has to agree to the proposal on a voluntary basis. This creates a challenge for tax design, which has no direct counterpart in national tax policy.

In spite of this, it is of considerable interest to analyse the problem of optimal tax design from the viewpoint of global welfare maximization.[9] This must not be taken to imply that there is in fact some world authority that can actually implement such a policy, but it is a theoretical approach that leads to a better understanding of the tradeoff between efficiency and equity considerations in global tax design. Thus, one issue that can be discussed in this framework is whether such a globally optimal tax should reflect equity consideration. Some proponents of the CO_2 tax, which will be discussed in more detail below, claim that it should be designed so as to satisfy the conditions for world production efficiency. Indeed, to ensure that emissions will be reduced the most where the marginal cost is lowest is claimed to be the main advantage of the tax. The question is whether this will lead to an ethically acceptable distribution of the cost between rich and poor countries. If not, should one design compensatory transfers, or should the design of the environmental taxes themselves have built-in distributional elements?

Suppose for simplicity that the world consists of two countries, one rich and one developing.[10] Consumers in each of the two countries have preferences defined on their own consumption of private goods; in addition, their utility or standard of living is affected by a negative global externality, which is caused by total world production of a particular commodity. Each country would have an incentive to impose a tax on the commodity in question, but since it cannot be expected to take account of the damage caused in the rest of the world, there is a strong presumption that the taxes in all countries would be too low compared to the global cooperative optimum.[11] Global welfare maximization would imply a tax that is related to the global sum of marginal benefits to world consumers. This is obtained by first computing the sum for all consumers in each of the countries and then summing across countries.

An important question is whether, in assessing the global sum of benefits, the benefits received by consumers in rich and poor countries should receive the same weight. The benefit received by each consumer is his marginal willingness to pay for environmental improvement, and this benefit, assuming that it could be elicited

---

[9] Although the analysis of this chapter relates to optimal *tax design*, the results are also applicable to the problem of *tax reform*. The insights that we get from studying, for example, the optimal combination of environmental and other indirect taxes have a direct application to the study of the welfare effects from substituting environmental for other indirect taxes.

[10] Appendix B develops a mathematical model of this case.

[11] For theoretical analyses of this presumption and the extent of its validity, see Williams (1966) and Boskin (1973). Their discussions are set in the related context of local governments providing public goods with jurisdictional spillovers.

in an empirically reliable manner, would reflect both his preferences and his ability to pay. We may not find it ethically acceptable that the benefit received by a poor African peasant should count for so little in the assessment of the global benefit just because he is so poor, and from an egalitarian perspective it would seem reasonable to give a higher weight to his benefit than to a representative consumer in a rich country. This problem is of special importance in an international context because redistributive taxation and transfers are clearly of much less importance internationally than within any particular country. Appendix B analyses two polar cases of international redistribution. In the first case, there is perfect redistribution in each country, but no international redistribution. In the second case, the assumption of perfect within-country redistribution is preserved, while now perfect international redistribution is also assumed. The analysis then focuses on the characterization of the optimal environmental tax under the two polar assumptions.[12]

Should the tax be uniform or differentiated between rich and poor countries? With perfect international transfers and free international trade, the answer is clear: the tax should be uniform. In this case, the world—at least in economic terms—is like the single jurisdiction of the original Samuelson (1954) analysis of optimal public goods supply. Then the policy objectives of efficiency and equity can be separated from each other, and in particular we would have production efficiency: the marginal cost of environmental improvement should be the same in rich and poor countries. However, if there are no transfers and the social welfare function is egalitarian, more weight should be placed on the willingness of the citizens in the poor country to pay. In that case, production efficiency is no longer desirable, and the global optimum is a situation where the tax and thus the marginal cost of improving the environment is lower in the developing country.[13] From the viewpoint of world welfare, it is rational to increase the global cost of environmental improvement if by so doing one can ensure that the poor country bears less of the cost burden. When lumpsum transfers are ruled out, we are in the world of the second best where redistributive concerns may have to be reflected in the design of the system of commodity taxes.

Which of the two polar assumptions is the more realistic one? Anyone who observes the extent of world income inequality and the amount of international transfers will have difficulties with concluding that his observations can be interpreted as the outcome of global welfare maximization; the case without international transfers is therefore the

---

[12] Both of the two polar cases are obviously unrealistic. National redistribution is not perfect and non-distortionary, and international redistribution, while it does occur, is far from the lumpsum ideal of welfare economics. But the study of polar cases has a long history in economics. In international economics, in particular, there is a long tradition for studying the contrast between autarky and perfectly free trade, none of which are realistic descriptions of actual economies. Another polar case assumption in international economics of the Heckscher–Ohlin variety is that factors of production are perfectly mobile within the national economies, but completely immobile internationally.

[13] In the limit, as the relative weight put on the consumption of people in the poor country becomes very large, the whole burden of reducing global pollution should fall on the rich country, and the tax on the poor country should be zero. This case could be seen as an application of Rawls' difference principle to the problem of international redistribution. However, Rawls (1999) warns against a simple-minded application of the principle to international relations.

one that comes closest to reality. To implement such a scheme is, however, far from simple. A major difficulty is that in the real world of many countries, there is no simple division of countries into the 'developing' and 'rich' categories, and a system by which every country pays the tax at a different rate raises major political and administrative difficulties. The problem is even more complicated if one envisages several global pollutants with associated tax rates, where for each tax rate one needs to strike a balance between cost efficiency and distributional equity.

The approach to tax design via global welfare optimization leaves open the question of its institutional and political foundation. Clearly, such a tax will have to be based on some kind of international agreement, possibly in combination with the creation of a world tax authority. To ensure voluntary participation by all countries, the tax would have to be designed in such a way that all countries gain by it. All countries will gain from a better global environment, but since both the gains and the tax payments are likely to be unevenly distributed between countries, it is not clear that the *net gain*—the environmental gain minus taxes paid—will be positive for all countries. But the income received by the world tax authority could be redistributed to the participating countries so that net gains are assured for all participants; the redistribution scheme could also be designed such that the poor countries would gain more than the rich. These issues are considered further below.

3.8. TAX DESIGN AND POLITICAL ACCEPTABILITY

What are the prospects for establishing a system of global environmental taxation? We have seen that a strong case can be established for such a system on the basis of welfare economics, but what are the prospects for its implementation? With regard to the case of greenhouse gas emissions, James Poterba no doubt expresses a common view among economists when he writes 'while efficiency considerations create a presumption for using coordinated international policies to alter greenhouse gas emissions, the prospects for such action are bleak' (Poterba 1993: 48).

There are two main reasons for the pessimistic view. One is that actions taken to prevent or slow down global warming involve the certainty of present costs against the uncertainty of future benefits. The uncertainty element comes in because of our incomplete knowledge concerning the effects of greenhouse gas emissions on the global climate in the future. The time element is also of major importance in judging the probability of political enactment. The time perspective in global warming is so long that even with moderate rates of time discounting, the costs will easily come to dominate the benefits. This particular ground for pessimism, it should be stressed, applies both to a single country and to the world community.

The second reason for pessimism is the fact that an efficient tax policy for global environmental improvement presupposes coordinated action among countries, but with each country knowing that the main beneficiaries from its own actions will be other countries. This creates an incentive for each country to be a freerider on the policies of the others, leading to a political equilibrium where all countries believe that inadequate action is taken, but where all feel powerless to break out of the low tax equilibrium trap.

It would seem fruitful, therefore, to try to search for arguments that would increase the probability of political adoption of global environmental taxes.

One such argument would be that of the double dividend. From a domestic point of view, increasing the tax on fossil fuels would not only correct a market failure, it would also enable the national government to cut other taxes or to expand public expenditure at a lower efficiency cost. Note, however, that this argument provides no answer to the pessimism stemming from the long time-horizon and the freerider problem.

Another approach would be to introduce global environmental taxes in conjunction with a commitment to use the revenue for a specific purpose, as in the current proposal to use it for promoting economic development. The emission of greenhouse gases contributes to a deterioration of the quality of the atmosphere, the most global of all commons. Taxes on emissions could then be seen as charges for use of the common property, to be redistributed to the owners—all the world's countries—on the basis of some criterion of distributive justice. Exactly what that criterion should be, would be a matter for deliberation between the parties to the treaty, but it would clearly have to favour the developing world, while the rich countries would pay the larger share of the taxes. In coupling proposals of new taxes to improve the global efficiency of resource allocation and redistributing income in favour of the poor, the approach might stand a better chance of political acceptance than either of the two proposals would be likely to muster on their own.

Is such a scheme likely to attract the support of the rich countries? The presumption is that a slow-down of global warming would be a benefit to all;[14] at the same time, however, there would be a net transfer of tax revenue from the rich to the developing countries. On a narrow calculation of national self-interest, some rich countries might find the proposal unattractive. However, wider considerations of the fairness involved in charging for the use of the global commons as well as the attainment of a more equitable distribution of world income might still appeal to an extended notion of the national self-interest.[15]

There are several alternatives regarding the construction of a system of global environmental taxation that combines efficiency and equity considerations. From the previous discussion two main alternatives emerge:

(A) A uniform tax designed to promote production efficiency combined with a separate system for equity-based distribution of the tax revenue;

---

[14] Cooper (1998) and Poterba (1993) cite evidence that countries like Canada and Russia might profit from global warming mainly because of higher agricultural yields. This might seem a narrow concept of the national interest, but in any case the possibility that a few countries could come to gain from global warming is not a crucial argument against the scheme.

[15] Newbery (1990) and Mäler (1991) analyse cost-efficient reduction of sulfur emissions in a European context and identify the countries that gain or lose by an efficient policy. Mäler also develops a system for revenue distribution that makes all countries that participate in the policy into net beneficiaries by the arrangement. Something similar could clearly be worked out on a global scale, which would imply that the rich countries would also get a share of the tax revenue.

(B) A non-uniform tax with rates depending on the income level of the tax-collecting country.

In addition, a simplified case of B would be:

(C) A positive efficiency-based rate of tax on the rich countries combined with a zero tax on developing countries.

An important issue of system design is that a politically acceptable treaty needs to be based to the largest extent possible on criteria that are capable of empirical verification and are easy to understand. None of the three alternatives satisfy this requirement completely; this is unavoidable because they all involve an element of redistribution, which clearly must be based on value judgements. My own view is that alternative A is better than B and C on this score. The basic issues involved are the same, but A has a separation of efficiency and equity considerations which implies that the tax rate and the redistribution system could more easily be negotiated separately than in the other two cases. The ranking of alternatives B and C is more difficult.[16] Alternative C has much to recommend it in the way of simplicity. On the other hand, the redistributive element is weaker than in B, since countries are simply divided into two groups with no within-group redistribution. Having just two tax rates instead of the several rates required by alternative B may be an advantage from an administrative and political point of view; on the other hand, setting the dividing line (presumably in terms of per capita income) between the two groups becomes significant, imposing a high marginal tax on the country, which makes the transition from developing to 'rich'.[17] Perhaps the simplicity of alternative C should be decisive in ranking it ahead of B.

It needs to be kept in mind that countries at present have widely different effective rates of tax on the emission of greenhouse gases; even within each country there will be a variety of effective rates, depending on the source of emissions. If countries were to impose a new uniform tax on themselves, effective tax rates would not be equal. It is the effective post-reform rate of tax which, according to alternative A, should be equalized across countries, and this means that allowance must be made for pre-existing taxes. Effective rates of tax should then be equalized within each country, and the single effective rate should be brought in line with the international rate. In all probability, this would lead to an increase of the overall rate of tax in a global perspective, but it is also likely that some rates in some countries would have to be cut in order to achieve global uniformity. This argument obviously has to be modified if one were to adopt any one of the tax systems B or C instead of A, but there would still be a strong case for a uniform rate of tax within each rich country and between the rich countries.

---

[16] The analysis of Appendix B does not provide much help in this ranking, since it assumes just two countries, and the difference between alternatives B and C becomes really significant when there are several countries.

[17] However, even a developing country not obliged to pay any tax under the treaty could find it in its own interest to levy such taxes for the purely domestic interest in reaping one or more of the second dividends discussed above.

3.9. COLLECTING THE TAX

The argument in favour of environmental taxes is that they change the incentives of the individual economic agents whose actions are the causes of the externalities. A treaty between countries which merely obliges the individual country to pay taxes in proportion to its emissions leaves open the question of how the country passes this obligation on to its citizens; see the more detailed discussion of 'fiscal architecture' in Atkinson (Chapter 2, this volume). If the government in question decides to finance this tax payment out of its general tax revenue, the individual incentives would not be such as to promote domestic or global efficiency. On the other hand, the domestic government clearly has an interest in designing a tax system with the right incentives; giving firms and consumers incentives to cut back on emissions would at the same time diminish the government's tax obligations under the treaty. This issue is discussed in more detail in the study by Boadway (Chapter 11, this volume).

As regards the institutional framework for collecting the tax and spending the revenue, several arrangements might be considered, and the detailed institutional framework would obviously have to be considered later. Nevertheless, a few general remarks are in order. Taxes in each individual country, for example, on the use of fossil fuels, would have to be collected by the domestic government and paid by it to an international agency. Whether this should be a new and separate institution or whether the tax-collecting task could be incorporated in an existing institution, is difficult to say. There are presumably cost advantages to not having to build a new international agency from the ground. However, if the agency is put in charge of collecting revenue from a number of different sources (global environmental taxes, the Tobin tax, a global lottery, etc.) there is more to be said for establishing it as a separate institution. One also needs to consider the next step of channelling the revenue into development finance. The agency would need to develop a system for passing the revenue on to institutions that are actually in charge of allocating resources to development projects. A crucial question is then whether the transfer of funds should take place according to some fixed rule or whether the agency itself should develop priorities among projects and receiving institutions. This should probably be among the first issues to be discussed among the parties to international treaties about the various new sources of development funding.

3.10. REVENUE POTENTIAL OF ENVIRONMENTAL TAXES

There are a number of activities that give rise to external effects that cross borders and could be said to be harmful to the global environment. However, at least for the purpose of the present discussion, it will be useful to limit discussion to the types of pollution that most directly affect the global commons, viz. the emission of greenhouse gases, in particular a tax on carbon (CO_2) emissions. What is the revenue potential of such taxes? How important could they be in providing additional funds for development finance?

The answer seems to be that they could be very important, but that there are a number of uncertainties attached to the estimation of their revenue potential. The

World Development Report 1999/2000 estimates world emissions of carbon dioxide at 22,754 million metric tons in 1996 (World Bank 2000: 249), equivalent at a conversion factor of 3.67–6.2 billion metric tons of carbon. Clunies-Ross (2003) points out that a uniform tax on carbon use at a rate of US$21 per metric ton of carbon (equivalent to a gasoline tax of 4.8 cents per US gallon or roughly 0.01 EUR per litre)[18] would yield annual revenue of about US$130 billion per year. This assumes that the tax is levied at a uniform rate on all countries. If instead it is assumed that it is levied only on those countries that according to the World Bank are classified as 'high income', having a per capita income of at least US$9361 in 1996, the figure drops to about US$61 billion per year. When these figures are compared to estimates of the additional resources required to reach the Millennium Development Goals (MDGs) by 2015, which are in the range of US$30–70 billion per year (Atkinson, Chapter 1, this volume), it is clear that the revenue potential is indeed very large, even for such a modest rate of tax. Cooper (1998) cites an OECD (organization for Economic Cooperation and Development) study that estimates the revenue from a carbon tax on a lower taxbase (5.2 billion metric tons) at US$750 billion per year. This is almost six times the amount suggested by Clunies-Ross, being based on a tax rate of approximately US$150 per metric ton (the equivalent of approximately 35 cents per US gallon or 0.08 EUR per litre.[19] Both this and the more modest Clunies-Ross revenue estimates are very high. Thus, even the latter would amount to about 2.5 times the current level of official development assistance in the case of a worldwide tax, and to 1.2 times the level of official development assistance (ODA) if only high-income countries are included. The significance of the estimates lies of course not in the precise numbers, but in the indications they give of the order of magnitude involved.

There are both economic and political reasons why these estimates might be too high. One is that the calculations assume that carbon use is unaffected by the tax, presumably because of an assumption that the demand price elasticity is very low. The assumption of a zero price elasticity is of course somewhat paradoxical, because it means that the tax has in fact no effect on CO_2 emissions and that there is no environmental benefit from it. Although the assumption appears to be consistent with experiences of short-run fluctuations in, for example, gasoline prices, it is clearly the more long-run elasticities that are relevant in this context. These are likely to be negative, which must lead to a downward adjustment of the taxbase. There seems to be a consensus that although short-run elasticities might well be close to zero, long-run elasticities are more likely to be in the neighbourhood of -0.5 to -1.5 (Pindyck 1979). For illustrative purposes, let us assume that the relevant long-run elasticity is -1. The Clunies-Ross proposal of a tax equivalent to 0.01 EUR per litre of gasoline implies a price increase (assuming the producer price to be constant at about 1.00 EUR) of roughly 1 per cent, which would lead to a 1 per cent reduction of the taxbase. Thus, his revenue estimates would have

---

[18] For comparison, this is about one-tenth of the current Norwegian carbon tax.

[19] This is approximately 60% of the current carbon component of the Norwegian gasoline tax and less than 10% of the total gasoline tax.

to be reduced downwards by about 1 per cent, clearly a very insignificant revision of the original calculations.

It should be kept in mind, however, that the rate of tax envisaged by Clunies-Ross is very low compared to those suggested in the literature on global warming. For example, Cooper (1998) and Poterba (1991) suggest that in order to achieve a significant reduction of emissions, a tax in the range of US$100–120 per metric ton would be necessary. Whalley and Wiggle (1991) estimate that a tax of about US$450—more than twenty times the level assumed by Clunies-Ross—is needed to reduce carbon use by 50 per cent. With a tax rate of this magnitude, the calculation of revenue on the basis of a constant taxbase is apt to be more misleading. The size of the taxbase will in fact have to be adjusted downwards by a percentage equal to the product of the tax rate and the price elasticity. To illustrate, take again the Clunies-Ross case of 6.2 million metric tons as the initial taxbase. With an elasticity of -1 and a tax rate of 20 per cent, the taxbase must be reduced by a factor of 20 per cent. However, with the higher tax rate, the tax revenue is still higher than with the lower tax rate; in fact, with an elasticity of -1 revenue is increasing for all tax rates up to one hundred per cent.[20]

The role of the price elasticity of carbon use is worth emphasizing. If policymakers want to use the tax in order to reach both a target level of emissions and a revenue target, achieving the emissions target requires a lower tax, the more elastic the taxbase is. On the other hand, a high elasticity means that a higher tax is needed to meet the revenue target. If the elasticity is in fact quite low, it is therefore likely that a carbon tax, which is decided with the objective of raising certain revenue for development purposes, is likely to be lower than that required to meet environmental objectives.

In spite of the uncertainty that is attached to the magnitude of the relevant elasticities, there can be no doubt that the revenue potential of a global carbon tax is very high. A modest rate of tax, whether levelled globally or only on the rich countries' emissions, would likely raise huge revenues that could potentially be channelled into economic development. But one needs to keep in mind that the estimate of the revenue potential of the carbon tax might not reflect a corresponding increase in tax revenue available for development assistance. Adoption of the global carbon tax would imply a large increase in the outflow of resources for development purposes, and the political system could well react to this by cutting back the amount of ODA over time, or increasing it by less than they would have done, had the global carbon tax not been in place.

3.11. CONCLUDING REMARKS

The economic case for global environmental taxes, primarily to control the climate externalities that are of increasing concern to public opinion, is very strong. Since these taxes can be seen as charges for use of the global commons, there is also a strong moral case for earmarking the revenue for global development purposes. There

---

[20] If t is the tax rate and x is the taxbase, revenue is $R = tx$. The effect of a tax increase on revenue, assuming the producer price to be constant, can be written as $\partial R / \partial t = x(1 + \theta \varepsilon)$, where θ is the tax rate in percentage terms and ε is the price elasticity of demand. For the special case where $\varepsilon = -1$, we accordingly have that $\partial R / \partial t = x(1 - \theta)$.

is at present wide-spread pessimism concerning the political realism of introducing such taxes; however, earmarking the revenue for development purposes might in fact enhance their political acceptability. The revenue potential of this type of tax appears to be large. A global carbon tax even at modest rates could alone generate sufficient revenue to finance the MDGs, and with a higher tax rate—one that is designed to achieve a substantial environmental improvement—the potential could be increased even further.

If such a system of taxes were to become enacted, one would clearly be justified in speaking of an international double dividend. First, there would be an improvement of the global environment. Second, there would be an increased flow of resources into economic development, and at a lower marginal source of public funds than is the case for most other taxes currently being used to fund development aid. Whether this argument is persuasive enough to overcome the freerider problems inherent in all issues involving global public goods and externalities, remains to be seen.

3.12. APPENDIX A

3.12.1. *A Formal Model of Environmental Taxation: The Single Country Case* [21]

It will be useful to establish a theoretical frame of reference in the form of a simple model for a single country. It has a number of consumers, indexed by $i (i = 1, \ldots, n)$, with utility functions that depend on the quantity consumed of two commodities, indexed 0 and 1, as well as on the amount of environmental pollution, e:

$$u^i = u^i(x_0^i, x_1^i, e). \tag{3.A1}$$

The utility functions are increasing in the first two arguments and decreasing in the third. Let total production of the two goods be y_0 and y_1, respectively, so that

$$\Sigma_i x_0^i = y_0 \quad \text{and} \quad \Sigma_i x_1^i = y_1. \tag{3.A2}$$

The amount of environmental pollution is an increasing function of the output of commodity 1, so that without loss of generality[22] we may simply write

$$e = y_1. \tag{3.A3}$$

Industry 1 is cast in the role of the 'dirty industry', but the pollution technology is of course a drastic simplification of real-life situations, where pollution is likely to depend on the specific technology used in production. It would not be conceptually difficult to take account of this, but it makes the analysis less transparent and does not add much in the way of interesting economic insights.

[21] The analysis in this and the following appendix is a further development of the model in Sandmo (2003).
[22] The unit function could be replaced by any increasing function without affecting the conclusions of the analysis.

We assume that there is an aggregate production constraint for the economy as a whole, which has the quasi-linear form

$$y_0 + C(y_1) - \omega = 0, \quad C(0) = 0, \quad C'(y_1) > 0, \quad C''(y_1) > 0. \tag{3.A4}$$

We now characterize the optimal allocation of resources in this economy as the maximum of a Bergson–Samuelson social welfare function

$$W = W(u^1, \ldots, u^n). \tag{3.A5}$$

Letting subscripts denote partial derivatives, it is easy to show that the optimum can be characterized by the conditions

$$(u_1^h/u_0^h) + \Sigma_i(u_e^i/u_0^i) = C_1(y_1) \quad (h = 1, \ldots, n). \tag{3.A6}$$

The first term on the left is the private marginal benefit to consumer h of an additional unit of commodity 1. The second term, which is negative, is the marginal social damage of increased pollution. This affects all n consumers—including consumer h himself—in a negative way. The condition implies, first, that at the optimum the private marginal benefit of consumption should be the same for all consumers, and, second, that the private marginal benefit adjusted for the marginal social damage, should be equal to the marginal cost of production.

Let us now confront this optimality condition with a competitive equilibrium in which consumers and producers face prices P and p, respectively, using commodity 0 as the *numéraire*. Utility-maximizing consumers, who take the level of environmental pollution as given,[23] will equate their marginal willingness to pay (their marginal rate of substitution) to the consumer price. Profit-maximizing firms will set marginal cost equal to the producer price, so that competitive equilibrium will be characterized by the conditions

$$u_1^h/u_0^h = P \quad (h = 1, \ldots, n) \tag{3.A7}$$

$$C_1(y_1) = p. \tag{3.A8}$$

One sees immediately that the equilibrium will satisfy the optimality condition (3.A6) only if a tax wedge is driven between the consumer and producer price, so that

$$P - t = p \quad \text{and} \quad t = -\Sigma_i(u_e^i/u_0^i). \tag{3.A9}$$

The optimal environmental tax is the aggregate marginal willingness to pay for environmental improvement. It is of course no coincidence that the tax formula is reminiscent of the Samuelson (1954) condition for the optimal supply of public goods, for the effect of the tax discouragement of consumption is precisely to improve the quality of the environment as a public good.

This is a very simple model in a number of respects. Most importantly, it assumes—rather implicitly, as presented here—that lumpsum redistribution between consumers

---

[23] This is equivalent to taking the total output of the dirty commodity as given and is just the standard competitive assumption.

is possible, so that the environmental tax can be set without any regard for distributional effects.[24] Moreover, it presents a very aggregate view of the production side of the economy. However, we shall use the formulation as a building block for the construction of a model of global externalities and environmental taxes, in which these complications will in fact be moved to the forefront of the analysis. From this perspective, it is useful to keep the single country case as simple as possible.

3.13. APPENDIX B

3.13.1. *Extensions to a Two-Country Model*—To make matters simple, we assume that the world consists of just two countries, one rich and one developing country. The model does not attempt to explain why one country is rich and one poor; this could be either because of differences in productive resources or because of differences in the technology of production. The environmental externality in question is global in nature, being a global 'bad' for all consumers in the two countries.

Country-specific variables are distinguished by superscripts D and R, so that the utility functions of consumers are written as

$$u^{iD} = u^{iD}(x_0^{iD}, x_1^{iD}, e) \quad (i = 1, \ldots, n), \tag{3.A10a}$$

$$u^{jR} = u^{jR}(x_0^{jR}, x_1^{jR}, e) \quad (j = 1, \ldots, m). \tag{3.A10b}$$

The materials balance equations (3.A2) become

$$\Sigma_i x_0^{iD} = y_0^D \quad \text{and} \quad \Sigma_i x_1^{iD} = y_1^D. \tag{3.A11a}$$

$$\Sigma_j x_0^{jR} = y_0^R \quad \text{and} \quad \Sigma_j x_1^{jR} = y_1^R. \tag{3.A11b}$$

For each commodity, domestic consumption should be equal to domestic production. Note that there are no other constraints on individuals' consumption than aggregate output in the domestic economy. This is equivalent to assuming lumpsum redistribution between individual consumers in each country; however, it is also assumed that there is no redistribution between countries. This is clearly not realistic. Domestic redistribution has in fact to rely on second best instruments like income and commodity taxes while on the other hand there exists a significant amount of international redistribution. The assumption must be seen as a simplified representation of the fact that redistribution in most countries is carried out on a scale far exceeding anything that exists for the world community as a whole, and with a set of instruments that, if far from perfect, are much more targeted on transferring resources from the rich to the poor.

---

[24] Formally, one set of first order conditions requires that the marginal contribution to social welfare of the consumption of the *numéraire* good is the same for all consumers.

Environmental pollution is assumed to be global in nature and to depend on the sum of the outputs in industry 1 in the two countries, so that

$$e = y_1^D + y_1^R. \tag{3.A12}$$

The production constraints of the two countries may differ both with respect to the availability of resources and alternative costs; in other words, production possibility curves may vary with respect to both location and slope:

$$y_0^D + C^D(y_1^D) - \omega^D = 0, \tag{3.A13a}$$

$$y_0^R + C^R(y_1^R) - \omega^R = 0. \tag{3.A13b}$$

We now wish to study the implications of global welfare maximization. The global social welfare function is

$$W = W(u^{1D}, \dots, u^{nD}; u^{1R}, \dots, u^{mR}). \tag{3.A14}$$

Before turning to the formal analysis, it is useful to think about the questions that the analysis of this model can help us to clarify. An interesting question is whether it is desirable to have world production efficiency. Since equation (3.A12) shows the amount of international pollution to be a function of the sum of output from the dirty industries of the two countries, a natural feature of the optimum would be equality of the marginal costs of reducing pollution. Another issue is to what extent distributional weights on the two countries' preferences should be taken into account in the design of the optimal policy. These two issues turn out, in fact, to be closely related.

Consider first the condition for global production efficiency. The problem can be formulated as the maximization of the output of commodity 0, subject to the condition that the output of commodity 1 is equal to some constant level, so that $y_1^D + y_1^R = y^*$. Using equations (3.A13a–b), we can write the maximization problem as

$$\max(y_0^D + y_0^R) = \omega^D + \omega^R - C^D(y_1^D) - C^R(y^* - y_1^D).$$

Setting the derivative of this expression with respect to y_1^D equal to zero, we obtain the condition for global production efficiency:

$$C_1^D(y_1^D) = C_1^R(y_1^R). \tag{3.A15}$$

The marginal cost of producing the dirty good, which is the same as the marginal cost of reducing pollution, should be the same in both countries.

The more general welfare problem is to maximize the social welfare function (3.A14), subject to the four materials balance equations (3.A11a–b) and the two production constraints (3.A13a–b). We skip the details of the derivation and move directly to the two conditions corresponding to (3.A6) for the single country case. For the developing country we have that

$$(u_1^{hD}/u_0^{hD}) + [\Sigma_i(u_e^{iD}/u_0^{iD}) + \Sigma_j(u_e^{jR}/u_0^{jR})(\lambda^R/\lambda^D)] = C_1^D(y_1^D) \quad (h = 1, \dots, n). \tag{3.A16}$$

The expression in square brackets is now the marginal global damage from the production of the dirty good. It has two terms, the first being the damage caused in the poor country while the second term is the damage to the rich country, multiplied by the term λ^R/λ^D. This term is the ratio of the social marginal utilities of income in the two countries; these are equal between individuals within each of the countries because of the assumption of domestic lumpsum redistribution. The social marginal utility of income is actually the marginal contribution to welfare of increasing an individual's consumption of the *numéraire* commodity 0, that is:

$$\lambda^D = W_i u_0^{iD} \quad \text{and} \quad \lambda^R = W_j u_0^{jR} \quad (i = 1, \ldots, n; j = 1, \ldots, m). \tag{3.A17}$$

We assume that the global welfare function is egalitarian, which implies the relative welfare weight λ^R/λ^D will be less than one. This means that the weight accorded to the marginal social damage for the rich country consumers will be less than that of the consumers in the developing country. Let P^D and p^D be the consumer and producer prices in the developing country, with the tax rate being $t^D = P^D - p^D$. From (3.A16) and the competitive assumption (see equations (3.A7) and (3.A8)) we may then conclude that the optimal tax in the developing country is

$$t^D = [\Sigma_i(u_e^{iD}/u_0^{iD}) + \Sigma_j(u_e^{jR}/u_0^{jR})(\lambda^R/\lambda^D)]. \tag{3.A18}$$

How does this correspond to the optimal tax rate in the rich country? This turns out to satisfy the following condition:

$$(u_1^{kR}/u_0^{kR})(\lambda^R/\lambda^D) + [\Sigma_i(u_e^{iD}/u_0^{iD}) + \Sigma_j(u_e^{jR}/u_0^{jR})(\lambda^R/\lambda^D)]$$
$$= C_1^R(y_1^R)(\lambda^R/\lambda^D) \quad (k = 1, \ldots, m). \tag{3.A19}$$

Let P^R and p^R be the prices in the rich country and the tax rate the difference between the two. Then we can write the optimal tax rate in the rich country as

$$t^R = [\Sigma_i(u_e^{iD}/u_0^{iD})(\lambda^D/\lambda^R) + \Sigma_j(u_e^{jR}/u_0^{jR})]. \tag{3.A20}$$

Comparing (3.A20) with (3.A18), we see immediately that

$$t^D = t^R(\lambda^R/\lambda^D). \tag{3.A21}$$

Since the relative welfare weight is less than one, this implies that $t^D < t^R$. At the optimum the optimal tax in the developing country is lower than in the rich country. We may think of the ratio of welfare weights as expressing the degree of egalitarianism embedded in the global social welfare function. In the limit, as the ratio λ^R/λ^D approaches zero, giving all weight to the welfare of the developing country, the tax in the developing country goes to zero, and the whole burden of discouraging global pollution falls on tax policy of the rich country.

What about global production efficiency? Using the competitive equilibrium conditions (3.A7) and (3.A8), we can rewrite (3.A21) as

$$P^D - C_1^D = (\lambda^R/\lambda^D)(P^R - C_1^R). \tag{3.A22}$$

We cannot conclude from the lower tax rate in the developing country that the marginal cost of reducing pollution should be higher in the developing country. However, in the important special case in which international trade causes equality of commodity prices, so that $P^D = P^R$, we can indeed conclude that at the optimum

$$C_1^D > C_1^R. \tag{3.A23}$$

The reasons for the difference between the first-best optimal tax rates and the desirability of global production inefficiency are clearly distributional. Both countries contribute to a cleaner global environment by discouraging the production and consumption of the dirty good, but the poorer country contributes less. Only in the case where the marginal utilities of income are the same in the two countries, so that $(\lambda^R / \lambda^D) = 1$, will there be a globally uniform tax rate. In the model, this will be the case if the first part of the materials balance equations (3.A11) is replaced by[25]

$$\Sigma_i x_0^{iD} + \Sigma_j x_0^{jR} = y_0^D + y_0^R, \tag{3.A24}$$

which says simply that world consumption must equal world production of the *numéraire* commodity. With this formulation, the only constraint on the consumption of each country is the aggregate production of commodity 0 in the world as a whole; domestic production is no longer a limit on domestic consumption. Clearly, this is equivalent to assuming lumpsum transfers between the two countries, since the only way in which a country can consume more than its domestic output (without paying for it in the form of international trade) is through transfers from other countries. With this assumption, there is no longer any egalitarian case for differentiating the tax rates, since any adverse distributional effect of the environmental tax is compensated by the transfers.

Will this assumption also imply world production efficiency? As condition (3.A22) makes clear this is not necessarily the case, since in equilibrium we have equality between marginal cost and the producer price. Equality of producer prices between countries will only result, except by coincidence, through free international trade. Thus, it is the twin assumptions of lumpsum international transfers and free trade that make the global community into one integrated economy, just like the single country of Appendix A. In this perfectly competitive global economy with no constraints on tax and transfer policies, there is perfect separation of efficiency and equity issues of economic policy, and environmental policy should accordingly be based solely on efficiency considerations.[26]

---

[25] Equation (3.A24) should not be confused with a balance of payments equation, which is a constraint on values, not quantities. Both versions of the model, with or without international transfers, are consistent with the presence of international trade; see Sandmo (2003). Without trade, producer prices will differ between countries; with trade, they will be the same.

[26] Chichilnisky and Heal (1994) discuss the problem of international production efficiency in a multi-country model with a similar structure to the one used here, but they do not discuss the tax implications. Keen and Wildasin (2004) and Edwards (2002) discuss the desirability of world production efficiency in more general settings, including second best situations where domestic tax systems are distortionary, an obviously important set of cases that is neglected in the present analysis.

REFERENCES

Boskin, M. J. (1973). 'Local Government Tax and Product Competition and the Optimal Provision of Public Goods'. *Journal of Political Economy*, 81: 203–10.

Bovenberg, A. L. (1999). 'Green Tax Reforms and the Double Dividend: An Updated Reader's Guide'. *International Tax and Public Finance*, 6: 421–43.

Chichilnisky, G. and G. Heal (1994). 'Who Should Abate Carbon Emissions?'. *Economics Letters*, 44: 443–9.

Clunies-Ross, A. (2003). 'Resources for Social Development'. Paper prepared for the World Commission on the Social Dimensions of Globalization, ILO, Geneva.

Coase, R. H. (1960). 'The Problem of Social Cost'. *Journal of Law and Economics*, 3: 1–44.

Cooper, R. A. (1998). 'Toward a Real Global Warming Treaty'. *Foreign Affairs*, 77(2): 66–79.

Dasgupta, P. (2001). *Human Well-Being and the Natural Environment*. Oxford: Oxford University Press.

Dinan, T. and D. L. Rogers (2002). 'Distributional Effects of Carbon Allowance Trading: How Government Decisions Determine Winners and Losers'. *National Tax Journal*, 55: 199–221.

Edwards, J. (2002). 'Global Production Efficiency and Pareto-efficient International Taxation. Cambridge: University of Cambridge. Mimeo.

Goulder, L. (1995). 'Environmental Taxation and the Double Dividend: A Reader's Guide'. *International Tax and Public Finance*, 2: 157–83.

Hardin, G. (1968). 'The Tragedy of the Commons'. *Science*, 162: 1243–8.

Keen, M. and D. Wildasin (2004). 'Pareto Efficient International Taxation'. *The American Economic Review*, 94(1): 259–75.

Mäler, K.-G. (1991). 'Environmental Issues in the New Europe', in A. B. Atkinson and R. Brunetta (eds), *Economics for the New Europe*. London: Macmillan, in association with the International Economic Association, 262–87.

Newbery, D. M. G. (1990). 'Acid Rain'. *Economic Policy*, 11: 297–346.

Pigou, A. C. (1920). *The Economics of Welfare*, 4th edition 1932. London: Macmillan.

Pindyck, R. S. (1979). 'Interfuel Substitution and the Industrial Demand for Energy: An International Comparison'. *Review of Economics and Statistics*, 61: 169–79.

Poterba, J. M. (1991). 'Tax Policy to Combat Global Warming: On Designing a Carbon Tax', in R. Dornbusch and J. M. Poterba (eds), *Global Warming: Economic Policy Responses*. Cambridge, MA: MIT Press.

—— (1993). 'Global Warming Policy: A Public Finance Perspective'. *Journal of Economic Perspectives*, 7(4): 47–63.

Rawls, J. (1999). *The Law of Peoples*. Cambridge, MA: Harvard University Press.

Samuelson, P. A. (1954). 'The Pure Theory of Public Expenditure'. *Review of Economics and Statistics*, 36: 387–9.

Sandmo, A. (1975). 'Optimal Taxation in the Presence of Externalities'. *Swedish Journal of Economics*, 77: 86–98. Reprinted in L. H. Goulder (ed.) (2002), *Environmental Policy Making in Economies with Prior Tax Distortions*. Cheltenham: Edward Elgar.

—— (2000). *The Public Economics of the Environment*. Oxford: Oxford University Press.

—— (2002). 'Efficient Environmental Policy with Imperfect Compliance'. *Environmental and Resource Economics*, 23: 85–103.

—— (2003). 'International Aspects of Public Goods Provision', in I. Kaul, P. Conceição, K. Le Goulven, and R. U. Mendoza (eds), *Providing Global Public Goods*. Oxford: Oxford University Press.

Schöb, R. (2003). 'The Double Dividend Hypotheses of Environmental Taxes: A Survey'. *CESifo Working Paper* No 946. Munich: CESifo.

Stigler, G. J. (1957). 'Perfect Competition, Historically Contemplated'. *Journal of Political Economy*, 65, 1–17. Reprinted in G. J. Stigler (1965). *Essays in the History of Economics*. Chicago: The University of Chicago Press.

Whalley, J. and R. Wiggle (1991). 'The International Incidence of Carbon Taxes', in R. Dornbusch and J. M. Poterba (eds), *Global Warming: Economic Policy Responses*. Cambridge, MA: MIT Press.

Williams, A. (1966). 'The Optimal Provision of Public Goods in a System of Local Government'. *Journal of Political Economy*, 74: 18–33.

World Bank (2000). *World Development Report 1999/2000*. New York: Oxford University Press for the World Bank.

4

Revenue Potential of the Tobin Tax for Development Finance: A Critical Appraisal

MACHIKO NISSANKE

4.1. INTRODUCTION

The dramatic rise in cross-border financial flows in the post–Bretton Woods period has been associated with the unprecedented increase in financial instability and crisis.

Indeed, while economic theory emphasizes the potential advantage of global financial trading for economic development and world welfare, it is by now abundantly clear that financial globalization entails genuine costs, risks, and hazards for participating countries not only in their increased susceptibility to financial instability and crisis but in the loss of autonomy in macroeconomic management—a condition known as the 'macroeconomic policy trilemma for open economies' or the 'inconsistent trinity' thesis.[1] The thesis stipulates that an open capital market deprives a government of the ability simultaneously to target its exchange rate and to use monetary policy in pursuit of other economic objectives.[2]

Financial globalization can also lead to a loss of fiscal autonomy, if financial openness makes it hard to tax internationally footloose capital relative to labour due to the

The author gratefully acknowledges invaluable comments and suggestions received on early versions of the chapter from the project director, Tony Atkinson. She has also benefited from helpful comments received from Tony Addison, Anthony Clunies-Ross, Ilene Grabel, John Langmore, George Mavrotas, Alice Sindzingre and participants at the UNU–WIDER project meeting in May 2003 and conference in September 2003. She extends her gratitude to anonymous referees for their detailed comments for improving the clarity of the chapter.

[1] See Obstfeld (1998) for a summary exposition how economic theory weighs costs and benefits associated with financial globalization. For a more critical literature review of economic propositions concerning the effects of financial globalization on economic development and welfare, see Nissanke and Stein (2003).

[2] Interestingly, the very constraints that financial openness places on the policymakers of emerging market economies in macroeconomic management are often treated as beneficiary, since the international capital market is seen to play the role of 'disciplining' policymakers 'who might be tempted to exploit a captive domestic market' (Obstfeld 1998: 10).

competition for foreign savings through tax incentives and general financial arbitrage.[3] Many countries reduced or eliminated taxes on capital transactions and lessened the rate of capital gain taxes or corporate taxes considerably in this process of tax competition and in fear of asset migration and capital flight. A critical analytical work is required to examine whether or not international tax coordination is welfare increasing nationally as well as globally.[4]

The Tobin tax has been debated in the context of this particular historical trend towards an accelerated pace of financial globalization over the recent decades. Tobin proposed a currency transaction tax first at the Janeway Lectures delivered at Princeton in 1972 and again at the presidential address to the Eastern Economic Association in 1977 (Tobin 1974, 1978). The currency transaction tax (CTT), widely known as the Tobin tax, was initially proposed, therefore, for enhancing the efficacy of national macroeconomic policy and the operation of the international monetary system by reducing short-term speculative currency flows.

However, as Tobin himself notes (1996), his proposal did not receive serious consideration from fellow academics or policymakers in the 1970s and 1980s. It was either dismissed almost at stroke as impractical on the grounds of technical and political unfeasibility or rejected as an unnecessary intervention that interferes with the efficient functioning of markets by injecting 'distortions'. However, in contrast to the its disappointing response in the 1970s, followed by the long silence on the subject in the 1980s, there has been a sudden surge of interest in the Tobin tax since the early 1990s.

The renewed interest in the Tobin tax in recent years certainly reflects the growing recognition that there is an urgent need for creating a new international financial architecture governing cross-border capital flows in face of the repeated severe financial crises, including self-fulfilling currency crises in a large number of European countries in the exchange rate mechanism (ERM) and emerging market economies. In particular, in developing and transitional economies, some small initial changes in perception towards their currencies could cascade into generalized financial and economic crises in no time.

For the purpose of this chapter, however, it is critical to note that the surge of interests in the scheme is also explained by its potential for generating a tax revenue of substantial size, which could more than offset the declines in official aid from OECD countries to developing and transitional economies. It has been argued widely that the revenue from CTTs has the potential to serve as an important source of finance for 'global public goods'. Responding to these emerging interests, a number of recent studies have assessed the potential of CTTs, not only for taming exchange rate volatility and averting financial crises but also as an important tax instrument to generate revenue for global development. Many of these studies have articulated modifications to Tobin's original CTT proposal in order to address a variety of technical and political concerns.

[3] This also means less freedom for providing social safety nets to people adversely affected by globalization (Rodrik 1997).
[4] See Boadway (Chapter 11, this volume) and Fuest *et al.* (2003) for a detailed discussion on this issue.

The principal objective of this chapter is to assess the potential of taxes on the CTTs to raise revenues that can be used for developmental purposes. Thus, though Tobin proposed and others assessed CTTs in terms of reducing exchange rate volatility and improving macroeconomic policy environments, this chapter considers the CTT first and foremost from the standpoint of revenue. Unlike other papers on this subject, this chapter treats the assessment of the potential of the CTT to achieve valuable double dividends, such as the promotion of financial stability and policy autonomy, as a subsidiary objective.

With a view of establishing the 'permissible' range of tax rates to obtain realistic estimates of revenue potential from CTTs, Section 4.2 reviews the debate on the effects of CTTs on market liquidity and the efficiency of foreign exchange markets, and assesses briefly the Spahn proposal for a two-tier currency tax. Section 4.3 discusses a number of issues raised in the debate on the technical and political feasibility of CTTs, followed by an evaluation of several new proposals, such as those advanced by Schmidt and Mendez. Section 4.4 presents my estimates of the potential revenue from CTTs in light of recent changes in the composition and structure of foreign exchange markets. Section 4.5 presents my concluding assessment of the potential of CTTs as a revenue-raising tax instrument. It also evaluates CTTs' ability to achieve double dividends.

4.2. THE DEBATE OVER THE EFFECTS OF THE CTTs ON MARKET LIQUIDITY AND EFFICIENCY

At the breakdown of the Bretton Woods system of adjustable pegged exchange rate regimes with capital controls, Tobin proposed an idea of instituting a currency transaction tax to tackle excessive exchange rate fluctuations, promote autonomy of national macroeconomic policies, and to improve the operation of the international monetary system by reducing short-term speculative currency flows. Acting as 'sand in the wheels', Tobin suggested that CTT could make short-term trades more costly and by doing so, would increase the maturity structure of international capital flows (Tobin 1994, 1996).[5] In particular, it was conjectured to considerably reduce exchange

---

[5] See Frankel (1996) for a mathematical model illustration of how a Tobin tax discourages short-term destabilizing speculation without discouraging investment and trade flows with longer maturities. Indeed, Frankel identifies the ability of the Tobin tax to penalize short-term roundtrips relative to transactions with longer maturities as their most attractive attributes. Davidson (1997) argues, however, that the effect of the Tobin tax on speculative flows is overstated when it is derived from calculations based on annualized rates. He suggests that the Tobin tax, like all transactions costs, is independent of the roundtrip time interval and therefore its deterrent capability is not a function of the time period. He argues instead that investors/traders base their decisions in relation to transaction costs and that as long as the Tobin tax rate is an insignificant addition to transaction costs and very marginal compared to expected gains from speculation, it does not deter short-term roundtrip transactions. In my view, so long as a trader's/investor's decision on asset portfolio is made in relation to a certain asset-holding period, calculation on relative returns based on uncovered interest parity condition is relevant in measuring the effect of the Tobin tax on short-term interest arbitrage. However, since traders' decisions are also based on the relative cost–benefit configuration in the immediate future, transaction costs are undoubtedly a critical parameter against which the tax rate has to be evaluated (see Section 4.4).

rate volatility by 'penalizing short-horizon roundtrips, while negligibly affecting the incentives for commodity trade and long-term capital investments' (Tobin 1996: x).

Filtering transactions by maturity on the understanding that speculators would have shorter horizons and holding periods, Tobin predicted that CTT is capable of reducing 'noise trading' from foreign exchange markets. In Tobin's own words, the tax is to set to 'make exchange rates reflect to a larger degree long-run fundamentals relative to short-range expectations and risks by strengthening the weight of regressive expectations relative to extrapolative expectations' (Tobin 1996: xii).[6]

The proposal has drawn strong criticism on efficiency and liquidity grounds.[7] Indeed, the debate on the effects of CTT on market liquidity and efficiency is inevitably shaped by varied perceptions about how well foreign exchange markets function and whether or not short-term speculation is destabilizing. A question is raised whether speculators or traders make exchange rates excessively more volatile than warranted by fundamentals.

Critics of the Tobin tax claim that speculators would not increase exchange rate volatility as their expectations are guided by fundamentals, and that their presence tends to reduce volatility by providing necessary liquidity to markets.[8] In particular, speculators, who could act as informed investors guided by their expectations about future underlying fundamentals (i.e. as traditional fundamentalists or 'informed' traders), are seen to keep exchange rate in line with the macroeconomic fundamentals and help to stabilize markets around new equilibrium.

From the perspective of opponents, the Tobin tax is a device that tends to decrease market efficiency by creating liquidity problems for the day-to-day operation of currency markets, adversely affecting the bid-ask spreads and hence deterring arbitrage transactions. In the 'wholesale' segments of currency markets in particular,[9] market-makers' position, whose act as arbitrageur provides a guaranteed counterpart, is seen to be compromised with reduced liquidity by CTT, as they need liquid markets to avoid large fluctuations in their net positions. It is thus clear that in most of the arguments against the Tobin tax, the concept of speculation is conflated with that of arbitrage, as noted by Davidson (1997).

In contrast, proponents of the Tobin tax argue that markets function inefficiently. For example, Frankel (1996) notes that speculative bubbles—a deviation from the value justified by fundamentals—are generated, as 'noise traders' (as opposed to 'traditional

---

[6] In this connection, it is also worth noting that in Dornbusch's overshooting model, the assumption of *regressive* expectations plays a critical role in ensuring a return of short-run overshooting exchange rates to the long-run equilibrium level dictated by the purchasing power parity (Dornbusch 1976).

[7] See Dooley (1996), Davidson (1997), Habermeier and Kirilenko (2003), and Dodd (2003), among other numerous papers.

[8] Habermeier and Kirilenko (2003), emphasizing the informational role of liquidity in the price discovery process, argue that taxing financial transactions introduces additional friction into this process.

[9] Interdealers and interbank transactions are referred to as 'wholesale' transactions, as opposed to transactions involving non-financial customers in 'retail' segments. See Section 4.4 for the composition of currency transactions by counter-party and its recent shifts in markets.

fundamentalists' or 'informed traders') follow the herd in the face of uncertainty.[10] In the analyses, a critical distinction is usually made between informed traders and noise traders: while informed traders act on homogeneous rational expectation, noise traders make their decisions on the basis of 'fads', which are unrelated to fundamentals.

In this context, Jeanne and Rose (1999) suggest that while the volatility in exchange rates is generated both by fundamentals and noise, the source of excessive exchange rate volatility (that is, speculative bubbles) is attributed to the presence of noise traders. In particular, their model shows that noise traders are attracted to the market in search for a risk premium, and that as the number of noise traders increases, so does the volatility of exchange rates. It predicts that when the volatility of fundamentals is low, there is a single equilibrium where noise traders are not active, resulting in a low volatility in exchange rates. Conversely, when the volatility of fundamentals is high, a large number of noise traders enter the market, producing a high volatility in exchange rates. When the volatility of fundamentals is in the intermediate range, however, multiple stable equilibria are possible, depending on the number of noise traders seeking for a risk premium.

The excess volatility generated by noise traders is also analysed in the model of asset markets, advanced by De Long *et al.* (1990*a*, *b*), with focus on the interesting interface between arbitrageurs and noise traders. 'Arbitrage does not eliminate the effects of noise because noise itself creates risk' (De Long *et al.* 1990*b*: 705). That is, the unpredictability of noise traders' beliefs and expectations, which can be erroneous and stochastic in light of fundamentals, could create a 'noise trader risk'—a risk in the price of assets that deters rational arbitrageurs from aggressively betting against them. This is because arbitrageurs are likely to be risk averse, acting with a short time-horizon. Hence, they tend to have limited willingness to take position against risks created by noise traders. As a result, 'prices can diverge significantly from fundamental values even in the absence of fundamental risk' (De Long *et al.* 1990*b*: 705). Moreover, bearing a disproportionate amount of risk thus generated enables noise traders to earn a higher expected return than rational investors engaged in arbitrage against noise. Clearly, their model challenges the standard proposition made by Friedman (1953) that irrational noise traders are counteracted by rational arbitrageurs who trade against them and in the process drive asset prices close to fundamental values.

Overall, these models support the view that speculators—acting on 'fads' or guided by extrapolative expectations at short-term horizon—can exert destabilizing effects on markets and 'overshooting of the overshooting equilibrium' takes place.[11] Furthermore, destabilizing speculation of this type can be profitable, contrary to Friedman's reasoning. The Tobin tax is often viewed by its proponents as particularly effective to

---

[10] Keynes (1936) uses a 'beauty contest' analogy to describe fund managers' herd behaviour, in that they must guess in an instant how other market players will interpret a new event and follow them accordingly.

[11] In this context, it is worth noting that in Krugman's model of the target zone (1991), the result that speculators could have a stabilizing effect at margins of the target zone depends critically on two assumptions: (i) speculators' expectations are guided by macroeconomic fundamentals; and (ii) the government's credible commitment to intervene prevails.

countering such speculation and speculative bubbles in the floating currency markets on short horizons by eliminating destabilizing noise trading.[12] It is also argued that the Tobin tax, by breaking the interest parity condition, could in principle allow policymakers to pursue monetary policy for domestic consideration without a fear of impending large exchange rate fluctuations (Eichengreen 1996).

Interestingly, Frankel (1996) reports survey results, which show that traders, using the 'Chartist technical analysis' or the 'momentum' models, act on extrapolative expectations at short horizon of under three months, while they act on adaptive, regressive or distributed lag expectations at longer horizons of three months to one year. Hence, he suggests that the former generates destabilizing speculations, while the latter produces stabilizing effects. Further, Spahn (2002) notes that more chartists may be found among the institutional investors such as investment fund managers than among dealers-arbitrageurs. These empirical observations point to the importance of distinguishing those who act as arbitrageurs from those whose behaviour tends to be speculative, pushing markets away from equilibrium.

On one hand, Frankel's empirical results tend to suggest that traders' behavioural pattern is a function of time-horizons over which they act, so the Tobin tax is seen as effective for moderating destabilizing speculation by penalizing trading with a short-term horizon. On the other hand, Spahn's observation implies that traders' behaviour depends upon their motivation for participating in currency trading. However, a complication arises, in my view, because the interaction between arbitrageurs and noise traders in currency markets is very complex, as the former often has to respond to the unpredictable behaviour of the latter rather than to expected changes in fundamentals (De Long *et al.* 1990*a*). Further, the market composition between the two types of traders shifts, as market conditions change because the entry and behaviour of noise traders are influenced by the level of volatility of fundamentals and the size of risk premium, as shown by Jeanne and Rose (1999). Equally, depending on market conditions, traders could switch their position from arbitrageurs to 'destabilizing' speculators.

Now, a critical issue is whether the Tobin tax could always be successful in distinguishing between these two types of traders. Williamson (1997) notes it is naïve to equate short-term movements with market destabilization. Spahn (2002) further remarks that the Tobin tax unfortunately cannot discriminate between destabilizing noise trading and stabilizing liquidity trading. Davidson (1997) goes a step further to suggest that the Tobin tax is more likely to be a constraint on arbitrage flows rather than on speculative flows. If this is the case, the Tobin tax could adversely affect market efficiency. Hence, critics argue forcefully that this 'liquidity' consideration alone provides sufficient grounds to oppose the Tobin tax.

---

[12] Applying the interest parity condition, Frankel (1996) estimates that even at the very modest rate of transaction tax rate of 0.001%, for traders with a one-day time horizon to engage in speculative transaction, the foreign yield would have to rise to 46.5%, compared to domestic yield of 10%. Similarly, Spahn (2002) estimates that at a tax rate of 0.1%, foreign yields would have to rise to 50.7%, 18.5%, and 10.7% compared to domestic yield of 5%, for traders with one-day, three-day, and one-week time-horizon, respectively.

Certainly, the liquidity-efficiency dimension has a critical bearing on the question of what the optimal (or permissible) range of the tax rate could be, when one attempts to estimate the revenue potential of the Tobin tax.[13] Liquid markets are certainly necessary for arbitrageurs to perform the important functions of reducing price volatility, settlement risk, and the cost of hedging. As discussed above, Jeanne and Rose (1999) show that markets are likely to be dominated by arbitrageurs rather than noise traders under 'tranquil' market conditions with a low volatility of fundamentals. Hence, the tax rate cannot be set at a very low threshold level to undermine liquidity and market efficiency. Rates that are too high certainly risk reducing unduly liquidity necessary for arbitrage operations as well as deterring international trade transactions and long-term investment.

While Kaul and Langmore (1996) set a ceiling at 0.25 per cent absolute maximum, Felix and Sau (1996) assess tax rates at less than 0.05 per cent (5 basis point) as those with no 'sand in the gears'. Hence, these authors use tax rates between 0.25 per cent and 0.05 per cent for their revenue calculation. Although we suggest in the following the use of a much lower rate of 0.01–0.02 per cent (1 or 2 basis points) for revenue estimation on the grounds of efficiency and feasibility, some consensus in literature had emerged by the mid-1990s that the liquidity question is likely to favour 0.1 per cent or lower as the tax rate ceiling. The lower rates are favoured on the basis of the growing recognition that a loss of liquidity resulting from CTT should be kept to a minimum, so that transaction costs and spreads as well as the trade volume and market structures would not be affected adversely.

It is assumed that at a modest tax rate of 0.1 per cent or lower, CTT would not entail a discernible disincentive to long-term investments or international trade, as the tax could be a very marginal part of other larger trade- and investment-related transaction costs. It can also be argued that a tax burden at this low rate is less likely to exceed the cost of using derivative instruments to hedge against currency fluctuations (Eichengreen and Wyplosz 1996). By affecting the cost of trading with a very short-term horizon (see note 12), it has been argued that CTT at these low tax rates could still reduce currency speculation and swings at margin.[14]

However, the low tax rates such as discussed here would certainly not be effective in countering large-scale speculative attacks on pegged exchange rates, as observed in recent currency crises. Yet, currency crises have increasingly become 'self-fulfilling' in character, where substantial financial gains are assured for speculators who take a position against the viability of currency pegs as in the ERM crisis. In the self-fulfilling crises, even though a fixed exchange rate is sustainable in terms of consistency between exchange rate policy and other macroeconomic fundamentals as it stands, agents'

[13] It has been suggested that the Tobin tax could be set as a percentage of spreads, which can eliminate the need for setting a tax rate as a percentage of trade turnover. However, in our view, because of the fragmented nature of the retail segments of currency markets, this would simplify neither tax administration nor revenue estimation as such. We shall return to this question in Section 4.4.

[14] Responding to Davidson's arguments that the effect on trade volume of Tobin tax at a low rate is minimum, Korkut (2002) suggests that the stabilizing effect of the Tobin tax is realized more through its negative impact on the *speed* of reaction of market traders to price changes.

expectations about possible inconsistency in the future can trigger a speculative attack (Obstfeld 1996).

As in the first generation model of currency crises (Krugman 1979), the main issue at stake here is still the credibility of a government committing to a fixed exchange rate regime in the presence of market speculation. However, instead of facing a real reserve constraint as a result of a deterioration of economic fundamentals as in the first generation model, the government facing a possible attack from speculators tries to address a tradeoff between the benefits of continuing to defend the currency and costs of doing so in terms of hardships resulting from such economic costs as high interest rates and unemployment. Speculators in turn try to second-guess the government's capabilities and intentions. A speculative attack occurs when the government is not believed to be able or willing to defend the peg at high cost and is expected to devalue.

Importantly, agents' expectations about possible future depreciation feed into current economic variables and increase wages and prices. In short, speculation in itself creates objective economic conditions that make devaluation likely, while macroeconomic fundamentals determine the existence and multiplicity of possible equilibria. In the end, the government is forced to validate the expectations *ex post* by devaluing. Thus, the inability to maintain credibility has become self-fulfilling, as the expectations of speculators regarding the behaviour of the government in a crisis situation might per se generate the crisis. Under such conditions, a regime that could have been viable in terms of economic fundamentals collapses. In effect, crises are not precipitated so much by the actual mechanisms of the economy, but rather by the speculators' expectations of the choices that a government would make in a tight crisis situation. Thus, mechanisms of self-fulfilling crises work through market expectations.

Under these crisis conditions, the issue at stake is not merely whether speculators increase exchange rate volatility, but also whether they generate and exacerbate exchange rate misalignments in terms of fundamentals. This is because noise traders could trigger a shift of exchange rate from an equilibrium with a low volatility of fundamentals to the one with a high volatility of fundamentals, by generating destabilizing speculative bubbles, as shown by Jeanne and Rose (1999).

In this regard, Williamson (1997) raises an interesting question whether the Tobin tax would curb misalignments. Referring to the fact that transaction tax would penalize both stabilizing and destabilizing speculators, he observes: 'if the object is to curb misalignments, it seems inefficient to penalize all transactions rather than those that are subverting policy' (1997: 336). Hence, he regards the Tobin tax as an inferior instrument to more discriminatory types of capital controls in its capacity to stabilize the currency market.

Certainly, if CTT is considered as an instrument for dampening speculation to avert self-fulfilling crises, the tax rate has to be set at a much higher rate than the one envisaged to deal with 'noise-trading' speculators operating under less volatile market conditions.[15] The low range of the tax rates referred to above would not deter

[15] Davidson (1997) emphasizes this problem, noting that to avert the speculative surge of the Mexican peso crisis of 1994–5, Tobin tax exceeding 23% would have needed.

speculative attacks on pegs, when much higher gains are at stake. Yet, as discussed above, a high tax rate would create severe liquidity problems for normal market operations. In order to address this tradeoff and to deal effectively with speculators' different motivations depending on market conditions, a flexible multi-tier system of taxes would be required, rather than a time-invariant uniform currency tax.

This issue is directly addressed in the two-tier tax system proposed by Spahn (1996, 2002). The two-tier structure embedded in Spahn's proposal consists of 'a low tax rate for normal transactions and an exchange surcharge on profits from very short-term transactions deemed to be speculative attacks on currencies' (1996: 24), as applied to a target zone.[16] Under this system, 'an exchange rate would be allowed to move freely within a band, but overshooting the band would result in a tax on the discrepancy between the market exchange rate and the closest margin of the band', while the low transaction tax is levied on a continual basis, raising substantial and stable revenues. Importantly, this system has to be executed under a two-tier structure, since credibility of the surcharge levy is anchored in the fact that the transaction tax system is already in place. Thus, Spahn proposes that the exchange surcharge would be administered in conjunction with the underlying transaction tax. The transaction tax would serve 'as a monitoring and controlling device for the exchange surcharge, which would be zero so long as foreign exchange markets are operating normally within a band, but would function as an automatic circuit-breaker at times of speculative attacks' (1996: 24). Thus, the exchange surcharge would be applied temporarily on a unilateral basis at the 'speculative end' and would not affect the liquidity or the efficiency of market functioning in a less volatile condition.

Indeed, once such a system is seen to be operating efficiently with credibility, the threat of a surcharge levy alone may be sufficient to keep exchange rates within a target zone, without depletion of official reserves or other interventions such as high premium on overnight money deposits or excessively high interest rates as observed during the ERM crises. The system is seen as providing monetary authorities with breathing space for orderly realignment of exchange rates, which would reflect the development of economic fundamentals. In this context, it should be noted that the band in the proposed scheme would be a moving one that continuously reflects changes in fundamentals. Thus, authorities would not choose to set and defend a particular parity and its associated band, but rather their aim would be to prevent self-fulfilling panic in the currency markets.

In my view, one of interesting aspects of this scheme is that its implementation is deemed successful, when the exchange surcharge is never levied, while the background low transaction tax generates steady revenues, as the two-tier currency tax manages to drive 'destabilizing' speculation from the system. In particular, in relation to potential revenue estimate, which is the main objective of this chapter, it is important to

---

[16] Spahn (2002) refers the exchange surcharge as an exchange-rate normalization duty (ENRD). Further, Grabel (2003) classifies potential measures managing cross-border capital flows into 'trip wires' and 'speed bumps'. An exchange surcharge in the Spahn proposal is an example of a speed bump measure that might be activated whenever trip wires reveal that a currency is vulnerable to speculative attack.

emphasize that the two-tier system proposed by Spahn allows the first-tier tax to be kept as low as 0.01–0.02 per cent (1 or 2 basis points).

Now, following on this scheme proposed by Spahn, others have proposed dual taxation as a way of increasing the 'double dividend' through schemes such as the 'dual currency and securities transaction tax'. We shall come back to the issue of appropriate exchange rate regime as well as the issue of achieving effective double dividends with the use of the Tobin tax in the concluding section. However, it may be worth noting here in passing that a multi-tier CTT such as Spahn's proposal is not universally accepted as a solution for averting self-fulfilling currency crises. For example, Williamson (2000) sees no role of any variation of CTT in managing the intermediate regimes against speculative attacks, while recommending the intermediate 'target zone' regime, governed by the BBC rule (where BBC stands for basket, band, and crawl), as a more appropriate exchange rate regime for most emerging market economies in preference over one of the two corner solutions of pure floating or hard pegs.[17] Naturally, bands are stabilizing when the credibility to defend is maintained.[18] He argues, hence, that it is important first and foremost to build credibility so that expectations are formed in a stabilizing manner.

However, Williamson recommends 'soft margins' of the bands rather than 'hard margins' as appropriate policy for emerging market economies in order to build credibility over time. He endorses the soft target zone system, analysed by Bartolini and Prati (1997, 1998), in which the exchange rate is allowed to move outside the band in the short run, at times of shocks to 'the fundamentals', in order to diffuse tension. According to Bartolini and Prati (1998), such a softening of the target zone makes the system less vulnerable to speculative pressures, as the edges to bands provide the market with targets to attack. In their view, government interventions should instead be focused on maintaining the obligation to hold the rate within the band in the long run.

Thus, Williamson argues that during times of large speculation the soft bands would remove the source of vulnerability without losing the main advantage of the BBC arrangement. By allowing a quick, temporary exit from commitments when a crisis situation develops, it is conjectured that credibility to commitments is not eroded permanently, while the exchange rate could revert back to the parity in the process of crisis resolution. Obviously, under such a soft target zone regime, there is no role for a circuit-breaker embedded in the two-tier CTT proposal, as commitments to defend the edges of the zone are abandoned altogether.

---

[17] In the recent literature on the appropriate exchange regime for emerging market economies, the term of 'two-corner solutions' is used to refer to a freely floating exchange rate or hard pegs such as currency boards, dollarization, or regional monetary union in the context of discussing the 'impossible trinity' thesis (see Frankel 1999, for example).

[18] Williamson (2000) lists the fundamental reasons found in literature for preferring a band system over floating: (i) the band performs the function of crystallizing market expectations of where the equilibrium exchange rate may lay, thus making expectations stable at the time-horizons relevant for influencing market behaviour (Svensson 1992); (ii) a band has a pronounced effect in limiting exchange rate variability by preventing noise traders, particularly stop-loss traders, from making money by introducing noise into the exchange market (Rose 1996).

However, it should be recalled that in the classic model on target zones (Krugman 1991), speculators could act in a stabilizing manner at the margin of the zone precisely because of their confidence in the government's commitment and ability to intervene.[19] A credible commitment to the exchange rate target would have a stabilizing effect on market expectations by discouraging the entry of destabilizing noise traders. Further, the 'hard' margin could avoid the large misalignments associated with the soft margin in terms of very high adjustment costs (even though they are claimed to be temporary).

Ultimately, in my view, several critical questions should be addressed in deciding which target zone system (soft or hard margins) is appropriate: (i) how credibility to commitment to the target zone can be best maintained; (ii) how costly is it to abandon the zone even temporarily in terms of macroeconomic fundamentals and adjustments; (iii) how quickly can market confidence be restored to allow the exchange rate to gravitate back towards the reference rate or the parity if a soft band option is adopted. The answer to these questions appears to vary case by case. If a soft band is too costly for the economy, a hard band incorporating the two-tier CTT system remains an attractive instrument to consider.

4.3. THE DEBATE ON THE TECHNICAL AND POLITICAL FEASIBILITY OF CTT

4.3.1. *Earlier Debate on the Technical Feasibility of CTT*

In Tobin's *original* proposal, a currency transaction tax is applied on a universal basis to spot transactions only. This raised strong scepticism on the grounds of technical and political feasibility. In particular, it has been argued that such a tax could be evaded too easily by market migration to offshore tax havens as well as asset substitutions.[20]

Kenen (1996) addresses these concerns in a comprehensive manner. To counter the shifting of transactions to tax-free jurisdictions, he proposes two measures: imposition of a punitive rate on transfers of funds to or from such locations,[21] and taxing at the site where the deal is made (at dealing sites) rather than at the site where the transaction occurs, that is, at settlement or booking sites. The reason for the second measure is both because too many transactions are netted out before they are settled and because tax-free jurisdictions can be used for booking all transactions with minimum cost. For example, booking and settlement sites could be easily relocated by just installing computers without moving dealing rooms or dealers, whereas relocation of dealing sites is far more costly. Hence, Kenen also proposes that tax collection is made on

---

[19] The empirical rejection of this model is usually explained in terms of imperfect credibility and intramarginal interventions (Garber and Svensson 1995; Sarno and Taylor 2003).

[20] Tobin (1996) remarks that the concerns about tax evasion may be generally overblown. Baker (2001) also argues that the 'evasion issue' has got too much attention in relation to CTTs and even capital controls. However, though this may be the case, a possibility of evasion can affect the efficacy of any tax as well as the cost of enforcement, so the evasion issue should be carefully examined. See Umlauf (1993) for the asset migration effects of transaction taxes on the Swedish stock market.

[21] Kenen suggests imposing a 5% punitive tax on transactions with a new dealing site, rather than one-half of the standard rate of 0.05% (i.e. 0.025% for wholesale trading).

a market basis where the dealing site is located and each party involved in wholesale transactions would pay half the tax in retail transactions in order to equalize the tax burden across wholesale interbank transactions and retail transactions.

As regards to addressing the possibility of tax evasion by asset substitutions, Kenen points to the need to extend the transaction base to derivatives such as forward and swap contracts, which could be used as close substitutions for spot transactions.[22] The case for taxing futures and options contracts is more complicated, as they are not perfect substitutes for spot transactions or forward contracts and they are not typically settled by delivering currencies. However, Kenen reckons that if substantial changes to derivative markets are to be avoided, both futures and option contracts need to be taxed as well.

However, those derivatives, which require high-frequency trading involving four or more transactions per contract instead of two transactions, should not be subject to double taxation. Further, these derivatives are risk-hedging instruments, so taxing them would make hedging very costly, as taxes would not eliminate exchange rate fluctuations from the market. At least, in order to remove the resulting bias against high-frequency trading for hedging purpose, Spahn (1996) suggests that transactions involving derivatives should be taxed at half the rate for spot transactions, which would allow the derivative markets to function for hedging purposes. In his more recent study, Spahn (2002) proposes that in addition to all spot transactions, outright forwards and swaps up to one month would be taxed, while options and other financial derivatives would not be taxed (though they are taxed indirectly through the spot and forward transactions they trigger).

Now, it could be envisaged that new 'cash substitute' instruments could emerge as tax avoidance mechanism. Garber and Taylor (1995) and Garber (1996) suggest that T-bills traded in liquid markets could be used for such a purpose, while Spahn (1996) foresees other possibilities involving bankers' acceptances, commercial papers, or repurchase agreements made against collateral without cash settlements. Since the use of these substitutes involve transactions costs and interest rate risks or other credit risks, both Kenen (1996) and Tobin (1996) assess that the possibility of large-scale use of these substituting instruments are rather exaggerated and could be avoided, if a low transaction tax is applied. However, a heavy tax burden may well encourage the development of liquid markets for new financial instruments and papers that could be used for cash substitutes.

Indeed, one of most efficient approaches to discourage all forms of tax avoidance, including migration and substitutions, is to keep the tax rate very low. Considering that spreads in the wholesale interbank market are well below 0.1 per cent, Kenen (1996) reckons a 0.05 per cent tax rate (5 basis point) to be the upper benchmark for CTT rather than the lower benchmark, as in the study by Felix and Sau (1996), while Spahn (1996) suggests an underlying tax rate of 0.02 per cent (2 basis point).

---

[22] While spot transactions are settled in less than three days, forward transactions take three or more days and swap transactions pair either a spot transaction with an offsetting forward transaction, or two forward contracts with different maturities. Hence, if only spot transactions are taxed, forward and swap contracts could easily be used as substitutes. Tobin acknowledges the need for this modification to the taxbase (1996).

Furthermore, both Tobin (1996) and Kenen (1996) suggest that for a CTT system to be operative, the currency transaction tax has to be adopted at least by the G7 countries and a few other major financial centres such as Singapore, Hong Kong, and Switzerland. Others argue, however, that for a more effective implementation and enforcement, a universal adoption of CTT under an international agreement is necessary. In particular, the universality was initially viewed as imperative in order to deal effectively with a race-to-the-bottom approach to tax competition for highly mobile financial services (Garber 1996).[23]

Such an agreement should specify uniform rules and procedures for subsequent amendments, as well as for the use of the tax revenue. Tobin forwarded a proposal in which the administration of a transactions tax is assigned to the IMF, so that a CTT levy can be tied to IMF membership and borrowing privileges, and hence, 'universality' can be ensured. While other existing international organizations such as Bank for International Settlement (BIS) and World Bank can be considered equally as the coordinating and enforcement agencies for CTT, the establishment of a specialized new institution under the UN system for this specific purpose (e.g. an international cooperation fund such as Global Development Fund or World Tax Authority) was also discussed. It was envisaged that under such a proposal, some agreed portion of tax collected by national authorities would be funnelled to a UN sanctioned fund management system or a specially established institution.

4.3.2. *New Schemes to Overcome Technical and Political Impediments to CTT*

While foreign exchange markets have hitherto been organized as decentralized dealer-driven markets, there appears to be a clear trend towards more centralized automated systems. While this rationalization may entail a reduction in the gross turnover of foreign exchange transactions, it may ease considerably the problem of administration and collection of CTT, as well as that of enforcement. In fact, as Frankel (1996) argues, a CTT may indeed accelerate this centralization process. It has been suggested that automated systems, increasingly used for currency interbank *settlements*, could be effectively used for tax administration. Proposals made by Schmidt and Mendez fall into this category (Mendez 1995; Schmidt 1999, 2001).

According to Schmidt's proposal, CTT would be collected and enforced at the settlement site, instead of the dealing site as in Kenen's proposal.[24] Currently, real time gross settlement systems (RTGS) for payment vs payment settlement (PVP) are used for eliminating settlement risk at the national level. In addition, the Continuous Linked Settlement (CLS) Bank is being developed as a global system of processing settlements involving a number of currencies. The CLS Bank's settlement operations would be linked to domestic systems to support PVP settlement for foreign exchange

---

[23] For a more recent proposal on CTT coverage, see discussion below.

[24] This means that tax revenues generated by the Schmidt scheme would be substantially lower than the estimates based on CTT imposed at the dealing site, as many foreign exchange transactions are netted out.

transactions. Seizing this new technological development, Schmidt proposes RTGS as a mechanism for levying a Tobin tax at the national level and CLS Bank's settlement operations for the imposition of CTT for cross-border flows in offshore netting systems. The latter will be monitored and supervised by central banks participating in CTT to deal with the threat of offshore tax avoidance. Schmidt (1999) further suggests that it is technologically easy to apply the Tobin tax to foreign exchange transactions intermediated by an exchange of securities, as securities exchanges around the world operate similar netting settlement schemes through clearing houses.

Mendez (1995, 2001) goes a step further to propose the establishment of a global 'foreign currency exchange' (FXE) under the UN system as alternative to the CTT to involve the setting-up of an extensive administrative structure for taxation. Under the Mendez' proposal, the centralized exchange, as a public owned entity in the form of a specialized agency, would be a global network of members comprising of frequent users as well as brokers and dealers, with trading facilities in the major financial centres and branches in other small cities. Members would pay a licensing fee as well as commission on each transaction. In place of CTT, these licensing and user fees would constitute revenues. Mendez predicts that the FXE would significantly lower the cost of changing money to end users by giving them competitive rates due to increased efficiency in exchange markets. In his view, it could also generate revenues of considerable size through transaction fees, rather than a transaction tax, while offering the potential of facilitating the operation of a Tobin type of tax with a view of reducing volatility. Mendez (2001) suggests that the distinctive advantage of FXE over CTT lies in the fact that it is a more market-based approach, and would therefore garner more political support than the Tobin tax. However, under the current international climate, it may be as equally difficult as with CTTs (if not more so), to reach an international agreement for creating and organizing such a global currency market under the UN system, as proposed by Mendez.

Adopting the Schmidt proposal of collecting CTT at the settlement site, Clunies-Ross (2003) argues that a virtually universal application of CTT on *wholesale* transactions could be achieved through the cooperation of five or so monetary authorities who issue 'vehicle' currencies, since almost all wholesale transactions have one of these vehicle currencies on one or both sides. He suggests that CTT at the settlement site would simplify the formidable technical issues associated with the Tobin tax imposed on largely unregulated, decentralized currency markets at the dealing site. It is worth noting here that taxing at settlement incidentally reduces risk penalizing arbitrage transactions considerably, as a tax is applied to a trader's netted out position, rather than to each of his or her transaction flows.[25] The problem associated with asset substitution can also be addressed through security exchange taxes or taxes on derivative instruments using a similar centralized mechanism, as suggested by Schmidt.

---

[25] Thus, taxing at the settlement site would mitigate, to a certain degree, the criticism against a transaction tax imposed on the *flow* in view of the understanding that speculative threats originate from an overhang of a *stock* of short-term claims. I am grateful to John Williamson for pointing to the need for drawing sufficient attention to this question.

Clunies-Ross (2003) assesses further that using the Schmidt scheme, the *higher tier* tax embedded in the Spahn proposal could be implemented unilaterally by countries facing impeding currency crises, without having an international agreement.

While all these authors emphasize the technical feasibility of CTT, they recognize that the most formidable obstacle is political (Mendez 2001). The main political obstacle in the way to making the CTT universal is the intense opposition anticipated from the US administration/congress and financial industry. So adoption of the CTT on a regional basis has been actively considered. For example, Cecil (2001) examines the possibility of domestic or regional adoptions of CTTs, such as the European Union, with international cooperation for enforcement. Spahn (2002) advances the distinct concept of a politically feasible Tobin tax (PFTT) in the prevailing political reality. Foreseeing fierce opposition from the US administration and Congress,[26] Spahn (2002) reckons with the fact that the Tobin tax cannot be introduced universally or multilaterally in the first instance, as the tax has to be legitimized first by existing parliamentary institutions, either national or regional (e.g. the European Council). In the light of the political reality faced by the international community, he actively considers the case in which the Tobin tax can be implemented unilaterally by a group of countries such as the European Union in cooperation with Switzerland.

Following on these arguments, Patomäki and Sehm-Patomäki (1999) also suggest an implementation of CTT in two phases: in the first phase, a group of countries, such as the Euro-EU, would establish an open agreement and a supranational body for tax administration. Member countries would agree to charge a small underlying CTT (e.g. 0.1 per cent) as well as high exchange surcharges, as the need arises. (Their proposed tax rate is much higher than the rates I consider realistic and permissible in the prevailing market and political conditions.) A higher CTT (e.g. 0.2 per cent) is charged in dealing with non-residents who are not in the tax regime, in order to solve the tax evasion problem as well as to exert pressure on outsiders to join. In the second phase, once all major financial centres and most other countries have joined, a universal and uniform CTT would be applied.

Patomäki and Denys (2002) develop this idea further in the 'draft treaty on global currency transactions tax' and propose the establishment of a CTT organization under a treaty, which will enter into force following the thirtieth ratification of the treaty or on the date on which the preparatory group has established that the contracting states, who have ratified the treaty account for at least 20 per cent of the global currency markets, whichever is later. The draft treaty has adopted the basic ideas contained in Spahn's two-tier scheme as well as the Schmidt system collection, though it stipulates that the CTT be levied on both wholesale Sand retail markets.

---

[26] In the Second Session of the 104th Congress of the United States, Senator Bob Dole and three other politicians introduced a bill to prohibit the UN and UN officials from developing and promoting Tobin's idea or any other international taxation scheme.

Table 4.1. *Global foreign exchange market turnover*[a] *daily averages in April, in billions of US$*

	1989	1992	1995	1998[b]	2001
Spot transactions	317	394	494	568	387
Outright forwards	27	58	97	128	131
Foreign exchange swaps	190	324	546	734	656
Estimated gaps in reporting	56	44	53	60	26
Total 'traditional' turnover	590	820	1,190	1,490	1,200
Memo: Turnover at April 2001 exchanges rates[c]	570	750	990	1,400	1,200

Notes:

[a] Adjusted for local and cross-border double-counting.

[b] Revised since the previous survey.

[c] Non-US dollar legs of foreign currency transactions were converted from current US dollar amounts into original currency amounts at average. Exchange rates for April of each survey year and then reconverted into US dollar amounts at average April 2001 exchange rates.

Source: BIS (2002: Table B1).

4.4. EVALUATION OF THE REVENUE POTENTIAL OF CTTs

4.4.1. *Recent Trends in the Composition and Structure of Currency Markets*

There are several important changes in foreign exchange markets in recent years, which can have a critical bearing on our estimates of CTT revenues. As shown in Table 4.1, according to the BIS survey data conducted in April 2001, average daily *net* turnover was US$1.2 trillion, compared to US$1.49 trillion in April 1998, which is a 19 per cent decline at current exchange rates and a 14 per cent fall at constant exchange rates as calculated by BIS (2002).[27] The decline in turnover between 1998 and 2001 is in sharp contrast to the rapid steady increase in turnover over the last two decades, found in the earlier surveys. The level of activities in currency markets in 2001 settled down to the level reported for 1995.

The decline is largely accounted for by a sharp fall in spot transactions, and to a lesser extent, in foreign exchange swaps, while outright forward transactions showed a slight increase. Thus, there are some notable changes in the market composition by type of transactions as shown in Fig. 4.1. The share of spot transactions has steadily declined since 1992, while that of foreign exchange swaps has risen, now accounting for over 55 per cent of transactions. According to the BIS survey, 38 per cent of outright forwards and 69 per cent of swaps are with a maturity of up to seven days. Together

[27] Forty-eight central banks and monetary authorities participated in the Triennial Central Bank Survey of Foreign Exchange and Derivatives Market Activities conducted by the Bank for International Settlement in 2001. The geographical coverage of the BIS survey has steadily expanded from the twenty-one countries in 1989.

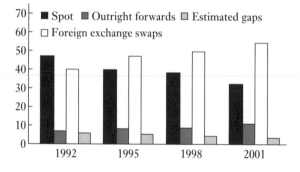

Figure 4.1. *Foreign exchange market turnover at constant April 2001 exchange rates by market segment in per cent of global turnover*

Note: Non-US dollar legs of foreign currency transactions were converted into original currency amounts at exchange rates for April of each survey year and then reconverted into US dollar amounts at average April 2001 exchange rates.

Source: BIS (2002: Graph B.1).

Table 4.2. *Reported foreign exchange market turnover by counterparty[a] daily averages in April, in billions of US$*

	1992	1995	1998[b]	2001
Total	776	1,137	1,429	1,173
With reporting dealers	540	729	908	689
With other financial institutions	97	230	279	329
With non-financial customers	137	178	242	156
Local	317	526	657	499
Cross-border	392	611	772	674

[a] Adjusted for local and cross-border double-counting. Excludes estimated gaps in reporting.

[b] Revised since the previous survey.

Source: BIS (2002: Table B3).

with spot transactions, this brings the share of transactions with maturity up to seven days to 76 per cent in 2001, close to the estimate of 80 per cent as transactions involving roundtrips of seven days or less, as noted in Tobin (1996).

There are also some changes in the relative market share accounted for by the different counterparties. As shown in Table 4.2, trading between reporting dealers declined sharply, bringing its share in total turnover from 70 per cent in 1992 to 59 per cent in 2001 (Fig. 4.2). A marked decline in trading between banks and non-financial customers is reported here, which now accounts only for 13 per cent of transactions. This may have reflected the acceleration of the consolidation process observed in the non-financial corporation sector. The increased transactions between banks and other financial institutions are accounted for by the increasing role of asset managers (BIS 2002: 2). At the same time, the role of hedge funds in foreign exchange transactions has declined since their debacle in 1998.

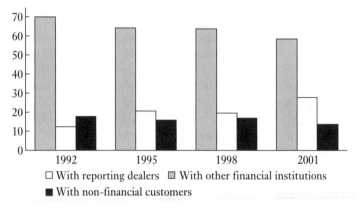

Figure 4.2. *Foreign exchange market turnover by counterparty as per cent of total reported turnover*

Source: BIS (2002: Graph B.2).

The marked decline in global foreign exchange market turnover in the 2001 survey undoubtedly reflects the general slowdown of the global economy and world trade as well as the increased economic and political uncertainty of recent years. However, a reduction of this scale as well as the significant changes in market structures is also an indication of the growing trend towards the centralized, automated systems in the settlement of wholesale currency transactions discussed above.[28] Thus, BIS (2002) also notes the growing role of electronic brokers in the spot interbank market, reducing the need for dealers to trade actively. The decline in wholesale interbank transactions is also explained by the steady trend towards concentration in the banking sector, observed in the major currency markets as well as globally, thus decreasing the number of trading desks (BIS 2002: Table B.5).[29]

The introduction of the euro has also reduced gross foreign exchange market turnover, as it eliminated the need for intra-EMS trading (Table 4.3). Dollar/euro trade constitutes 30 per cent of the global turnover, followed by dollar/yen with 20 per cent and dollar/GBP with 11 per cent (Table 4.4).

Major trading locations such as London, New York, and Tokyo continuously dominate foreign exchange transactions, accounting together for 56 per cent of global transactions (Table 4.5). London remains the largest centre, larger than New York and Tokyo combined. The ten trading centres listed in Table 4.5 handle 85 per cent of global currency transactions.

---

[28] However, as CLS Bank became operational only in autumn 2002, the trade volume revealed by the BIS survey conducted in April 2001 could not be affected by this new technology applied to settlements in global foreign exchange trade.

[29] BIS (2002) suggests the decline in turnover can also be explained by the decrease in the risk tolerance of banks after the financial crises in 1998, which led to a reduction in credit limits and proprietary trading.

Table 4.3. *Currency distribution of reported foreign exchange market turnover[a] percentage shares of average daily turnover in April*

	1989	1992	1995	1998[b]	2001
US dollar	90.0	82.0	83.3	87.3	90.4
Euro	—	—	—	—	37.6
Deutsche mark[c]	27.0	39.6	36.1	30.1	—
French franc	2.0	3.8	7.9	5.1	—
ECU and other EMS currencies	4.0	11.8	15.7	17.3	—
Japanese yen	27.0	23.4	24.1	20.2	22.7
Pound sterling	15.0	13.6	9.4	11.0	13.2
Swiss franc	10.0	8.4	7.3	7.1	6.1
Canadian dollar	1.0	3.3	3.4	3.6	4.5
Australian dollar	2.0	2.5	2.7	3.1	4.2
Swedish krona[d]	—	1.3	0.6	0.4	2.6
Hong Kong dollar[d]	—	1.1	0.9	1.3	2.3
Singapore dollar[d]	—	0.3	0.3	1.2	1.1
Emerging market currencies[d,e]	—	0.5	0.4	3.0	5.2
Other	22.0	8.5	7.9	9.3	10.1
All currencies	200.0	200.0	200.0	200.0	200.0

[a] Because two currencies are involved in each transaction, the sum of the percentage shares of individual currencies totals 200% instead of 100%. The figures relate to reported 'net-net' turnover, that is, they are adjusted for both local and cross-border double-counting, except for 1989 data, which are available only on a 'gross-gross' basis. More details about emerging market and other currencies are provided in BIS (2002: Annex Tables E.1.1 and E.1.2).
[b] Revised since the previous survey.
[c] Data for April 1989 exclude domestic trading involving the Deutsche mark in Germany.
[d] For 1992–8, the data cover home currency trading only.
[e] For 1992 and 1995, South African rand; for 1998 and 2001, Brazilian real, Chilean peso, Czech koruna, Indian rupee, Korean won, Malaysian ringgit, Mexican peso, Polish zloty, Russian rouble, Saudi riyal, South African rand, Taiwan dollar, and Thai baht.

Source: BIS (2002: Table B.4).

Despite the marked decline in market turnover between 1998 and 2001, the relative size of foreign exchange markets is still staggering, as shown in Table 4.6. Annual world exports stood at US$6,121 billion, compared to the annualized global foreign exchange market turnover of US$300 trillion. This means that the ratio of global exports to global foreign exchange turnover is 0.02—an increase from the low level of 0.015 in 1998, but far less than the ratios observed in the 1970s. Felix and Sau (1996) report that these ratios for 1977, 1980, and 1983 were 0.29, 0.09, and 0.06, respectively.

Critically, global official foreign exchange reserves, which have been increasing steadily since the ERM crises in 1992, are equal to merely 1.7 days of global currency transactions. This reveals the meagre capacity of monetary authorities to intervene

Table 4.4. *Reported foreign exchange market turnover by currency pair[a] daily averages in April, in billions of US$ and percentages*

	1992		1995		1998[b]		2001	
	Amount	% share	Amount	% share	Amount	% share	Amount	% share
US dollar/euro	—	—	—	—	—	—	354	30
US dollar/mark	192	25	254	22	290	20	—	—
US dollar/French franc	19	2	51	4	58	4	—	—
US dollar/ECU	13	2	18	2	17	1	—	—
US dollar/other EMS	43	6	104	9	172	12	—	—
US dollar/yen	155	20	242	21	256	18	231	20
US dollar/sterling	77	10	78	7	117	8	125	11
US dollar/Swiss franc	49	6	61	5	79	5	57	5
US/Canadian dollar	25	3	38	3	50	3	50	4
US/Australian dollar	18	2	29	3	42	3	47	4
US dollar/other	48	6	72	6	167	12	195	17
Euro/yen	—	—	—	—	—	—	30	3
Euro/sterling	—	—	—	—	—	—	24	2
Euro/Swiss franc	—	—	—	—	—	—	12	1
Euro/other	—	—	—	—	—	—	21	2
Mark/yen	18	2	24	2	24	2	—	—
Mark/sterling	23	3	21	2	31	2	—	—
Mark/Swiss franc	13	2	18	2	18	1	—	—
Mark/French franc	10	1	34	3	10	1	—	—
Mark/ECU	6	1	6	1	3	0	—	—
Mark/other EMS	21	3	38	3	34	2	—	—
Mark/other	20	3	16	1	20	1	—	—
Other EMS/other EMS[c]	3	0	3	0	4	0	—	—
Other currency pairs	23	3	30	3	38	2	27	2
All currency pairs	776	100	1,137	100	1,430	100	1,173	100

[a] Adjusted for local and cross-border double-counting. Data in this table are not directly comparable with Table 4.4 for currency groups.
[b] Revised since the previous survey.
[c] The data cover home currency trading only.

Source: BIS (2002: Table B.6).

Table 4.5. *Geographical distribution of reported foreign exchange market turnover daily averages in April, in billions of US$ and percentages*

	1989		1992		1995		1998		2001	
	Amount	% share	Amount	% share	Amount	% share	Amount	% share	Amount	% share
United Kingdom	184	25.6	291	27.0	464	29.5	637	32.5	504	31.1
United States	115	16.0	167	15.5	244	15.5	351	17.9	254	15.7
Japan	111	15.5	120	11.2	161	10.2	136	6.9	147	9.1
Singapore	55	7.7	74	6.9	105	6.7	139	7.1	101	6.2
Germany	—	—	55	5.1	76	4.8	94	4.8	88	5.4
Switzerland	56	7.8	66	6.1	87	5.5	82	4.2	71	4.4
Hong Kong SAR	49	6.8	60	5.6	90	5.7	79	4.0	67	4.1
Australia	29	4.0	29	2.7	40	2.5	47	2.4	52	3.2
France	23	3.2	33	3.1	58	3.7	72	3.7	48	3.0
Canada	15	2.1	22	2.0	30	1.9	37	1.9	42	2.6

Source: Compiled from Table B.7 in BIS (2002).

Table 4.6. *Foreign exchange trading, world trade and global official reserves, in billions of US$ and percentages*

	1989	1992	1995	1998	2001
Annual world exports	3,027	3,762	5,130	5,444	6,121
Annual exports of developing countries	899	1,112	1,661	1,779	2,252
% share of developing country exports	29.7	29.6	32.4	32.7	36.9
Global official foreign exchange reserves	715	925	1,385	1,638	2,039
Foreign exchange reserves of developing countries	262	434	729	968	1,260
% share of developing country reserves	36.6	46.9	52.6	59.1	61.8
Annual global foreign exchange turnover (250 trading days)	147,500	205,000	297,500	372,500	300,000
Exports/foreign exchange turnover (%)	2.05	1.83	1.72	1.46	2.04
Reserves/exports (%)	23.6	24.6	27.0	30.1	33.3
Reserves/daily turnover (days)	1.21	1.13	1.16	1.10	1.70

Source: Author's calculation, based on data in International Financial Statistics (IMF) and BIS (2002).

in foreign exchange markets in the face of speculative self-fulfilling attacks on their currencies. Monetary authorities have been trying to improve their defence capacity by raising official reserve holdings from 25 per cent of global exports in 1992 to 33 per cent in 2001. Table 4.6 shows clearly that developing countries, which are more likely to face currency crises, are forced to hold larger reserves in relation to the size of their economies at very high opportunity costs. The share of developing countries in global reserve holdings has increased consistently from 37 per cent in 1989 to 62 per cent in 2001, in contrast to their share in world exports of 37 per cent in 2001.

4.4.2. *Revenue Potential and Tax Implementation*

Previous studies produced various estimates of potential revenue from the Tobin tax, predicting a very considerable tax revenue, as tax rates of 0.25–0.05 per cent are commonly used for calculation. For example, Frankel (1996) estimates that the 0.1 per cent tax applied to the 1995 global foreign exchange would generate an annual tax revenue of US$176 billion, after taking into account that the 0.1 per cent tax would reduce transaction volume by 45 per cent and allowing for a 20 per cent deduction for exempted official trading and tax evasion. Applied to the volume reached in 1995, Tobin (1996) reckons that the revenue is more likely to be US$94 billion maximum. His estimate is based on the assumption that only 30 per cent of the gross volume of transactions constitutes a taxbase if banks' end-of-day open positions only are taxed with a 0.1 per cent one-way tax. He concedes revenue could be less than US$50 billion if the tax-induced reduction of volume is taken into account.

Felix and Sau (1996) produce a range of potential revenue estimates, applying varying assumptions with regard to: (i) tax rates of 0.25, 0.1, and 0.05 per cent; (ii) pre-tax transaction costs, ranging from 0.1 to 1 per cent; and (iii) elasticities of trade volume in response to tax-induced changes in transaction costs, ranging from 0.3 to 1.75.[30] According to their estimates, the 0.1 per cent tax applied to the 1995 global foreign exchange would generate tax revenue of US$148 billion and US$180 billion, under the assumption of pre-tax transaction costs of 0.5 and 1.0 per cent, respectively. The 0.05 per cent tax rate, suggested by Kenen (1996), is estimated to produce tax revenue of US$90 billion and US$97 billion.

Felix and Sau are correct in estimating revenue potential on the basis of the elasticity of the volume with respect to currency transaction costs, which should absorb a tax burden. They note, 'by adding to transaction costs, a Tobin tax not only reduces the foreign exchange volume by an amount determined by the weighted average elasticity of volume with respect to costs, but alters its composition by squeezing hardest the low-unit-profit, high elasticity transactions such as covered interest arbitraging' (Felix and Sau 1996: 228). However, their estimated pre-tax transaction costs of 0.1–1.0 per cent appear to be too high in relation to the wholesale segments of foreign exchange markets as observed today.[31]

Transaction costs are reflected in the bid-ask spreads observed in markets.[32] The more liquid markets are, the lower spreads can be. Spahn reports that the spreads currently observed in highly liquid interbank wholesale markets are 0.011 per cent for the US dollar/euro transactions, 0.023 per cent for the US dollar/yen transactions, and 0.021 per cent for the US dollar/GB pound (Spahn 2002: appendix 4). However, reflecting a more fragmented nature with less competition because of asymmetric information disadvantages affecting retail, non-financial customers, spreads observed in retail segments are much larger and vary widely across markets.[33]

While CTT is supposed to reduce the transaction volume in short-horizon roundtrips or to affect the speed of traders' responses, it is unable to differentiate between destabilizing noise trading and stabilizing liquid trading in the wholesale markets. Given the substantial changes taking place in market structures in the wholesale interbank segments as a result of the new technological development discussed above, it is now unwise to impose a high tax rate to trigger further significant disturbances to market liquidity in the wholesale segments. Indeed, as many argue, it is best to adopt a

[30] Felix and Sau (1996) allow a 35% reduction for exempted official trading and tax evasion, compared to the 20% allowed in Frankel's estimate.

[31] Especially, it is not correct to assume uniform transaction costs across different market segments in their model and estimation, where Felix and Sau use the weighted average size of pre-tax transaction costs.

[32] The spreads also include risk premium and premium arising out of asymmetric information.

[33] For this reason, the revenue calculation presented here is not based on an alternative method of calculating tax revenue as a unified percentage of spreads (see note 13 above). Indeed, a unified CTT calculated as a percentage of spreads across the two market segments could make tax effects on real cross-border trade and investment more (not less) in most cases.

phase-in approach, whereby markets would have time to respond to the introduction of CTT gradually and in a stable manner.[34]

This line of thinking would set an upper limit to the CTT levied on interbank transactions at 0.01–0.02 per cent (1 or 2 basis points) as a 'permissible rate' in the light of the spreads in the wholesale segments reported above.[35] Hence, these very low tax rates, much lower than those used in previous studies, are selected and used in the revenue estimation produced below with a view of minimizing the adverse effects on the liquidity of the wholesale dealer markets, where also profit margins are known to be very thin. Indeed, for this very reason, the transaction cost reflected in the prevailing bid-ask spread in the wholesale segments is used as a yardstick for setting the permissible tax rate. At the same time, I conjecture that, based on calculations made by Frankel and Spahn,[36] the tax rates considered here could still provide enough disincentives to traders not to engage *excessively* in noise trading.

As mentioned above, the spreads are higher in less liquid retail foreign exchange markets, where transactions are much less cost-elastic. From this point of view, retail markets can in principle absorb a higher tax rate in transaction costs. However, the tax imposed on wholesale trading is more likely to be passed to less competitive retail transactions in the form of higher spreads, especially given the cost-inelastic demand. Since a single retail transaction typically gives rise to a chain of subsequent interbank transactions until a dealer closes his or her ensuing open position, an effective tax rate resulting from the 0.01 to 0.02 per cent tax imposed on wholesale transactions could be translated into additional spreads of 0.04–0.1 per cent or more in retail market segments. This suggests that there may be a heavier tax burden on international trade transactions than hitherto acknowledged and tax incidence of CTT may go far beyond financial institutions, contrary to the claim made otherwise.[37] For this reason, the scale of the rise in the spreads as result of the CTT at 1 or 2 basis points proposed here would, in my view, approach the maximum level that could be introduced to retail segments. This transfer of burden across segments eliminates, at least partially, the need to levy differentiated tax rates to wholesale and retail segments, as suggested by Kenen (1996).

Hence, in my calculation of potential revenue from CTTs, two estimates are produced: (i) one estimate is based on the assumption that the tax rate to wholesale transactions is one-half of that applied to retail transactions; and the other estimate (ii) on the assumption that a unified tax rate is applied across the two segments of foreign exchange markets. It is further assumed that a tax applied to all derivative

---

[34] Felix and Sau (1996: 230) suggest that as 'the increments to the Tobin tax rates are phased in, the reduced annual global foreign exchange will become more stable, at least regarding further changes in transaction costs'.

[35] Spahn (2002) suggests that given that spreads in interbank transactions were in the range of 0.04–0.05 in 1995 when the traded volume was roughly similar to that observed in 2001, the 0.02% tax would not damage market liquidity too much.   [36] See footnote 12.

[37] Considering this possibility, Davidson (1997: 679) suggests that 'a Tobin transaction tax might throw larger grains of sand into the wheels of international real commerce than it does into speculative hot money flows'.

transactions will be one-half of the rate applied to spot transactions, as derivative deal-ings are high-frequency trading by their nature and function. The taxbase is assumed to be virtually global in my estimate.

In my calculation I have also made the assumption that both retail and wholesale transactions are taxed at the dealing site on a market basis, as suggested by Kenen (1996). This assumption was adopted simply because the turnover at the settlement site is not made available in the BIS survey. Hence, I assume that the major trading cites listed in Table 4.5 would agree to participate in CTT. I also conjecture, for the purpose of simplifying revenue estimates, that the very low tax rate used in my estimate will produce a light tax burden on all transaction parties and considerably reduce the incentive for tax avoidance through migration and asset substitution. The latter possibility is minimized particularly if CTT is adopted universally, as assumed in the estimates produced here.

My estimates presented below are based on the assumption that alternative tax rates of 1 or 2 basis points are applied to the global taxbase as described earlier. It is also assumed that the share of official transactions carried out by monetary authorities in global turnover is about 8 per cent.[38] Hence, this amount and other possible leakages, amounting to 10 per cent of total turnover, are deducted from the taxbase as non-taxed instruments. At these moderate tax rates, retail transaction volume is assumed to be virtually unaffected, while *excessive* noise trading in wholesale segments would respond to an introduction of CTT at these rates.

In this respect, my approach differs from the assessment by Felix and Sau, who regard tax rates of less than 5 basis points as tax rates with no 'sand in the gears'. Instead, I reckon that tax rates of 1 or 2 basis points would still act as 'sand in the wheels' in the environment with equally low transaction costs and profit margins as observed in interbank markets today. Naturally, a reduction in volume would be much less at these low rates than the 33 per cent obtained with the elasticity about 0.32 used by Felix and Sau (1996) and Frankel (1996). In my estimates, it is assumed that a 0.02 per cent tax and 0.01 per cent tax would reduce the volume of wholesale transactions (i.e. excluding transactions with non-financial customers) by 15 and 5 per cent, respectively. These are somewhat arbitrary numbers as was the case in other estimates, since no estimate on the cost-elasticity of foreign exchange trading volume is known a priori. I have also proceeded with the calculations on the basis of additional information available in the BIS survey on the share of transactions with non-financial customers in outright forwards transactions (29 per cent) and foreign exchange swaps (9 per cent).

My estimates of the CTT revenue potential under alternative tax rates applied to different modes of transactions are shown in Table 4.7. My estimates show that CTT

---

[38] This figure is derived from the information in Table 4.4, where the share of the pair transactions between US dollar and others is reported as 17% in 2001. It is assumed that about one-half of this was carried out by monetary authorities of emerging markets and transitional economies who typically exhibit 'fear of floating' (Calvo and Reinhart 2002), whereas interventions by monetary authorities in transactions between vehicle currencies were less in relative terms. With a view that a half leg of the US dollar/other currencies would constitute 4% of global transactions, it is assumed that the share of official transactions globally is about 8%.

at 2 basis points applied to wholesale transactions would generate a annual revenue of about US$30–35 billion, while CTT at 1 basis point would produce US$17–19 billion. My revenue estimates are much lower than the US$53 billion suggested by Clunies-Ross (2003). My lower estimate of US$35 billion at 2 basis points under the scenario of no volume reduction is accounted for by the half rate applied to derivatives transactions. I have taken a view that CTT should not discriminate against high-frequency transactions conducted for risk-hedging purposes, unless it could greatly reduce exchange rate volatilities. In general, I applied an estimation procedure, so that the estimate could provide us with a clue of the revenue size that the global community could expect from CTT at the prevailing level of foreign exchange trading activities.

These revenues would be collected on a market basis by monetary or tax authorities of the countries where these markets are located (see Table 4.5 for geographical location of major market sites).[39] Clunies-Ross (2003) regards CTT as ideal for global use, since the burden would be borne more or less proportionately to a country's income, adjusted by the degree of openness. He continues to suggest that 'whereas those that would be collecting it would be rich countries, and even among those countries themselves, the revenue collected would bear little or no relationship to the burden borne' (2003: 7). Hence, he concludes that revenue retention by the tax collecting governments would be highly objectionable in a moral/political sense.

While CTTs should be carefully evaluated according to economic criteria set out by Atkinson (Chapter 2, in this volume), CTTs present the potential of generating approximately US$15–28 billion for global public use, if the national retention rate from CTT revenues is agreed at 20 and 70 per cent for developed and developing countries, respectively (Patomäki and Denys 2002) (though many argue that the retention rate for developing countries could be 100 per cent).

4.5. CONCLUDING REMARKS

In this chapter, I have argued that the currency transaction taxes should be implemented in an extremely cautious manner, starting with a very low tax rate. This is deemed necessary in light of the recent structural changes in foreign exchange markets as well as considerations of market efficiency, liquidity, and technical and political feasibility. According to my preliminary estimates and assessments based on these considerations, the contribution that CTT could make towards generating innovative sources for global finance may be much smaller than those derived from earlier studies. If CTT is collected and enforced on the netting settlement sites with the use of new technology such as the CLS Bank's operations, revenue from CTT may even be smaller than those presented here. In my view, therefore, the very high expectations raised with respect to CTT's revenue-generating capacity on its own are not as yet warranted, in light of the prevailing economic and political reality today.

[39] Since banks and exchange transactions are under the supervision and regulation of the monetary authorities, CTTs could be administered by monetary authorities rather than by tax authorities. Alternatively, tax authorities could administer and collect CTT in cooperation with monetary authorities and with access to information generated by CLS Bank as suggested by Patomäki and Denys (2002).

Table 4.7. *CTT revenue estimate applied to 2001 foreign exchange trade volumes*

	Daily average transactions[a]	Adjusted by trade volume reduction at:		0.02% Tax applied to wholesale transactions					0.01% Tax applied to wholesale transactions				
	Daily turnover	0.02%	0.01%	Revenue with no volume reduction[b]	Tax rate A	Tax rate B	Revenue with volume reduction[b] A	Revenue with volume reduction[b] B	Revenue with no volume reduction[b]	Tax rate A	Tax rate B	Revenue with volume reduction[b] A	Revenue with volume reduction[b] B
Total turnover	1,200												
BIS adjusted turnover	1,173												
less non-taxed instruments	−117												
Taxable base	1,056												
of which:													
1) Spot transactions	348	304	333	69.6	—	0.02	50.4	60.8	34.8	—	0.01	—	33.3
wholesale	296	252	281	—	0.02	—	—	—	—	0.01	—	28.1	—
retail	52	52	52	—	0.04	—	20.8	—	—	0.02	—	10.4	—
2) Outright forward	118	105	114	11.8	—	0.01	—	10.5	5.9	—	0.005	—	5.7
wholesale	85	72	81	—	0.01	—	7.2	—	—	0.005	—	4.1	—
retail	33	33	33	—	0.02	—	6.6	—	—	0.01	—	3.3	—
3) Foreign exchange swaps	590	510	563	59	—	0.01	45.6	51.0	29.5	—	0.005	—	28.2
wholesale	536	456	509	—	0.01	—	—	—	—	0.005	—	25.5	—
retail	54	54	54	—	0.02	—	10.8	—	—	0.01	—	5.4	—
Daily revenue				**140.4**	—	—	**141.4**	**122.3**	**70.2**	—	—	**76.8**	**67.2**
Annual CTT revenue[a]				**35.1**	—	—	**35.4**	**30.6**	**17.5**	—	—	**19.2**	**16.8**

Notes:

[a] Billions of US dollars.

[b] Millions of US dollars.

Case A refers to the estimates made on the assumption that the tax rate to wholesale transactions is one-half of that applied to retail transactions.

Case B refers to the estimates made on the assumption that a unified tax rate is applied across two segments of currency markets.

Source: Author's calculations based on BIS data.

Nor does CTT by itself, implemented at low rates, have sizeable effects on restoring macroeconomic policy autonomy. However, if CTT is successfully administered in the two-tier structure as stipulated by Spahn or in conjunction with other measures such as capital controls or security transaction tax (STT) in a coordinated fashion, potential benefits in double dividends from these measures would render support to the debate over its implementation. The revenue generated by CTT and STT combined could indeed far surpass the currently stagnating flows of official aid from OECD countries to developing and transitional economies, which in recent years has been running at the level of US$50 billions (see Atkinson, Chapter 2, this volume).[40] At the same time, these measures combined may create a new condition, in which many emerging economies would no longer be forced into a *two-corner solution* of either 'fearful floating' with high, variable interest rates or 'hard pegs' such as full dollarization or monetary unions at the cost of involuntarily losing an independent monetary policy.[41]

Indeed, the two-tier CTT structure proposed by Spahn or other dual taxation schemes could have the potential of achieving what the unified single transaction tax at a low tax rate alone would fail to deliver—the restoration of credibility to intermediate exchange rate regimes and some autonomy of macroeconomic policy. That is, the 'impossible trinity' could be mitigated with the application of this system, as three objectives—financial openness, exchange rate stability and monetary independence—become more compatible in the *triad*.

Furthermore, the coordinated approach considered here would curtail the potential for leakages from these policies, such as might result from asset substitution, market migration, or tax evasion. Indeed, there are substantial economies of scale to be gained from the combined application of CTTs and STTs with the use of centralized settlement mechanisms, as discussed above. The coordinated approach also increases the political feasibility of these measures by substantially lowering further the tax rate necessary on any single tax measure. Finally, the cross-border harmonization of these tax measures would reduce the potential for leakages.

The official development aid available today is vastly inadequate for the needs of developing countries.[42] The currency transaction taxes considered in this chapter could serve as one critical innovative financial source for development finance. In this context, possible merits of taxing capital transactions should be evaluated against the historical background of the progressively reduced tax burden on capital income, relative to labour income, in the current era of financial globalization.

The CTT may be regarded more as a new additional source for development finance, rather than as a possible substitute for (or alternative to) official development assistance

---

[40] UNCTAD (United Nations Conference on Trade and Development) estimates that in 2000 the total value of world stocks, bonds, securities amounted to US$50 trillion, while total global equity market capitalization is estimated at US$37 trillion.

[41] See Frankel (1999) and Nissanke and Stein (2003) for a critical literature review on the exchange rate policy regime choice faced by emerging market economies.

[42] In particular, an allocation of bilateral aid tends to be at least partially used by donor countries as a foreign policy tool or for their economic gains (Maizels and Nissanke 1984).

(ODA). Naturally, this may not be the case if the availability of vast revenues from CTT would make ODA less generously available.

The technical feasibility of implementation and enforcement can be substantially enhanced, and the cost of tax administration of CTT can also be reduced correspondingly, with the introduction of automated clearing and settlement mechanisms adopted globally, such as the CLS Bank settlement scheme discussed here. However, the cost of reaching a political consensus and commitment towards the universal adoption of CTT remains high. In light of this high political (and administration) cost, many regard CTT as a 'leaky bucket', to use Atkinson's terminology. Dodd (2003) argues, for example, that the Tobin tax cannot be achieved politically, and hence the pursuit wastes much effort and resources.

Furthermore, an introduction of CTT will trigger a further change in foreign exchange market structures as well as in the structure of the financial industry. With their small profit margins, smaller traders and dealers may be hurt more, leading to a further consolidation of the industry.

Whether or not a *flexible geometry*—considered the practical way forward with a subset of countries (Chapter 2, this volume)—can be successfully applied to this politically contentious tax instrument has been debated, and several schemes in this regard have been proposed, though yet to be carefully evaluated. The fiscal architecture emerging from such an analysis would certainly involve not only tight coordination of the taxbase, but also close cooperation in the implementation and administration of CTT under an international agreement, such as envisaged in the treaty proposal by Patomäki and his associates.[43]

Naturally, CTT implemented partially on the basis of regional tax coordination alone is a *second-best* solution compared to global implementation, and would produce a negative effect akin to 'trade diversion effect' found in literature on custom unions. Indeed, Fuest *et al.* (2003) find that there are welfare gains from regional tax coordination, but that these gains are lower than those from worldwide coordination. Further, the application of CTT, for example, for the euro-zone only would certainly induce changes in the relative position of the euro versus the US dollar, as the vehicle currency used in international trade and financial transactions as well as in official reserve holdings. However, the direction of these changes may not necessarily be uni-directional as often predicted by the financial community. The euro may—as result of CTT and despite the penalty of transaction tax—become the more stable (and hence preferred) currency for holding in agents' portfolio. If the tax rate is kept small as considered here, the positive effect of CTT on the euro may, indeed, outweigh the negative effect vis-à-vis the dollar or yen. While the fears expressed by the financial community would justify the lower end of the tax rate, the euro may emerge stronger rather than weaker after an introduction of CTT.

It should also be noted that the tax incidence of CTT could be much deeper and wider than hitherto suggested. An impact of CTT on real economic activities, as

---

[43] See Boadway (Chapter 11, this volume) on the economics of global taxation and Sandmo (Chapter 3, this volume) for similar issues facing environmental taxation.

opposed to purely speculative financial activities, could be greater than what has been acknowledged so far in literature. Hence, this is an additional factor for considering a very low tax rate. CTT could become indeed a leaky bucket in this aspect, if it discourages people from participating in international trade and investment. However, these possible negative effects of CTT on the cross-border trade of goods and services and direct investment should be assessed and balanced carefully in light of the sizeable negative effects that excessively volatile exchange rates can have on international trade and investment flows. The welfare loss from a currency or financial crisis that is endured by the affected emerging economies and the global community at large is immeasurably large. Hence, in assessing CTT as a tax instrument for global finance, it is important to keep in mind that its benefits for achieving a global double dividend for the world economy may not be negligible, particularly if CTT is successfully implemented in conjunction with other measures of capital controls or in a multi-tier system.

REFERENCES

Baker, D. (2001). 'Why do we Avoid Financial-transaction Taxes?'. *Challenge*, 44(3): 90–6.

Bank for International Settlement (BIS) (2002). *Triennial Central Bank Survey: Foreign Exchange and Derivatives Market Activity in 2001*, March 2002.

Bartolini, L. and A. Prati (1997). 'Soft versus Hard Targets for Exchange Rate Intervention'. *Economic Policy*, 24(April): 15–52.

—— —— (1998). 'Soft Exchange Rate Bands and Speculative Attacks: Theory and Evidence from the ERM since August 1993'. *IMF Working Paper* 98/156. Washington, DC: IMF.

Calvo, G. and C. Reinhart (2002). 'Fear of Floating'. *Quarterly Journal of Economics*, CXVII (May): 379–408.

Cecil, R. (2001). 'Sovereignty, Automaticity and International Trust Funds: A Proposal for Implementation of Tobin-Style Taxes'. Arcata, CA: The Center for Environmental Economic Development (CEED), September.

Clunies-Ross, A. (2003). 'Resources for Social Development'. Paper for the World Commission on the Social Dimensions of Globalization. ILO, Geneva.

Davidson, P. (1997). 'Are Grains of Sand in the Wheels of International Finance Sufficient to do the Job When Boulders are Often Required?'. *The Economic Journal*, 107(442): 671–86.

De Long, J. B., A. Sheleifer, L. H. Summers, and R. J. Waldmann (1990a). 'Positive Feedback Investment Strategies and Destabilizing Rational Speculation'. *The Journal of Finance*, 45(2): 379–95.

—— —— —— —— (1990b). 'Noise Trader Risk in Financial Markets'. *Journal of Political Economy*, 98: 703–38.

Dodd, R. (2003). 'Lessons for Tobin Tax Advocates: The Politics of Policy and the Economics of Market Micro-Structure'. Paper presented at Financial Policy Forum, 6 January, Washington, DC.

Dooley, M. P. (1996). 'The Tobin Tax: Good Theory, Weak Evidence, Questionable Policy', in M. ul Haq, I. Kaul, and I. Grunberg (eds), *The Tobin Tax*. Oxford: Oxford University Press.

Dornbusch, R. (1976). 'Expectations and Exchange Rate Dynamics'. *Journal of Political Economy*, 84: 1161–76.

Eichengreen, B. (1996). 'The Tobin Tax: What Have We Learned?', in M. ul Haq, I. Kaul, and I. Grunberg (eds), *The Tobin Tax*. Oxford: Oxford University Press.

Eichengreen, B. and C. Wyplosz (1996). 'Taxing International Financial Transactions to Enhance the Operation of the International Monetary System', in M. ul Haq, I. Kaul and I. Grunberg (eds), *The Tobin Tax*. Oxford: Oxford University Press.

Felix, D. and R. Sau (1996). 'On the Revenue Potential and Phasing in of the Tobin Tax', in M. ul Haq, I. Kaul, and I. Grunberg (eds), *The Tobin Tax*. Oxford: Oxford University Press.

Friedman, M. (1953). 'The Case for Flexible Exchange Rates', *Essays in Positive Economics*. Chicago: University Chicago Press.

Frankel, J. (1996). 'How Well Do Markets Work: Might a Tobin Tax Help?', in M. ul Haq, I. Kaul, and I. Grunberg (eds), *The Tobin Tax*. Oxford: Oxford University Press.

Frankel, J. A. (1999). 'No Single Currency Regime is Right for All Countries or At All Times'. *NBER Working Paper* 7338. Cambridge, MA: National Bureau of Economic Research.

Fuest, C., B. Huber, and J. Mintz (2003). 'Capital Mobility and Tax Competition: A Survey'. *CESifo Working Paper* No. 956. München: Center for Economic Studies (at the University of Munich) and the Ifo Institute for Economic Research.

Garber, P. (1996). 'Enforcement and Evasion in a Tax on Foreign Exchange Transactions', in M. ul Haq, I. Kaul, and I. Grunberg (eds), *The Tobin Tax*. Oxford: Oxford University Press.

—— and L. E. O. Svensson (1995). 'The Operation and Collapse of Fixed Exchange Rate Regimes', in G. Grossman and K. Rogoff (eds), *Handbook of International Economics*, Vol. 3. Amsterdam: North-Holland, 1865–911.

—— and M. P. Taylor (1995). 'Sand in the Wheels of Foreign Exchange Markets: A Sceptical Note'. *The Economic Journal*, 105(428): 173–80.

Grabel, I. (2003). 'Averting Crisis: Assessing Measures to Manage Financial Integration in Emerging Economies'. *Cambridge Journal of Economics*, 27(3): 317–36.

Habermeier, K. and A. A. Kirilenko (2003). 'Securities Transaction Taxes and Financial Markets'. *IMF Staff Papers*, 50: Special Issues. Washington, DC: IMF.

Jeanne, O. and A. Rose (1999). 'Noise Trading and Exchange Rate Regimes'. *NBER Working Paper* W7104. Cambridge, MA: National Bureau of Economic Research.

Kaul, I. and J. Langmore (1996). 'Potential Uses of the Revenue from a Tobin Tax', in M. ul Haq, I. Kaul, and I. Grunberg (eds), *The Tobin Tax*. Oxford: Oxford University Press.

Kenen, P. B. (1996). 'The Feasibility of Taxing Foreign Exchange Transactions', in M. ul Haq, I. Kaul, and I. Grunberg (eds), *The Tobin Tax*. Oxford: Oxford University Press.

Keynes, J. M. (1936). *The General Theory of Employment, Interest and Money*. New York: Harcourt, Brace and Co.

Korkut, E. (2002). 'Why the Tobin Tax Can Be Stabilizing'. *Working Paper* No. 366. New York: The Levy Economics Institute.

Krugman, P. (1979). 'A Model of Balance-of-Payments Crises'. *Journal of Money, Credit and Banking*, 11: 311–25.

—— (1991). 'Target Zones and Exchange Rate Dynamics'. *Quarterly Journal of Economics*, 106: 669–82.

Maizels, A. and M. Nissanke (1984). 'Motivations for Aid to Developing Countries'. *World Development*, 12(9): 879–900.

Mendez, R. P. (1995). 'Paying for Peace and Development'. *Foreign Policy*, 100: 19–31.

—— (2001). 'The Case for Global Taxes: An Overview'. Paper presented to the United Nations ad hoc Expert Group Meeting on Innovations in Mobilising Global Resources for Development', 25–26 June, United Nations, New York.

Nissanke, M. and H. Stein (2003). 'Financial Globalisation and Economic Development: Towards an Institutional Foundation'. *Eastern Economic Journal*, 29(2): 289–311.

Obstfeld, M. (1996). 'Models of Currency Crises with Self-Fulfilling Features'. *European Economic Review*, 40: 1037–47.

——(1998). 'The Global Capital Market: Benefactor or Menace?'. *Journal of Economic Perspectives*, 12: 9–30.

Patomäki, H. and K. Sehm-Patomäki (1999). 'The Tobin Tax: How to Make it Real'. Helsinki: The Network Institute for Global Democratisation.

Patomäki, H. and L. A Denys (2002). 'Draft Treaty on Global Currency Transaction Tax'. *NIGD Discussion Paper*. Helsinki: The Network Institute for Global Democratisation.

Rodrik, D. (1997). *Has Globalization Gone Too Far?*. Washington, DC: Institute for International Economics.

Rose, A. (1996). 'Exploring Exchange Rate Volatility: An Empirical Analysis of "The Holy Trinity" of Monetary Independence, Fixed Exchange Rates, and Capital Mobility'. *Journal of International Money and Finance*, 15(6): 925–45.

Sarno, L. and M. P. Taylor (2003). 'Currency Unions, Pegged Exchange Rates and Target Zone Models', *The Economics of Exchange Rates*. Cambridge: Cambridge University Press, Chapter 6.

Schmidt, R. (1999). 'A Feasible Foreign Exchange Transaction Tax'. Ottawa: North–South Institute.

Spahn, P. B. (1996). 'The Tobin Tax and Exchange Rate Stability'. *Finance and Development*, June: 24–7.

—— (2002). 'On the Feasibility of a Tax on Foreign Exchange Transactions'. Report commissioned by the city. Bonn: Federal Ministry for Economic Cooperation and Development, February.

Svensson, L. E. O. (1992). 'An Interpretation of Recent Research on Exchange Target Zones'. *Journal of Economic Perspectives*, 6(4): 119–44.

Tobin, J. (1974). *The New Economics One Decade Older*. The Eliot Janeway Lectures on Historical Economics in Honour of Joseph Schumpeter. Princeton, NJ: Princeton University Press.

——(1978). 'A Proposal for International Monetary Reform', *Eastern Economic Journal*, 4 (July–October): 153–9.

——(1996). 'Prologue', in M. ul Haq, I. Kaul, and I. Grunberg (eds), *The Tobin Tax*. Oxford: Oxford University Press.

Umlauf, S. R. (1993). 'Transaction Taxes and the Behaviour of the Swedish Stock Market'. *Journal of Financial Economics*, 33: 227–40.

Williamson, J. (1997). 'Public Policy Towards International Capital Flows', in I. P. Szekely and R. Sabot (eds), *Development Strategy and Management of the Market Economy*. New York: Oxford University Press, 325–47.

——(2000). 'Exchange Rate Regimes for Emerging Markets: Reviving the Intermediate Option'. Washington, DC: Institute for International Economics.

5

A Development-Focused Allocation of the Special Drawing Rights

ERNEST ARYEETEY

5.1. INTRODUCTION

The campaign for the issue of development-focused Special Drawing Rights (SDRs) by the International Monetary Fund (IMF) has been on the development agenda for many years. This was certainly reflected by the Brandt Commission's report (1970). In more recent times the campaign has been propelled, first, by the Asian financial crises as the liquidity problems of developing nations took a new dimension with the collapse of private capital markets, and then second, with the search for financing options towards the achievement of the Millennium Development Goals (MDGs). Since the Asian crises broke, there has been a shrinking of capital flows to small nations, making it more difficult for them to hold adequate reserves, even if they chose to borrow for that. It is reckoned that when borrowing for reserves becomes difficult and a need is felt to increase reserves, as after the Asian crisis, many poor nations are obliged to make consumption and investment decisions that harm future growth and development. This is one of the reasons for the growing calls for multilateral finance institutions to be innovative in increasing the financing options available to these countries, including an expanded and enhanced role for SDRs.

The SDRs are international finance instruments created for the purpose of providing an increase in the world stock of monetary reserves from time to time without making countries run surpluses or deficits. Indeed, the idea behind the SDRs is that large imbalances force countries to incur costs in earning or borrowing reserves, and this should be contained with the IMF allocation of SDRs. It was born out of what has been referred to as Triffin's dilemma (Triffin 1960): 'whereby additions to official dollar holdings were seen as undermining the stability of the system, given the tendency on the part of some central banks to convert their dollar reserves into gold, thereby drawing down the limited US gold stock' (Clark and Polak 2002: 3).

Extending the uses to which SDRs can be put results from the growing demands on the international financial system to respond to the development finance needs of poor nations. Apart from the need to provide emergency funds in times of crises and the whole area of crisis prevention, increasingly the facilitation of development in poor countries and assistance for making the best policy decisions are considered crucial. It is the growing complexity of the requirements of the international financial system that leads to the frequent suggestion that the IMF should increasingly play the role of a lender of last resort, including the issuing of SDRs from time to time. Some of the strongest advocates for this idea have been associated with the Fund. Shortly before retirement as IMF managing director, Michel Camdessus proposed that in times of a systemic credit crunch, 'the IMF be authorized to inject additional liquidity—and to withdraw it when the need has passed—in a manner analogous to that of a national central bank, through the creation and selective allocation of SDRs' (Camdessus 2000: 3).

But this chapter on SDRs separates, despite the obvious links, the issues of international liquidity reform and development finance. The focus here is on development finance. The recent calls to redistribute SDRs for development purposes were given a boost by the Zedillo Report (UN 2001) and by the appeal from George Soros (2002), and the contributions from Stiglitz (2003). Proponents for the creation of development SDRs argue that such additional funds for development can assist in meeting the MDGs. Such SDR creation would be the means for reducing the costs to developing countries of the increased holding of reserves, which has become quite common after the 1997–8 East Asian crises. In the report of the Zedillo Panel, it is argued that a resumption of the issue of SDRs would reduce the demand for US-dollar holdings, a development that might discourage the indefinite increase of US short-term debt. Soros (2002) suggests that there should be a resumption of SDRs, by which developed countries would re-allocate their share first to the provision of global public goods, and secondly to supplement aid flows to individual countries. If the approved allocation of 1997 were made active and the re-allocation took place, he expects that US$18 billion could be made available for global public goods or additional aid.

It is important that the arguments for the creation of SDRs for development are explored in some detail, particularly from a developing-country perspective. While showing the likely benefits of such SDRs on the development process in poor economies, the arguments that are often raised against such an endeavour must be explored, both with regard to the global economy and to the poor nations. The entire exploration should investigate the feasibility (both technical and political) of the undertaking, and the likely consequences on the overall flow of resources for development.

This chapter discusses in Section 5.2 the historical development of SDRs, including their purpose and how they are created. This is basically about regular SDRs and the problems associated with their creation and allocation. Section 5.3 introduces the recent proposals for development-oriented SDRs, and Section 5.4 analyses these proposals with a focus on the arguments for and against them. In Section 5.5, the chapter discusses the mechanisms proposed for the creation of development SDRs, including the institutional and structural changes in international finance that may support their creation. Section 5.6 concludes with an assessment of the effects of development SDRs on the resource situation in poor countries and how they will be perceived.

5.2. THE DEVELOPMENT OF SDRs

The SDRs are a special reserve asset allocated to IMF member countries participating in the SDR department proportionate to their IMF quotas. SDRs are not a claim on the IMF but are potentially a claim on the freely usable currencies of IMF members, in that holders of SDRs can exchange their SDRs for these currencies (IMF 2002*a*). Its value as a reserve asset comes from the commitments of members to hold and accept it. The IMF members have, indeed, undertaken to honour all obligations related to the SDR system. The Fund ensures that the SDRs' claim on freely usable currencies is honoured by first 'designating IMF members with a strong external position to purchase SDRs from members with weak external positions, and through the arrangement of voluntary exchanges between participating members in a managed market' (IMF 2002*a*). The least developed countries (LDCs) may use the SDRs (i) to repay the IMF; (ii) to repay Paris Club debt; (iii) to help countries in foreign exchange crisis get hard currency from IMF by exchanging at the Fund their SDRs for US dollars with the IMF matching them up with a source of dollars, and (iv) to release hard currency reserves for use in such transactions.

Indeed, in the basic form, SDRs are promissory notes issued by the IMF to member states on the basis of a quota that is related to their relative strength in the world economy. Members that receive these notes may either hold them or exchange a part of them over time for hard currency, through the Fund itself and through central banks. In a regular sense, SDRs may be perceived as liquid assets that are created by the IMF in the same manner that national monetary authorities issue their currencies as liabilities against themselves and can affect the supply of money. In this limited context, the Fund may behave like a central bank so long as it commands sufficient credibility. On the other hand, however, because of the peculiar treatment that SDRs are given, such as the fact that they are allocated by quotas and only central banks can hold them. No other asset has to be exchanged for them, and they cannot be treated as money. If countries received their allocations of SDRs and held them, there is no interest cost to them.[1] Countries actually receive interest income from the Fund for their SDR holdings, but they only pay interest at the same rate on their total cumulative allocations. When countries seek to exchange SDRs for hard currencies, the new holders then earn the accompanying interest from the Fund (Fig. 5.1). In effect, it is only when a country's holdings of SDRs are less than its cumulative allocation that it becomes a net payer of interest. So, obviously when poor countries exchange SDRs for hard currency, they have to pay the interest on these.

[1] The SDR interest rate provides the basis for calculating the interest charges on regular (i.e. to say, non-concessional) IMF financing and the interest paid to members who are creditors to the IMF. The SDR interest rate is determined weekly and is based on a weighted average of representative interest rates on short-term debt in the money markets of the SDR basket countries. The yields on three-month treasury bills serve as the representative interest rates for the United States and the United Kingdom. In keeping with the changes introduced to the SDR basket on 1 January 2001, the three-month Euribor (Euro Interbank Offered Rate) became the representative rate for the euro area, replacing the national financial instruments of France and Germany. The representative interest rate for the Japanese yen was changed from the three-month rate on certificates of deposit to the yield on Japanese government thirteen-week financing bills.

Figure 5.1. *SDR flows*

In addition to the general allocations of SDRs for the purpose of supplementing existing official reserve assets of member countries, there is currently a proposal to create a special one-time allocation of SDRs that would enable all IMF members to receive such SDRs on an equitable basis, making amends for the fact that a fifth of the membership have never received an SDR allocation. The proposal followed the fourth amendment of the Articles of Agreement by the IMF board of governors in 1997, and will be effective only when the United States gives its backing to what 73.34 per cent of the total voting power already supports.

Even though the original intention behind the creation of SDRs was to increase what was thought of as a total international liquidity, Clark and Polak (2002) argue that that rationale is no longer relevant. They maintain that if international liquidity were simply an aggregation of the foreign currency and gold holdings of all the economies of the world, then there was adequate liquidity and this had been growing as fast as the world's economies, if not faster. Hence, the concept of aggregate international liquidity was no longer relevant for creating SDRs. They also point out that the conditions in the global economy that necessitated the creation of SDRs changed shortly after these reserves were created. This included the adoption of flexible exchange rate regimes, which may have reduced the size of the reserves needed, compared to what was required to maintain a fixed exchange rate regime. But they argue that this situation notwithstanding, there were still good enough reasons to create SDRs in view of efficiency gains resulting from the low-cost access to reserves and the reduction in systemic risk. Developing countries, which would otherwise incur costs in adding to their international reserves, would thereby be enabled to do so costlessly. Their subsequent increased readiness to hold reserves would reduce the risk of financial crisis to them—and to the international system.

5.2.1. *Trends in SDR Allocation and the Global Reserve System*

There have so far been only two rounds of creation of SDRs, each spread over three years. The first allocation was in 1970, for a total amount of SDR9.3 billion. The most recent allocation, made on 1 January 1981, brought the cumulative total of SDR allocations to SDR21.4 billion. The IMF executive board discussed the possibility of an SDR allocation during the fourth, fifth, sixth, and seventh basic periods, that is up to 31 December 2001, but there has not been enough support for an allocation.

A major reason for no SDRs being allocated since 1981 is that industrial countries no longer see clear benefits from receiving such allocations, particularly in the presence of thriving capital markets with full capital mobility. Low-income developing countries, with generally far less stable international earnings, could make very good use of SDRs, but their small quotas mean that they get very small shares of any allocation in relation to those of the big industrial countries that do not want or need them. But any allocation that is not in accordance with IMF quotas would require amendment of the Articles of Agreement. Thus, because of the need to amend the Articles, the 1997 agreement on a special one-time allocation of SDRs, which would equalize the ratio of cumulative allocations to current quotas for all member countries, is unratified six years later.

The situation has extensively reduced the role of SDRs as a reserve asset. By April 2002, SDRs accounted for less than 1.25 per cent of IMF members' non-gold reserves, even though the holding of reserves was growing worldwide (see Table 5.1). Indeed, the developing countries added little to reserves between 1980 and 1995, but then

Table 5.1. *Worldwide non-gold reserves, 1970–2000*[a] *(in billions of SDRs)*

	1970	1975	1980	1985	1990	1995	2000
Advanced economies, of which:[b]	41.9	89.1	196.4	247.6	466.7	599.3	860.4
Canada	3.9	3.8	2.4	2.3	12.5	10.1	24.5
Hong Kong SAR	—	—	—	—	17.3	37.3	82.5
Japan	4.3	10.2	19.3	24.3	55.2	123.3	272.4
Korea	0.6	0.7	2.3	2.6	10.4	22.0	73.8
Emerging markets, of which:[b]	8.8	42.3	70.9	93.8	100.3	278.2	470.0
China	—	—	2.0	11.6	20.8	50.7	129.2
India	0.8	0.9	5.4	5.8	1.1	12.1	29.1
Mexico	0.6	1.2	2.3	4.5	6.9	11.3	27.3
Poland	—	—	0.1	0.8	3.2	9.9	20.4
Developing countries[c] of which:[b]	3.7	9.4	25.5	25.5	19.2	31.1	65.8
Algeria	0.1	1.0	3.0	2.6	0.5	1.3	9.2
Kuwait	0.1	1.3	3.1	5.0	1.4	2.4	5.4
Libya	1.5	1.8	10.3	5.4	4.1	4.1	9.6
United Arab Emirates	—	0.8	1.6	2.9	3.2	5.0	10.4
Total	54.3	140.8	292.8	366.9	586.1	908.7	1 398.9

[a] The increase in worldwide reserves between 1970 and 1995 is slightly overestimated because data for a few economies become available only in the latter part of the period.

[b] Economies with the largest increase in reserves (in billions of SDRs) between 1995 and 2000.

[c] Excluding economies that are included as emerging markets.

Source: Clark and Polak (2002).

added SDR 37 billion in the following five years.[2] When the Zedillo Panel called for the resumption of the issue of SDRs, the panel members argued that, 'the cessation of allocations has severely prejudiced the interests of developing countries' (UN 2001). They suggested that developing countries were not in a position to borrow additional reserves in the market on terms similar to SDRs. But many developing countries were trying to build up their reserves in order to reduce their vulnerability to crises. With the emerging markets included, they were estimated to hold reserves of over US$850 billion, which was almost US$300 billion more than before the Asian crisis. These additional reserves had been borrowed largely on terms clearly more difficult than the SDR issues. At the time, emerging markets paid an average premium of about 8 per cent more than the US Treasury bond rates. The panel noted that, 'the result is a large flow of what is sometimes called 'reverse aid', which in the aggregate is not far short of the flow of conventional aid from the DAC countries' (UN 2001).

Stiglitz estimates that there are currently US$2.4 trillion held in reserves around the world, held in a variety of forms including US Treasury Bills for most developing countries:

While the United States may benefit from the resulting increased demand for US Treasury Bills, the cost to the developing countries is high. Today they receive a return of 1.25 per cent—a negative real return rate—even though investments yield high returns in their own countries. This is the price developing states have to pay to insure against unpredictable market events. (Stiglitz 2003: 56)

There are a limited number of private financial instruments that are denominated in SDRs. Because of their limited use, the main function of the SDRs' is to serve as the unit of account of the IMF and some other international organizations (IMF 2002a). It is thus used almost exclusively in transactions between the IMF and its members.

5.2.2. *The IMF, Developing Countries, and SDR Creation*

The creation of SDRs has always been seen in developing countries as an inadequate but necessary tool for countering the usual problem of low reserves. It has been perceived as inadequate in relation to the financing needs arising from increasing volatility in exchange rate instability and foreign exchange earnings. While inadequate, its creation has sometimes been seen as an attempt by developed or industrial economies to cover their reluctance to deal with the real financing issues confronting developing countries through IMF that has for long been seen as a rich men's club. Aboyade (1983) notes strongly that,

The Fund has always related its (foreign) currency sales and stand-by facilities for member countries to their respective quotas. This means the richer countries, which have (and have always had) the highest quotas, can also borrow the most ... It is generally unsympathetic to exchange rate policies, which offer any strong prospect of affecting the existing pattern and structure of international economic power, with the excuse that they may hurt international

---

[2] This does not include the emerging markets.

trade. Most of its innovations over the last decade (for example, the creation of SDRs and the establishment of a Substitution Account) are more to help the currencies of the rich nations and preserve international stability, than as direct answers to the clamour of the poor countries. (Aboyade 1983: 30)

Wade (2002) comments on similar sentiments expressed by Triffin (1968) who had suggested that since the allocation went strictly in proportion to the countries' quotas, it was 'as indefensible economically as it (was) morally'. At the time, the two biggest economies received one-third of the total. In Triffin's (1968) view, 'the SDR designers had created an asset that made the rich even better off'.

The role that the Fund's board plays is crucial in understanding some of the sentiments often expressed about the issue of SDRs. The board of governors of the IMF (in which all member governments are represented) has to approve each issue of SDRs by an 85 per cent majority.[3] The voting system is weighted so that a small number of industrial countries can veto any new creation. This allows the United States alone to do the same. It is the lack of interest of the industrial economies, for reasons already provided, that has ensured that there was no new approval between 1978 and 1997. Opposition from Germany, Japan, the United Kingdom, and the United States effectively made new allocations impossible in the period. The *status quo* is that any changes in the quota arrangements would require an amendment to the IMF's Articles of Agreement.

It is interesting that in 1997 when an attempt was made to issue new allocations in order to make the cumulative proportions of SDRs received up to that time equal to the various member-countries' current quotas, this received a negative response only outside of the Fund itself. Indeed, the necessary changes to bring about the Fourth Amendment to the Articles of Agreement, which would allow an allocation other than in proportion to current quotas, had been made, but the amendment failed year after year to reach the required level of ratification by the 110 members who constitute 85 per cent of the voting power. By the end of April 2001, only 107 members had ratified it. The main obstacle has been that the US Congress remained opposed to it, despite the support of the Clinton administration.

The US Congress and other industrial country governments believe that there are a number of good reasons why they should worry about changes in the power structure that pertains at the IMF, particularly if that change means an increasing use of SDRs for reserve holdings in many countries. Increasing the stock of SDRs would mean a likely reduction in the holding for reserves of US bonds, 'Certainly expansion of the SDR stock touches America closely because of the prominence of US dollar holdings among existing reserves. Cutting the world's dependence on dollar reserves would reduce Americans' access to a deepening well of cheap credit' (Clunies-Ross 2002: 30).

But economists at the Fund have made some of the strongest arguments for the resumption of regular SDRs. Clark and Polak (2002) provide an interesting argument

[3] The decision to make a general allocation has to be based on the finding that there is a long-term global need to supplement existing reserve assets. The decision of the board of governors is on the basis of a proposal by the managing director with the concurrence of the executive board, with an 85% majority of the total voting power. Decisions on general allocations are made in the context of five-year basic periods.

for allocating new SDRs. After indicating that the original justifications for creating SDRs were no longer relevant as the concept of aggregate international liquidity lost its meaning in the post-Bretton Woods era, they argue strongly that the individual developing countries' need for reserves was still significant, and this was important for improving the operation of the international monetary system. Considering that most countries still needed to increase their reserve holdings in view of expanding current and capital account fluctuations, if countries were to attempt doing this by generating a balance-of-payments surplus this would be costly in terms of foregone consumption and investment. On the other hand, attempting to borrow such reserves on the international capital markets is very costly for poor countries, while some countries have no access to such markets. They also indicate that while borrowed reserves may substitute, to some extent, for owned reserves, 'volatile capital flows demonstrate that undue reliance on international capital markets for (the) purpose (of holding reserves) can be risky' (Clark and Polak 2002: 11). Their main argument (following an earlier point of Mussa 1996) is that SDRs offer a costless reserve asset which, if properly managed as required by the Articles of Agreement, leads to enormous efficiency gains for the world economy compared to the cost of foregoing consumption and investment, and the cost of borrowing from the capital markets. The risk involved in increasing SDR allocations to developing countries can also be shown to not worsen. They observe that:

a number of considerations suggest that the provision of reserves in the form of SDRs would in fact reduce credit risk. Allocations of SDRs make more external resources available to a country, enabling it to weather potential balance-of-payments crises without undue reliance on import compression or the imposition of trade and other restrictions. (Clark and Polak 2002: 19)

Clark and Polak (2002) additionally argue that SDR allocations would contribute to reducing systemic risk. This is because they are a permanent addition to the world's stock of reserves since the Fund is unlikely to cancel any stock of SDR holdings. They contrast this with reserves acquired from borrowing on the capital market, which may be 'withdrawn under inauspicious circumstances'. The example from the crises of the 1990s that made it difficult for countries to refinance their debt is given to support this point.

In the Zedillo Report, the panel members argue that now will be a good time for resuming allocations, 'in that the original concern was not just with the cost to a typical country of having to earn or borrow a secular increase in its reserve holding, but also with the impact on the financial fragility of the country issuing reserves' (UN 2001).

They argue that the financial fragility of the countries that issued the reserves was not much of a concern before, but it is now. This they attribute to the unprecedented size of the US current account deficit. This is partly a consequence of the desire all over to build up dollar reserves. These have become too large for comfort and a source of discomfort in the financial markets. 'Substantial SDR allocations might help to shrink the US deficit while allowing other countries to continue to build up the reserves they feel they need to guard against financial crises' (UN 2001).

5.3. PROPOSALS FOR A DEVELOPMENT-ORIENTED SDR

As already mentioned, there is a long history of proposals to resume allocations of SDRs for specific purposes, often development, or to redistribute holdings of SDRs. Indeed, it would appear that the campaign for SDRs to support development is being pushed along two complementary lines. The first is for the resumption of the regular SDRs to deal with what has become the frequent shortage of liquidity in developing countries (Stiglitz 2003), while the second looks at the occasional injection that mainly targets the developing countries (Soros 2002). The second is intended to be an allocation beyond the scope of the regular SDR. It might have elements of regular SDRs (allocation by quota) with a modification coming by way of donations to other users. Further extensions of this might take the form of alterations to the agreed quota as was, indeed, negotiated in 1997. It might, therefore, favour some countries and institutions, namely those that may be assessed to be in need of development assistance well beyond what traditional assistance packages may afford.

The IMF, as an institution, however, has tended over the years to view proposals to finance specific development initiatives with SDRs more cautiously, suggesting that the use of SDRs for such purposes would generally require a change in the Articles of Agreement, except if industrialized countries voluntarily transferred their SDRs to other countries. The Fund has always observed that there was nothing preventing countries from engaging in such voluntary transfers. On the proposals to supplement fund resources, the Fund has responded that:

> To the extent that these proposals involve balance-of-payments financing with conditionality they can be viewed as essentially substituting for an increase in IMF quotas or IMF borrowing. The key difference among them is the degree of IMF involvement in intermediating redistributed SDRs, and the implications of this for conditionality and the assumption of credit risk. (IMF 2002*b*)

The IMF places SDR proposals into two broad categories as follows:

- Proposals to supplement Fund resources. These proposals seek to direct SDRs allocated to industrial countries to countries with more severe international liquidity needs.

- Proposals to finance development. These are generally of two types, those that may involve voluntary donations to a prescribed holder or to another country and not requiring a change in the Articles of Agreement; and those that call for a redistribution of quotas.

These proposals may be classified further as those requiring mild reforms in the international financial system or no change to the *status quo*, and those requiring more radical or substantial reforms that would imply changes to the governance arrangements of the IMF. While the proposals from the Zedillo Panel seem to call for both broad categories of change in the way SDRs were allocated, it may be noted that most of the calls over the years have been related to the first category of change. A slight departure from the category of mild reforms is the Soros proposal, the best-known scheme. A central part of the proposal from his book *George Soros on Globalization* (2002), is that there should be periodic creations of SDRs and that the rich countries should agree to make their allocations available for global public goods and for aid to development in individual countries. He would like to see the process started with the activation of the proposed allocation of 1997. The Soros proposal was intended to achieve additional aid resources in a manner that was more or less automatic. The pooling of funds was also expected to engender proper coordination. In this proposal, SDR donations from the industrial economies would first be paid into an escrow account, and there would be no recorded budgetary cost to them until the SDRs were withdrawn from the account in order to pay for the approved development projects.

Stiglitz (2003) has suggested clearly there is a need for more than just a one-time issuance of SDRs. He calls for a complete overhaul of the global reserve system, which he blames for being at the centre of the failures of the global financial system. His argument is also based on the fact that developing countries' reserves are growing much faster than they can afford to, as they set aside huge reserves against a variety of contingencies, including decreases in foreign investor confidence and declines in export demand. With imports growing at 10 per cent per annum, about US$160 billion has to be set aside each year for reserves, and a part of this could easily be made available for health and education. In advocating more frequent issues of SDRs to finance development, Stiglitz writes that:

Keynes, during the founding of the IMF, envisaged the issuance of 'global greenbacks', more familiarly known as Special Drawing Rights (SDR)... Global greenbacks could be used to finance global public goods, such as improving the environment, preventing the spread of diseases like AIDS, increasing literacy in the developing world, and providing humanitarian and broader development assistance. (Stiglitz 2003: 57)

Some countries may receive more than they put into reserves, which they can exchange for conventional currencies, while countries receiving less than they put into reserves may supplement these reserves, freeing up money that would otherwise have been set aside.

Richard Cooper (2002) has proposed an amendment of the Articles of Agreement to allow the IMF to create SDRs on a large enough and temporary basis to counter financial crises and to forestall creditor panic (Fig. 5.2). Interestingly, while the Monterrey Conference on Financing Development discussed the various proposals for using SDRs among other schemes, it did not provide support for any particular scheme.

5.4. ANALYSIS OF PROPOSALS FOR DEVELOPMENT SDR

The discussion here focuses on the perceived role of SDRs within the context of the debate for and against the issuance of such development focused SDRs. Noting the general concern about the effect of development SDRs on international stabilization, Clunies-Ross (2002) poses the question of whether the use of specific-purpose SDRs for allocating resources to global public goods is consistent with their use for stabilization purposes as originally intended, and if so what should be the nature of the institutional

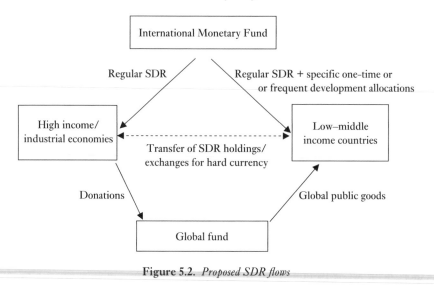

Figure 5.2. *Proposed SDR flows*

changes required to bring that about. His response to these questions is that, with minor modifications, it is possible to issue development SDRs for supplementing aid and providing global public goods in a manner that does not compromise international stabilization.

The idea that development SDRs will not harm global stabilization is even more strongly put across by both Clark and Polak (2002) and also by Stiglitz (2003). The latter has written that: 'this scheme would not be inflationary: rather it would offset the inherent downward bias of the current regime. Relative to global income—some US$40 trillion—the magnitudes of monetary emissions would be minuscule' (Stiglitz 2003: 5).

There appear to be quite strong arguments for the issuance of SDRs, both the regular and the specific. But the arguments against cannot be dismissed.

5.4.1. *The Argument for a Development SDR*

Stiglitz sums up his discussion of the need for development SDRs as follows: 'In effect, these reserves are a commitment of the world to help each other in times of difficulty . . . This policy would end the logic of instability that is built into the current system, for it would allow some deficits without inevitable crisis' (2003: 5).

As noted earlier, the idea behind the calls for these new issues of SDRs is basically to provide developing countries an opportunity to devote resources that would otherwise have been devoted to enlarging reserves to providing services that facilitate development.

But the calls for development SDRs go beyond the need for less expensive reserves, as we saw with Stiglitz (2003). The growing calls for the creation of development

SDRs are also closely associated with the need for a faster development of global public goods *a la* Soros (2002) and Stiglitz (2003). The argument is that effective delivery of global public goods enhances the achievement of the development goals of poor nations. Some of the more comprehensive argumentation for the creation of development SDRs has been put together by Clunies-Ross (2002). In his preamble to the arguments for considering various ways for mobilizing resources for social and economic development, including development SDRs, he indicates that the methods and resources must be (i) technically and administratively accessible; (ii) unlikely to impose any unduly high excess burden of costs through misallocation; (iii) equitably distributed; (iv) not politically out of the question for ever, and (v) so far not fully exploited. Clunies-Ross (2002) sees the attraction of SDRs as a source of globally available funds, first, in the fact that it is created by an international institution, hence belonging to the world as a whole, and making it useful for the maintenance of the global public goods for global stability and full employment of resources. Second, he anticipates that in certain circumstances the rise in the resulting world income and output may either equal or exceed the value of the funds assigned for the purpose. Third, since SDRs come to national monetary authorities without payment, and their uses are somewhat restricted, those countries with more than adequate reserves could give them up for global causes while incurring minimal overt sacrifices (Clunies-Ross 2002: 26).

Wade (2002) has had an interesting look at the Soros proposal for new SDRs, and notes that, the 'proposal focuses public attention on apparently arcane monetary issues, which have a huge impact on the performance of the world economy yet receive rather little public attention'. He suggests that the injection of a modest amount of US$27 billion of SDR equivalent under the proposal for the first issue makes it doable, and this could produce better performance from the world economy as a whole. Wade (2002) sees the link made by Soros between monetary/payment issues and the supply of global public goods as credible 'and the mechanism of choosing which goods will be supplied, by whom, and financed by whom, is an interesting one when put alongside the present arrangements'. In Soros' proposal there is a group of eminent persons or an independent jury, working with a trust fund, and chosen for the purpose of deciding which global public goods may be funded. This is not left for the World Bank, currently the most significant supplier of global public goods, to determine.

Wade (2002) notes that even though the proposal is quite modest in scale, it could easily be enlarged to make it a significant contributor 'to solving the chronic tendency in the world economy at large towards excess capacity reflecting insufficient demand'. If the possible uses of SDRs were broadened, Wade expects the allocations of these development SDRs, which favour poor nations, to raise their consumption significantly. He expects such a growing consumption to lead largely to an increasing demand for goods from industrial economies. In effect, industrial economies do not necessarily lose by consenting to the creation of the development SDRs.

Having observed that international agreement on assistance to poor nations often takes too long to achieve, Clunies-Ross (2002) notes that the Soros proposal for regular SDRs to be issued to member countries, with the richer ones among them donating theirs to aid and global public goods, has the advantage of ensuring that allocations to such aid and global public goods do not have to wait for universal agreement.

5.4.2. *The Argument 'Against' Development SDRs*

The arguments against the issuance of development SDRs are basically an extension of the arguments made against regular SDRs. These have been summarized by Lissaker's in the Pocantico Report (2003) as (i) legal, referring to the requirement that there must be long-term global need to supplement international liquidity; (ii) moral, in that non-conditional financing encourages bad policies; (iii) efficiency, implying that the SDRs are unlikely to go to the developing countries; and (iv) historical, suggesting that the environment of floating exchange rate regimes and the existence of multiple media for reserve holdings made SDRs unnecessary. But these are the points that Clark and Polak (2002) strongly argue against. In effect, the main arguments against the issue of development SDRs on account of international stabilization derive from the anxiety that not enough measures are being put in place to restrain the IMF from 'flooding' the financial markets with excess new liquidity and cash-strapped poor nations will go on a spending spree.

In addition to the above arguments, most of the points of concern that have often been raised about the use of SDRs for development are centred on a couple of issues. First, it is not obvious what advantages the use of SDRs brings to poor developing nations that are not derived from traditional aid packages. And second, the impact on the stability of the world economy is not clear, and finally, the institutional adjustments that are required for creating the special SDRs that affect country quotas are probably not politically appealing to industrial economies and hence not likely to happen.

Wade (2002) points out the fact that Soros is not clear on what the poorer countries would do with their SDR allocations. He notes that beyond the effect to be generated by the global public goods, it is not obvious what direct benefits countries would receive. 'Presumably, the direct benefits are those they could have had all along from conventional SDRs, and the Soros proposal does not contain anything new in this respect.'

But Clunies-Ross discusses even more extensively the difficulty in identifying the potential benefits from development SDRs. He sees a possible problem with generating enough desire on the part of potential SDR holders to want them, particularly when the recipient of the SDRs is not a central bank but a trust set up to administer global public goods after these allocations have been transferred to the trust by a recipient central bank. The problem arises from the obligation of interest payments on total cumulative allocation. The interest would, in that case, have to be transferred to whoever held the donated SDRs or spent their proceeds. Thus, the 'development SDRs' would come to the governments or other agents representing their beneficiaries not in the form of grants, but rather in the form of low-interest term loans. He explores a number of possible uses of the development SDRs as follows:

If the global fund were to provide guarantees, for example, of markets for new drugs or vaccines, these assets could be held costlessly against the call to make good the guarantees without having in that contingency to raise large amounts in the financial markets. Or, if one of the functions of the fund were to reduce the debt burden of highly indebted poor countries, buying out their debt by exchanging it for the proceeds (and the obligations) of SDRs could be valuable to these debtor countries even though it left them with interest obligations at international short-term rates. The servicing obligations would be much more favourable than those attached to many of the loans that might be available to developing and transitional economies (though less so than those on IDA loans). (Clunies-Ross 2002: 29)

He admits, however, that this 'quirk of SDR arrangements does take some of the attractiveness from the Soros and similar schemes' (Clunies-Ross 2002: 28).

It has been suggested that new proposals for the creation of development SDRs ignore the question of how to entice the US government into accepting the proposals (Wade 2002). In view of this, it is obvious that if the new SDRs are seen as additional grants to developing nations the US government will not be enthused about it. Aside from its reluctance to see a reduction in the demand for dollar reserves, the US government is also not very interested in seeing the IMF become a central bank to the world.

Indeed, Wade (2002) also suggests that the Soros proposal does not say enough on the governance issues related to the creation of SDRs. The lack of clarity leaves the question of how the global public goods would be prioritized unresolved. In the Soros proposal, infectious diseases, judicial reform, education, and bridging the digital divide are prioritized for attention. But this is observed to be different from the priority list of the G7 countries. For the World Bank, infectious diseases, environmental improvement, trade promotion, and greater financial stability should be at the top of the list for global public goods. Under the New Partnership for African Development (NEPAD), the priority areas are given as (i) peace, security, and governance; (ii) investing in Africa's people; (iii) diversification of Africa's production and exports; (iv) investing in ICT (information and communication technology) and other basic infrastructure, and (v) developing financing mechanisms. It is obvious that several different lists are possible and accommodating all of them may lead to a longer list that may not easily lend itself to feasible agreed actions. This point is buttressed by the fact that the Stiglitz list is only a subset of all of these.

5.5. PROPOSED MECHANISMS FOR CREATING DEVELOPMENT SDRs

A number of the proposals for the issue of development SDRs do not provide details of how this can be done. A good example of this is the Stiglitz (2003) paper. Details of what mechanisms may be applied in creating new SDRs for development can at best be pieced together from several sources, and this is done in this section.

5.5.1. *The IMF Articles of Agreement and the Creation of a Development SDR*

A complication would arise in the creation of development SDRs if the proposed scheme were to make an allocation in other than exact proportion to IMF quotas. This would require an amendment of the IMF Articles of Agreement, and the difficulty of meeting this requirement would, therefore, impede the use of SDRs in ad hoc schemes intended to benefit particular groups of countries. If there were no changes in the allocation quotas, in order for high-income recipients of SDRs to give them up simply as grants to others would require no alteration to the Articles. It has been pointed out by Boughton (2001) that the Fund's executive board has already altered the working practice to allow recipients of SDRs to use them as grants. The Fund is, indeed, in a position to name a global fund that receives the grants from SDR recipients as a 'prescribed holder', as has been done for some international institutions. This will allow the global fund to hold SDRs and also to trade them with central banks.

As indicated earlier, however, someone must bear the net interest cost of the SDRs once they have been spent on global public goods or spent by recipient developing countries. If it is not to be the donor countries themselves, then it must presumably be the bodies (recipient governments or other agencies) that do the spending. From their point of view, spending of the proceeds would in that case be like spending financed by a low-interest loan. On the other hand if the donors were to bear the full interest burden, the transfers of SDRs would entail the same costs to the donors themselves as equal amounts of official development assistance (ODA) given in the form of grants, and there would be no advantage in undertaking the process through SDRs.

Clunies-Ross (2002) discusses at length various scenarios for dealing with the interest payment issue, if industrial countries were to decide to follow the Soros proposal for donating any new issues of SDRs immediately to a global fund. The likely outcome would be that the wealthier nations would essentially be providing only a termless loan at a standard short-term interest rate to the global fund or poorer recipient countries, and this may be utilized in any of the manners discussed earlier. It is, indeed, the lack of clarity of whether or not donor countries should continue with the interest payment that is the main issue. Making donor countries pay the interest effectively turns the SDRs into additional financial assistance to the recipient.

5.5.2. *Conditions for Creating Development SDRs and Links to Debt Relief*

It is important to point out that the Soros proposal for donations was intended to overcome the difficulty that an alteration to the SDRs allocation by quotas was considered unlikely to happen soon. While the quotas remained, voluntary donations were thus a way of ensuring less antagonism from some industrial economies. Clunies-Ross (2002) suggests, however, that eventually there might be possibilities for other allocations, as was indeed the case with the (unratified) 1997 Fourth Amendment of the Articles of Agreement, and that considerable discretion might be given (under guidelines) to the management of the Fund.

If there is to be a special allocation outside the quotas, who should be eligible for it? In the Soros proposal, the SDRs going to the global fund are all from donations, so there is not a major problem. But it should be possible to link the gains from the new development SDRs to current initiatives on debt relief and the attainment of the MDGs. If the concern with the new SDRs is the likely effect of rapid expansion in international liquidity, one could limit the consideration for special allocation to the heavily indebted poor country (HIPCs) only, instead of the low–income and middle-income countries, as proposed by Clunies-Ross. It is observed from the enhanced HIPC Initiative that countries will continue to borrow even as they receive relief in order to settle other obligations in the pursuit of poverty reduction goals. It is import-ant that payments on these do not slow down growth. It is obvious that debt relief must be recognized by creditor countries as additional to new and increased ODA with a focus on enhancing and sustaining both growth and poverty reduction expli-citly. New SDRs that provide HIPC countries with an opportunity to engage in further debt exchanges certainly enhance the benefits of their involvement in the HIPC Initiative.

There is tension between quick debt relief and comprehensive country-owned poverty reduction strategies. The solution to this problem is to make countries focus on their medium- and long-term development frameworks, showing the anticipated growth paths and how these promote poverty reduction. In this situation, new SDRs that create new comfort levels in reserve holdings allow countries to pursue develop-ment programmes of a longer orientation than the shorter-term programmes of the last two decades under the direction of the Bretton Woods institutions. Essentially, the development SDRs will provide them with termless credit facilities that have some-what reduced short-term interest rates. In effect, specific or development SDRs may be essential so long as there are HIPC countries that need greater liquidity than their trade volumes would permit and want greater flexibility in the international financial markets.

Linked to the conditions for creating development SDRs is the issue of their timing. The report of the Zedillo Panel (UN 2001) indicates that there should be an immediate resumption of the issue of regular SDRs. Throughout that report, there is emphasis on the need to augment financial support to developing countries in a manner that deals with their cyclical problems related to the nature of their engagement with world trade. When compounded with the cyclical nature of international capital flows, especially private, the need to develop mechanisms that are counter-cyclical cannot be overemphasized.

5.5.3. *Proposed Institutional Re-organization for Creating a Development SDR*

The forms that development SDRs may take are often linked to the question of whether the IMF should behave increasingly like a central bank. Mohammed has noted that: 'developing countries would continue to press for an exploration of the merits of establishing an effective international lender of last resort, that is, one able to create international liquidity freely and to deploy it rapidly to deal with widespread financial crises' (2000: 201).

If SDRs are to be used actively to provide global public goods or aid to developing countries, it is argued that the IMF needs to have the authority and structure to take decisions and act upon them (though probably under imposed guidelines) as independent central banks do. While the Soros proposal deals with the problems of providing support for development largely through informal agreements to transfer reserves from one party to another, there appears to be a major demand from developing countries for the formalization of such arrangements (Wade 2002). Clunies-Ross (2002) suggests that it might be possible to begin with the informal approach to providing additional support for development with SDRs, but eventually to move to a more formalized way of using SDR allocations so as to bring about both more targeted development finance and counter-cyclical activity for international stabilization. This would be effected by giving greater discretionary authority to the Fund's structures, working through the managing director's recommendations, in concert with the executive board, to the board of governors. The managing director might, for example, be empowered to seek authorization for allocation in a particular year to be made to a certain group of countries only.

As the process of selective allocations of SDRs is formalized, it is inevitable that the IMF would have to act a little more like a central bank—and that requires an amendment of the Articles of Agreement: 'to provide more powers to its existing governing institutions, and possibly also delegation by them, or further amendment, to give more actual decision-making power to say a technical committee [operating of course under guidelines that the governing institutions had laid down]' (Clunies-Ross 2002).

Putting together ideas from Soros' proposal and sentiments from the Zedillo Panel, Clunies-Ross (2002) outlines five stages that could be followed in promoting the use of SDRs for stabilization and for the provision of global public goods. At the first stage, the Fourth Amendment to the Articles of Agreement is to be ratified by the US Congress in order to allow the 1997 allocation to proceed. This is followed at the second stage by the high-income or industrial economies agreeing to donate their new holdings to an appropriately constituted international body for the delivery of global public goods. That body is to be accepted by all and made a prescribed holder by the IMF. At the third stage, the IMF board of governors agree informally over a period to accept recommendations from the managing director and the executive board to issue and cancel SDRs according to an agreed formula that reflects a relationship between the growth rate of total international reserves and the trend rate of growth of real international transactions. At the fourth stage, the Articles of Agreement are altered to allow the distribution to be done possibly according to criteria other than the prescribed quota, while such alterations are approved each time by the board of governors, following proposals from the managing director and the executive board. Finally, the Articles of Agreement could be further altered to create a technical body, which will work on the appropriate quantities of SDRs to be allocated and how these can be timed. It is this body, guided by the executive board and the managing director, which will generate the information necessary for decisionmaking by the board of governors.

5.6. AN ASSESSMENT OF THE PROPOSALS FOR DEVELOPMENT SDRs

There are two issues that we address in this concluding assessment, namely whether development SDRs are likely to bring significant additional benefit to developing countries, and the manner in which new SDR issues can be managed.

5.6.1. *Development SDRs versus Other Forms of Assistance*

In the work by Clark and Polak (2002) on regular SDRs, they draw attention to what they refer to as 'the allocation of SDRs versus the provision of conditional Fund credit'. The question suggests that the perceived direct benefits of an expanded SDR allocation to developing countries, even if it is not directed at development, need to be more clearly identified. They are obviously concerned about the question of whether regular conditional credit from the Fund does not deal with the problems that new and regular SDRs are supposed to tackle, namely creating the means for increasing reserve holdings. Clark and Polak (2002) cite the IMF's 1965 annual report, which observed that, 'ideally countries' need for additional liquidity could be met by adequate increases in conditional liquidity. In practice, however, countries do not appear to treat conditional and unconditional liquidity as interchangeable'. Clark and Polak (2002) fear that inducing countries to meet their liquidity constraints with increased conditional lending from the Fund would force them to adopt balance of payments programmes that may have largely negative consequences for growth and development. But this does not deal with the substitution of conditional credit by new grants. Ultimately, should new grants not be preferred to new SDRs? Maybe that is what is intended by proposing the new development SDRs.[4]

As indicated earlier, Wade (2002) questions in his critique of the Soros proposal how developing countries would gain directly from a large increase in SDRs. He then proposes his own list of what could be done with SDRs, but these are a basic extension of what countries would generally do with owned reserves as opposed to borrowed reserves.

Indeed, there are a number of people who have suggested that if the idea behind the campaign for new development SDRs is simply a matter of getting more development assistance for developing countries, then one should tackle the issue directly. In response, it should be pointed out that it is more difficult to argue for increased ODA which involves a significant direct cost to one party, namely the development assistance donor, than for the SDRs, which involve no direct cost to those developed countries.

In our view, given the existence of traditional ODA, the question of whether or not new SDRs should be created should ultimately be tied to the issue of whether such SDRs are a substitute for ODA or complement it. The difference between SDRs and other flows to developing countries lies in the fact that the use of SDRs is determined

---

[4] Wade (2002) suggests that, 'it is basically a way to arrange for the rich countries to cough up more grants to poor countries. All the fancy talk is really just an elaboration of this very familiar idea'.

largely by the recipient, and not by the donor. Recipient countries, therefore, are free to use these essentially termless facilities over a period, despite the possible low short-term interest costs if the recipients have to transact business with the development SDR provider. A developing country that receives an SDR allocation targeted at such countries basically has the option of using the opportunities created by the facility to increase spending on items not typically funded by donor ODA. This includes the massively expanded support to the private sector. This characteristic ensures that additional SDRs without a decline in ODA will give developing countries greater flexibility in managing their economies than they possibly will have with ODA only. Using the development SDRs in a complementary manner is what may be useful.

If donor countries accept to continue paying the interest discussed earlier, this, in effect, would be the main form of support for development that they are providing under this arrangement. But such interest payment cannot be expected to continue indefinitely. The time limits will be determined largely by the usual requirements for assisting developing countries to overcome structural deficiencies.

5.6.2. *Structuring the Issuance and Management of New SDR*

There is the obvious question of how much development SDRs can be issued at a time. Wade's estimate of an equivalent of US$27 billion of SDR as the amount required to satisfy the needs of the Soros' proposal is comparable to the Clark and Polak (2002) suggestion. They propose an annual issue of regular SDRs with an upper limit of 10 per cent of combined quotas, which would yield about SDR20 billion. Assuming that the annual issues suggested by Clark and Polak were utilized mainly for development finance, with industrial economies donating their quota share for the purpose, an amount of US$25–30 billion would be available as an additional resource for development finance. And this is about one-half of the initial additional resources needed for the achievement of the MDGs.

One area in which the creation of SDRs for global public goods is seen to be likely to generate good outcomes for developing countries is governance. Wade (2002) thinks that Soros' ideas of establishing a trust fund with an independent jury, the shopping for recipient programmes, and the addition of SDRs to the reserves of the poorer member countries are important and should be treated seriously. The element of having an independent third party organize the distribution of global public goods reduces the influence of the World Bank in this area and supposedly brings greater transparency and accountability into what poor nations may or may not have. Shopping for recipient programmes ensures that developing countries are not saddled with what some international technocrat believes is good for them.

But even more important is the question of which of the three possibilities should be adopted in resuming SDR issues: (i) should the IMF allocate the SDRs differentially? (ii) should the IMF allocation follow quotas, and should there be an international agreement of donors to transfer according to some formula? and (iii) should the IMF allocation follow quotas and individual members decide how to transfer their allocation? This takes us back to the issue of whether or not the transfer arrangements should be more formalized. There seems to be the growing consensus that the third option is the way to start, with a gradual shift to more structured transfers later. This is generally seen by the supporters of the resumption of SDRs as the best chance of gaining wider support.

REFERENCES

Aboyade, O. (1983). *Integrated Economics, A Study of Developing Economies*. London: Addison-Wesley Publishers.

Boughton, J. M. (2001). *Silent Revolution: The International Monetary Fund 1979–1989*. Washington, DC: IMF.

Camdessus, M. (2000). 'An Agenda for the IMF at the Start of the 21st Century'. Remarks at the Council on Foreign Relations, February, New York.

Clark, P. B. and J. J. Polak (2002). 'International Liquidity and the Role of the SDR in the International Monetary System'. *IMF Working Paper* WP/02/217. Washington, DC: IMF.

Clunies-Ross, A. (2002). 'Resources for Social Development'. Paper prepared for the World Commission on the Social Dimensions of Globalization.

Cooper, R. (2002). 'Chapter 11 for Countries?' *Foreign Affairs*, 81(4): 90–103.

International Monetary Fund (IMF) (2002a). 'Special Drawing Rights (SDRs): A Factsheet'. IMF Website. Available at: www.imf.org/external/np/exr/facts/sdr.htm. Accessed 20 August.

—— (2002b). 'Allocations of Special Drawing Rights (SDRs): A Factsheet'. IMF Website. Available at: www.imf.org/external/np/exr/facts/sdrall.htm. Accessed 22 August.

Mohammed, A. A. (2000). 'The Future Role of the IMF: A Developing Country Point of View', in J. J. Tuenissen (ed.), *Reforming the International Financial System*. The Hague: FONDAD.

Mussa, M. (1996). 'Is There a Case for Allocation Under the Present Articles?', in M. Mussa, J. M. Boughton, and P. Isard (eds), *The Future of the SDR in the Light of Changes in the International Financial System*. Washington, DC: IMF.

Pocantico Report (2003). Report of the Conference on Additional Sources of Finance for Development, 29–31 May, Pocantico, Tarrytown, NY. New York: Friedrich Ebert Stiftung.

Soros, G. (2002). *George Soros on Globalization*. Oxford: Public Affairs.

Stiglitz, J. (2003). 'How to Reform the Global Financial System'. *Harvard Relations Council International Review*, 25(1): 54–9.

Triffin, R. (1960). *Gold and the Dollar Crisis*. New Haven: Yale University Press.

—— (1968). *Our International Monetary System: Yesterday, Today, and Tomorrow*. New York: Random House.

United Nations (UN) (2001). 'Technical Report of the High-level Panel on Financing for Development'. Available at: www.tradeobservatory.org/library/uploadedfiles/Technical_Report_of_the_High-Level_Panel_on_Fi.htm. Accessed 20 August.

Wade, R. H. (2002). 'On Soros: Are Special Drawing Rights the Deus ex Machina of the World Economy?'. *Challenge*, September–October. Available at: www.findarticles.com/cf_dls/m1093/5_45/91659838/p1/article.jhtml. Accessed 18 June.

6

The International Finance Facility Proposal

GEORGE MAVROTAS

6.1. INTRODUCTION

Proposals for new institutional arrangements for official development assistance (ODA) that exploit techniques for securitization in the capital market can function as an innovative source for generating funds necessary for the achievement of Millennium Development Goals (MDGs). The present chapter takes the proposal for an International Finance Facility (IFF), published in the United Kingdom in January 2003 jointly by HM Treasury and the UK Department for International Development (DFID) (HM Treasury–DFID 2003a,b) as a concrete illustration of this type of proposals.[1]

The IFF proposal could be viewed as part of the 'Global New Deal: A Modern Marshall Plan for the Developing World', which was put forward by the UK Treasury in 2002 (HM Treasury 2002) to tackle poverty in the developing world.[2]

The generic features of the HM Treasury–DFID proposal on IFF are as follows:

1. A substantial increase in ODA of US$50 billion a year today to US$100 billion per year.
2. Making a pre-commitment, so that the promises can be 'banked'.

The chapter is part of the UNU–WIDER and UN–DESA project on Innovative Sources for Development Finance directed by Tony Atkinson, Nuffield College, University of Oxford. The views expressed in the chapter are those of the author and do not necessarily represent UN–DESA and UNU–WIDER. I am most grateful to Tony Atkinson, Ernest Aryeetey, Nicholas Vaughan, and two anonymous referees for comments and suggestions which substantially improved the Chapter. I am also indebted to Tony Addison, Yilmaz Akyuz, Tony Burdon, Andrew Kenningham, Ian Kinniburgh, Tony Shorrocks, and Rachel Turner for helpful background discussions. I would like also to thank the participants of the project meeting on Innovative Sources for Development Finance (WIDER, Helsinki, May 2003) as well as the participants of the Sharing Global Prosperity WIDER Conference (Helsinki, 6–7 September 2003) for their constructive comments and suggestions. None of the above should, however, be held responsible for the views expressed in the chapter.

[1] The scheme has the full support, at the time of writing, of the United Kingdom and France while other donors are still considering their position (Report of Pocantico Conference, New York, 29–31 May 2003).

[2] See the HM Treasury website: www.hm-treasury.gov.uk/documents/international_issues/global_new_deal.

3. Annual commitments would start from the roughly US$15–16 billion of aggregate Monterrey and post-Monterrey additional sums pledged and would rise by 4 per cent (in real terms) per year.
4. The increase is of limited duration, timed to achieve the internationally agreed MDGs by 2015.

The above generic features of the IFF scheme seem to suggest that the proposal can be analysed *either* as a net addition to existing development aid, *or* as a comparison with 'straight' ODA of the same net present value (NPV), *or* as a comparison with ODA with the same time path.[3] In the first case, we have all the benefits of the increased flows, together with some potential problems related to absorptive-capacity constraints of aid recipients. In the second case, we have the benefit of being able to bring forward disbursements. Finally, in the third case, we have the certainty of the flows with the difference being much smaller.

It is notable that the internationally agreed MDGs in Monterrey pose an important challenge to the international community, namely to increase aid flows substantially to meet the MDGs or to think of alternative ways of development financing.[4] The joint HM Treasury–DFID proposal on IFF focuses exactly on this important issue.[5]

In view of the significance of the above interesting and promising IFF proposal, the present chapter will seek *inter alia* to contribute to the current debate on exploring innovative ways to raise funds to meet the MDGs by:

1. Discussing in detail the IFF proposal, its main technical details and financial structure (Section 6.2).
2. Elaborating administration and implementation issues of crucial importance in the current proposal (Section 6.3).
3. Evaluating the proposal in terms of both its potential advantages (substantial increase in aid flows, predictable and stable nature of flows over the next ten years, tried and tested principle for raising finance in international capital markets, among others) and its shortcomings (heavy reliance on political coordination among donor countries, possible absorptive-capacity constraints in aid-recipient countries related to the substantial increase in aid and continuous commitment on behalf of the donor community towards the implementation of the IFF during the thirty years of its life among others), as well as suggesting ways to strengthen further the proposal (Section 6.4).
4. Summing up the key challenges for IFF (concluding Section 6.5).

---

[3] Note that ODA flows are defined from the perspective of the donor countries.

[4] See Atkinson (2003) for a detailed discussion on this.

[5] It is notable that the IFF is an ongoing and evolving process at the time of writing thus the present study cannot be considered as a final assessment of the proposal since its technical details, implementation procedure, and overall administration structure can change dramatically in the very near future. Indeed, HM Treasury and DFID are currently trying to iron out the technical details of the current proposal in the aftermath of discussions at the G7 Meeting in Paris in February 2003 and the IMF–World Bank Spring Meetings in April 2003.

6.2. KEY FEATURES AND TECHNICAL DETAILS OF THE PROPOSED FACILITY

According to the HM Treasury–DFID proposal on IFF, the Facility is specifically designed to achieve both the additional finance and the value for money necessary to reach the MDGs.[6] The whole idea is based on securitization structures used extensively in the capital markets, that is, leverage in additional finance by borrowing through bonds issued in the international capital markets against long-term commitments for aid by donor countries. Along these lines, the Facility would essentially frontload long-term aid flows so that the MDGs are reached by 2015. The Facility will be structured so that the bonds it issues can achieve the highest possible ratings. This will result in a cost of leverage, which would be comparable to that achieved by existing multilateral organizations.

At the same time, it is argued that the Facility is designed so that aid effectiveness can be improved substantially by focusing aid disbursement on pro-poor priorities of IFF aid-recipient countries and also by improving the predictability and stability of longer-term aid. This, as has been recently argued, would strengthen recipients' efforts to adopt policies that foster sustainable growth, create the right environment for trade and investment, and ensure that the new resources are used efficiently for poverty reduction.[7]

The Facility would involve two main parties, the donor countries and the recipient countries. The donor countries will be the shareholders of the IFF and at the same time party to the IFF's Articles of Association; they will also make commitments to provide annual payments to the Facility. Finally, they need to agree to a set of overarching principles in relation to the effectiveness of their aid management and aid policies. On the other hand, the recipient countries, according to the IFF proposal, will be the world's poorest countries. It is notable that the relevant HM Treasury–DFID documents on IFF are not clear at all at this stage regarding which countries will be in the final list of the world's poorest countries eligible for IFF funding; obviously the final decision/list of countries will be reached by discussion between all countries, both donor and recipient, in future meetings in which the final proposal on IFF will be discussed in detail. On this front, the IFF proposal states that countries which received financing in the last IDA replenishment could be potential IFF–recipient countries (although there is not any clear commitment in the proposal regarding this).[8]

---

[6] The present section (as well as Section 6.3) draws heavily on recent documents published by the HM Treasury and DFID on IFF (see www.hmtreasury.gov.uk/documents/international_issues/ int_gnd_intfinance.cfm) as well a technical note from the HM Treasury–DFID not in the public domain at the time of writing. It is notable that there is no other bibliography on IFF (external to the HM Treasury–DFID) at present apart from the relevant documents published by HM Treasury–DFID as well as press releases following the Chancellor's presentation of the Facility in recent G7 Meetings in Paris (February 2003) and Washington DC (IMF–World Bank Spring Meetings, April 2003).

[7] Speech given by the Chancellor of the Exchequer, Gordon Brown, at the Financing Sustainable Development, Poverty Reduction, and the Private Sector Conference, London, 22 January 2003.

[8] In view of the fact that the IFF is designed to help achieve the MDGs, and since its niche is in grants, this would suggest the poorest countries.

It is notable that the IFF will not disburse funds directly to recipient countries. On the basis of the agreed IFF overarching principles (see relevant discussion below) it will instead provide funds for disbursement by existing bilateral and multilateral aid-delivery channels, which may include the World Bank and the Global Health Fund as well as specific agencies of the governments of donor countries (e.g. DFID in the United Kingdom). These agencies, both bilateral and multilateral, would be acting as agents on behalf of the IFF. They would also manage the disbursements in line with the allocation of funds agreed by the Facility.

The life of the Facility will be rather limited, in the sense that the IFF will terminate upon repayment in full of all bonds issued and other liabilities incurred by the IFF. A rough idea on how the Facility would work can be provided by the flow diagram (Fig. 6.1).

The IFF proposal states that the Facility will be created by an international treaty among participating donor countries (the shareholders of the IFF). Issues related to the principal objectives of the IFF, its constitution and governance structure would not be covered by the Articles of Association, which would be negotiated at an IFF founding conference. The overarching principles (OPs) would also be defined by the Articles of Association. The OPs, to which all donors would sign up, would have to be met for the disbursement of all funds raised through the IFF. The plan is for OPs to be agreed by donor countries at the founding conference and they could include conditions such as that funds raised by the Facility must be disbursed to recipients on the basis of sound aid-effectiveness principles as well as the domestic policy environment and need. Although the proposal does not provide (at least at this stage) further details regarding the precise nature of the OPs, it clearly states that the funds should be (i) used for poverty reduction; (ii) not tied to contracts using specific national suppliers; (iii) provided in multi-year programmes of at least three years' duration; (iv) disbursed

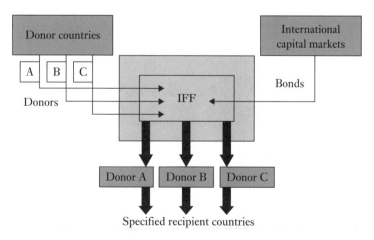

Figure 6.1. *Overview of the IFF*

Source: HM Treasury–DFID (2003*a*).

mainly in grant form, including debt relief, with some highly concessional loans where appropriate; and (v) targeted at low-income countries.

The assets of the Facility will consist primarily of donor commitments to provide streams of annual payments to the IFF. Thus, the Facility will be relying on donor commitments to meet its obligations under the bonds. The proposal also states that the IFF's ability to service the debt under the bonds will not depend on any repayment by the recipient countries of the aid disbursed to them.[9]

Donors will contractually commit to provide streams of payments annually to the Facility. The plan is for each stream to comprise fifteen annual payments (under discussion at the moment). To decide on these commitments, donor countries should meet on a regular basis. One option is for shareholders to participate in pledging rounds on a tri-annual basis. Another option is that donor countries should participate in rolling annual pledging rounds. It is notable that participation in one pledging round would not commit a donor country to participate in following pledging rounds. This is a potential weakness of the proposal in the sense that the continuous commitment of the donor countries to the Facility, absolutely vital for its sustainability and success, is not guaranteed (see Section 6.4 for further discussion).

Furthermore, donors will be contractually bound to make annual payments subject to certain fundamental conditions being met by the recipient countries (called 'high-level financing conditions'; not precisely defined at the moment). These conditions would be few according to the proposal, clearly defined in advance and capable of independent determination; a possible financing condition is that a recipient is not in protracted arrears to the IMF (International Monetary Fund); defined as continuous arrears for more than six months. Note, however, that an IFF donor will not be legally bound to make its annual payments to the Facility in regard to notional amounts for a particular recipient if that recipient fails to meet the high-level financing conditions.

Also, donors would be separately, not jointly, liable for making their payments to the Facility and they would not have any responsibility for making good on payments for which another donor country had defaulted. The IFF, on the other hand, will have the right to suspend disbursements to programmes if any donor countries are in arrears on any payments due to the Facility.

Regarding disbursements by the IFF, these will be linked to a stream of annual payments. In the case where a recipient country programme disburses over five years, it will be financed via payments from five streams. Furthermore, it would be possible for donors to change the length of a specific stream subject to the minimum length necessary to support a bond issuance. Note also that it is not necessary that every payment profile should be considered as attached to a particular stream. The IFF income will be the result of annual payments made each year by donor countries to the Facility of an amount equal to their share of each outstanding committed stream.

---

[9] It is notable that the bonds issued by the IFF will be backed by the aggregate of all donor commitments; this will essentially provide bondholders with a direct claim against the IFF, if it fails to meet its obligations under the bonds.

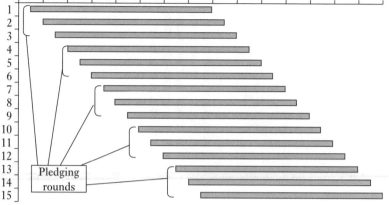

Figure 6.2. *Stylized representation of donor commitments*
Source: HM Treasury–DFID (2003*a*).

Figure 6.2 shows how donor commitments to the Facility can be made through a number of pledging rounds.

The above-stylized representation feeds into a broader illustrative model, which assumes the following parameters:

(i) fifteen funding rounds, one every year;

(ii) a defined life-span of thirty years for the IFF;

(iii) disbursements of funds from the Facility increase from US$10 billion in the first year to US$50 billion in 5 years, to remain constant for five years before declining to zero over the final 5 years;

(iv) the average cost of funds for the IFF is 5 per cent;

(v) no more than 85 per cent of the net present value is raised as debt (the leverage limit; see below).

In line with the above assumptions, Figs 6.3 and 6.4 show the funds which could be raised based on annual donor contributions starting at US$3.65 billion, rising to US$44 billion from 2017 to 2020 and thereafter falling (Fig. 6.3) and the resulting profile of IFF bonds outstanding (Fig. 6.4).

The underlying assumption of the illustrative example of IFF income and disbursement in Fig. 6.3 is that donors will commit themselves to provide constant nominal streams of annual payments to the Facility. However, it may be possible that donor commitments will be phased in a different way. It may be preferable, for instance, for donors to provide a more even spread of aggregate payments across the lifetime of the Facility, rising in line with donor income. This will result in the phased streams illustrated in Fig. 6.5.

It is notable that in line with Fig. 6.5, disbursements as projected fall away sharply after 2015. Most conventional wisdom would suppose, however, that if we were planning a pattern of aid flows, we would not necessarily plan it like this. *Inter alia*, it would

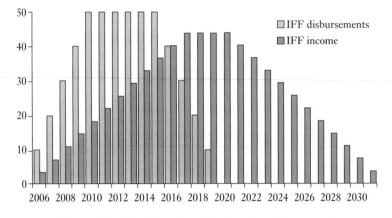

Figure 6.3. *IFF inflows (income) and outflows (disbursements)*
Source: HM Treasury–DFID (2003*a*).

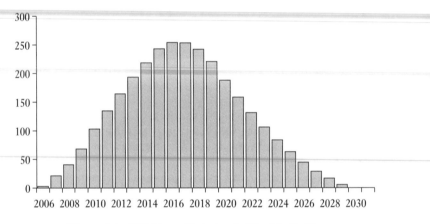

Figure 6.4. *IFF debt profile during the life of the Facility*
Source: HM Treasury–DFID (2003*a*).

rather tend to disrupt economic stability. Added to this is the situation projected in which (according to Fig. 6.5), from 2020 on to 2032, the extra donor contributions (above the 2002 base) gradually rise until they are running at more than US$40 billion a year (in 2002 prices) without a cent of this extra going to the recipient countries; it is all debt-servicing and replenishment of the Facility's reserves.[10]

Turning to leverage issues of crucial importance in the proposed Facility, in order to achieve and preserve the highest possible ratings of all bonds issued by the IFF, the Facility will limit the degree to which the donor commitments may be levered. More

---

[10] We would like to thank an anonymous referee for raising this issue.

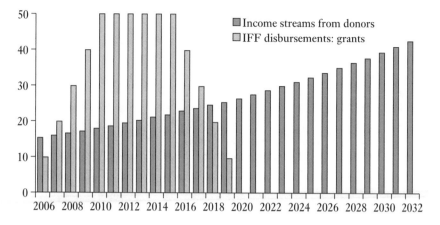

Figure 6.5. *Illustrative example of IFF income and disbursement patterns—phased streams*
Source: HM Treasury–DFID (2003*a*).

precisely, at each disbursement the Facility will allocate a fixed proportion of the donor commitment made by a donor country in the pledging round to that disbursement. This allocation needs to take into account the prevailing cost of long-term debt for the IFF in the donor country's currency and the leverage limit.[11]

Under the assumption that donor commitments are binding and perceived as credible by financial markets, the IFF leverage would depend on a careful assessment of the likelihood that the high-level financing conditions (see above) are met by the recipients to whom finance raised through the Facility is disbursed. In case the high-level financing condition is that recipients are not in protracted arrears to the IMF (see above) then a careful assessment of the historical data, according to internal work by HM Treasury, could provide a sound basis for preliminary work to evaluate the possible leverage limit.

Internal work by HM Treasury includes some examples to illustrate the above. For instance, the historical record of all IDA-eligible countries' experience in going into protracted arrears with the IMF has been considered and has been used as a basis for projections. Under the assumption that commitments by donors are evenly distributed across the 75 countries receiving funds in the IDA-13 replenishment, it was calculated that it is 99 per cent likely that at least 87 per cent of the NPV of donor commitments would actually be paid to the Facility.[12]

Relaxing the unrealistic assumption that donor countries are evenly distributed across the IDA countries and in line with the disbursement profile of IDA-13, the

[11] By the leverage limit it is assumed that only a certain proportion of the donors' commitment would be allocated to loan servicing; the rest would be a reserve kept in the Facility, principally to cover donor default, either under the 'high-level funding condition' or otherwise.

[12] This means that if the IFF were to borrow 87% of the net present value of donor commitments over the next fifteen years, there would only be a 1% chance of the IFF not having sufficient funds to repay its borrowings.

leverage limit would now need to be lower in order to achieve and maintain AAA equivalent ratings. The estimates in this case seem to suggest that it is 99 per cent likely that at least 80 per cent of the net present value of donor commitments would actually be paid to the Facility, compared to 87 per cent in the previous case.[13]

It is also notable that although the leverage applied to donor commitments will be restricted by the leverage limit, the full value of donor commitments will be disbursed over time in the sense that a lower leverage limit would affect the volume of funds that could be disbursed in the early years of the Facility but not the cost of these funds. More precisely, as the Facility receives annual payments from donors, the value of donor commitments will rise relative to the funds disbursed. This will have two possible effects: it will either reduce the level of commitments donors would need to make for new programmes or release additional funds that may be disbursed under existing (or proposed) programmes.

A relevant issue to the above discussion of the leverage limit is the rating of bonds. The working assumption in the IFF proposal is that the Facility will operate under a leverage limit that will enable bonds issued by the Facility to secure AAA/Aaa/AAA ratings by Fitch/IBCA, Moody's, and Standard & Poor's, respectively.

The HM Treasury–DFID argue that under the assumption that the Facility operates under a prudent leverage limit (in the range 80–87 per cent) and with AAA credit ratings, it is expected that the IFF's debt will be perceived by the market as a risk comparable to the existing multilateral debt.

A rather dubious feature of the above interesting proposal and, at the same time, an issue that possibly deserves further discussion is related to the 'high-level financing condition', that is, the licence for a donor to stop servicing portion of the debt for which it is responsible if the relevant recipient has, for example, defaulted on its obligations to the IMF. It might well be argued that the servicing obligations should be treated instead in the normal way (especially since the failings of the recipient country in no way affect the capacity of the donor to service the loan) and since the cessation of servicing by the donor constitutes in itself no punishment or deterrent for the erring recipient. Building on this it might be suggested, for instance, to drop the high-level financing condition and raise the leverage limit since no one would suffer from this or would be subjected to moral hazard as a result.[14]

6.3. ADMINISTRATION AND IMPLEMENTATION ISSUES

The present section briefly discusses a possible governance structure of the IFF by drawing on an illustrative model used in the internal work by the HM Treasury

---

[13] Clearly, the larger the portfolio of commitments and the more even the distribution, then the greater the leverage, all other things being equal. However, it is rather unrealistic to assume that all countries have the same probability of entering protracted arrears with the IMF. Countries receiving a high proportion of funds within the IDA-13 replenishment would tend to have a lower probability of entering protracted arrears with the IMF. Hence, while the more unequal distribution within IDA-13 would tend to lower the leverage, this would be offset, to some extent, by the better creditworthiness of countries receiving an above-average proportion of funds. [14] We thank an anonymous referee for alerting us on this issue.

(work still in progress at the time of writing). Obviously, the final governance structure has to be agreed at the establishment of the IFF at the founding conference. One possible governance structure of the IFF might comprise two main committees:

1. A shareholders' committee comprising all of the shareholders of the IFF, each appointed by a donor country. The committee would be responsible for ensuring that the Facility is managed according to the Articles of Association (see Section 6.2). The committee should meet annually to review the activities of the IFF.
2. A management committee, which would be appointed by the shareholders, comprising the executive directors (each one to be appointed by the shareholders) in the board of executive directors. The board of executive directors would be responsible for overseeing the overall management of the IFF. It would be also responsible for approving programmes to which the Facility can disburse and ensuring a prudent borrowing strategy such that the IFF retains the highest possible credit ratings (e.g., AAA type ratings). The committee would be chaired by a chief executive who could be appointed for a fixed term by the shareholders by means of a transparent and open process (further details on this not available at the time of writing).

A small team of professional staff might also be appointed by the chief executive to carry out the treasury function of the Facility and to oversee the allocation of funds.

Regarding the voting rights of the members of the management committee, it could be suggested that these rights should reflect the level of participation of the shareholders in the IFF. This would be subject to a maximum limit in the sense that no shareholder can hold more than 49 per cent of the voting rights. In relation to the above, it might be prudent for certain matters to be subject to approval by super-majority and/or veto by one or more shareholders (again, discussion on these issues is still ongoing and a final decision will be reached at the founding conference).

The main duties of the management committee would be to maintain the financial integrity of the Facility, which may involve *inter alia*:

(i) deciding on the level of leverage to be achieved by the IFF;
(ii) establishing the bond issuance programme of the IFF;
(iii) deciding how much cash reserve the IFF will hold and how this will be managed;
(iv) deciding the appropriate strategy for the allocation of funds across recipient countries to achieve an acceptable spread of risk;
(v) deciding how much finance will be disbursed each year.

Finally, the location of the main offices of the Facility needs to be decided at the IFF founding conference.

6.4. POTENTIAL ADVANTAGES AND DISADVANTAGES OF THE IFF PROPOSAL

6.4.1. *Potential advantages of the IFF*

Revenue-raising potential and accelerating progress regarding the MDGs
Undoubtedly, a key advantage of the proposed Facility is its revenue-raising potential. Indeed, the revenue-raising potential of the IFF is quite substantial. The Facility could double existing ODA from US$50–100 billion per year during the crucial years of 2010-15, thus allowing the MDGs to be met.[15] This is a great advantage of the proposed Facility combined with the plan to disburse grants rather than loans to the recipient countries participating in the IFF, although some concessional loans will also be disbursed where appropriate.[16] In view of the above, the scheme can deploy a critical mass of aid flows as investment over the next few years (in line with the worked examples of Section 6.2 when it will have the most impact on achieving the MDGs.

Predictable and stable aid
Another major advantage of the proposed Facility is related to the nature of the aid flows, which will be disbursed to the IFF-recipient countries. The proposal clearly states that the aid flows will be predictable and stable, thus minimizing the negative effects associated with unpredictable and volatile aid. Indeed, unpredictable aid imposes a serious constraint in recipient countries with regard to future public expenditure planning and causes problems related to the achievement of sound macroeconomic management.[17]

Distinguishing predictable from unpredictable aid flows is also relevant to the issue of aid heterogeneity, which has been neglected (until very recently) by the vast literature analysing the impact of aid in aid-recipient countries. More precisely, until very recently existing evidence on the macroeconomic impact of aid lacked a systematic treatment of the aid disaggregation issue and of the way different types of aid affect key macroeconomic variables in aid-recipient countries. One of the main features of the vast quantitative literature of the effectiveness of development aid in recipient countries has been the employment of a single figure for aid. However, this is likely to be misleading for reaching conclusions on aid effectiveness, since we can distinguish at least four different categories of aid: project aid with a rather lengthy gestation period, programme aid that disburses rapidly as free foreign exchange, technical assistance, and food aid and other commodity aid which adds directly to consumption (Cassen 1994; Mavrotas 2002*a*, *b*). To the above four types of foreign aid, emergency or relief

[15] This is equivalent to an average aid ratio of 0.47% of GNP, a clear departure from current levels.

[16] This is an important comparative advantage of IFF in accelerating grant finance in view of the need to make substantial progress regarding the MDGs.

[17] Empirical findings of an important early study on the negative effects of unanticipated aid (Levy 1987), clearly indicate different tendencies of anticipated and unanticipated aid in thirty-nine countries over the period 1970-80: unanticipated aid was fully consumed but more than 40% of predictable aid was invested thus contributing significantly to the growth process in recipient countries.

aid could be added as a separate category, given its increasing importance in recent years (Addison 2000).[18]

Recent work in this promising research area seems to suggest that aid disaggregation does matter for our overall understanding of the macroeconomic impact of aid in aid-recipients (Mavrotas 2002*a*, 2003*a*, *b*; Mavrotas and Ouattara 2003*a*, *b*). The relevant policy lessons for both the donor and aid-recipient communities are quite significant: understanding *how aid works*, and in particular, *how different types of aid work* is of paramount importance for designing and implementing policies aiming at improving further aid effectiveness. However, there is a clear need for further work in this promising area at the individual country, regional and global level so that important conclusions and robust policy guidelines can be derived.

Comparative advantage compared to other proposed funding additional to existing ODA: IFF vis-à-vis MCA

An advantage of IFF as compared to other possible ways of increasing aid flows so that MDGs are achieved, and in particular the much discussed recently Millennium Challenge Account (MCA) of the US administration, is that the IFF does not deal with recipient countries on a bilateral basis only, as the MCA does.[19] By doing so, the MCA could possibly undermine significant progress made recently in improving donor coordination (see, for instance, the recent Aid Harmonization Initiative on this front). As has been recently argued, 'backsliding in this area could condemn poor countries to the unhappy position of having to court myriad donors and wade through competing and conflicting regulations' (Sperling and Hart 2003: 10).

A relevant question here might be, what would happen if the rest of the donor countries, apart from the United States, set up a fund (let us say the IFF) with the United States going its own way (with the MCA, for instance)—which, indeed, is the most likely outcome in view of the recent US (but also German) opposition to the IFF proposal at the IMF–WB Spring Meetings in Washington DC in April 2003 (see further details later). Crowding-out issues are of relevance in this case (i.e. introducing a new revenue source may displace other sources for development funding) under the assumption that the IFF proposal would be finally accepted by some donor countries. A proper discussion of the above issue should adopt a common framework to evaluate

---

[18] There are three relevant points here: (i) different types of aid operate in different ways (and with different lag-structure) in the recipient country thus resulting in different macro effects; (ii) because of different conditions regarding each in different countries (e.g. the state of aid coordination may vary among aid recipients), there is also an extra reason to expect different effects of aid in each country—the *ceteris paribus* assumptions of the econometrics of aid may be disturbed by such considerations; (iii) and perhaps most important, aid disaggregation might not matter so much if the proportions of different types of aid were constant; if they were, there could be sense in a coefficient relating aid (measured by one number) to some aspect of effectiveness; but if the proportions are changing, as they are, and changing in different degrees for different countries, this will definitely disturb the empirical results (Mavrotas 2002*a*, *b*).

[19] The US administration has recently proposed the creation of a federal corporation, separate from the Agency for International Development, to administer its proposed fund by targeting a small group of 'high-performing' countries on the basis of some eligibility criteria. For a detailed discussion of MCA see Radelet (2003), Brainard *et al.* (2003), and Catholic Relief Services Report on MCA (2002) among others.

different forms of development financing including the proposed Facility (Atkinson, Chapter 1, this volume).[20]

Indeed, this is also relevant to the IFF as compared to the IDA. IDA disbursed US$5.6 billion (US$5 in 2001 [World Bank 2003]) in 2002. Recently there has been a lot of discussion regarding the restructuring of IDA with a part of its lending being in the form of grants rather than loans. The IDA-13 replenishment was approved in mid-2002 and it was agreed that between 18 and 21 per cent of its overall resources would be provided in the form of grants. Bearing also in mind that IDA focuses on low-income countries, the question is, what would happen if the IFF was finally set up to disburse aid (mostly in the form of grants as discussed in Section 6.2 with a focus on low-income countries also). Most likely, the countries receiving aid flows from the IFF would be the same countries receiving grants (but also loans) from IDA. This is an important issue that needs to be addressed by the IFF proposal in view of the above recent developments in the IDA.[21]

IFF is based on a tried and tested principle for raising finance in international capital markets

It could be well argued that the securitization principle for raising finance through the IFF has been tried and tested for raising finance in international capital markets, thus adding significantly to the robustness of the overall proposal. Needless to say, the overall success of the proposed Facility will also be determined by other factors, such as the number of donors participating in the Facility (as well as their importance as perceived in international capital markets) and their continuous commitment to the Facility during its thirty-year life (see below for a discussion).

6.4.2. *Potential Disadvantages of the Proposed Facility and Issues for Further Discussion*

Possible undesirable effects of increasing aid flows through the IFF

Doubling aid through IFF may cause some potential undesirable effects in aid-recipient countries such as:

1. Absorptive-capacity problems (i.e. how recipient countries can cope with high levels of aid) and diminishing marginal rates of return to increased aid;[22]

---

[20] Obviously, in considering the likely extent of crowding out, the specification of the counter-factual is also crucial (Atkinson 2003).

[21] The reader can refer to a recent paper by Kapur (2002) on MDBs and IDA for a detailed discussion of IDA restructuring and the 'aidization' of the World Bank.

[22] It is notable that even if aid increases substantially by US$50 billion a year up to 2015, as the IFF proposal predicts, this does not necessarily guarantee that the MDGs will be reached. This is also relevant to absorptive-capacity issues; needless to say, this might be also the case with other types of development financing under discussion in the international community at the time of writing. There is some degree of optimism in the IFF proposal regarding this issue. It is assumed that by doubling aid flows through the Facility the targets will be met. However, we should be a little sceptical about this, in view of the lessons emerged from the voluminous literature on aid effectiveness, and particularly recent developments on this front.

2. Dutch-disease type of effects (i.e. the impact of aid on relative prices in aid-recipient countries);

3. The impact of aid on the public sector in recipient countries (i.e. does aid result in reduced taxation effort in recipient countries? How aid affects the fiscal sector of the aid recipient).[23]

Absorptive-capacity issues

It has been recently estimated that if aid donors were to meet the ODA target of 0.7 per cent of donor country GNP, aid flows would increase to about US$175 billion, that is more than three times the current levels. This, obviously, would help a lot with the achievement of the MDGs, but at the same time it would pose a number of challenges for aid-recipient countries at both the micro and the macro level (Heller and Gupta 2002). Although not implying an increase of aid flows equivalent to 0.7 per cent of donor country GNP, the proposed IFF is associated with a sharp increase in aid in the next decade up to 2015, which may pose crucial challenges for potential recipients of IFF flows. An important relevant issue is the possible absorptive-capacity constraint in a number of aid-recipient countries.[24] More precisely, doubling aid through the Facility would face diminishing marginal rates of return and this could become a serious problem at very high aid-to-GDP ratios. However, doubling aid in real terms by 2005 would bring only fourteen countries with a combined population of 109 million above 20 per cent aid/GNI. At the same time, it would be fair to say that there is no evidence that countries which receive high levels of aid have performed poorly. Some recent success stories in Africa clearly show how large amounts of aid can yield substantial rates of return: Uganda received more than 20 per cent of aid as share of GDP in the early 1990s but managed to register high growth rates above 7 per cent, reducing at the same time poverty (mainly through the Poverty Eradication Action Fund) by 20 per cent. Mozambique, with a 50 per cent aid-to-GDP ratio in the 1990s, achieved high growth rates, reaching 12 per cent in 1998. Recipients with high aid levels (above 20 per cent of income), most of them in Africa, increased on average their per capita GDP by 1.3 per cent per year over the period 1995–2000 (World Bank 2003).[25] Needless to say, these trends cannot suggest a robust conclusion regarding the impact of aid on growth (and the overall effectiveness of development aid) in countries receiving huge amounts of aid, since the aid-growth nexus can be affected by a number of factors which are not captured by simple correlation statistics.

[23] The above issues may be also relevant to all forms of increased transfer; for example, the absorptive-capacity issue, the Dutch disease problem, and issues related to fiscal response could all arise if the transfer was funded by a Tobin tax.

[24] Absorptive-capacity constraints and recipient need may be more unpredictable and uncontrollable than the steep bell-curve of rising and declining aid flows during the life of the Facility that the IFF seems to suggest. Heller and Gupta (2002) have recently argued that donors should put funds in trust today in order to finance increased aid in future when absorptive capacity allows.

[25] This is lower than China and India but greater than the average for all low-income countries (World Bank 2003).

On the issue of diminishing marginal rates of return related to increased aid, HM Treasury has recently argued that a minimum criterion for public investment, including what comes through aid, is that the test discount rate must not be less than the rate used by the donor country for domestic spending (currently 3.5 per cent in the United Kingdom) or the social time preference rate of the recipient country, estimated at 5.8 per cent for low-income countries. IFF-related assistance at average rates of return of 25 per cent (HM Treasury estimate) would yield returns of more than three times the borrowing rate of 6 per cent, and far above test discount, and social time preference rates.

Dutch disease effects

Regarding the Dutch disease type of effects, it may be well argued that large and sustained aid flows (i.e. IFF-type flows) may cause some appreciation of the nominal and real exchange rates in recipient countries. Indeed, since most aid is provided to governments whose expenditure is mainly on non-tradables such as public services, there is clearly a likelihood of short-run Dutch disease effects. In this case, aid may have two effects: a distortionary effect on price incentives and a direct positive income effect. Obviously, the final outcome will be determined by how the economy responds to the distortion. However, if substantial aid flows are supported by appropriate economic policies in recipient countries, the net gains to higher sustained levels of aid will remain strongly positive and donors should therefore continue to make these resources available to recipient countries pursuing sound macroeconomic policies (DFID 2002).[26]

The impact of aid on the public sector

An issue relevant to potential absorptive-capacity problems in countries receiving large amounts of aid through the IFF concerns the impact of aid on the public sector in the aid-recipient economy. One of the key criticisms of the aid–growth literature is that it fails to recognize explicitly that aid is given primarily to governments in aid-recipient countries, and hence any impact of aid on the macroeconomy will depend on government behaviour, in particular how fiscal decisions on taxation and expenditure are effected by the presence of aid. This is exactly what motivates the so-called 'fiscal response' literature, that is, modelling how the impact of aid is mediated by public sector behaviour.[27] The analysis of fiscal response is also important because it helps to open one of the many 'black boxes' of the aid–growth nexus (McGillivray and Morrissey 2000; Mavrotas 2002a; Mavrotas and Ouattara 2003a). Long ago it was argued that aid, *inter alia*, may have a negative effect on recipient economies

---

[26] Potential Dutch disease effects of increased aid flows are also related to the classical 'resource transfer problem' that has been discussed extensively in the trade literature. In the case of IFF, since the pattern of transfers is advanced, the terms of trade effect may become more conspicuous relative to a smoother time path; this may not necessarily outweigh the advantages of earlier disbursement, however, it needs to be put into balance (see Atkinson, Chapter 2 in this volume).   [27] The term is attributed to White (1992).

since recipient-country governments often use aid money to increase government consumption rather than direct aid flows towards developmental government investment (Griffin 1970). These potential negative effects of foreign aid could be viewed further within the context of the fungibility literature; the impact of aid on fiscal variables in the recipient economy and the related issue of aid fungibility have been the subject of a booming empirical literature in recent years. The 'fiscal response' literature, however, is not conclusive about the overall impact of aid on the fiscal sector of recipient countries.[28]

Issues related to donor coordination and commitment: the key-challenge
An issue very relevant to the overall success of proposals like the IFF is donor coordination: improving donor coordination (as well as maintaining it throughout the life of the Facility) is absolutely vital for the successful completion of the IFF. This is one of the disadvantages of the proposal, namely its heavy reliance on political coordination among the donor countries that will finally participate in the Facility. At the same time, the underlying assumption in the IFF proposal is that there will be continuous commitment on behalf of the donor community towards the implementation of the IFF during the thirty years of its life. This, to our view, is rather optimistic since, in a dynamic and uncertain world, this type of commitment is rather difficult to guarantee.

The conditions to be attached to the outflows from the Facility would be politically difficult to be agreed by all donors participating in the IFF
The conditions related to the IFF (see the discussion on OPs in Section 6.2) will be rather difficult to be agreed among donors and multilateral agencies participating in the Facility. Since the delivery channels of the IFF will be various (including multilateral agencies and bilateral channels), there is no guarantee that the conditions to be met by the recipients will necessarily be the same in all cases. Indeed, there are plenty of reasons to argue the opposite, in view of the lack of consensus among donors on issues related to the role of conditionality in development aid in the past. This may also undermine one of the main advantages of the current IFF proposal, namely that it will channel predictable and stable flows to low-income countries, thus allowing them to adopt pro-poor growth strategies. If we assume that there will be no widespread agreement regarding the OPs among donors participating in the IFF but that instead different conditions will be adopted by different donors, this may possibly make the disbursements less predictable and stable thus affecting the achievement of MDGs. However, possibly the right route for the IFF to take at this stage is to link the whole effort with recent initiatives on the aid harmonization front.[29]

---

[28] See McGillivray and Morrissey (2000), McGillivray (2000), Mavrotas (2002*a*), and Mavrotas and Ouattara (2003*b*) for a detailed discussion of the relevant literature.

[29] See the High-Level Aid Harmonization Meeting in Rome, February 2003.

Would the IFF be large enough (in terms of donor participation)
to be able to deliver what is being proposed?

Obviously, the issue (and the main challenge for the proposed Facility) is really whether enough donor governments will commit enough money to get the Facility working to the right scale (*Financial Times* 2003a). This clearly emphasizes that the biggest task in the implementation of the IFF proposal is political. The proposal does not discuss details regarding possible donor participation in the Facility in terms of the 'right' number and/or size needed to raise US$50 billion a year until 2015. However, this is a crucial factor, which will eventually determine the future of this promising proposal. If the HM Treasury–DFID manage to convince a substantial number of donors to go ahead with the proposed Facility, even without the United States as an IFF donor country (in view of the recent developments related to the MCA, see above), the Facility may be in a position to deliver what it is promising at the moment. In the opposite case, the prospects for the Facility would be rather bleak.

How would the IFF be treated in the national accounts of donor governments?:
Implications for debt/GDP ratios

Another potential disadvantage of the proposed Facility is related to the way it may be treated in the national accounts of the donor countries participating in the Facility. It may well be argued here that the future commitments of donor countries to the Facility will be registered as government liabilities in the national accounts of the donor countries resulting in higher debt-to-GDP ratios in these countries. This would make the Facility rather unattractive to those donor countries wishing to reduce their debt-to-GDP ratios.

Regarding the above issue, the HM Treasury–DFID argues in the revised proposal (work still in progress) that the IFF is expected to be classified as an international organization (under Eurostat guidelines) and so within in-the-rest-of-the-world sector in national accounts and therefore outside the general government sector in individual countries' national accounts. Along these lines, the proposal goes further by arguing that the Facility will be 'owned' by the several donor governments but will be responsible for its own debt servicing, that is, bondholders will have no call on donor governments participating in the Facility. HM Treasury–DFID also argue that donor countries will need to consider whether, under their own accounting conventions, the funds raised through the securitization process would be classified as IFF borrowing rather than as borrowing by the individual donor governments.[30]

Under the assumption that the IFF will be classified in this manner, there is no potential disadvantage arising from the Facility regarding its treatment in the national accounts of the participating donor governments. However, as the proponents of the Facility also admit, this will crucially depend on two factors, namely (i) the nature of the donor commitments and (ii) the IFF's decisionmaking process for allocating

---

[30] In the former case, it is argued that the Facility's disbursement of those funds would be recorded as IFF expenditure rather than expenditure by the donor governments and government expenditure would be recorded when donor governments make their actual payments to the Facility.

funds for disbursement (to be agreed at the proposed founding conference). Needless to say, even on the assumption that there is some ineluctable logic determining how the presentation for national-accounts purposes should be done given the nature of the financial obligations (which might make the first condition important), it is very hard to see how the manner in which the allocation decisions are made with the borrowed funds (the second condition) has any bearing on whether those funds should be counted as donor-government borrowing.[31]

The IFF may imply a significant change in organizational terms since it would involve a new international treaty and possibly substantial organizational costs

It could well be argued that a new scheme, along the lines of the proposed IFF, implies a significant change in organizational terms since it would involve a new international treaty as well as potentially substantial organizational costs as compared to the existing institutions. One might even go further to argue that it is rather unclear what advantage the new Facility would provide as compared to existing institutional structures. Along these lines, one might possibly wonder whether increasing the callable capital of the existing MDBs could achieve similar results.

However, distinguishing between grants and non-concessional loans is crucial in dealing with the above issue. In the case of non-concessional loans (which is not the focus of the proposed Facility) the most efficient means would probably be an increase in the callable capital of the existing MDBs. This would not be the case if we considered grants (and concessional loans) as in the case of IFF, since the IFF would be a more efficient way to finance grants and concessional loans than the callable-capital structure of the MDBs. For example, IDA cannot borrow in the international capital markets and the International Bank for Reconstruction and Development (IBRD) may not give grants. In the latter case, internal work by the HM Treasury seems to suggest that, if the World Bank itself were to finance loans on IDA-type concessional terms through market borrowing, and wanted to maintain its status as a stand-alone financial institution (without any donor subsidy), it would require an increase in capital at least equal to the grant element of the loans and probably significantly more, reflecting credit risk; this would result in a leverage which would be very low. Thus, it would be fair to conclude that increasing the callable capital of the existing MDBs would be unable to accelerate grant finance the way the IFF does.

Could the additionality of the money committed through the IFF be guaranteed?

Finally, an important issue is related to the additionality element of the proposed Facility regarding existing ODA flows from donor countries. It would be difficult (if not impossible) to guarantee that the money committed through the IFF would be additional to ODA flows. Regarding this, it could possibly be argued that, even if contributions are not entirely additional, the IFF process will bind them in and give

---

[31] We are grateful to an anonymous referee on this point.

them leverage. This is clearly an issue that needs further discussion and elaboration in forthcoming G7 meetings.[32]

6.5. CONCLUDING REMARKS

In a globalized world, we need solutions of a global scale to deal with important global issues (such as the MDGs). In view of this, a proposal to set up an IFF should, in principle, be welcomed by the international community. In the present chapter, we have discussed in detail the IFF, the joint HM Treasury–DFID proposal to increase development aid substantially so that the MDGs are achieved by 2015. The main conclusion of the chapter is that the proposed IFF is a promising and forward-looking proposal, in view of the substantial increase in fresh, predictable, and stable aid it is envisaging as well as its robust financial structure.

However, there are a number of concerns about some potential shortcomings of the proposal, namely its underlying assumptions of continuous commitment on behalf of the donor community towards the implementation of the IFF during the thirty years of its life, and most importantly its heavy reliance on political coordination among donor countries participating in the proposed Facility. Achieving its huge political task as well as relaxing the crucial constraints on the successful implementation of this innovative proposal would be the main future challenge of the IFF.[33]

Furthermore, the discussion of potential disadvantages of the proposed Facility, particularly those related to donor coordination and continuous commitment of the donor community during the life of the Facility to contribute to the IFF in line with the Articles of Association, clearly suggests the need for future research to discuss in-depth political economy aspects of sources of development finance, including the IFF, since 'the political economy of different proposals is an important part of the story, requiring a nuanced political analysis of the likely coalitions of support and opposition, as well as a careful specification of the exact nature of the proposals' (Atkinson 2003: 22).

To sum up, our own view is that this is a promising, forward-looking, and creative proposal which needs to be carefully considered at international fora in the very near future so that it is turned from a proposal into a practical solution to the problem of development financing for the achievement of the MDGs. Obviously the political constraints regarding the possible implementation of the proposal in the near future are extremely important and should not be overlooked. Many donor countries and international agencies may be sceptical about a proposal which may reduce part of their autonomy and independence regarding aid allocation. Indeed this sort of scepticism is reflected in some of the comments already made by some donors at the IMF–WB Spring Meetings in April 2003. The United States and Germany, for instance, fear that

[32] Furthermore, it is not very clear from the above proposal what happens after 2015 when a part of the aid budget is diverted into funding the bonds that have been issued to support increased transfers prior to 2015; in particular, it is not certain whether this intertemporal change in resource transfer will increase welfare.

[33] As has been correctly argued recently, 'unless there is the commitment to implement the IFF, the Facility will remain just a proposal' (*Financial Times*, 21 February 2003a).

the proposal may be impractical since it would bind the hands of future governments and mortgage future aid budgets to repay the borrowings (*Financial Times* 2003*b*). Others, however, including the IMF's former managing director Horst Kohler and France, welcomed the proposal thus crediting it with more time for further discussions and revision at this stage.[34]

At the Pocantico Conference on Feasible Additional Sources of Finance for Development (May 2003) an alternative option was discussed in case binding explicit commitments from all potential major donors proved impossible to achieve. It has been argued that it might be fruitful to ask the potential donors to issue the relevant volumes of bonds on an individual basis, with the proceeds still to be used under whatever ground-rules the donors corporately could agree to follow; each donor country's own credit would then be at issue in maintaining the annual payments. Along these lines, whatever bonds each had issued, these it would certainly service. However, in view of the Facility's multilateral approach to aid allocation, coordination issues could be more difficult to deal with here as compared to the IFF option.

Accelerating aid flows through the IFF needs to take into account absorptive-capacity constraints in aid-dependent economies to ensure that marginal returns do not fall below the minimum thresholds we derived. In view of this, borrowing against future aid, as proposed by the IFF, can be worthwhile provided returns exceed the borrowing cost (Foster 2003).[35]

The final point to make is that arguing as well as campaigning for the IFF (as is the case with other sources of development finance), even if the proposed Facility finally does not succeed in being adopted in the near future, can be extremely valuable in maintaining a sense of urgency over the need for additional finance for the achievement of MDGs and in challenging the major economic powers to find an efficient way of providing it. Furthermore, coalitions among donors trying to promote new major

---

[34] The recent response of the IMF to the IFF proposal was overall positive, as reflected in the comments made by its managing director at the recent Spring IMF–World Bank Meetings in Washington, DC: 'I think this is an intelligent idea. It raises a number of questions. I know that there is some skepticism, but I do think we should remain open to this suggestion, because we need more financing for development. We know that public budgets are tight and, therefore, we should also look to some creative ideas, and this is one.' Press conference at the IMF following the Spring Meetings, Washington, DC, April 2003 (www.imf.org/external/np/tr/2003/tr030410.htm).

[35] Another fair point (raised by an anonymous referee) is that behind the IFF proposal seems to lie a supposition about a rather strange pattern of discount rates (and productivity rates on investment) over time within the recipient countries. The pattern of disbursements (as illustrated in Figs 6.3 and 6.5) seems to make sense only on the assumption that the marginal productivity-of-investment function moves sharply downward from 2015 to 2020. Although it makes sense (in view of the need to meet the internationally agreed MDGs by 2015) to assume an upward sloping marginal productivity-of-investment function prior to 2015, it is not necessarily reasonable to assume a downward sloping curve after 2015. The present chapter examines whether returns on investment in the recipients are likely to be high enough to justify borrowing at AAA rates to finance them and concludes that they very probably are. However, one of the distinctive features of the IFF is that it not only increases disbursements up to 2015 but also (in comparison with a straight disbursement of the projected donor contributions as they occur) reduces them thereafter. Do we know of any good reason why that is likely to be efficient? Or is it just an inefficiency that is worth accepting because the whole package will generate more predictable donor contributions, one of the main advantages of the above proposal?

initiatives on the development finance front (such as the IFF) could be possibly more efficient if they included politicians representing both North and South; this would give to the proposed initiatives more international support and credibility as well as higher chances of being finally adopted.

REFERENCES

Atkinson, A. (2003). 'Innovative Sources for Development Finance: Global Public Economics'. Paper presented at the World Bank ABCDE Conference, 15–16 May, Paris.

Addison, T. (2000). 'Aid and Conflict', in F. Tarp (ed.), *Foreign Aid and Development: Lessons Learnt and Directions for the Future*. London: Routledge Studies in Development Economics 17.

Brainard, L., C. Graham, N. Purvis, S. Radelet, and G. Smith (2003). *The Other War: Global Poverty and the Millennium Challenge Account*. Washington, DC: Centre for Global Development and Brookings Institution.

Cassen, R. (1994). *Does Aid Work?*, 2nd edition. Oxford: Oxford University Press.

Catholic Relief Services (CRS) (2002). 'Improving Development Effectiveness: Recommendations for the Millennium Challenge Account'. Report, June.

DFID (2002). 'The Macroeconomic Effects of Aid'. A policy paper by the Department for International Development. London, December.

Financial Times (2003a). 'G-7 to Hear Brown's Anti-Poverty Plan'. 21 February.

—— (2003b). 'Brown Plan to Reform Global Financial System Meets Opposition'. 14 April.

Foster, M. (2003). 'Criteria for Assessing the Case for Overseas Aid: A Note'. *Development Policy Review*, 21(3): 293–300.

Griffin, K. (1970). 'Foreign, Domestic savings and Economic Development'. *Oxford Bulletin of Economics and Statistics*, 32(2): 99–112.

Heller, P. and S. Gupta (2002). 'More Aid—Making It Work for the Poor'. *World Economics*, 3(4): 131–46.

HM Treasury (2002). *Tackling Poverty: A Global New Deal—A Modern Marshall Plan for the Developing World*. London, February.

HM Treasury–DFID (2003a). *International Finance Facility*. London, January.

—— (2003b). *International Finance Facility: A Technical Note*. London, February.

Kapur, D. (2002). 'Do As I Say Not As I Do: A Critique of G-7 Proposals on Reforming the MDBs'. *Working Paper* No 16. Washington, DC: Centre for Global Development.

Levy, V. (1987). 'Anticipated Development Assistance, Temporary Relief Aid, and Consumption Behaviour of Low-Income Countries'. *Economic Journal*, 97(June): 446–58.

Mavrotas, G. (2002a). 'Foreign Aid and Fiscal Response: Does Aid Disaggregation Matter?'. *Weltwirtschaftliches Archiv*, 138(3): 534–59.

—— (2002b). 'Aid and Growth in India: Some Evidence from Disaggregated Aid Data'. *South Asia Economic Journal*, 3(1): 19–49.

—— (2003a). 'Which Types of Aid Have the Most Impact?'. *WIDER Discussion Paper* No. 2003/85. Helsinki: UNU-WIDER.

—— (2003b). 'Assessing Aid Effectiveness in Uganda: An Aid Disaggregation Approach'. Report to the UK Department for International Development, January.

—— and B. Ouattara (2003a). 'The Composition of Aid and the Fiscal Sector in an Aid-Recipient Economy: A Model'. *WIDER Discussion Paper* No. 2003/11. Helsinki: UNU-WIDER.

—————— (2003*b*). 'Aid Disaggregation, Endogenous Aid and the Public Sector in Aid-Recipient Economies: Evidence from Côte d'Ivoire'. *WIDER Discussion Paper* No. 2003/15. Helsinki: UNU-WIDER.

McGillivray, M. (2000). 'Aid and Public Sector Fiscal Behaviour in Developing Countries'. *Review of Development Economics*, 2(2): 156–63.

—— and O. Morrissey (2000). 'Aid Fungibility in Assessing Aid: Red Herring or True Concern?'. *Journal of International Development*, 12: 413–28.

Radelet, S. (2003). *Challenging Foreign Aid: A Policymaker's Guide to the Millennium Challenge Account*. Washington, DC: Center for Global Development.

Sperling, G. and T. Hart (2003). 'A Better Way to Fight Global Poverty: Broadening the Millennium Challenge Account'. *Foreign Affairs*, 82 (March/April): 9–14.

White, H. (1992). 'The Macroeconomic Impact of Development Aid: A Critical Survey'. *Journal of Development Studies*, 28: 163–240.

World Bank (2003). *Global Development Finance 2003*. Washington, DC: World Bank.

7

Private Donations for International Development

JOHN MICKLEWRIGHT AND ANNA WRIGHT

> How selfish soever man may be supposed, there are evidently some principles in
> his nature, which interest him in the fortune of others, and render their happiness
> necessary to him, though he derives nothing from it except the pleasure of seeing it.
>
> Adam Smith (1759), *The Theory of Moral Sentiments*, chapter 1.

7.1. INTRODUCTION

Charitable giving is common, reflecting various 'principles' in human nature alluded to
by Adam Smith, as well as others that he did not identify. For example, 70 per cent of
American households give money to charity, with their donations summing to almost
US$150 billion in 1999—more than one and a half per cent of US national income.[1] The
US heads the giving league in per capita terms as well as total amounts but there is a lot
of giving in other Organization for Economic Cooperation and Development (OECD)
countries as well. Two-thirds of UK adults report making charitable donations in
2001, with an annual total of nearly US$10 billion. Recent changes to the UK tax
system have tried to encourage private philanthropy, and the evidence suggests that
much of the donor response could still be to come. Donations by private individuals
in Germany totalled about US$4 billion in 2000 and a similar amount was given in the
Netherlands in 1999.[2] Econometric estimates of the response of charitable giving to
changes in incomes and prices imply that rising real income over the next 15–20 years

Very useful comments on earlier drafts were made by Tony Atkinson (several of which helped shape our
conclusions), other project participants, David Lewis, Sylke Schnepf, and OUP's referees. We are grateful
for help in various ways to Jonathan Burton, Catherine Carnie, Susan Chisnall, Bill Cottle, Stephen Lee,
Liz Markus, Marjorie Newman Williams, Caroline Thomas, and Della Weight.

[1] See www.access.mpr.org/civic_j/giving/resources/factoids.shtml. More recent figures for 2001 come
from www.independentsector.org/PDFs/GV01keyfind.pdf and show an even higher involvement in philanthropy. See also the summary statistics in Andreoni (2001) who provides a concise review of the economic
theory of philanthropy, empirical literature from the United States and policy issues surrounding the tax
treatment of donations.

[2] Figures for the United Kingdom and Germany taken from NCVO (2002) and Bundesarbeitsgemeinschaft Sozialmarketing (2002). Figure for the Netherlands from Helmich (2003: 161). US dollar values obtained
with annual average exchange rates from the Bank of England website. The definition of donations may not
be the same in each country.

should result in substantial additions to total donations and that tax incentives, where not currently in place, could lever further sums.[3]

Philanthropy can come in-kind as well as cash. Gifts of time—'volunteering'—are the most important form to consider. Like charitable gifts in monetary form, voluntary work is widespread in industrialized countries. In the twelve OECD countries covered by Salamon *et al.* (1999), volunteer work was estimated to total over 16 million full-time equivalent jobs, and to average nearly 7 per cent of all full-time non-agricultural employment. This too could rise as a result, for example, of the ageing of OECD countries' populations and any trend towards early retirement.

But to what extent does *development* benefit from all this philanthropic effort? This is the subject of Section 7.2. The answer is mixed. A great deal of philanthropy in rich industrialized countries is aimed at domestic concerns, although the evidence we have been able to assemble suggests that the picture is not the same in every country. We discuss how donations for development may vary with household income, of particular interest given a trend towards greater income inequality in some industrialized countries. The super-rich are treated as a special case. Their ranks have recently produced several prominent examples of philanthropy aimed at international development, notably the large sums given by Bill Gates and Ted Turner.

The next question is *why* development may command only a small share of charitable donations. Until we know this, the way forward for the future remains unclear. This is dealt with in Section 7.3. The economic literature on philanthropy provides only limited help and we, therefore, draw on literature on donor behaviour from other disciplines, notably marketing.

Section 7.4 considers the special case of private donations to the UN agencies, one group of major players in financing and promoting development. We consider the particular problems faced by the UN and then focus on the Children's Fund, United Nations Children's Fund (UNICEF). This is by far and away the most successful UN agency at collecting money from private individuals, raising more than US$350 million each year (although we highlight the large variation in the per capita amounts among OECD members). Could UNICEF's success be emulated by other agencies? And does the relationship between UNICEF donations and official overseas development assistance suggest there is a problem of crowding-out?

Future prospects are discussed in Section 7.5. We include measures designed to promote charitable donations in general, but focus on their particular relevance for development. We cover the old issue of tax deductions, the new 'global funds' (intended partly to attract money from the super-rich), corporate social responsibility and 'cause-related marketing', the use of the Internet, and long-term donor education. Section 7.6 concludes.

---

[3] For example, a regression of log gifts on log personal income for the US using annual data for 1974–95 given in Clotfelter (1997: table 2) yields an estimated elasticity of 1.12 (SE 0.03). The fact that the estimated elasticity is greater than one means that gifts can be expected to rise more than proportionately with income.

Three caveats on the scope of the chapter: first, we include under 'development' those donations that go for emergency relief, for example, the alleviation of famine or the consequences of floods. The long-term impact of donations for emergencies is clearly different from those for several other causes, for example, education or vaccine research. Second, we focus much more on giving by households than by firms. Direct corporate donations to charities are far smaller in aggregate than those by private individuals and there is no particular reason to believe that they will expand sharply.[4] However, Section 7.5 provides some balance with our discussion of corporate social responsibility and cause-related marketing. Third, for reasons of space we concentrate on private donations in rich industrialized countries, ignoring important traditions of domestic charity in developing countries, including volunteering.[5]

7.2. DEVELOPMENT'S SHARE OF PHILANTHROPY

Oxfam, an international development charity, raised more voluntary income in 1996 than any other registered UK charity. But if one takes the top thirty fundraising UK charities in that year, development's share of their total voluntary income was less than a quarter.[6] Development's share of private donations in the Netherlands is rather lower, about 15 per cent (Helmich 2003: 161). The massive philanthropic effort in the United States seems, on the face of it, to be even more domestically orientated. Less than 2 per cent of total household contributions went to 'international' charities in 1999.[7] This contrasts with the 60 per cent that went to religious organizations although, as we illustrate below, a slice of this may in fact be furthering international causes, including development. On the other hand, Germany seems to be a country where a large share of charitable donations go to fund overseas development, but we do not know whether the situation there is more representative of other OECD countries than that in the United Kingdom or the Netherlands. Almost three-quarters of total donations to the

---

[4] Corporate donations in the United States to all causes totalled US$9 billion in 1998, far below the US$135 billion of households (Andreoni 2001). Similarly, donations by firms in the UK in 2000/1 are estimated to have been only £286 million compared to some £6 billion from households (Charities Aid Foundation Briefing Paper March 2003).

[5] For example, the giving of alms to the needy in one's own society, the practice of *zakat*, is one of the five main tenets of Islam. (*Zakat* should normally be paid at the rate of 2.5 per cent of annual income.) On volunteering, the Comparative Nonprofit Sector Project at Johns Hopkins University has produced several papers on developing countries that include this form of giving. (The border-line between 'volunteering' and inter-household transfers of time is a hazy one—helping family and neighbours is clearly very common in all cultures.)

[6] Pharoah and Tanner (1997) list the top thirty fundraising charities in 1996 by name of which we have classified as 'development' the following: Oxfam, Red Cross, Save the Children, Actionaid, Christian Aid, The Tear Fund, and WWWF. These seven charities' voluntary income amounted to 23% of the total.

[7] Sourced from www.independentsector.org/GandV/s_hous2.htm.

sixteen German charities with the highest volume of gifts in 2000 were to what can be classified broadly as development charities.[8,9]

Tastes for international development may, therefore, vary from country to country as far as cash giving is concerned. Turning to volunteering however, the picture right across the industrialized countries is one in which the great bulk of the labour involved does not benefit international development charities.[10] This comes as little surprise, given that voluntary labour must typically be used domestically.[11]

The situation where development's share is low might, paradoxically, seem encouraging for the future. The argument would run as follows. The evidence shows there to be a great deal of philanthropy. Some of this could be shifted towards development and away from the causes to which it is currently directed. Private donations for development could, therefore, rise very substantially without households having to give any more time or money in total. Imagine that households adopt a two-stage budgeting process, first deciding on total allocations of time and money to charity and then deciding how to divide those allocations between different causes. The job, it would seem, is to influence the second-stage allocation. To date, economists have tended to look only at the results of the first-stage allocation—at total donations. Theoretical models of philanthropic behaviour do not identify motives for gifts to particular causes, and empirical models of giving are estimated on data that measure just total gifts. But richer data could be collected and insight gained into how donations could be shifted away from domestic causes and towards development assistance.

But there is little reason to believe that households do allocate their time and money to charity in this way. Gifts to one cause may not represent resources that can be competed away by another. We have no direct evidence to cite on this issue, but simple reflection on why people may donate to some specific named charities provides food for thought. Table 7.1 shows the total annual income from all sources of several UK development charities, both large and small, together with examples of charities serving other causes that have similar income levels.

---

[8] Eleven of the sixteen can be classified as development charities and their donations sum to 72% of the total. We are grateful to Sylke Schnepf for this estimate. (Source as in footnote 3, although this source also cites an earlier estimate by the Deutschen Spendeninstitus Krefeld that 75% of donations go to 'national projects'.)

[9] Anheier and List (2000) attempt to bring together data for the mid-1990s on cross-border philanthropy for the United States, the United Kingdom, Germany, and Japan. Definitions vary substantially but broadly speaking, their results suggest that private sector giving for development as the final cause was at the level of about US$1–2 billion per year in the United States, US$1.5 billion in Germany, about US$1 billion in the United Kingdom, and well less than these levels in Japan.

[10] We base this conclusion on the data in Salamon *et al.* (1999) and Salamon and Sokolowski (2001). The categories the authors use for 'development' and 'international' are probably too broad and narrow respectively for our purposes.

[11] Schemes also exist to transfer gifts in-kind in physical form to developing countries, for example, old sewing machines and other tools (e.g. see www.findit.co.uk/charities/519568.htm). However, there are obvious limits to this form of philanthropy. Transport costs may be excessive, many goods would be inappropriate for the local setting, and there is the risk of undermining local production. This could be a useful form for some corporate donations however, for example, medical supplies.

Table 7.1. *Examples of UK charities*

Development charity	Income (£s, m)	Other charity	Cause	Income (£s, m)
Oxfam	187	The National Trust	Architecture & landscape	188
Red Cross	138	Barnado's	Children	125
Save the Children	116	Imperial Cancer	Health	122
Action Aid	62	RSPCA	Animal welfare	65
Catholic Agency for International Development	40	Guide Dogs for the Blind	Blind people	38
UNICEF	28	Shelter	The homeless	27
Sightsavers International	14	NACRO	Former criminal offenders	13

Notes: Income is for 2000 and from all sources, including government grants, contributions from other charities, donations from firms, investment income and the proceeds of trading, as well as gifts and legacies from private individuals.

Source: Charity Commission on-line register.

Non-development charities cover many causes of which the table illustrates just some of the main ones. The examples in the table include cases where it is possible to imagine development charities being able to compete away part of the funding (although whether that would be desirable for human welfare overall requires a value judgement that we do not make here). Charities working for children in the developing world such as Save the Children and UNICEF might view Barnado's income as money that could in principle come their way. Sightsavers International might consider the resources of Guide Dogs for the Blind in the same light. But money given to the National Trust for the preservation of Britain's architectural heritage and landscape does not seem an obvious target for a development charity. Similarly, the large sums of money given for animal welfare in the United Kingdom may be hard to shift to the cause of human welfare in developing countries.[12]

The table also illustrates the difficulties in classifying charities and hence in measuring how much philanthropy is directed towards overseas development. We have labelled both the Red Cross and Save the Children as development charities, but both have programmes in the United Kingdom, with the Red Cross being particularly

---

[12] We suspect that animal welfare charities may do particularly well in the United Kingdom compared with those in other countries. Among charities with incomes in excess of £10 million in 2000, total income of obvious animal charities came to about £250 million (including £17 million for the Cats' Protection League, £13 million for the Donkey Sanctuary, and £10 million for Battersea Dogs' Home). (Our analysis of information from the Charity Commission register.)

active.[13] The Catholic Agency for International Development (the English and Welsh arm of Caritas Internationalis) is clearly a religious charity in one sense and we suspect that in some classifications it would be labelled as such, despite its activity being firmly in the field of development. Similarly, Save the Children and UNICEF could obviously be labelled as children's charities.[14]

Another implication of recognizing that people give to a wide variety of types of charity is that the estimates of the response of total giving to changes in incomes and prices from the empirical literature on the economics of philanthropy may not be very useful in providing guidance into how donations for development will respond to future changes in real income or tax treatment. Estimates vary considerably but a figure of 0.8 to 1.0 for the income 'elasticity' of total donations is perhaps broadly representative (Clotfelter 1997; see also footnote 4). An elasticity of 1.0 implies that donations rise proportionately with income. However, if charity indeed 'begins at home', and then extends elsewhere, perhaps donations to fund development are a luxury in economic terms, implying that donations rise more than proportionately with income. This would mean a strong response of donations for development to rising incomes in the future. The economic literature alas seems silent on this issue. It should also be noted that the great bulk of empirical studies are from the United States and behavioural response to income may be different in other countries. (We discuss price elasticities in Section 7.5.) The notion of donations for development as a luxury would be consistent with the rise of international development charities as a largely post-Second World War phenomenon, something underlined by Mullin (2002) in the case of the United Kingdom.[15]

The picture for total gifts, at least from US and UK data, seems to be that the rich and the poor give higher proportions of their income than those on middle incomes. This means that richer households provide the lion's share of charitable donations. For example, the one-in-seven American households with incomes of US$75,000 or more in 1996 provided about half of total contributions (Clotfelter 1997: table 3). In the United Kingdom, persons giving more than £50 per month—'elite donors' in UK charity parlance—represent just one in twelve of all persons who give, but their donations make up nearly 60 per cent of the total; elite donors are concentrated in higher social classes (NCVO 2002). Any greater propensity of the rich to donate means that there is a silver lining to the cloud of sharply higher income inequality in recent years in the United States and the United Kingdom (trends in other countries are less clear). The share of the top 1 per cent in the United States rose from about 9 to 15 per cent of

[13] The Red Cross spent £47 million in 2001 on 'UK services' and £70 million abroad. Save the Children spent about £7.5 million on UK programmes from its total programme expenditure of £90 million. Oxfam also has a small UK programme, spending less than £1 million in 2001. (Information taken from annual reports available at www.redcross.org.uk, www.scfuk.org.uk and www.oxfam.org.uk.)

[14] The UK survey drawn in footnote 3 shows 13% of donations going to 'children and young people' with 'overseas relief' and 'disaster relief' receiving just 12%. We do not know how Save the Children and UNICEF were treated in this classification.

[15] A different explanation in the case of the United Kingdom is that the rise coincided with the end of the empire and tapped into some of the same motives that led people to work in colonial administration.

gross personal income between the mid-1980s and late 1990s and from about 6 to 10 per cent in the United Kingdom (Atkinson 2002; Piketty and Saez 2003).

The case of the super-rich deserves special attention. Many large charitable foundations in existence today are the result of a gift by a very rich individual in the past. While the activities of a foundation are constrained by the original donor's wishes, boards of trustees may be able to interpret their trust deeds in ways that give them a wide scope. This form of philanthropy typically has a firmly domestic concern in the United States. For example, only US$1 billion of the 11 billion total given by US foundations in 1994 was devoted to 'international activities', including those that do not fund development in poorer countries (Anheier and List 2000: 108). However, large foundations such as Ford and Rockefeller clearly do have development concerns. With Rockefeller they have always been there, the trustees being charged to further 'the well-being of mankind throughout the world'. Ford, on the other hand, acted as a local philanthropy in Michigan from its founding in 1936 until 1950. The foundation now has thirteen offices outside the United States: in Latin America, Africa, Asia, and Russia. The Soros Foundations, a recent creation, have been prominent in the former Soviet bloc countries in the 1990s.

Two prominent examples come from the United States in recent years of foundations that have been established to finance aspects of international development. The UN Foundation was set up in 1997 by Ted Turner with a promised endowment of US$1 billion, about equivalent to the annual budget at that time of the UN Children's Fund, UNICEF. The Foundation works exclusively through UN agencies and provides funds in four areas: (i) children's health, (ii) the environment, (iii) peace, security and human rights, and (iv) women and population. The Bill and Melinda Gates Foundation, established in 2000, has a much weaker relationship with the UN as we will explain later in the chapter—and a much larger budget following an endowment of about US$24 billion. (To give a point of reference, the Ford Foundation's assets are currently about US$10 billion and the Rockefeller's US$2.6 billion.) This is clearly an absolutely vast sum of money for one individual to give to good causes, although in fact it represents less than a fifth of what all US households give to charity every year. Global health is one of the foundations' four areas of activity and as of June 2003, this had accounted for just over £3 billion in grants, or about half the total of all grants to that date.[16] The expenditure on health is focused on the prevention of transmission of HIV in developing countries and the search for vaccines to combat AIDS, malaria, and tuberculosis.

7.3. WHY DO PEOPLE GIVE—OR NOT GIVE—TO DEVELOPMENT?

The economic literature on philanthropy has not typically sought to explain donations to different causes, as we have already noted. Nor has it focused much on the demand

---

[16] The Gates Foundation's other concerns are domestic US causes relating to education, libraries and the US Pacific North–West. See www.gatesfoundation.org.

side of the market—it has been the behaviour of donors rather than the actions of different charities that has been the subject of attention.[17] The behaviour of charitable organizations in trying to attract funds to their particular causes is important to understand and, obviously, this behaviour is revealing about how the demand side of the market actually perceives donor motives in relation to different aims.

The motives for giving identified in the economic literature include (i) altruism, (ii) the 'warm glow' obtained from the act of giving, (iii) the receipt of material benefit in return for the gift, and (iv) simple morality.[18] To some extent, these are useful in helping understand development's share of charitable donations. Material benefit is a clear motive for donation to some domestic charities. For example, giving to the National Trust in the United Kingdom in the form of a subscription to membership gives free access to a large number of stately homes and landscaped gardens. It is not easy for a development charity to match such an offer. On the other hand, higher-order morality may generate more funds for development than for dogs' homes. Altruism could lead donations to be skewed towards places where living standards are lowest in order to get more 'bang for the buck' (development charities are quick to emphasize the very low cost in Western terms of many of their interventions). Charities try to generate 'warm glow' through such measures as sponsoring a child.

The marketing literature, as applied to charitable giving, provides more insight on both motives for donors and the behaviour of charities. We draw on the review in Sargeant (1999) who considers the insights from clinical psychology, social psychology, anthropology, and sociology as well as economics. In trying to apply these insights to the case of development we do not tailor our comments to particular countries, but the apparent variation in development's share of total donations discussed in Section 7.2 suggests that no common explanation exists across the OECD area. Giving for international development must in part have specific national determinants.

The marketing literature provides a quick answer to why 'development' charities exist at all, rather than general-purpose charities that aim to help the poor wherever they may be. A positive response from individuals to charities' efforts to solicit contributions is helped by branding and by a clear projection by a charity of its brand identity. Potential contributors want a firm picture of the cause they are being asked to give in aid of, and the brands they will be attracted to are those that are well-known and trusted.

Individuals' reaction to the 'ask' (which may come in a variety of forms) depends on various factors, including the portrayal of the individuals in need, the fit of the charity with a donor's self image, and the degree of perceptual noise (whether competition from other charities so confuses the donor that a lower level of total contributions results).

---

[17] Andreoni (1998) is a rare exception.

[18] This listing follows the summary in Clotfelter (1997). The first three motives are consistent with utility-maximization. Vickery (1962) and Boulding (1962) mention most of the motives that economists have subsequently considered.

The stimulus to the individual to donate is believed to be stronger the more urgent the need can be demonstrated to be and the greater the degree of personal link that the donor feels with the (eventual) recipient. The cause of long-term development does not score well on either factor. A criterion of urgency obviously works in favour of appeals for disaster relief in developing countries following, for example, a flood or a famine. But by definition the achievement by 2015 of the Millennium Development Goals (MDGs) hardly seems an urgent task. Similarly, long-term development suffers in the competition for funds due to many donors' desire to support short-term need for a fairly narrow section of the community, factors that encourage donors to feel that their relatively small contribution can make a real and immediate difference. In many areas of development, however, need is typically persistent and very widespread.

One question here is how attitudes to urgency and duration of need vary across the income distribution and by level of education. Higher socioeconomic status appears to be associated with a greater willingness to give for longer-term causes. The Gates and UN (i.e. Turner) Foundations would certainly seem to reflect this. But a longer-term view may not necessarily help international causes. US data for 1973 show high–income philanthropists (those with incomes of over US$0.7 million in 2003 terms) giving a quarter of their donations to education, compared to only 1 per cent for those under US$80,000 in current-day prices (Clotfelter 1997: table 5). But the vast majority of this was almost certainly to benefit domestic causes, for example, alumni donations to the alma mater. More research is needed on how giving for development varies by income level.

Another factor found to favour donations is the existence of a sense of personal contact with the beneficiary. This must have been in Adam Smith's mind when he wrote the words in the quotation at the start of the chapter: giving alms to the local poor in the past would typically have meant that one saw the impact on welfare achieved by the gift.[19] Some donations of cash may continue to reflect personal contact in the modern age. This is most obvious in the case of donations to local causes—again development misses out—but it can be found in other situations too.[20] For example, the huge funds raised for cancer research and for the relief of those with cancer presumably reflect the importance of cancer as a cause of death in rich industrialized countries. Cancer sufferers and relatives of sufferers are obvious potential donors, as indeed is the population as a whole—everyone is a potential sufferer with a non-negligible probability, such is the sheer prevalence of different forms of this disease in OECD countries.[21] But fighting HIV, malaria, and tuberculosis—diseases so prevalent in the south—seems much more remote.

[19] Conniff (2003: 102) writes of the Duchess of Marlborough visiting the homes of poor families near Blenheim Palace to distribute leftover food.

[20] The network of about 1400 United Way organizations in the United States expressly raise money for local purposes (to the tune of about US$4 billion per year).

[21] The website of Cancer Research UK notes prominently that 'more than one in three of us will develop cancer at some point. Few of us go through life without coming into contact with the disease in some way—either through personal experience or through that of a friend or family member'.

Development charities sometimes find ways of introducing personal contact between the donor and the needy. Charities that enable the donor to sponsor a child's education are one example. (We have already noted the 'warm glow' that this may generate.) This also scores highly on the criterion of meeting long-term need and may appeal especially to educated higher-income donors. However, such schemes are not without their critics. They risk creating inequalities within families and within local communities, and they may perpetuate a patriarchal relationship between North and South.

What about motives for giving in-kind? A lot of volunteering provides personal contact with the recipient, but typically this will only be the case when the gift of time benefits a local cause. An exception is when a person volunteers to go and work in a developing country, organized for example by the US Peace Corps, the UK charity Voluntary Service Overseas, or UN Volunteers. However, the opportunities for doing this are obviously limited and the commitment of time is huge compared to that involved with most local volunteering.

The final motive to consider, identified in both the economic and marketing literatures on philanthropy, is the notion of obtaining visibility or standing in one's social group or in society at large. This may be particularly important for super-rich donors. (Think of all the foundations named after their benefactors.) As we have emphasized earlier, the motives and donor behaviour of the extreme upper tail of the income distribution need special treatment, and the very rich have indeed been the subject of considerable attention. Lundberg, in his 1960s investigation of *The Rich and the Super-Rich*, argued that 'the founding of foundations has the effect of altering opinion in an unsophisticated population, turning the supposed bad guy into a supposed good guy' (1968: 467–8). Conniff, in his recent *Natural History of the Rich*, argues for a more direct motive, reporting Ted Turner as saying 'the more good I do, the more the money has come in' (2003: 104). On this view, improving one's standing in society by a spectacularly large gift can have very positive effects for the donor.

The different motives and behaviour of the super-rich have clear potential for generating additional resources for development. Compared to small-scale donors, who may favour a local or national cause with which they can easily identify, the super-rich may be more likely to seek a global cause with a global stage as a return for their generosity—the chance to be seen worldwide as a benefactor of mankind. (This can be thought of as a material benefit that cannot be bought by smaller-scale donations.) Of course, this is unlikely to be their only motive. Notions of civic responsibility figure highly in the behaviour of some of the super-rich (the 'simple morality' listed at the start of this section), as may the idea that their money could really help overcome the immense challenges posed by human development in poor countries. (In this, the super-rich donor may simply be mirroring on a large scale the desire of the low-income donor to make a difference, which we argue above works against giving for long-term development.) This is not to argue that the super-rich will always favour international development in their philanthropic behaviour (and the evidence is clearly to the contrary) but it does mean that there may be significantly greater potential for international development to benefit from the behaviour of the super-rich than from the average donor.

However, there are also many aspects of development activity and the working systems of development agencies that discourage the wealthy potential donor. The super-rich will demand a high degree of accountability and feedback on how their money is used. They may also seek a high degree of involvement with the causes selected for support—they are rarely passive donors. Large intergovernmental bodies and international non-governmental organizaions (NGOs) have great difficulty delivering on both these requirements. Complex and decentralized systems of programme delivery make the right kind of specific and individualized feedback almost impossible. Governance structures may not permit the level of involvement that is sought. In Section 7.5, we describe the 'global funds' that have been set up by the G8 governments with the express purpose of brokering funds for development from the super-rich and other large donors. This has been done in a way that is intended to surmount problems of a lack of donor confidence.

To summarize: a range of motives affect philanthropic behaviour, and a consideration of the factors at play in donor decisionmaking helps one understand why the cause of development struggles at times to compete. Factors like scale and persistence of need, empathy and relationship to recipient do not work in favour of development. However, the possible motives of the super-rich provide some encouragement, although there are practical constraints here that need to be overcome.

7.4. GIVING TO THE UN

Why does the UN need money from private individuals at all—surely it receives its money from government contributions according to formulae that are laid down in international treaties? This is a misconception of the UN's organization and finances. The development activities of the UN take place through its autonomous agencies—the Children's Fund (UNICEF), the Development Programme (UNDP), the World Food Programme (WFP), the Food and Agriculture Organization (FAO), the World Health Organization (WHO), the Population Fund (UNFPA), and so on.[22] These agencies are not 'formula-funded' and each relies on voluntary contributions. The contributions come mainly from governments, but private individuals are another potential source.

What attractions do the UN agencies present to private donors? On the one hand, they may be seen as able to work with and maybe influence governments in ways that charities cannot. Their status as 'international organizations' and their senior staff's status as diplomats help in this respect. For the same reason, they may be able to convey more status on the large-scale donor. These are presumably the factors that led Ted Turner to give US$1 billion to the UN rather than to a large international charity.[23] However, the money was not given directly to the UN's development agencies but

[22] Technically the UN has agencies, funds, and programmes, each of which has slightly different status. We term all of them here as 'agencies'.

[23] The UN Foundation's website argues that 'Mr Turner chose the United Nations as the vehicle for his global gift because the UN alone provides the machinery to help find solutions to international challenges, and to deal with pressing concerns facing people everywhere' (www.unfoundation.org/about/about_overview.htm).

was used to set-up the UN Foundation, which then makes grants to UN agencies for specific projects within the Foundation's areas of interest. The Foundation's website notes that Turner chose the president of the board of directors and that he is also a member of the board himself.

The perceived power of the UN may encourage small-scale donors as well. However, as with large donors, perceptions of waste and bloated bureaucracy need to be overcome. Unlike Turner, the small donor cannot set up his or her own foundation and appoint its board to control where the money goes, although anyone in fact is free to contribute to the UN Foundation (via the Internet) and benefit from its independence from the agencies' control.[24] And 'brand' is likely to be more important for the small donor who may have difficulty in perceiving what the UN and its aims are, even at the level of the individual agency.

The problems of the UN in raising money from the household sector are underlined by considering the essentials of the process of private fundraising: selling 'conceptual goods' and interpreting a donor country's local culture in a way that helps sales. This requires the fundraiser to be closely in touch with the local market. But the UN and other international agencies exist outside of national structures, in the world of international civil service and intergovernmental relationships. Inevitably, this makes them out of touch with national societies from which they might raise money.

The implication is that, if UN agencies are to raise funds from households (and firms) at the national level, then they must have a national presence at the country level to do the job. The only agency with this in place is the Children's Fund, UNICEF, which has a system of 'national committees' in thirty-seven countries. These committees are *not* local branches of the UN agency. Rather, they are fully autonomous national charities that are in effect franchized by UNICEF to use the name and logo of the agency in order to raise money on its behalf. The national committees are able to pitch their fundraising in line with local custom (e.g. children help the US committee to raise money through 'trick or treat' at Halloween). As they are national charities, donations to the committees qualify for income tax deductions in countries where there is tax deductibility of charitable gifts, overcoming one of the problems that is present in cross-border philanthropy. UNICEF is, indeed, the only part of the UN to raise substantial sums of money from private individuals (leaving aside the money donated by Ted Turner). The national committees raised some US$380 million in 2001, net of administration costs, or about one-third of UNICEF's annual budget.[25]

The varying degree of success with which the national committees ('natcoms' in UNICEF parlance) raise money is illustrated in Figs 7.1 and 7.2. The analysis is restricted to the twenty-two committees in countries that are members of the

---

[24] See www.unfoundation.org/donate/donate.htm.

[25] By this we mean that the national committees transferred about US$380 million to UNICEF headquarters after taking into account all local expenditures on fundraising and administration (UNICEF Annual Report 2001). The amounts shown in Figs 7.1 and 7.2 refer to the same definition.

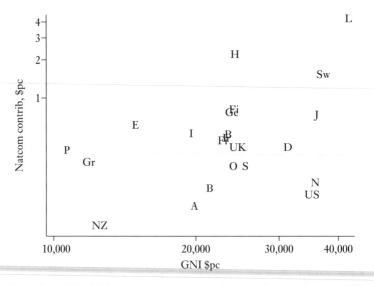

Figure 7.1. *UNICEF national committee contribution and national income, 2001 (US$ per capita)*

Source: UNICEF *Annual Report 2002* and World Bank (2003). The figure for New Zealand natcom contribution is for 2002 and was kindly provided by the natcom itself (the UNICEF *Annual Reports* for 2002 and 2003 do not include the full amounts for this country).

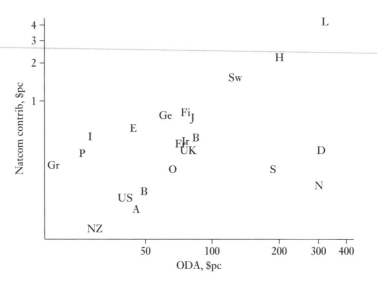

Figure 7.2. *UNICEF national committee contribution and official ODA, 2001 (US$ per capita)*

Source: UNICEF *Annual Report 2002* and OECD DAC website. See sources for Fig. 7.1 on the New Zealand natcom contribution.

OECD Development Assistance Committee (DAC).[26] Figure 7.1 plots the natcom contribution to UNICEF's funds in 2001 against national income, while Fig. 7.2 shows how this contribution varies with each country's level of official ODA, as measured by the DAC. All amounts are shown in US dollars per capita. The natcom contributions include resources raised from all sources except governments and hence include profits from trading (e.g. greeting card sales) and corporate (cash) contributions, but private donations should dominate the totals.

The range of natcom contributions is huge—from 9 cents per capita in New Zealand to nearly $4 in Luxembourg. These extremes and the Netherlands and Switzerland aside, other countries raised between 15 and 75 cents per capita. On average people in richer countries do give more to UNICEF than people in poorer countries. The elasticity estimated from the data implies that a 10 per cent increase in national income leads to a 10 per cent increase in giving, but the relationship is not well determined.[27] The natcoms' success in raising funds must depend in addition on various other factors, including national tastes for donating for development, competition from other child and development charities, and the size and professionalism of the natcoms' staff. For example, contributions to UNICEF and to Save the Children may be viewed by donors as close substitutes in countries where the latter organization is present.

One possibility is that private donations to natcoms are crowded-out by government contributions to UNICEF, households withholding their contributions in the face of government donations derived from their taxes. This would imply a degree of sophistication that we do not believe is present in the typical UNICEF donor (the vast majority of whom must be ignorant of the level of their government's contribution). But a negative association between government and private contributions could also be observed as a result of natcom behaviour, with some natcoms focusing on soliciting government funds on behalf of UNICEF (these do not enter the natcom figures in the graphs) rather than going all-out for private donations. In fact, the correlation between natcom contributions and government contributions to UNICEF turns out to be zero.

Figure 7.2 looks at what is probably a more interesting relationship—the association between the natcom contributions and total government ODA (official development assistance). Private individuals should be more aware of their government's over-all stance on overseas assistance than they are of government contributions to just UNICEF. There seems no obvious picture of crowding-out, and if anything the opposite. Natcom contributions are higher where ODA is higher.[28] Three Scandinavian countries are exceptions to the rule, with much lower natcom contributions than one would expect, given their levels of ODA. But these are all countries in which Save the Children is very active, raising much more money than UNICEF.

---

[26] These twenty-two committees account for over 95% of funds raised. The committees not included in Figs 7.1 and 7.2 are those in Central and Eastern European countries, Hong Kong, South Korea, Andorra, and San Marino.

[27] A regression of log natcom contribution on log GNI (gross national income) yields a slope coefficient of 0.97 with a standard error of 0.49 and a r-squared of 0.17.

[28] The correlation between log natcom contribution and log ODA is 0.47. (A regression of the former on the latter yields a slope parameter of 0.51 with standard error 0.21.)

Could other UN agencies emulate UNICEF and develop networks of national committees to collect funds? We do not see this as very feasible (although UNHCR is making moves in this direction). UNICEF's natcoms have three advantages: (i) children are a natural selling point; (ii) UNICEF is perceived as an agency that 'does' things (and the great majority of its staff do indeed work in developing countries rather than in New York or regional headquarters); and (iii) its history as a post-Second World War emergency relief organization in Western Europe.[29] Some of these are shared by other agencies, but the combination is probably unique.

7.5. SOME POSSIBLE WAYS FORWARD

Ways forward for increasing private donations for international development need to neutralize the limiting factors we have identified in earlier sections and to exploit what few advantages development may have in attracting funds. We do not attempt to list all possible ways for raising more donations of money or time. Rather, our purpose is to cover several areas that seem worthy of more thought or where prospects may be particularly encouraging.

7.5.1. *Tax Incentives to Donors*

We start with an old issue—the tax incentives for charitable giving. These have been the subject of intense investigation by economists since Vickery (1962) drew attention to the anomalous state of the treatment of donations in the United States. In contrast to other initiatives that try to change underlying attitudes towards giving, the aim here can be seen as more limited: to change individuals' budget constraints and in so doing stimulate more donations conditional on their existing preferences.

What is the particular angle here for development finance? First, in countries where charitable contributions do not benefit from deductibility for income tax purposes, development would share in the increased philanthropy that a more favourable tax treatment could induce. (The United Kingdom is an example of a country that has recently introduced a much more favourable tax treatment of donations.) There appears to be no special development angle in this case. But we have noted the absence of econometric estimates of the price elasticity of donations by cause. It is possible that donations to development are more price elastic than donations to other causes. And with a progressive income tax, development will benefit more from deductibility than other causes if the rich have a greater propensity to give for the needy in other countries, since the price of giving falls as an individual's marginal tax rate rises.

Second, governments could give more favourable tax treatment to donations to development. After all, the case for *any* donation attracting a deduction depends in part on whether it is aimed at furthering social objectives (e.g. Atkinson and Stiglitz 1980: 568). One could argue that governments have signed up to the MDGs in a way that

---

[29] The Italian UNICEF natcom website notes the number of Italian women and children helped by UNICEF in the late 1940s.

they have not to the aims of many domestic charities. There would be administrative difficulties in defining a qualifying donation. Charities could be classified as eligible according to a criterion of, for example, the share of expenditure directed to developing countries. Not only should this stimulate more donations to such charities, but it would provide an incentive to other charities to spend money abroad so as to satisfy the rules on qualification.[30] That such a scheme is feasible in practice is demonstrated by an example from the United Kingdom, in operation during 1998–2000 prior to the extension of tax deductibility to donations to all causes. To qualify, donations had to be to UK charities running projects in the areas of health, education, or poverty-relief in eighty countries eligible for IDA/IBRD funding from the World Bank.[31]

The case for tax deductions has always been seen to rest as well on the size of the price elasticity. With an elasticity greater than one in absolute size, the additional contributions induced by the tax deduction outweigh the loss in government revenue that the tax deduction implies. In this case, tax deductibility is an efficient way of channelling resources to good causes, compared to a situation where no deduction is given. Private individuals are induced to give more to charity by an extent that exceeds the amount of foregone tax revenue the government could have contributed to charities in the absence of the deduction. Curiously, there seems no mention of this in the case made for the recent tax changes in the United Kingdom, where the arguments seem based more on the notion of stimulating a culture of giving, that is, changing underlying attitudes (HM Treasury and Home Office 2002). Put optimistically, if 'herd behaviour' to donate more is induced as a result of just some individuals responding to the tax incentive, the long-run price elasticity for aggregate donations could exceed unity even if the individual level short-run elasticities do not.

One means of providing a tax deduction is through employers. This method of donation has the attraction to fundraisers of 'locking-in' the donor, if only due to the effort required to overcome inertia to discontinue payments once started. 'Payroll-giving' is widespread in the United States. By contrast, it is at a much lower level in the United Kingdom, for example, only 20 per cent of employees have access to a payroll-giving scheme and only about 2 per cent use it, a take-up rate of around 10 per cent compared to one of 35 per cent in the United States (HM Treasury and Home Office 2002: para 2.12; CAF Research 2003). Organizing payroll-giving schemes may also be seen as an example of 'corporate social responsibility' (see below).

7.5.2. *The Super-rich and the Global Funds*

Funds from the super-rich need to be attracted in ways that provide accountability and visibility for the donor. Setting up the UN Foundation was the route chosen by Ted Turner. But money from Bill Gates and others has been tempted into 'global funds'.

---

[30] Inducing domestic charities to take on a more international role might seem only a good thing: but the change would threaten their brand identity and hence their donations, as well as create substantial administrative costs as domestic charities sought international partners.

[31] The scheme was known as Millennium Gift Aid. See Inland Revenue Press Release 111/98 31 July 1998 (www.inlandrevenue.gov.uk/news/press.htm).

These have been set-up in the last few years with the express purpose of raising money from governments, private individuals, and the corporate sector in a way that avoids all these potential contributors' concerns with traditional ways of giving large sums of money to development, for example, direct to UN agencies. The funds, well described by Clunies-Ross (2003), include the Vaccine Fund/Global Alliance for Vaccines and Immunization (GAVI), the International Aids Vaccine Initiative (IAVI) and the Global Fund to Fight AIDS, Tuberculosis, and Malaria. But as the names indicate, these funds are exclusively in the area of health—there is no global fund to fight illiteracy, for example. Health seems especially attractive to a large donor looking for a problem that can be solved by funding a 'technical' solution.

A natural reaction when thinking of the super-rich is to look to the United States, as we have done in earlier sections of the chapter. But other countries also have many very rich people, including some where we have seen a greater propensity among the population at large to donate to development. Germany has the largest number of billionaires outside the United States. Next comes Japan. Perhaps these are countries where the super-rich need more courting. Surprisingly, after Germany, the European country with the highest number of billionaires is Russia where most of them made their fortunes in the 1990s by buying up the state oil industry when it was privatized.[32] Important as the global funds are, the job in capturing some of the wealth of the super-rich for international development is not just one of devising a suitable vehicle to receive it. The wealth needs to be actively courted wherever it exists.

One hope is that the super-rich may compete for attention in their gifts so that imitative behaviour results in positive spillovers. Conniff (2003) argues that Ted Turner's gift helped prod Bill Gates into action.

7.5.3. *New Forms of Corporate Giving*

We noted in the Introduction that cash donations by corporations to charitable causes are minor compared to those by households and they seem likely to stay that way, at least in the form that they have often taken in the past. The future of giving by firms is seen by many to be in two areas: 'cause-related marketing', which started in earnest in the 1980s, and 'corporate social responsibility', which has attracted a lot of recent interest. An international development angle can be identified in both cases.

These forms of corporate giving have grown for two main reasons. First, businesses have recognized that positive use of ethical messages can benefit their brands. Associating a product with a 'good cause' helps sales. The natural choice of good cause for a multinational firm may be a development charity.

Second, firms are increasingly aware that their reputation for social responsibility—in broad terms—is an important asset, to be developed and maintained from their core budgets rather than from a peripheral benevolence fund. Seventy per cent of people interviewed in a poll conducted in twelve European countries in 2000 said

---

[32] See www.bbc.co.uk/worldservice/learningenglish/news/words/business/030228_witn.shtml and www.forbes.com/free_forbes/2003/0317/087.html.

that a company's commitment to social responsibility was important to them when buying a product or service and around half said they would be willing to pay more for products that are environmentally and socially responsible.[33] Global corporations working in developing countries have realized that they have to be particularly careful in this regard. There is now greater awareness among the public in rich countries of their activities and their employees' working conditions due to various factors including investigative journalism and improvements in communications via the Internet.

Multinationals have always had an interest in improving the education, health, and other aspects of the living standards of their developing country workforces, although this may have been muted when their demand was largely for unskilled labour that was in abundant supply. This interest now works in constructive combination with the public pressure that companies increasingly feel from their customer base in rich countries. Customers and the media are now much more sensitive to issues around the exploitation of labour by multinationals, for example, the alleged use in the past of child workers by Nike and Gap.

Cause-related marketing is 'a commercial activity by which businesses and charities or causes form a partnership with each other to market an image, product or service for mutual benefit' (Business in the Community 2002). Carrying a charity logo or associating with a charity in some other way is simply another form of product differentiation under imperfect competition. And buying products and services with these logos or other association is argued to be an 'easy, quick and efficient method for consumers to support charities and good causes whilst going about their daily routine' (Business in the Community 2002). Some might argue that it is too quick and easy—with the 'warm glow' of donation emphasized in the economic theory of philanthropy coming for too small an effort (i.e. the cost of purchase to the consumer of the warm-glow is made too small).[34]

The sums that are currently raised for international development by cause-related marketing are unclear. In the United Kingdom, Business in the Community has identified over £30 million for all causes during 2001 (not including the value of the advertising achieved in the process for the charities concerned). But the top ten charities that benefited are all domestic in purpose. This presumably reflects companies' perceptions that most people want to help domestic rather than international causes, as we have seen earlier to be the case with households' cash donations. One international example expressly benefiting development is the Change for Good scheme in which international airlines collect leftover coins and notes for UNICEF from their passengers. This has raised US$44 million since 1991 (UNICEF 2003: 31).

---

[33] See www.mori.com/pubinfo/pdf/csrupdate.pdf. The same source contains examples of corporate executives' responses to surveys in which they recognize the consumer concern. See also www2.bitc.org.uk/resources/research/statbank.

[34] Cause-related marketing illustrates the fact that corporate and household sector giving are not always separable—this is giving that results from the combined action of individuals and firms. This includes situations where the firm donates following a private individual's action, as is the case for example with the Hunger Site, and those where the individual donates within a framework organized by a firm, as in Change for Good.

'Corporate social responsibility' could cover a very wide range of possible activities and many firms, including multinationals working in developing countries, now express an open commitment to behaviour that would seem encouraging for the cause of international development. (See, for example, the 'business principles' listed on the Shell website.)[35] However, the interpretation of what this implies needs leadership within the development arena so as to maximize the return from the apparent willingness to act. Capacity is also needed at the local level within developing countries.

One example of global leadership is the Global Alliance for Improved Nutrition (GAIN), which establishes national food fortification networks. GAIN operates as a power broker to get the multinational food companies to adopt goals that local and national companies actually set and share. The aim in effect is to lock a multinational corporation into a national plan that is beyond its own goals.

The cynic might argue that a cover of 'social responsibility' may allow corporations to interpret development policy in the way that suits them best and such fears may be natural in view of past exploitation. However, we tend towards the pragmatic view that there can be benefits for all if corporations are not treated like the enemy, and we see this as a largely untapped resource for development with important potential. While cause-related marketing may generate extra cash to meet the cost of reaching the MDGs, corporate social responsibility might be seen as reducing that cost.

7.5.4. *The Internet*

Continued growth in the use of the Internet can benefit development giving in at least four ways. First, the Internet helps global communication and the provision of information about the needs of developing countries. (An example is OneWorld.net.) We have noted how this may increase the pressure on firms to act in socially responsible ways. It should also help development education more broadly (see below).

Second, online giving is an additional method of delivering a cash donation to a charity. The effort needed to donate in this way is in general less than that with postal donations or those made via the telephone. The donor's transaction costs in the broad sense are reduced. While online giving benefits all charitable causes (and the same is true of online charity auctions), international development might arguably benefit more due to the inherently global nature of the Internet. There is no physical border to overcome in this form of cross-border giving. For example, we noted earlier that anyone can donate to the UN Foundation online. On the other hand, residents of countries with tax-deductibility for charitable donations will typically be unable to deduct a direct cross-border donation. (The World Food Programme circumvents this problem for US citizens by directing the donor to the US Friends of the WFP while

---

[35] Available at: www.shell.com/home/Framework?siteId=shellreport2002–en. Under the heading 'Social performance' elsewhere in the website, Shell argues that 'wherever we work we are part of a local community. We will constantly look for appropriate ways to contribute to the general wellbeing of the community and the broader societies that grant our licence to operate'. As part of this, about US$40 million was spent by individual Shell companies on 'social investment' in low- and middle-income countries in 2002.

the main UNICEF website invites donors to go to the site of their country's natcom.) Removing such blocks to cross-border giving would be a useful step, although many donors may still prefer to give to a domestic branch of an international charity on grounds of trust.

Third, the Internet also provides another medium for donation of time, through 'online volunteering'. In this case, an even more obvious constraint to cross-border giving is removed. The organization NetAid works with UN Volunteers to enable people in industrialized countries (or indeed anywhere) to contribute their time to work on development projects from home. NetAid brings together individuals wanting to volunteer with organizations needing labour.

Fourth, there are the 'click for good' websites. The individual clicks on a button and a sponsoring firm makes a donation to a named charity, typically worth a few US cents.[36] This is a form of cause-related marketing and the site itself may in fact be run for profit. Again, these schemes can benefit all causes but one of the most successful, which is said to have inspired others, was originally aimed firmly at international development: the Hunger Site. Visits to the Hunger Site raised US$0.5 million for the World Food Programme in 1999 and US$2.6 million in 2000—with an average of nearly 8 million visits per month.[37] However, the history of the site also illustrates the shifting nature of this form of funding. The Hunger Site changed hands in 2001. Funds raised are now split between two charities working to alleviate hunger—one of them solely in the United States. The Hunger Site still receives over 3 million visits per month (and the sister site the Child Health site, which largely benefits the developing world, about 2 million visits) but the amount of food donated in 2002 as a result was less than a third of that in 2000.[38]

7.5.5. *Donor Education*

One long-term objective of the development charities must be to change donor preferences towards giving for international development (as distinct from lobbying for changes to their budget constraints via tax deductions or by reducing their transaction costs via expansion of online donation). The importance of 'donor education' has long been recognized in, for example, the United Kingdom where investment in advocacy campaigns by the large development charities (e.g. Oxfam, Save the Children, Action Aid, and the UNICEF Natcom) has been partly justified on these grounds. The hope is that a sense of global responsibility will be encouraged by educating the public on the complex inter-relationships between the north and south (including perhaps that

[36] Summaries and lists of click for good sites can be found for example at www.quickdonations.com/ and dir.yahoo.com/society_and_culture/issues_and_causes/philanthropy/free_donations/.

[37] Statistics on visits to the Hunger Site and its sister sites are from www.thehungersite.com. The sums raised for the World Food Programme (WFP) are given in annual reports available from www.wfp.org.

[38] Figures for visits refer to 2003. The owners' more recent Animal Rescue site, devoted to animal welfare in the United States, became their leader during 2003 with over 3.5 million visits per month. In June 2003 the Hunger Site provided 198 tons of food for people while the Animal Rescue Site provided 530 tons for animals.

'misery breeds hate') and by challenging the traditional views of charitable giving as passive handouts from the powerful to the powerless.

Advocacy campaigns by charities are entirely complementary to the aim of changing public attitudes so as to support higher tax-financed government spending on ODA. McDonnell *et al.* (2003: 15) argue that more is being done in OECD countries by charities to inform the public about development cooperation than is done by governments. Not surprisingly, government spending on development information varies substantially from country to country. While the US government spent less than 1 US cent per capita in 2001, and several other countries (including Germany, France, Japan and Italy) spent less than 10 cents, Belgium, the Netherlands, Denmark, Norway, and Sweden all spent more than $1 (McDonnell *et al.* 2003: figure 2). Television is probably the primary medium through which people receive information about development, so trends in the amount and content of television coverage are important. In the United Kingdom, there has been a long-term decline in factual coverage of developing world issues since the late 1980s.[39] Media coverage of developing countries is also reported to have fallen in Italy (McDonnell *et al.* 2003: 13).

Investment in 'education for development' among young people through the formal school system has been considered by some to hold particular potential. The belief is that promoting a change in behaviour among the older generation may be a losing battle but that young people can be encouraged to see that tackling the extremes of global inequality is essential for the future survival of the planet. School age children obviously make only very small contributions to charity but, if their commitment to global development causes is won, the young are likely to demonstrate great longevity as donors. And some of them will grow up to hold influence in politics and business and be able to exert power in favour of development objectives. Investment in educating (and courting) the super-rich may also be sensible.

7.6. CONCLUSIONS

Faced with an estimated cost each year of US$50 billion for meeting the MDGs, there is a temptation to dismiss private donations as a marginal source of funding. Even Ted Turner's endowment of US$1 billion seems small compared to the extent of the need, while such sums as the US$4 million per year raised by UNICEF's Change for Good may appear tiny. But taken together, the sums currently being given from all sources, big and small, are substantial. Our 'back of the envelope' estimate is about US$17 billion from the OECD countries for 2001, which may be compared with the total for their ODA in that year of US$52 billion (although we stress that the former is a very rough guess while the latter is a fact).[40] We have also identified a number

---

[39] This is the conclusion of a series of reports from the Third World and Environmental Broadcasting Project, 3WE (available at: www.epolitix.com/forum/3we?default.htm).

[40] These figures both refer to the DAC countries only. Our figure of US$17 billion for private donations assumes that the share of national income going to all forms of charity is 0.5% (other than in countries where we have a better estimate: Germany 0.25%, Netherlands 1.0%, United Kingdom 0.7%, and the United States 1.5%). We then assume that development gets 15% of these total donations (again with variation

of possibilities for expansion. Were these to produce an increase of 30 per cent in the total given for development, then our estimate of the current level of donations implies that US$5 billion of the estimated US$50 billion needed would be raised. And even if this total seems relatively minor compared to the need, private donations play an important psychological role. Individuals' example may encourage governments to be more generous.

If private donations stimulate government generosity, then notions of crowding-out of donations for development by ODA are way off the mark, both in terms of the sign of the association and the direction of causality. However, this is not something we have been able to assess properly. (Our data show UNICEF donations and ODA to be positively correlated, but more investigation is needed, taking donations to other organizations into account as well.)

Private donations are also likely to be affected by some other forms of development finance covered in the UNU-WIDER project on Innovative Sources for Development Finance. In the case of an international lottery, considered by Addison and Chowdhury (Chapter 8, this volume), the impact might be negative, with lottery ticket purchasers reducing their direct donations to 'good causes'. (This possibility was the subject of much discussion when the United Kingdom introduced a national lottery in the 1990s.) In the case of remittances, dealt with by Solimano (Chapter 9, this volume), it is more a question of the dividing line being blurred. Where an individual migrant sends money to his or her relatives back home, this is clearly a remittance. The status is less clear for organized donations from associations of the South's diaspora who are resident in the North, for example, expatriate Bangladeshi communities.[41] Such associations are structures outside of the main development charities and are an important and under-researched resource. A migrant may stimulate donations from others as well as remit to his or her own family.

This leads logically to our final comment: it is important to repeat our warning in the introduction that the chapter concentrates on donations from the North, to the exclusion of domestic philanthropy in the South. A complete appraisal of the potential for private donations to help the funding of the MDGs would clearly cover both North and South.

REFERENCES

Andreoni, J. (1998). 'Toward a Theory of Charitable Fund Raising'. *Journal of Political Economy*, 106: 1186–213.
—— (2001). 'The Economics of Philanthropy', in N. J. Smelser and P. B. Baltes (eds), *The International Encyclopedia of the Social and Behavioral Sciences*. London: Elsevier, 11369–76. Available at: www.ssc.wisc.edu/~andreoni/ Publications/IESBS-Andreoni.pdf.

where we have better estimates or reason to assume a different figure: Germany 50%, Japan 10%, UK 25%, United States 3.5%).

[41] See www.eb2000.org/. Another example is the African Foundation for Development (www.afford-uk.org).

Anheier, H. K., and R. List (eds) (2000). *Cross-Border Philanthropy*. West Malling: Charities Aid Foundation.

Atkinson, A. B. (2002). 'Top Incomes in the United Kingdom over the Twentieth Century'. *Discussion Paper* 43 in Economic and Social History. Oxford: University of Oxford.

——, and J. Stiglitz (1980). *Lectures in Public Economics*. New York: McGraw-Hill.

Boulding, K. (1962). 'Notes on a Theory of Philanthropy', in F. Dickinson (ed.), *Philanthropy and Public Policy*. Cambridge, MA: National Bureau of Economic Research.

Bundesarbeitsgemeinschaft Sozialmarketing-Deutscher Fundraising Verband (2002). 'Zahlen zum Fundraising in Deutschland'. 6 February. Frankfurt: BSM–Deutscher Fundraising Verband.

Business in the Community (2002). 'Is there a Revolution in 21st Century Giving?'. 9 July. Available at: www2.bitc.org.uk/news/news_directory/21stcgiving.html .

Charities Aid Foundaton (CAF) Research (2003). 'Payroll Giving 2001–02 Update'. *Dimensions Online Briefing Paper*. London: Charities Aid Foundation. Available at: www.cafonline.org/research.

Clotfelter, C. (1997). 'The Economics of Giving', in J. Barry and B. Manno (eds), *Giving Better, Giving Smarter*. Washington, DC: National Commission on Philanthropy and Civic Renewal. Available at: www.pubpol.duke.edu/people/faculty/clotfelter/giving.pdf .

Clunies-Ross, A. (2003). 'Resources for Social Development'. Paper prepared for the World Commission on the Social Dimensions of Globalization. ILO, Geneva.

Conniff, R. (2003). *A Natural History of the Rich: A Field Guide*. London: William Heinemann.

Helmich, H. (2003). 'The Netherlands', in I. McDonnell, H.-B. Solignac Lecomte, and L. Wegimont (eds), *Public Opinion and the Fight against Poverty*. Paris: OECD.

HM Treasury and Home Office (2002). *Next Steps on Volunteering and Giving in the UK: A Discussion Document*. London: The Stationary Office.

Lundberg, F. (1968). *The Rich and the Super-Rich*. New York: Bantam Books.

McDonnell, I., H.-B. Solignac Lecomte, and L. Wegimont (2003). 'Public Opinion Research, Global Education and Development Co-operation Reform: In Search of a Virtuous Circle'. *Webdocs* No. 10. Paris: OECD Development Centre. Available at: www.oecd.org/dev/technics.

Mullin, R. (2002). 'The Evolution of Charitable Giving', in C. Walker and C. Pharoah (eds), *A Lot of Give. Trends in Charitable Giving for the 21st Century*. London: Hodder & Stoughton.

National Council for Voluntary Organizations (NCVO) (2002). 'Charitable Giving in 2001'. *Inside Research*, June (16).

OECD (2003). Development Assistance Committee website. Available at: www.oecd.org/xls/M00037000/M00037875.xls. Accessed 10 April 2003.

Pharoah, C. and S. Tanner (1997). 'Trends in Charitable Giving'. *Fiscal Studies*, 18(4): 427–43.

Piketty, T. and E. Saez (2003). 'Income Inequality in the United States'. *Quarterly Journal of Economics*, 118(1): 1–40.

Salamon, L. and W. Sokolowski (2001). 'Volunteering in Cross-National Perspective: Evidence from 24 Countries'. *Working Papers of the Johns Hopkins Comparative Nonprofit Sector Project* No. 40. Baltimore: The Johns Hopkins Center for Civil Society Studies.

——, H. Anheier, R. List, S. Toepler, W. Sokolowski *et al.* (1999). *Global Civil Society: Dimensions of the Nonprofit Sector*. Baltimore: The Johns Hopkins Center for Civil Society Studies.

Sargeant, A. (1999). 'Charitable Giving: Towards a Model of Donor Behaviour'. *Journal of Marketing Management*, 12: 215–38.

UNICEF (various years). *Annual Report*, for various years. New York: UNICEF.

Vickery, W. (1962). 'One Economist's View of Philanthropy', in F. Dickinson (ed.), *Philanthropy and Public Policy*. Cambridge, MA: National Bureau of Economic Research.

World Bank (2003). *World Development Indicators.* Available at: www.devdata.worldbank.org/data-query: Accessed 31 March 2003.

8

A Global Lottery and a Global Premium Bond

TONY ADDISON AND ABDUR R. CHOWDHURY

8.1. INTRODUCTION

The use of lotteries by national and local/regional governments to raise funds for public sector and charity projects is now commonplace across the world. In 2001, there were at least 177 public (national and local government) lotteries in operation, with combined sales amounting to over US$120 billion (see Table 8.1). Given the scale of the revenues raised, it is natural to ask whether lotteries could also be used to provide funds for global development programmes. Proposals to establish a global lottery to fund UN development activities have circulated since at least the early 1970s. In 1994, Erskine Childers and Brian Urquhart proposed that: 'One possibility for income moving more directly to the UN—but still with government licensing in each country—would be an annual United Nations Lottery, administered by a special authority under the Secretary-General' (Childers and Urquhart 1994: 155). The idea of a global lottery has recently been given a major impetus by a former President of Finland, Mr Martti Ahtisaari, together with the Finnish NGO (non-governmental organization), Crisis Management Initiative (CMI), and the Ministry for Foreign Affairs of Finland.

In this chapter, we evaluate proposals for a global lottery. We also propose a complement to the global lottery, namely a global premium bond (which we dub the 'global ERNIE', after the UK's long-running premium bond scheme). The return on both a lottery ticket and a premium bond depends on a random prize draw but, unlike a lottery ticket, a buyer of a premium bond does not lose the initial stake: consequently this instrument has the characteristics of a savings product, making it potentially attractive to ethical investors.

Paper prepared for the UN-DESA and UNU-WIDER project on 'Innovative Sources for Development Finance' directed by Tony Atkinson, Nuffield College, University of Oxford. We thank Tony Atkinson, John Micklewright, David Mayes, and Antti Pentikäinen as well as other participants in the first project meeting and the conference 'Sharing Global Prosperity' (Helsinki, September 2003) for useful comments on earlier drafts. Hirut Arega-Pentikäinen provided excellent research assistance. Helpful points arose in discussions with Tilman Brück, Alberta Hagan, Ian Kinniburgh, Mark McGillivray, and Adam Swallow. Any remaining errors are our own. The views expressed are those of the authors alone, and should not necessarily be attributed to UN-DESA, UNU-WIDER, or UN-ECE.

Table 8.1. *World lottery sales by region, 1996–2001 (US$ millions)*

	Africa	Asia & Middle East	Australia & New Zealand	Europe	North America	Central & South America	Total
1996	289.0	14,900.0	2,888.7	56,274.4	42,394.3	3,951.9	120,698.3
1997	280.0	14,300.0	2,600.0	55,000.0	42,600.0	4,200.0	118,980.0
1998	272.8	13,391.0	2,334.8	61,246.6	42,825.6	4,114.9	124,185.7
1999	190.8	14,561.6	2,469.5	63,481.1	43,607.4	3,738.3	128,048.7
2000	289.0	36,200.0	3,100.0	54,455.5	45,997.0	na	140,041.5
2001	621.6	16,649.7	2,039.4	54,821.5	49,390.0	2,888.9	126,411.1

Source: The Gaming Industry News Site, available at: www.lotteryinsider.com.au/stats/world.htm.

The structure of the chapter is as follows. Section 8.2 discusses how a global lottery might work and evaluates the issues in the following sub-sections: lottery operators and their regulation (8.2.1), the market for lotteries (8.2.2), competition between the global lottery and national lotteries (8.2.3), the challenge posed by Internet gambling (8.2.4), revenue-raising potential (8.2.5), cross-county equity (8.2.6), distributional and welfare effects (8.2.7), ethical issues (8.2.8), and development education (8.2.9). Section 8.3 discusses the potential for a global premium bond; we summarize the UK scheme as a model for a global version (8.3.1) and we set out the modalities of a global premium bond and highlight its differences with a global lottery (8.3.2). We conclude (Section 8.4) that global versions of both a lottery and a premium bond are viable and complementary in mobilizing more development finance.

8.2. A GLOBAL LOTTERY

How would a global lottery function? Discussions of a global lottery yield two basic possibilities. The first is for national lotteries to run national versions of the global lottery game. The second is a single global lottery sold worldwide and run by one organization. The proposal developed by the CMI, hereafter referred to as the CMI proposal, adopts the first approach (see Ahde *et al.* 2002). As far as we know, the second approach has not been formally proposed by anyone, but it comes up in discussion because of the possibilities now offered by the Internet. In both versions an agreed international framework is necessary to regulate the lottery organizer(s) and to transfer the money into a global lottery fund to be run by the UN or another agency (and distributed from there to programmes engaged in development and the provision of global public goods).[1]

---

[1] On global public goods see Kaul *et al.* (2003).

Lottery products consist of games such as Lotto where the winners are determined by a random draw of numbers, conducted at regular intervals (often weekly in national lotteries) and instant products such as ticket lotteries ('scratch cards') and video lottery terminals (electronic games of chance often simulating popular casino games). A national Lotto game is organizationally more complex and requires more infrastructure than instant games (for this reason, the CMI proposal argues for the introduction of instant ticket lotteries first and a Lotto game at a later stage). Lottery proceeds are divided between winning players, administrative costs, and beneficiaries. In state lotteries in the United States, the proportions are roughly 40–50 per cent (winners), 15–20 per cent (administration), and 30–45 per cent (beneficiaries) (Clotfelter and Cook 1989: 164–5) and the proportions are roughly similar in European lotteries. A key issue for the global lottery is whether to share some of the beneficiaries' portion with national beneficiaries before transferring any money to a global lottery fund. This is a feature of the CMI proposal, which argues that otherwise a global lottery, in competing against national lotteries, may be opposed by governments and national charities. We return to the issue of competition between the global lottery and national lotteries later in the chapter.

National legislatures would be subject to lobbying for and against the global lottery and national debates would inevitably (and rightly) raise questions regarding the basic structure of the global lottery as well as its objectives and ethics. This needs to be paralleled by a well-structured and focused international debate, and international civil society has become very active on issues of international finance in recent years.

Before proceeding further, we must note several other lottery possibilities which are distinct from the global lottery itself. The first is to make development a beneficiary of existing national lotteries. The second is to liberalize national lottery markets in developed countries to permit the marketing of developing-country lotteries. The third is for a developing country (or group of countries) to create their own world lottery product, with themselves as the main beneficiaries. We do not discuss these options in this chapter, but if properly organized they could provide further sources of development finance in addition to the global lottery.

Having set the scene, we now turn to the issues in detail, including our evaluation of the global lottery and its possible *modus operandi*.

8.2.1. *Lottery Operators and Their Regulation*

National lottery operators range from government agencies and state-owned corporations (as in Sweden) to private corporations, licensed and regulated by government (as in the United Kingdom). About one-third of the world's lotteries are government agencies, and two-thirds are private corporations operating under licence or corporations owned by local or national governments. Accordingly, there is a range of options regarding private versus public providers—whichever version of the global lottery is adopted (the single global lottery or national global lotteries).

The alternative merits of private versus public lottery operation have been extensively debated; older lotteries are often state-run, but newer lotteries tend to be private operators who hold the license until the next round of competitive tendering (the United Kingdom, a latecomer to national lotteries, opted for private operation on the grounds that it would raise more revenue than a state-run lottery). If the global lottery is put out to competitive tender for private operation, then the process must be transparent and well regulated. Competitive tendering captures some of the monopoly rents associated with being a lottery provider, thereby raising the amount generated for beneficiaries (development programmes in the case of the global lottery). However, in countries where private operators hold the market monopoly for a fixed period, a national version of the global lottery could not be introduced until the expiry (or renegotiation) of their licenses. Current as well as prospective lottery providers would inevitably lobby to influence the process by which a global lottery is introduced.

It is imperative to run the global lottery efficiently and honestly. This requires a governance structure—to set policy in an overall framework of objectives—as well as regulatory mechanisms. Regulation is by no means straightforward, and economics now has much to say on such problems as 'regulatory capture'. Regulating a single global lottery provider, but with a worldwide operation, is obviously a different challenge to regulating numerous, but national, providers of a global lottery. If the single global provider sells the lottery through the Internet, then the issue of regulation becomes bound up with the larger issue of how to effectively regulate e-commerce (Clarke and Dempsey 2001; O'Connor 2003). If the national variant of the global lottery is chosen, then national lottery operators will fall under the purview of national regulatory authorities, but these vary considerably in their effectiveness. Hence, national regulatory authorities must be overseen by an international authority to ensure that the high standards of a global lottery are met. The World Lottery Association (WLA), a respected international organization with a large membership of national and state lotteries, could play an important role in this regard. Whatever form of international regulatory system is chosen, it must have the ability to impose sanctions and to deregister national global lotteries, which fail to meet the required standards. This will necessitate the creation of a suitable legal framework. And international bodies such as the UN will have to exercise final oversight.

8.2.2. *The Market for Lotteries*

In a Lotto game, players buy tickets where they choose n numbers from a possible available N numbers and winners receive a share of the prize pool; the design of the game affects the mean, variance and skewness of the prize distribution (Walker and Young 2001: 703; Garrett and Sobel 2002). Empirical evidence shows that ticket sales are an increasing function of the skewness of the prize distribution; players display a preference for games with very few large prizes and some small prizes (Creigh-Tyte and Farrell 1998: 4; Walker and Young 2000: 15). This 'long-shot' bias is evident in other types of gambling (Forrest 2003). Empirical studies show that rollovers (when nobody wins the top prize and the jackpot is added to the jackpot of the next draw) raise sales not only for the draw in question but also for successive draws (Farrell *et al.* 1999). This is referred to as the 'halo' effect in the industry. Most lotteries suffer from 'fatigue'; once the initial excitement of the launch wears off, revenues tend to stagnate or even decline (Creigh-Tyte and Farrell 2003). Periodic redesigns of lotteries are often used to raise excitement and bolster flagging sales—for instance reducing the probability of jackpot winners (e.g. by raising N) thereby making rollovers more likely.

Since the *expected* return is lower than the stake, lottery-ticket purchases have puzzled economists and non-pecuniary motives have been much emphasized (Farrell and Hartley 1998). There is a tendency to focus on *altruism* as a motive for buyers if the lottery funds 'good causes', as with the proposed global lottery or the existing UK national lottery. It is certainly the case that charity-run lotteries can raise size-able sums; in the United States about US$6 billion is raised annually in this way, while UK charities derive 8 per cent of their income from their own lotteries (Douglas 1995; Morgan 2000). But some of this may simply be substitution from other forms of charitable giving; there is no evidence on *additionality*. Evidence on whether the use of funds affects the demand for lottery products is decidedly mixed. In the case of the UK national lottery, 'there is no evidence to suggest that play would be sensitive to the distribution of funds even though individuals may express disapproval over it' (Walker and Young 2000: 29). However, the US state-governments, which earmark lottery proceeds to public goods (e.g. to education), have higher average per capita lottery expenditures than the states which do not (Morgan 2000). And experimental evidence—whereby laboratory participants are asked to choose between lotteries—shows that changes in the desirability of the public good significantly affect gambling behaviour, with gambling falling as the desirability of the offered good falls (Morgan and Sefton 2000). The public goods provided by US state-lotteries benefit many players personally (e.g. as parents). This effect may arise for global lottery players in developing countries, but for players in developed countries it may be of little importance unless development education convinces them that the global lottery will fund global public goods that benefit them personally (see Section 8.2.9 on development education).

In summary, it appears that the global lottery will face the same design issues as existing lotteries if the objective is to maximize revenues, that is, skew the prize structure towards a few large prizes and encourage rollovers to combat lottery fatigue. The development and global public goods funded by the global lottery will attract people (who we shall call 'global altruists') who are motivated by a desire to help poor countries and combat world problems. And the global lottery's design will determine its entertainment value relative to other lotteries and other forms of gambling, and its entertainment characteristics will significantly affect sales. However, we have not yet finished discussing the market for the global lottery since there is the important issue of competition between the global lottery and national lotteries, to which we must now turn.

8.2.3. *Competition Between the Global Lottery and National Lotteries*

Running right through the debate is a concern that the global lottery may take too much market share from existing national lotteries, leading to opposition by the beneficiaries of existing lotteries (national charities as well as regional and central governments).

The fear is, therefore, that the global lottery may never get off the ground. Such opposition can certainly be vocal. In the United Kingdom, for instance, charities lobbied hard against the introduction of a national lottery in 1994, fearing its effects on their own charity-lotteries as well as charitable donations overall (UK Parliament 2001). A global lottery would also take market share from private gambling operators; these might be considered 'fair game' for competition—especially when they are unregulated and untaxed Internet operations (see next section). However, the taxation of licensed gambling provides substantial revenue (especially for state governments in Australia and the United States). Private commercial operators will therefore have powerful political friends to lobby against the global lottery's introduction.

Recall that the mean, variance, and skewness of the prize distribution all affect lottery demand, with the empirical evidence showing that ticket buyers prefer higher mean, lower variance, and skewness towards very large prizes (Clotfelter and Cook 1989; Walker and Young 2000: 25). For buyers the global lottery may be more (or less) attractive than competing lotteries along some or all of these moments of the prize-distribution.[2] Moreover, if a single global lottery is run through the Internet, it will have large economies of scale and its administrative costs will be lower than the aggregate of the administrative costs of existing national lotteries. It would, therefore, have more money to distribute as prizes, another factor giving the global lottery a competitive edge.[3] Hence, in order to reduce opposition by stakeholders in national lotteries to the global lottery's introduction, it would be necessary to reduce the size of the top prize and the frequency of rollovers (by increasing the odds of winning the top prize). If the global lottery is adjusted in this way, then it will not maximize sales or funds for development, given what we know about the demand for lottery products.

One extra twist arises when the global lottery takes the form of national versions rather than a single globally marketed version. If a national version of the global lottery is designed to have the same prize distribution as the existing national lottery (in order to equalize its attractiveness), then national versions of the global lottery will have different prize distributions *across* countries since the prize distributions of national lotteries show cross-country variation. If the differences in the distributions of national global lotteries are significantly large, and the transactions costs of cross-border purchase are low, then buyers may prefer to purchase another country's version of the global lottery. There already exist cross-border 'grey markets' in national lotteries, despite national legal prohibitions (e.g. intermediaries sell UK national lottery tickets at a premium in

---

[2] Assessing the attractiveness of different lotteries to ticket buyers is complicated by the fact that the comparison is between different prize distributions, and not just over the mean prize (given that buyers are influenced by variance and skewness of the distribution in addition to the mean). Such comparisons therefore face the same issues encountered in comparing, for example, distributions of household income and expenditure.

[3] Note that a single monopoly lottery can maximize its revenues by offering a very large jackpot but if a new entrant into a field with a number of existing lotteries attempts to maximize revenues in this way, it will face retaliation; for example, existing lotteries will raise their maximum prize above the level offered by the new entrant, and will reduce the number of smaller prizes. Some existing national lotteries might respond in this way to the introduction of a global lottery.

Hong Kong). Hence, national lotteries could lose revenues even if their own national global lottery is designed to give an equivalent return.[4]

Any opposition to the global lottery may be reduced if the formula for distributing the resulting global lottery funds (together with their use) are perceived to be in national interests, particularly when global concerns regarding the environment, health and security are seen as bearing on national interests (Section 8.2.6 below discusses the formula). Moreover, if a single global lottery had jackpots sufficiently large to attract pure gamblers, then it might take substantial market shares away from private commercial gambling (which is a US$1 trillion market, Gaming Board for Great Britain 2003); this would then permit generous 'compensation' to national causes that lose market share to the global lottery.

In summary, to get the necessary support to sell the global lottery in national markets, it is probably the case that the global lottery has to be designed so that it does not maximize sales. Nevertheless, it could still raise significant amounts given the size of the world market for gambling products (and the expected growth in that market).

8.2.4. *The Challenge Posed by Internet Gambling*

The first proposals for a global lottery arose before the Internet age. However, the revolution in information and communications technologies (ICT) is transforming the gambling industry, and this is challenging traditional gambling products including lotteries (the Internet reduces the transaction costs of gambling, especially across borders, and it offers new products which are attractive to gamblers).

A report undertaken for the UK Home Office by the Gaming Board for Great Britain estimates that Internet gambling contributes some US$32 billion to an annual global gambling turnover of close to US$1 trillion (a market share of about 3.2 per cent); online lotteries account for US$7.5 billion of the US$32 billion (Gaming Board for Great Britain 2003, data for 2001). Most of the online lotteries are run by private operators for private profit, although charities are now moving into this area. The growth of online lotteries (and online gambling) is not confined to developed countries. Indian states such as Maharashtra and Sikkim now operate competing online lotteries using public computer terminals, and private companies compete vigorously for the business of setting up and running India's online state lotteries (BBC 2002*a*).

Table 8.2 shows the wide range of countries, which provide a base for online gambling. Much of the online gambling is lightly regulated, if at all, and private operators tend to base themselves in jurisdictions with the least regulation, for example, small islands in the Caribbean but also traditional tax havens such as Gibraltar and the British Channel islands. Sophisticated Internet casinos targeted to the large Asian markets operate from the Caribbean. Case law is still being created in the area of Internet gambling as new operators seek to exploit loopholes in existing national laws, or

---

[4] A single global lottery would eliminate the international grey market arising from multiple national versions of the global lottery (and the rents to intermediaries running the grey market would be transferred to the global lottery operator, the prize winners and the beneficiaries).

Table 8.2. *Regions with online gambling*

Africa	Asia Pacific	Caribbean	Central &South America	Europe	North America
Comoros (Anjouan)	Australia (Capital Territory)	Antigua & Bermuda	Belize	Austria	Canada (Saskatchewan)
Mauritius	Australia (New South Wales)	Dominica	Costa Rica	Belgium	Canada (Kahnawake)
South Africa (Western Cape)	Australia (Northern Territory)	Dominican Republic	Nicaragua	British Channel Islands (Alderney)	US (New Jersey)
Swaziland	Australia (Queensland)	Grenada	Argentina	British Channel Islands (Sark)	US (California)
	Australia (Tasmania)	Jamaica	Brazil (Parana)	Czech Republic	US (Nevada)
	Australia (Victoria)	Netherlands Antilles (Curacao)	Brazil (Santa Catarina)	Denmark	
	Australia (Western)	St Kitts & Nevis	Columbia	Finland	
	Cook Islands	St Vincent	Venezuela	France	
	India (Maharashta)	Virgin Islands (US)		Germany	
	India (Rajasthan)			Gibraltar	
	New Zealand			Iceland	
	Norfolk Island			Ireland	
	South Korea			Isle of Man	
	North Korea			Jersey	
	Philippines			Liechtenstein	
	Solomon Islands			Luxembourg	
	Taiwan			Malta	
	Vanuatu			Monaco	
	Vietnam			Norway	
				Russia (Kalmykia)	
				Serbia	
				Spain	
				Sweden	
				Switzerland	
				The Netherlands	
				United Kingdom (Great Britain)	

Source: Gambling Licenses.com, available at: www.gamblinglicenses.com/licencesDatabase.cfm.

circumvent those laws entirely. The refusal of some credit card companies to process Internet bets has slowed the market's growth. Although this threatens some existing operators, the long-term prospects for the Internet market remain strong since major (licensed) casinos are determined to win market share and are influencing US legislation to this effect—and they have political allies in states keen to expand their revenues from gambling taxes (*Wall Street Journal* 2003).

In summary, the global lottery will enter a crowded market-place in many countries. In developed countries gamblers can choose not only between a variety of national lottery products but also between an increasingly large menu of gambling options, reflecting the growth of Internet gambling as well as the recent liberalization of major gambling markets such as the United Kingdom. Asia's high-growth gambling markets are now well-served by both domestic and Internet gambling products, many of which are provided by large commercial operators with a sophisticated knowledge of the market and the new technologies. A global lottery would face much less competition in the smaller countries of sub-Saharan Africa, but this is neither a large market nor a growing market. These are all factors to keep in mind as we now turn to the revenue-raising potential of the global lottery.

8.2.5. *Revenue-Raising Potential*

The global lottery will raise money from (i) people who substitute in from other forms of gambling (including national lotteries) or are so motivated that they increase their total gambling expenditures, and (ii) 'new players' who do not otherwise participate in lotteries but who are now motivated to do so (including global altruists).

Any assessment of the likely revenue-raising potential of the global lottery must be highly speculative. Table 8.1 shows recent trends in world lottery sales by region. The total size of world lottery market sales is over US$120 billion. The largest market is Europe (US$54.8 billion in 2001), followed by North America (US$49.4 billion) and Asia and the Middle East (US$16.7 billion). The global gambling industry had a gross turnover of US$950 billion in 2001, generating gross profits of about US$200 billion and net revenues for the industry of US$115 billion after taxes, levies, and payments to charities (Global Betting and Gaming Consultants 2002; Gaming Board for Great Britain 2003).

Of the gross profits (US$200 billion) the largest share is provided by lotteries (about US$62 billion), followed by gaming machines (US$58 billion) and casinos (US$50 billion) (Global Betting and Gaming Consultants 2002). The largest gambling profits are derived from the markets of United States (about US$61 billion) and Japan (US$48 billion), followed by the United Kingdom, Australia, Spain, Canada, Italy, France, India, and Germany; these markets range from US$10 billion in the United Kingdom to about US$4 billion in Germany (Global Betting and Gaming Consultants 2002).

From these data, we can make two points regarding revenue-raising potential. First, the global lottery will generate most of its funds from the developed countries (although India is a significant potential market in the developing world). Second, these large markets are subject to intense and growing competition in the provision of gambling products. Take, for example, the United States, which is the largest market. In 1975 there were thirteen US state-lotteries but by 1999 there were 37, and the 1990s saw the creation of hundreds of legal casinos as fiscal pressures on state governments, and a political reluctance to tax, drove the relaxation of previously tightly controlled markets (Shiller 2000: 41). Similar forces are evident in Australia, India, and South Africa.

If the global lottery took 10 per cent of the 2001 global lottery gross profit (US$62 billion), then it would raise US$6.2 billion annually. This compares to total official development assistance (ODA) of US$59.5 billion in 2001, or aid grants of US$38.3 billion in 2001 (OECD–DAC data from www.oecd.org/dac).

Developing more sophisticated estimates of global lottery revenues depends on making assumptions regarding the amount that the global lottery will 'capture' from the existing lotteries, substitution away from other forms of gambling, and the amount from new players (including global altruists). All of these assumptions hinge in one way or another on the effectiveness of the marketing of the global lottery, both to pure gamblers and global altruists.

Experience from introducing new national lotteries shows that revenue generation can stagnate as the novelty wears off. This may also be the case for the global lottery. This must be taken into account in the disbursement of funds to development programmes, so as not to endanger delivery (i.e. any special development fund for this purpose may need to retain sizeable reserves). However, the global lottery has a major advantage over national lotteries: its global sales will not suffer as much from the business cycle fluctuations that affect national lottery proceeds, and demand will grow with global income.

8.2.6. *Cross-Country Equity*

As we discussed, countries differ substantially in the potential national market for the lottery. The CMI proposal is for a portion of the national global lottery to be distributed within the country concerned, in order to offset any negative impact on the revenue raised through existing lotteries or the causes they fund.

How should that portion be determined? Should the portion retained by the country be the same across all countries or should it vary according to the level of development (weights based on per capita income) or some form of poverty weighting (using weights derived from UNDP's Human Development Index for instance?). This issue applies not just to the global lottery as an instrument of innovative finance for developing countries, but also to other instruments such as global taxation (and it is part and parcel of any discussion on regional fiscal arrangements such as the European Union's system of contributions and rebates).

We do not resolve this issue here, but a simple example highlights the problem. India has a gross national income of US$460 per capita and a population of over one billion; Nicaragua has roughly the same per capita income (US$420) and a population of only 5 million (World Bank 2002: 232–3). For simplicity, assume that per capita annual expenditure on the global lottery is one dollar in each country, so that India sells US$1 billion of tickets per year and Nicaragua sells US$5 million (Indians currently spend US$10 billion annually on lottery tickets; BBC 2002*a*). If each country transfers the same percentage to the global lottery fund, then India makes a much larger *absolute* transfer into the fund than Nicaragua. Although large countries will also retain higher absolute amounts for their own causes (including poverty reduction), they may still balk at the scale of their transfers to the global lottery fund and argue for higher percentage retentions for their national causes. There may be a case for a sliding scale; countries with a GNI (gross national income) below some pre-determined level (X) would keep 100 per cent, and countries with a GNI more than X would keep a fraction that falls as their GNI rises.

8.2.7. *Distributional and Welfare Effects*

Empirical evidence for developed countries shows that low-income groups spend a larger proportion of their income on lotteries than higher-income groups.[5] This implies that lotteries are a regressive way of financing public spending, an aspect that has been much emphasized by their critics (e.g. see, Reno 1997; Fekjoer 2002).[6] For each dollar bet, the average US state lottery pays 55 cents in prizes, spends 12 cents on retailer commissions and other operating costs, which leaves 33 cents for the state (Clotfelter 2000). Clotfelter and Cook (1989) call this an 'implicit tax' because it has the same effect as a tax on lottery expenditures. Clotfelter (2000: 4) concludes that 'if it were an excise tax, it would amount to a 50 per cent tax on the cost of operating a lottery (67 cents), making it much higher than the excise taxes we place on alcohol or tobacco products'.

UK evidence shows that higher-income groups are more likely to play in rollover weeks when the expected return is higher, presumably because their time carries a higher opportunity cost or they have many other forms of entertainment (Farrell and Walker 1997). Hence, lottery design affects the regressivity of the tax, and if the competitiveness of the global lottery relative to national lotteries is reduced by lowering the top prize (as discussed in Section 8.2.3) then the global lottery tax is likely to be more regressive than existing national and state lotteries.

Compared to ODA financed through an income tax, the global lottery is regressive in its effect on the distribution of income in developed countries. But compared to nothing (i.e. lower development financing in the lottery's absence), it is progressive in terms of the world income distribution—provided that the additional development programmes funded by the global lottery are pro-poor in their impact. When the lottery finances programmes with positive externalities for everyone (e.g. efforts to preserve environmental capital and combat global warming), then the poor benefit along with the non-poor, and these benefits increase when the 'global bad' is especially acute for

---

[5] In the United States, the 1999 national survey on gambling behaviour found that households with incomes in the range of US$50,000–99,000 spent an average of US$301 per year, while households with an income less than US$10,000 spent an average of US$520 on lotteries in a year (Federal Reserve Bank of Minneapolis 2003).

[6] See Clotfelter and Cook (1989: 222–3) on defining regressivity in the context of lotteries.

the poor (e.g. they suffer disproportionately from flooding and drought due to global climate change). Finally, when the poor themselves buy lottery tickets (as many do in South Asia) then as a group the expenditure effect is negative (recall that the expected return in buying a lottery ticket is less than the stake) but some individuals, the winners, may be lifted out of poverty. In summary, the lottery's welfare and distributional effects can be viewed from several different perspectives, some of them more favourable than others.

8.2.8. *Ethical Issues*

Although many countries run lotteries, there are also many critics, and the ethics of the global lottery must be taken seriously and debated at national and international levels. Some religious groups discourage their members from buying lottery tickets, but practices vary widely. Muslim countries vary in their tolerance for lotteries: Bangladesh, Malaysia, and Pakistan have active state lotteries, whereas Saudi Arabia does not. The Catholic religion does not expressly forbid lotteries or gambling, provided that the gambler acts freely and without unjust compulsion.[7] Many local-level church organizations raise funds from their own lotteries, but gambling is not universally tolerated across all Christian groups. Again, religious organizations would have an important part to play in the national and international debate on the global lottery.

Many people welcome the opportunity to participate in lotteries, judging by the numbers who buy tickets. But equally, gambling addiction can result in personal ruin; of the 125 million Americans who gambled in 1998, some 7.5 million were estimated to be 'problem gamblers' (Shiller 2000: 41 citing data collected by the National Gambling Impact Study Commission). Moreover, gambling addiction appears to be more prevalent in men than women, with catastrophic effects on the household when, as in many countries, men control most of the households' cash income by virtue of their greater participation in wage labour, etc. (see Kearney 2002 on the impact of US state lotteries on consumer expenditures).

So in 'social lotteries', there is always an uneasy tension between the desire to raise money to do good, and the recognition that one is providing a potentially addictive route to ruin, even if only for a small minority of people. For this reason some US state lotteries set aside funds for projects to reduce gambling addiction and some states impose strict controls on advertising (Clotfelter 2000).

The evidence on problem gambling in lotteries is mixed. Griffiths and Wood (1999) review the European research on addiction to lottery gambling. The most addictive forms of gambling are those that give purchasers the chance to gamble continuously (thus slot machines are the most addictive). This also makes scratch cards more of a problem than weekly or bi-weekly lotteries. They conclude that:

With regards to weekly or bi-weekly lotteries there is little evidence Europe-wide that they are addictive. This is primarily because of their low event frequency (i.e. there are a number of days

---

[7] See the *Catholic Encyclopaedia* at: www.newadvent.org/cathen/06375b.htm.

gap between knowing the result of each gamble) ... Scratch cards and VLTs [Video Lottery Terminals] appear to be a different proposition to a discontinuous lottery game and appear to have the potential to promote repetitive habit patterns. Although the evidence is somewhat sparse, there does appear to be evidence in a number of countries ... that scratch cards are a problem to a small minority of people .... (Griffiths and Wood 1999: 21)

In India, lottery gambling has become a matter of public debate, particularly regarding gambling addiction among the poor, and its encouragement by lottery companies.[8] India's Lotteries (Regulation) Act 1998, bans single digit lotteries and instant lotteries, and bills have been submitted to parliament to ban all lotteries (meeting fierce resistance from state governments, many of which have become increasingly dependent on lottery revenues).

There is also concern over the potentially negative effects of very large prizes on winners (e.g. in press reports regarding family breakdown following lottery wins), leading to the argument that small prizes may be preferable. However, this creates a problem for maximizing lottery revenues given the positive effect of very large prizes on demand. Prizes could be paid in annuities (an option that is offered to winners in the United States), which may reduce such negative social impact.

Despite these problems, many observers might reasonably argue that the ethical case for a global lottery is strong and, indeed, that it is stronger than the case for many existing national lotteries (where national taxation offers more possibilities for meeting social goals if the ethical case for lotteries is in doubt). That is, given the extent of current global problems as well the scale of world poverty and the urgent need to eradicate it— recently reaffirmed by the adoption of the Millennium Development Goals (MDGs)— 'exceptional' financing measures are required above and beyond raising foreign aid. And the ethical case for the global lottery will strengthen as the funds it raises deliver tangible progress in meeting the MDGs by their target date of 2015.

8.2.9. *The Global Lottery's Role in Development Education*

The global lottery has considerable potential as a vehicle for conveying information about development via local sales points together with the national and international media (e.g. through regular advertisements and programmes on commercial (e.g. CNN) and public/semi-commercial TV and radio services (e.g. BBC World).

A single global lottery might be superior to many national versions in its development education impact. Any global televised prize draw would command substantial audiences, affording a unique opportunity to publicize the impact of the funds raised. It would also provide potential for raising additional and large sums from the associated advertising in what could be a peak-viewing slot for a large global audience (for comparison, advertisers paid US$2 million for a 30-second TV spot during the broadcast of the 2002 US Super Bowl). Any hint of malpractice in the lottery operation or

[8] In 2002, an Indian builder earning US$3 a day won a US$1 million jackpot in an online lottery and was taken on a nationwide promotional tour by the lottery company (BBC 2002*b*).

misuse of funds would undermine the positive development-education role: caution is therefore recommended.

Development education might be promoted by offering, in addition to a standard global lottery ticket, a menu of lottery tickets (each with the same expected return), the funds from which are earmarked to important causes; for example, tickets to fund primary education, improvements in the livelihoods of poor women, or HIV/AIDS programmes. This might also have positive effects for total funds raised since prospective buyers favour different causes. However, this could reduce the incentive for governments to fund these activities from general taxation or appropriate user charges, thus reducing the net impact—in terms of actual services created—from lottery funds themselves. This issue needs further investigation.

8.3. A GLOBAL PREMIUM BOND

8.3.1. *Experiences with National Premium Bonds*

We now turn to a measure, which can complement the global lottery, namely a global premium savings bond modelled on the long-running and successful UK scheme. We describe the UK scheme (and other national premium bond schemes in this section) before turning to the possible structure of the global premium bond in the next section.

In the UK premium bond scheme, people buy savings bonds, each with a unique number that is entered every month in a prize draw, with prizes ranging from £50 to £1 million (a random number generator, nicknamed ERNIE, picks the winners).[9] The size of the total prize allocation is set so that the *expected* return is equivalent to the yield on UK government stock. Individual bondholders will receive a return above or below the average expected return—depending on their luck and the size of their bond holdings—but in aggregate bondholders get the average if they hold the maximum permitted amount of bonds (which is £30,000 per person). Winners can opt to reinvest their winnings and many people accumulate sizeable holdings in this way (and since the maximum is per person, not per household, families can potentially hold significant wealth in premium bonds). With average luck, a holder of £30,000 of bonds will win 12 prizes per year; given the minimum prize of £50, such an average winner will take home a minimum of £600 per year in prizes. Annual premium bond sales are presently running at £21.4 billion (US$34 billion) in the United Kingdom.

Bangladesh and Ireland have similar premium bond schemes. In Bangladesh the 'prize bond scheme' has operated for at least thirty years; the top prize is approximately US$2000 and there are many small prizes (there is no limit to the amount that may be held in prize bonds and the prizes are drawn quarterly). For fiscal year 2001–02, US$815 million was held in prize bonds (Bangladesh Bank 2003).

Premium bondholders never lose their investment (unless the government defaults) but the return depends on their luck. Hence, an individual's return can be above or below that on an interest-bearing deposit account or other types of government bonds.

---

[9] The UK premium bond is managed by the National Savings and Investments Office and is described at: www.nsandi.com.

Investors, who buy premium bonds rather than conventional government bonds, have a preference for skewness in the distribution of returns (also the characteristic of lottery tickets). Many investors favour premium bonds to interest-bearing deposits when interest rates are low (as at present). Their return may fail to match the inflation rate but this is the case for most government bonds.[10] Premium bonds are much less risky than equities and may produce higher returns than equities over the short-to-medium term given the greater volatility of equity markets. They are also suitable for people in retirement, or closer to retirement, when the main concern is to earn an income from investment in a way that protects the accumulated capital. In addition, winnings are tax free in the United Kingdom; accordingly, higher-rate taxpayers often hold the maximum allowable amount of premium bonds.

However, at this point we should issue a note of caution. Buying premium bonds *does* contain an element of gambling. You could view a premium bond as equivalent to saving in a savings bank and then using all of the interest in each period to buy lottery tickets. A premium bond offers you the ability to gamble with fewer transactions costs. That said, premium bonds and lottery tickets are incomplete substitutes for three reasons. First, the top prize on a UK premium bond is much less than a UK national lottery jackpot and the prize distribution is less skewed towards very large prizes than is the lottery; given gamblers' preference for skewness, many will still prefer to buy lottery tickets.[11] Second, you cannot choose the numbers of your UK premium bond (bondholders are allocated a number), whereas this is important to the lottery's entertainment value.[12] Third, a premium bond offers less *ex post regret*. If you buy £100 of lottery tickets over a year and win nothing, then you lose £100, but if you buy £100 of premium bonds and win nothing then you forfeit the interest from holding the money in a savings account (or other alternative investment). This is important given that most people consistently overestimate expected returns—whether on lottery tickets, premium bonds, or equities (see Clotfelter and Cook 1989 on lotteries and Shiller 2000: 142 on 'irrational exuberance' in equity markets).

In summary, a premium bond is like a lottery ticket in that the return depends on a random prize draw, but otherwise the premium bond is a savings instrument (with some entertainment value) whereas a lottery ticket is closer to other types of entertainment expenditure. Hence it can make financial sense to make a sizeable investment in premium bonds while it is very unwise to bet a large sum on a lottery. Premium bonds have a potentially wider market since their purchase is more socially acceptable to groups who otherwise avoid lotteries; in the United Kingdom, they are often given as gifts, especially to children (also the case with Bangladesh's prize bonds).

---

[10] United States Treasury Inflation Protected Securities (TIPS) are a major exception.

[11] The take-up of premium bonds in the United Kingdom was quite slow until the prize structure was redesigned to make it more appealing to gamblers (Rayner 1969, 1970).

[12] It may be possible to design a system whereby premium bondholders select their draw numbers each month if they wish; the bond number would then carry a permanent reference number purely to record ownership.

8.3.2. *The Modalities of A Global Premium Bond*

Whereas a global lottery can be run in either national versions or a single (international) version (see Section 8.2), a global premium bond (which henceforth we shall call a 'global ERNIE') is a more complex instrument and would be best managed by a single organization (selling the bonds through national sales offices and/or the Internet). It is advantageous, for reasons discussed later, for the global ERNIE to be denominated in a major currency (or basket of major currencies to offset exchange rate risk for bondholders). The flow of funds in and out of the global ERNIE will be subject to changes in its rate of return relative to other financial instruments (e.g. other bonds and equities). The global ERNIE must be liquid and well managed (and its credibility will be strengthened if the world's financial authorities conduct close oversight).

A premium bond is a *debt instrument*, the bondholder lends his or her money and is entitled to repayment upon request, in contrast to a lottery ticket that is a non-refundable expenditure.[13] This has implications for the use to which the money can be put. A global lottery can provide *grant* finance for development purposes, whereas a global ERNIE is more suited to providing *loan* finance. If the UK model is followed and the expected return for an individual holding the maximum permitted amount of bonds is linked to the return on a comparable financial instrument (for instance, a weighted average of the yield on a basket of developed-country government bonds) then this (plus associated administrative costs) sets a lower bound on the lending rate unless some element of subsidy from other sources is provided (from the funds raised by the global lottery, for example). This means that eligible borrowers, who could be developing-country governments, NGOs and international organizations, could borrow on terms as good as those facing rich-country governments (but on less concessional terms than IDA, unless a subsidy is provided).

Default by borrowers is always possible, but this is true for any loan instrument; thus the desirability of ERNIE funded-lending is bound up with the larger question of whether grants or loans are preferable for low-income countries, an issue which is hotly debated in the context of the heavily indebted poor country (HIPC) Initiative (Addison *et al.* 2004). Default could, *in extremis*, be absorbed by lowering the rate of expected return to bondholders and raising the lending rate to borrowers, but this would reduce the attractiveness of global ERNIEs to investors. Large-scale default would throw into question the repayment of the principal, with potentially fatal results for the viability of the scheme. In addition, since bonds are redeemable on demand, whereas loans are long-term, there is mismatch in the maturity structure of assets and liabilities. This mismatch is similar to that found in bond-financed mortgage markets and in the United States the government acts as the guarantor (through Freddie Mac and Fannie Mae). In the case of the global ERNIE, the guarantors could be rich-country governments (the G7 group) or emerging economies with sizeable foreign-exchange reserves (for instance, China and India).

---

[13] UK Premium bonds do not have a fixed term (as is the case with government and corporate debt).

As a financial instrument the global ERNIE would have the following qualities:

1. It would be an attractive savings instrument in its own right, particularly for 'ethical' investors. Ethical investment products are a rapidly growing market, both for individuals (e.g. pension investment) but also for charitable foundations (a large market). From the perspectives of risk management and return, ethical investors need to hold bonds but they face a dilemma in holding government paper; they cannot avoid financing categories of state spending (e.g. the military, nuclear power, etc.) that they deem to be unethical (whereas ethical investors in equities can pick and choose across companies, excluding those that are unethical). This class of investors will provide a strong source of demand for a global ERNIE.

2. The global ERNIE would widen the range of savings instruments open to individuals and organizations (including NGOs as well as private and public organizations) in developing countries that are often ill-served by domestic financial instruments. It would provide a useful hedge against the inflation and currency risk arising from holding savings in domestic assets, especially in countries with weak currencies and high inflation, since it will be denominated in a convertible foreign currency (or preferably a basket of foreign currencies so as to stabilize its global purchasing power—this also reduces the exchange rate risk for bond buyers in major currency countries). Migrants making remittances home could also purchase global ERNIEs for their families (see Chapter 9, this volume). Note that a conventional international bond, if made available to developing-country citizens, could also fulfil the function of widening the range of savings instruments, so this benefit is not exclusive to the global ERNIE alone.

3. Global ERNIE's would be a suitable charity gift, including transfers between individuals or groups in developed and developing countries, and such gifts and bequests could be exempted from taxation under national legislation to increase their attractiveness (however, a limit on purchases would be necessary to avoid the crowding-out of taxable bonds). International charities could also hold global ERNIEs on behalf of community organizations in countries and localities with insecure property rights and poor communications.

4. The global ERNIE may over time establish itself as a collateral instrument that people can borrow against in their domestic capital markets, both informal and formal (to the advantage of poorer ERNIE holders who can diversify their collateral away from traditional instruments such as land, cattle, jewellery, and bonded labour).[14]

These potential development and welfare benefits of a global ERNIE are independent of the use to which the funds are put by international development agencies (and would also apply to any conventional bond made available to developing-country buyers which

---

[14] If ERNIEs were *bearer bonds*, then their use as collateral would be facilitated but this is almost certainly ruled out by the necessity to impose a maximum limit on the holding per person (as in the UK scheme) and the ease with which bearer bonds can be used in money laundering.

indicates an important gap in the market irrespective of whether one favours a global premium bond or not).[15]

In summary, the global lottery is superior to the global ERNIE from the perspective of the final user of the funds, since the lottery can provide finance on grant terms. But the lottery does not offer a savings instrument, whereas the premium bond does and, provided that the risks of borrower default are contained, the global ERNIE could be attractive to investors in both developed and developing countries. This would facilitate ethical investment in developing countries and provide individuals and organizations in developing countries with access to an international financial instrument.

The global ERNIE may be more ethically acceptable to those who disagree with gambling in general. Since the funds raised by existing national premium bonds are not earmarked to charitable causes (as is often the case with government lotteries), but instead form part of general government funding, there would not be the level of resistance among national charities that poses a political problem for the global lottery (rather the opposition might arise from ministers of finance who see the global ERNIE as taking market share from their country's domestic debt instruments).

Finally there is an issue of sequencing the introduction of the global lottery and the global premium bond. As we noted in Section 8.2.1, the introduction of the global lottery may be delayed when national lottery suppliers hold licences for defined periods. Being a different product, the global premium bond could be introduced earlier.

8.4. CONCLUSION AND RECOMMENDATIONS

This chapter has discussed the present proposals for a global lottery. This has potential for raising finance for development programmes and programmes to provide global public goods. In addition, we have proposed a global premium bond as an additional instrument. Both the lottery and the global ERNIE could have strong development education benefits, an important consideration in these days of 'aid fatigue', when the case for helping poor countries and poor people must again capture the public's imagination. But for this reason, both schemes must meet the highest possible ethical standards.

The global ICT revolution is fundamentally changing the market for gambling. It is now possible to conceive of running the global lottery from a single organization via the Internet. This would have significantly lower administrative costs than selling national versions of the global lottery through national lottery agencies; a single authority would be easier to regulate than many national authorities and it would have potentially greater reach than national schemes. But for these reasons it may face more political opposition than nationally run versions of the global lottery if it is seen to take money from national charities and treasuries. We do not envision nationally run versions of the global ERNIE since this is a more complex financial instrument than the lottery.

---

[15] We are grateful to an anonymous referee for this point.

The market for gambling is also being liberalized in many countries. Liberalization is driven by the fiscal needs of central and local governments (including the increasing importance of gambling taxes arising from political opposition to other forms of taxation), the liberalization of cross-border transactions in services (e.g. EU harmonization) and more permissive social attitudes to gambling. In the United Kingdom for example, the report of the Gambling Review Body, chaired by Sir Alan Budd, recommended relaxing legal restrictions on the advertising and promotion of gambling, in part to create a fairer and more competitive market for gamblers (UK Department for Culture, Media and Sport 2003). A global lottery will have to compete in an increasingly vigorous market.

Global altruism can play a big role in encouraging sales of the global lottery—hence the importance of the development education component—but sizeable sales depend as well on its attractiveness to gamblers relative to other gambling products, including those now provided commercially via the Internet. In contrast, the attractiveness of the global ERNIE depends more on its merits as a savings instruments and we argue that it could find a strong place in the growing market for ethical investments. Whatever the final design of such schemes, it is imperative that we move ahead with further debate on these and other innovative forms of development finance.

REFERENCES

Addison, T., H. Hansen, and F. Tarp (eds) (2004). *Debt Relief for Poor Countries*. Basingstoke: Palgrave Macmillan for UNU-WIDER.

Ahde, M., A. Pentikäinen, and J-M. Seppänen (2002). 'Global Lottery'. Prepared for the Ministry of Foreign Affairs of Finland, 8 March. Helsinki: Office of President Ahtisaari (Crisis Management Initiative).

Bangladesh Bank (2003). 'Economic Trends'. Dhaka. Available at: www.bangladesh-bank.org/pub/monthly/econtrds/exnotes.html. Accessed 17 April 2003.

BBC (2002a). 'India's Online Lottery: It's a Rollover!'. BBC News, 30 March. Available at: news.bbc.co.uk/1/hi/world/south_asia/1901203.stm.

—— (2002b). 'Indian Pauper Strikes Lottery Gold'. BBC News, 3 July. Available at: news.bbc.co.uk/2/hi/south_asia/2091523.stm.

Childers, E. and B. Urquhart (1994). *Renewing the United Nations System*. Uppsala: Dag Hammarskjold Foundation.

Clarke, R. and G. Dempsey (2001). 'The Feasibility of Regulating Gambling on the Internet'. *Managerial and Decision Economics*, 22: 125–32.

Clotfelter, C. T. (2000). 'Do Lotteries Hurt the Poor? Well, Yes and No'. A Summary of Testimony Given to the House Select Committee on a State Lottery, 28 April.

—— and P. Cook (1989). *Selling Hope: State Lotteries in America*. Cambridge, MA: Harvard University Press.

Creigh-Tyte, S. and L. Farrell (1998). 'The Economics of the National Lottery'. *Working Paper* 190. Durham: University of Durham.

—— —— (2003). 'Is the UK National Lottery Experiencing Lottery Fatigue?', in L. V. Williams (ed.), *The Economics of Gambling*. London: Routledge, 165–81.

Douglas, A. (1995). *British Charitable Gambling 1956–1994*. London: Athlone Press.

Farrell, L. and I. Walker (1997). 'It Could Be You! But What's It Worth? The Welfare Gain from Lotto'. *Working Paper* 97/4. London: Institute of Fiscal Studies.

—— and R. Hartley (1998). 'Can Friedman-Savage Utility Functions Explain Gambling?'. *Working Paper* No. 98/02. Keele: Department of Economics, Keele University.

——, E. Morgenroth, and I. Walker (1999). 'A Time Series Analysis of UK Lottery Sales: The Long-Run Price Elasticity'. *Oxford Bulletin of Economics and Statistics*, 61(4): 513–26.

Federal Reserve Bank of Minneapolis (2003). 'Taking Food from Mouths?'. *FedGazzette*, March.

Fekjoer, H. O. (2002). 'Gambling as Taxation of the Poor'. Paper presented at the EASG Conference, 4 October, Barcelona. Available at: www.bks.no/barcelon.htm. Accessed on 16 April 2003.

Forrest, D. (2003). 'Time Series Modelling of Lotto Demand', in L. V. Williams (ed.), *The Economics of Gambling*. London: Routledge, 182–203.

(The) Gaming Industry News Site. Available at: www.lotteryinsider.com.au/stats/world.htm .

Gaming Board for Great Britain (2003). 'Internet Gambling: Report to the Home Secretary by the Gaming Board for Great Britain'. Available at: www.gbgb.org.uk/intgambling_main.html. Accessed on 2 April 2003.

Garrett, T. A. and R. S. Sobel (2002). 'State Lottery Revenue: The Importance of Game Characteristics'. *Working Paper* 2002-011A. St Louis, MO: Federal Reserve Bank of St Louis. Available at: www.research.stlouisfed.org/wp/2002/2002-011.pdf.

Global Betting and Gaming Consultants (2002). 'Betting and Gaming Industry Becomes a Global Proposition'. *Press Release*, 15 July. Available at: www.bettingconsultants.com.

Griffiths, M. D. and R. T. A. Wood (1999). 'Lottery Gambling and Addiction: An Overview of European Research'. Report compiled for the Association of European National Lotteries (AELLE) Lausanne, Switzerland. Nottingham: Psychology Division, Nottingham Trent University. Mimeo.

Kaul, I. P., P. Conceição, K. Le Goulven, and R. U. Mendoza (eds) (2003). *Providing Global Public Goods*. Oxford: Oxford University Press for UNDP.

Kearney, M. S. (2002). 'State Lotteries and Consumer Behaviour'. *NBER Working Paper* 9330. Cambridge, MA: National Bureau of Economic Research. Available at: www.nber.org/papers/w9330.

Morgan, J. (2000). 'Financing Public Goods by Means of Lotteries'. *Review of Economic Studies*, 67: 761–84.

—— and M. Sefton (2000). 'Funding Public Goods through Lotteries: Experimental Evidence'. *Review of Economic Studies*, 67: 785–810.

O'Connor, N. (2003). 'Online Betting and the Law'. Available at: www.bettingmarket.com/law2.htm. Accessed 6 March 2003.

Rayner, A. C. (1969). 'Premium Bonds—the Effect of the Prize Structure'. *Bulletin of the Oxford Institute of Economics and Statistics*, 31(4): 303–11.

—— (1970). 'Premium Bonds—A Postscript'. *Bulletin of the Oxford Institute of Economics and Statistics*, 32(2): 167–9.

Reno, R. (1997). 'Gambling and the Poor'. *Citizen Link*. Available at: www.family.org/cforum/research/papers/a0004190.html. Accessed 1 April 2003.

Shiller, R. J. (2000). *Irrational Exuberance*. Princeton, NJ: Princeton University Press.

UK Department for Culture, Media, and Sport (2003). 'Modernising Britain's Gambling Laws: Draft Gambling Bill'. London: The Stationary Office.

UK Parliament (2001). 'Memorandum Submitted by the National Council for Voluntary Organizations to the Select Committee on Culture, Media and Sport: Minutes of Evidence'. London: UK Parliament. Available at: www.parliament.the-stationary-office.co.uk.

Walker, I. and J. Young (2000). 'The Dummies' Guide to Lottery Design'. *Warwick Economic Research Papers* 572. Warwick: Department of Economics, University of Warwick.

————(2001). 'An Economist's Guide to Lottery Design'. *Economic Journal*, 111(November): F700–22.

Wall Street Journal (2003). 'Curbs on Web Gambling Supported'. 22 August.

World Bank (2002). *World Development Report 2002: Building Institutions for Markets*. Oxford: Oxford University Press for the World Bank.

9

Remittances by Emigrants: Issues and Evidence

ANDRÉS SOLIMANO

9.1. INTRODUCTION

Remittances from migrants are a growing and relatively stable, market-based external source of development finance. Remittances bring foreign exchange, are a complement for national savings, and provide a source of finance for capital formation (mainly small-scale projects). Through these mechanisms, remittances can support economic growth in recipient countries. As remittances depend on flows of people that are often less volatile than capital flows, remittances are expected to be more stable than such capital flows as portfolio investment and international bank credit. Remittances are also an international redistribution from low-income migrants to their families in the home country. These transfers act as the international mechanism of social protection based on private transfers. The sustainability of remittances over time depends on various factors such as the anticipated flow of migration, and whether the migrants come alone or with their family, and how this changes over time.[1]

It is also important to recognize that benefits from remittances for the receiving countries have to be compared with the potential costs of emigration for the developing countries in terms of the loss of scarce human skills (the so-called brain drain phenomenon). Thus, a certain tradeoff is generated between the inflow of foreign exchange and external savings through remittances and the outflow of skilled individuals.[2]

Currently, remittances—after foreign direct investment—are the second most important source of external finance for developing countries. Moreover, they surpass foreign aid. There are twenty countries that are the main recipients of remittances. These twenty low- to medium-income developing economies capture around 80 per cent of total worker remittances to the developing world. In terms of value, the

Very useful comments by Tony Atkinson are greatly appreciated, as are the comments received from participants at the workshop of the UNU-WIDER project 'Innovative Sources for Development Finance' in Helsinki on 17–18 May 2003. Efficient assistance by Claudio Aravena is greatly appreciated.

[1] Leaving their families at home, new immigrants may initially go to the foreign country alone. Later, as their employment situation in the host country is stabilized, they tend to bring their families. This may have implications for the flow of remittances and their persistence over time, as families are often the main recipients of remittances.   [2] See Ellerman (2003) and Solimano (2002a) for a discussion of these issues.

three main recipient countries are India, Mexico, and the Philippines, while the three main source countries are the United States, Saudi Arabia, and Germany.

The international market for remittances (from a social point of view) is segmented and inefficient, as is reflected by the high costs of intermediation. Money transmitter operators dominating the market charge high fees and use overvalued exchange rates. Commercial banks in both the source and recipient countries have a low share of the global remittances market. Empirical evidence, however, shows that the costs of remittances are lower when sent through banks than through money transfer operators (MTOs).

There is, however, room for leveraging a greater value for remittances if international money transfers were conducted at lower costs. The amount of remittances is below the socially optimal level associated with a more competitive cost structure in the market for remittances (causing, therefore, a deadweight loss for both the sender and the receiver of a remittance). The development potential of remittances is thus diminished under current market realities.

The chapter is organized in seven sections in addition to the introduction. Section 9.2 discusses global and regional trends in remittance flows and their growing import-ance as a source of external transfers to developing countries. Section 9.3 examines measurement issues and discusses the main micro-motives for remittances and their implications for stability across cycles, while Section 9.4 analyses the development impact of remittances (effects on savings, investment, growth, poverty, income distri-bution). Section 9.5 overviews the international market for remittances and provides evidence on the costs of sending remittances to various country groups. Section 9.6 highlights policies for reducing the costs of sending remittances and thus enhancing their developmental impact. Section 9.7 concludes.

9.2. GLOBAL AND REGIONAL TRENDS IN REMITTANCE FLOWS

In a world of volatile capital flows, remittances[3] are a stabilizing component of external resources transfers to the developing world. Remittances are the financial counter-part of the outflow of people, and migration flows have been growing in the last two decades in response to expanding opportunities in advanced economies compared to developing countries. Remittances to the developing world have increased steadily from around US$15 billion in 1980 to 80 billion in 2002. This represents an annual rate of increase of 7.7 per cent (see Table 9.1).[4] At the regional level, the highest rate of increase in the flow of remittances is to Latin American and the Caribbean with 12.4 per cent per annum, followed by East Asia and the Pacific with 11 per cent per year. The lowest annual growth rate in remittances is to sub-Saharan Africa with 5.2 per cent. As shown in Table 9.1, in 2002 Latin America and the Caribbean have

---

[3] Remittances are defined as the sum of workers remittances and compensation of employees.

[4] As remittances are also sent through informal and un-recorded channels, official data may underestimate actual remittances (see Section 9.3).

Table 9.1. *Remittances received by region, 1980–2002 (in billions of US$)*

Region	1980	1985	1990	1995	1996	1997	1998	1999	2000	2001	2002 (est.)	Annual rate of growth (%) 1980–2002
East Asia and Pacific	1.1	2.3	3.6	8.3	9.5	14.2	8.3	10.6	10.3	10.4	11.0	11.0
Share (%) of remittances in developing countries	7.1	12.7	12.4	17.3	18.1	22.6	13.9	16.4	15.9	14.4	13.8	
Europe and Central Asia	2.1	1.7	3.2	5.5	6.2	7.1	9.2	8.1	8.7	8.9	10.0	7.4
Share (%) of remittances in developing countries	13.5	9.4	11.0	11.5	11.8	11.3	15.5	12.5	13.5	12.3	12.5	
Latin America and the Caribbean	1.9	2.6	5.7	12.8	12.8	13.6	14.8	16.9	19.2	22.6	25.0	12.4
Share (%) of remittances in developing countries	12.3	14.4	19.6	26.7	24.3	21.7	24.9	26.1	29.7	31.3	31.3	
Middle East and North Africa	3.8	4.6	9.3	8.6	9.1	9.4	10.3	10.5	10.9	13.1	14.0	6.1
Share (%) of remittances in developing countries	24.5	25.4	32.0	18.0	17.3	15.0	17.3	16.2	16.9	18.1	17.5	
South Asia	5.3	5.8	5.6	10.0	12.3	14.6	13.3	15.1	13.5	14.9	16.0	5.2
Share (%) of remittances in developing countries	34.2	32.0	19.2	20.9	23.4	23.3	22.4	23.3	20.9	20.6	20.0	
Sub-Saharan Africa	1.3	1.1	1.7	2.7	2.7	3.8	3.6	3.5	2.0	2.4	4.0	5.2
Share (%) of remittances in developing countries	8.4	6.1	5.8	5.6	5.1	6.1	6.1	5.4	3.1	3.3	5.0	
Developing countries	15.5	18.1	29.1	47.9	52.6	62.7	59.5	64.7	64.6	72.3	80.0	7.7
Industrial countries	n.a.	n.a.	n.a.	37.2	35.7	40.5	41.0	40.2	40.1	39.3	n.a.	n.a.
All countries	n.a.	n.a.	n.a.	85.1	88.3	103.2	100.5	104.9	104.7	111.6	n.a.	n.a.

Notes: Remittances are calculated as the sum of workers remittances and compensation of employees; n.a. means not available.

Source: Source: IMF (2003).

Table 9.2. *Remittances*[a] *received by country groups, 1995–2001*
(in billions of US$)

Countries	1995	1996	1997	1998	1999	2000	2001
Upper middle income	13.7	13.6	14.3	16.3	15.7	16.6	17.2
Share of remittances in all countries	16.1	15.4	13.8	16.2	15.0	15.9	15.4
Lower middle income	20.7	21.2	24.2	24.1	27.2	28.3	30.0
Share of remittances in all countries	24.3	24.0	23.5	24.0	26.0	27.0	26.9
Low income	13.5	17.8	24.2	19.1	21.8	19.7	25.1
Share of remittances in all countries	15.9	20.2	23.5	19.0	20.8	18.8	22.5
All developing	47.9	52.6	62.7	59.5	64.7	64.6	72.3
Share of remittances in all countries	56.3	59.6	60.7	59.2	61.7	61.7	64.8
Industrial countries	37.2	35.7	40.5	41.0	40.2	40.1	39.3
Share of remittances in all countries	43.7	40.4	39.3	40.8	38.3	38.3	35.2
All countries	85.1	88.3	103.2	100.5	104.9	104.7	111.6
Share of remittances in all countries	100.0	100.0	100.0	100.0	100.0	100.0	100.0

Notes: [a] Remittances are calculated as the sum of workers' remittances and compensation of employees.
Source: IMF (2003).

the highest level of remittances, totalling US$25 billion, followed by South Asia with 16 billion, the Middle East and North Africa (MENA) with 14 billion, and East Asia and the Pacific with 11 billion. Sub-Saharan Africa has the lowest level of remittances, US$4 billion.

In terms of the distribution of remittances by levels of per capita income, the developing-country group received 65 per cent of world remittances. In turn, the lower middle-income and low-income groups received a higher proportion than the upper middle-income countries (Table 9.2).

In 2002, for the developing-country group, worker remittances represented on average 1.3 per cent of GDP, 55.9 per cent of FDI flows, and nearly 140 per cent of the aid flows (Table 9.3). These coefficients vary from region to region. The proportion of worker remittances in GDP is the highest in the MENA region (3 per cent in 2002) and the lowest in the East Asia and Pacific region (0.7 per cent). Remittances as a proportion of FDI are the highest in the MENA region (466.7 per cent in 2002) and the lowest in East Asia and Pacific (19.3 per cent). In turn, the proportion of remittances in foreign aid is the lowest in sub-Saharan Africa, reflecting both lower remittances and high aid flows to this region.

In terms of total resource flows, remittances are the second largest component of external resource flows to developing countries after FDI (Table 9.4 and Fig. 9.1). Remittances have been larger than aid flows as a source of external development finance since 1997. In 2001, foreign aid represented 18 per cent of total external finance flows while remittances were 25 per cent. Interestingly, as mentioned earlier, remittances are much more stable than other capital flows. Mainly bank credit and portfolio investment are considered volatile components of external resource flows.

Table 9.3. *Remittances*[a] *received by developing countries, 1996–2002*

Countries	1996	1997	1998	1999	2000	2001	2002 (est.)
East Asia and Pacific							
as % of GDP	1.0	1.3	0.7	0.8	0.7	0.7	0.7
as % of FDI inflows	16.2	22.8	14.4	21.7	23.4	21.3	19.3
as % of aid flows	125.0	215.2	103.8	112.8	128.8	152.9	n.a.
Europe and Central Asia							
as % of GDP	1.4	1.3	1.4	1.1	1.0	0.9	1.0
as % of FDI inflows	38.0	32.6	35.4	28.6	29.8	29.6	34.5
as % of aid flows	89.9	126.8	131.4	84.4	90.6	97.8	n.a.
Latin America and the Caribbean							
as % of GDP	1.3	1.2	1.1	1.1	1.2	1.3	1.4
as % of FDI inflows	28.8	20.6	20.2	19.2	25.3	32.6	59.5
as % of aid flows	232.7	302.2	328.9	359.6	505.3	434.6	n.a.
Middle East and North Africa							
as % of GDP	3.4	3.0	3.1	2.9	2.8	3.0	3.0
as % of FDI inflows	1,300.0	151.6	137.3	328.1	436.0	238.2	466.7
as % of aid flows	171.7	195.8	219.1	244.2	294.6	335.9	n.a.
South Asia							
as % of GDP	3.7	3.8	3.1	3.2	2.6	2.6	2.6
as % of FDI inflows	351.4	298.0	380.0	487.1	435.5	363.4	320.0
as % of aid flows	236.5	339.5	271.4	351.2	321.4	252.5	n.a.
Sub-Saharan Africa							
as % of GDP	1.4	1.7	1.4	1.3	0.7	0.7	1.1
as % of FDI inflows	62.8	46.9	55.4	43.2	32.8	17.4	57.1
as % of aid flows	18.0	28.6	27.1	28.7	16.4	18.9	n.a.
Developing countries							
as % of GDP	1.6	1.7	1.4	1.4	1.3	1.3	1.3
as % of FDI inflows	41.2	37.0	34.1	36.1	40.2	42.1	55.9
as % of aid flows	101.3	134.5	118.3	123.5	127.9	139.0	n.a.

Notes: [a] Remittances are calculated as the sum of workers' remittances and compensation of employees; FDI is foreign direct investment; Aid flows are official development assistance; n.a. means not available.
Source: IMF (2003).

The quantitative importance of these components of private capital flows is still significant (nearly 30 per cent of total resource flows, on average, to developing countries between 1991 and 2000). These components are an important source of macroeconomic volatility. Often private capital flows do *lead* the macroeconomic cycles. In contrast, remittances can be even counter-cyclical, as emigrants send money home during bad times to provide income support.

Table 9.4. *Resource flows to developing countries, 1991–2002*
(current US$ billions and %)

	Remittances[a]		Aid flows[b]		Other official flows[c]		FDI		Other private flows[d]		Total	
	US$	%	US$	%	US$	%	US$	%	US$	%	US$	%
1991	33.1	21	49.5	32	11.4	7	35.7	23	26.3	17	156	100
1992	37.2	19	46.4	24	10.1	5	47.1	24	52.2	27	193	100
1993	38.9	15	41.7	16	11.9	5	66.6	26	100.2	39	259.3	100
1994	44.1	16	48.1	18	−0.1	0	90.0	34	85.6	32	267.7	100
1995	47.9	15	61.0	19	8.9	3	105.0	33	99.1	31	322.3	100
1996	52.6	14	51.9	14	−7.8	−2	128.0	34	148.44	40	372.9	100
1997	62.7	15	46.6	11	7.2	2	169.0	41	131.37	31	417.2	100
1998	59.5	15	50.3	12	16.2	4	175.0	43	108.75	27	409.3	100
1999	64.7	19	52.4	15	5.0	1	179.0	52	45.09	13	346.6	100
2000	64.6	19	50.5	15	−3.0	−1	161.0	48	65.15	19	338.0	100
2001	72.3	25	52.0	18	n.a.	n.a.	172.0	60	−11.73	−4	284.3	100
2002 (est.)	80.0	36	n.a.	n.a.	n.a.	n.a.	143.0	64	n.a.	n.a.	223.0	100
Average: 1991–2001	52.51	18	50.04	18	5.98	2	120.75	38	77.32	25	306.04	100

Notes:
[a] Remittances are calculated as the sum of workers' remittances and compensation of employees;
[b] Aid flows are official development assistance and official aid;
[c] Other official flows are total official flows (official development fin.a.nce), net of aid flows;
[d] Other private flows are portfolio flows, and bank and trade; n.a. not available.

Source: IMF (2003) for remittances; World Bank (2003) for all other flows.

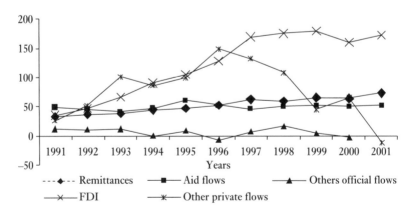

Figure 9.1. *Long-term resource flows to developing countries, 1991–2001*
Source: IMF (2003).

At the individual country level, remittances are relatively concentrated in the group of twenty developing countries that capture around 80 per cent of total remittances to the developing world (Fig. 9.2). In turn, the GDP of these twenty countries represents approximately 60 per cent of the GDP of the developing world (World Bank 2003). In 2001, the main recipient of worker remittances was India, receiving an annual flow of US$10 billion, followed by Mexico with 9.9 billion and the Philippines with 6.4 billion. At the lower end of this group of twenty developing-country recipients of worker remittances are Thailand, China, and Sri Lanka. The country ranking, however, changes, when remittances are measured as shares of GDP, on which measure the top three economies are Tonga, Lesotho, and Jordan with remittances ranging between 20 and 40 per cent of GDP. At the lower end are the Philippines, Uganda, Ecuador and Sri Lanka, with shares between 7 and 9 per cent of GDP (Fig. 9.3).

On the other side, the top twenty *source* countries of remittances in 2001 are headed by the United States with US$ 28.4 billion, followed by Saudi Arabia with 15.1 billion and Germany with 8.2 billion (see Fig. 9.4). At the lower end of the top twenty sending countries are Czech Republic, Venezuela, and Norway (all three with US$ 0.7 billion in 2001).

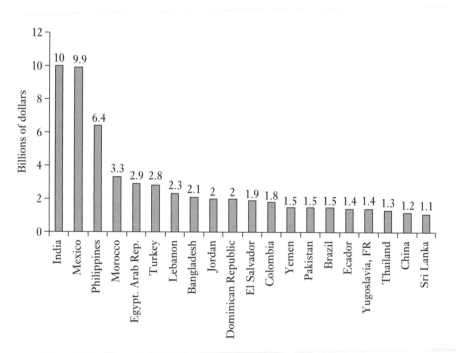

Figure 9.2. *Top twenty developing-country recipients of workers' remittances, 2001 (in billions of dollars)*

Source: World Bank (2003).

A. Solimano

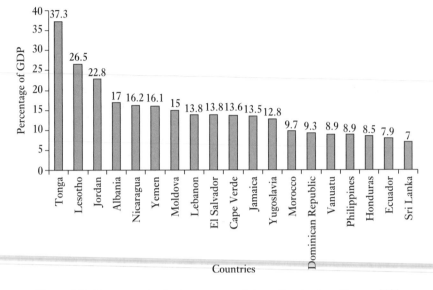

Figure 9.3. *Top twenty developing-country recipients of workers' remittances, 2001*
(as percentage of GDP)

Source: World Bank (2003).

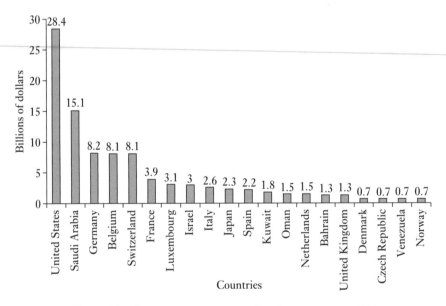

Figure 9.4. *Top twenty country sources of remittance payments, 2001*

Next we turn to the motives for remittances that may shed some light on the empirical behaviour of remittances reviewed in this section.

9.3. MEASUREMENT, MICRO-MOTIVES FOR REMITTANCES AND CYCLICAL BEHAVIOUR

In this section, we review (i) measurement issues; (ii) the micro-motives for remittances, and (iii) the stability of remittances during the cycle.[5]

9.3.1. *Definition and Measurement Issues*

The economic significance of remittances often goes beyond what is suggested by the official balance-of-payments statistics in the sending and receiving countries. The important concept for measuring the economic impact of remittances is the resource transfer—monetary or in-kind—made by a migrant to his home country. Monetary transfers in dollars directly increase the availability of foreign exchange in the migrant's country of origin, whereas remittances in-kind save foreign exchange for the recipient country. This distinction is important, as there are several modalities for sending remittances. Some of these are recorded while others are not. For example, when remittances are sent through the formal channels, they are recorded in the receiving country's balance-of-payments current account. Conversely, remittances sent informally in cash, for example through couriers, are unrecorded in official statistics. Remittances can be in-kind, for example, goods sent to households in the home country. Only part of the later are recorded as imports. Migrants may also make donations in the host country to institutions like the church or other charitable organizations formed by co-nationals. They can also make numerous payments (insurance premiums, school tuition, international airfares paid directly to airlines) on behalf of relatives or friends from their home country.[6] Although most of these payments should, in the economic sense, be treated as 'remittances', they rarely are recorded as such. In sum, these considerations should be borne in mind in assessing the true magnitude of remittance transfers based on official statistics, which as noted above, tend to *underestimate* their full economic impact.

In general, data on remittances are available from three items in balance-of-payments reports at country level:[7] (i) worker remittances (money sent by workers living abroad for more than one year); (ii) compensation of employees (gross earnings of foreigners residing abroad for less than a year; and (iii) migrant transfer (net worth of migrants moving from one country to another) (see Gammeltoft 2002).

---

[5] This section draws largely on Solimano (2003).   [6] See Brown (1997).
[7] Data for different countries are compiled in the IMF (International Monetary Fund) *Balance of Payments Statistical Yearbook*.

9.3.2. Microeconomic Motivations to Remit

The analytical literature[8] on motives for remittances can be summarized in four approaches.

The altruistic motive

Under the altruistic view, the migrant sends remittances home because he cares about the well-being of his or her family in the home country, and a remittance satisfies the emigrant's concern for the welfare of his family. Furthermore, it is an empirical regularity that the migrant generally has a higher education level than family members who stay at home. When a migrant goes to a country where the average wage and per capita income are higher than at home, his income level, once he secures a job, can be expected to be better than that of comparable workers at home. The main prediction of the altruistic motive is that remittances tend to decrease over time,[9] as the attachment to family gradually weakens over time when members are in different countries. Furthermore, the migrant may plan to stay abroad for an extended period (or eventually retire there), subsequently bringing his family to his adopted country. This, of course, reduces remittances. The converse case is the return–migration in which the migrant brings fresh funds on his return home, raising remittances the one time.

The self-interest motive

Opposite to the altruistic motive is the emigrant who sends remittances to the home country mainly for economic reasons and financial self-interest. In this scenario, the successful emigrant saves money in a foreign country, creating the dilemma as to how to accumulate wealth (in which assets) and where (in which country). An obvious place to invest at least part of the assets is in the home country, buying property, land, financial assets, etc., where these assets may earn a higher rate of return than in the host country, albeit with a greater risk profile. These assets can be administered on behalf of the migrant by the family, who acts as a trusted agent. Expectations of an inheritance from the emigrant's parents may be another motivation for remittances. In this case, family members who have contributed to the increasing family wealth (e.g., by sending remittances) become the obvious candidates of future inheritance.

Implicit family contract 1: loan repayment

Economic theory has developed explanations of the remittances process, which take the family—rather than the individual—as the main unit of analysis.[10] The theory assumes that a family develops an implicit contract with the individual (the migrant) who chooses to live abroad, and those who stay at home. The implicit contract has an intertemporal dimension, say various years or even decades, as the time-horizon, and combines elements of investment and repayment. In the loan repayment theory,

---

[8] References of this literature are Stark (1991), Brown (1997), Poirine (1997), Smith (2003).

[9] See Stark (1991, chapter 16).

[10] See Poirine (1997) and Brown (1997) for an elaboration on this specification of remittances.

the family invests in the education of the emigrant and usually finances the migration costs (travel and subsistence in the host country). This is the loan (investment) element of the theory. The repayment part comes after the migrant settles abroad, his income profile starts to rise over time and he is in a position to start repaying the loan (principal and interests) back to the family in the form of remittances. Thus the family invests in a higher yielding 'asset'—the migrant—who earns a higher income in a foreign country than other family members living and working at home. This model predicts various time profiles of remittances, depending on the length of time it takes for the migrant to become established in the foreign labour market and on the duration of his stay abroad. The quicker the migrant's integration into the labour market of the new country, the faster the flow of remittances. Amounts to be remitted will depend, among other things, on the income profile of the migrant. In this model, remittances do not need to decrease over time as they do in the altruistic model.

Implicit family contract 2: co-insurance
Another variant of the theory of remittances as an implicit family contract between the migrant and those at home is based on the notion of risk diversification. The idea is simple: insurance markets and capital markets in the real world are incomplete, and risks cannot be diversified because of the absence of financial assets that edge risk. In addition, constraints to borrowing, a particularly serious problem for poor migrants, limit the ability to smooth consumption or finance investment. Assuming that economic risks between the sending and foreign country are not positively correlated, then it becomes a convenient strategy for the family as a whole to send abroad some of its members (often the most educated) to diversify economic risks. The migrant, then, can help to support his family in bad times at home. Conversely, for the migrant, having a family in the home country is insurance against bad times that may also occur in the adopted country. Here, emigration becomes a co-insurance strategy, with remittance playing the role of an insurance claim. As in any contract, there is the potential problem of enforcement (e.g. ensuring that the terms of the contract are respected by all parties). However, in principle, enforcement can be expected to be simpler due to the fact that these are implicit family contracts, which are helped by family trust and altruism (a feature often absent in legally sanctioned contracts).

9.3.3. *Stability of Remittances in the Economic Cycle*

As mentioned in the previous section, worker remittances are more stable than portfolio investments and bank credit. Remittances can even be counter-cyclical. The different motives to remit reviewed above can shed some light in explaining this behaviour. In the model of remittances based on altruism, the migrant can increase his remittances when there is an economic downturn in the home country (as income of the migrant's family declines). In this case, a remittance would be the equivalent of a private 'welfare payment' sent from abroad to help smooth the consumption of the recipient at home. However, business cycles may be internationally synchronized. The growing economic interdependencies of globalization make this a more plausible case. In this situation, a recession in the receiving country may be positively correlated with a recession in the source country, so that the ability of the immigrant worker to send remittances may be hampered by economic conditions in the host country. This is a real possibility, although the sender may also draw on existing savings to maintain a steady flow of remittances.

If remittances were driven by the portfolio decisions of the migrant (remittances driven by investment), again the relevant issue would be the correlation between the rate of return of the assets in the host country and the rate of return on the assets at home. Here international correlation of the business cycle matters, as does the degree of financial integration between the source and the receiving country. In the model of remittances as mechanisms of co-insurance, risk diversification may call for a steady flow of remittances if business cycles are not fully positively correlated between the source and the receiving country.

9.4. THE DEVELOPMENT IMPACT OF REMITTANCES

Remittances have a potential positive impact as a development tool for the recipient countries. The development effects of remittances can be decomposed into its impact on savings, investment, growth, consumption, and poverty and income distribution. Remittances' *impact on growth* in the receiving economies is likely to act through savings and investment as well as short-run effects on the aggregate demand and output through consumption. Also the indirect effect of migration on output depends on the productivity level of the emigrant in the home country before departure. The *total saving effect* of remittances comes from the sum of foreign savings and domestic savings effects. Worker remittances are a component of foreign savings and they complement national savings by increasing the total pool of resources available for investment. Part of the savings effects of remittances takes place in the 'community'. In fact, migrant associations, often called hometown associations (HTAs) in the United States, organize migrants from various Latin American countries such as El Salvador, Guatemala, Honduras, Mexico, and the Dominican Republic. HTAs regularly send *donations* to finance investment in community projects and local development in the home countries.[11] Migrants' associations of former El Salvadorians send home donations of about US$10,000 per year, while those of Mexicans send home between US$5,000–25,000 per year (see Ellerman 2003). These are small numbers but in the recipient countries these sums can still have an impact. In the Mexican state of Zacatecas, the federal and local government match every dollar (it may be a two-for-one or three-for-one) donated by HTAs to local projects oriented to small infrastructure projects on water treatment, schools, roads, parks, etc. Through this programme, more than 400 projects

---

[11] See chapter by Micklewright and Wright in this volume on the role of private donations, mainly from foundations and other vehicles, as a source of development finance.

in Zacatecas have been completed in eight years. Total investment made by migrants to these projects amounts to around US$4.5 million (World Bank 2002). In this way, public savings are mobilized to finance small community projects, along with the remittances.

The previous discussion suggests that the direct effects of remittances on *investment* are bound to be on small community projects. Ratha (2003) cites instances of positive effects on investment in such receiving countries as Mexico, Egypt, and sub-Saharan Africa, where remittances have financed the building of schools, clinics, and other infrastructure. In addition, return-migrants bring fresh capital that can help finance investment projects.

Remittances also finance consumption; thus, private savings will increase proportionally less than an increase in income from external remittances. A study of remittances for Ecuador (Bendixen and Associates 2003) shows that around 60 per cent of remittances to that country are spent on food, medicine, housing rent, and other basic commodities; less than 5 per cent of remittances are used for the acquisition of residential property.

The combined effects of remittances on investment and consumption can increase output and growth. The sustainability of this effect is an open discussion. If remittances are a response to recent migration, remittances may be transitory and thus their effect on investment, consumption and growth can be more of a temporary nature. In contrast, if migrants form associations and their commitment to their home country becomes 'institutionalized', then the positive developmental effects of their remittances may become more permanent.

The indirect growth effect of remittances on *growth (or output)* depends on the type of emigrant leaving home, the state of the labour market, and the productivity of the emigrant. If the emigrant is unskilled with low productivity, or an unemployed worker, reflecting slack and excess supply in the labour market, then the effect of emigration on output in the home country is bound to be small. In contrast, if the emigrant is a highly skilled worker, an information technology expert or an entrepreneur with a high direct and indirect contribution to output, the adverse growth effect of high-skilled emigration is bound to be large (see Solimano 2001, 2002*a*).

One negative effect of (substantial) remittances is the possibility that they produce the so-called 'Dutch disease' effect.[12] In countries receiving substantial amounts in remittances, there is a tendency for the real exchange rate to appreciate which then penalizes non-traditional exports and hampers the development of the tradable goods sector.

Remittances may also have a *poverty reducing and income distribution effect*. As mentioned above, the recipient of remittances is often a low-income family whose offspring has left the country to work abroad. In a way, emigration is an effort to escape poverty

---

[12] This effect is extensive to all kinds of transfers, not only to remittances.

at home[13] and to improve the income-earning capacity of the emigrant by attempting to enter a foreign labour market in a richer country. At the same time, remittances serve to alleviate the poverty of the migrant's family in the home country by supplementing its income through transfers. The negative side of this is that remittances may create a 'culture of dependence' on the income from remittances. This, in turn, can impair efforts to escape poverty through education and work. The *distributive effect of remittances* is another dimension of the development effects of remittances.[14] Stark (1991) studies the effects of remittances on *domestic* inequality in two Mexican villages near the US border in which villagers engage in internal rural–urban migration as well as in migration to the United States. The study finds that remittances from internal migrants are correlated more with the years of schooling than remittances from international migrants to the United States, as the later often go to low-skilled labour-intensive jobs. Stark (1991) generalizes that the inequality impact of changes in remittances depends on the recipients' position in the village income distribution scale, the share of remittances in the village incomes and the distribution of the remittances themselves. These variables in turn depend on the distribution of human capital (education and skills) among the villagers and the migration opportunities of the villages. Another piece of evidence is provided by Ratha (2003) who reports that a household data survey for Pakistan shows that the share of income originating from external transfers increases with the income level (the households with the highest incomes receive the largest shares of their income from remittances). So remittances might appear to be increasing local inequality However, *income distribution between countries* may eventually improve with remittances, as income is redistributed from source countries with a higher income level to receiving countries with a lower income per capita. As seen in Section 9.2, remittances represent a very significant share of GDP in several low-income countries.

A final remark here: the development effect of remittances depends on the 'life-cycle' of the whole migration process at the country level. In fact, in instances where the source countries have expanding economies with rising per capita incomes, the differentials across countries in the income per head will diminish, reducing the incentives for emigration. Thus, the relative importance of remittances is likely to decline as a country moves up the development ladder. This is valid mainly for remittances from low-skilled migrants, however. In the case of highly skilled well-educated individuals, migration flows are likely to continue at the high per capita income levels, as has been seen within the European Union or between Europe and the United States. In this case, remittances may continue although their economic effects are probably quite different than those discussed earlier when the recipients of remittances are the developing countries.

---

[13] However, extreme poverty may also impede emigration, as the very poor may not be able to finance the costs of migrating to a foreign country.

[14] The distributive effects of remittances in the home country are more ambiguous. The issue is investigated in Barham and Boucher (1998).

9.5. THE INTERNATIONAL MARKETS FOR REMITTANCES

Remittances are channelled through financial entities such as MTOs, post offices, travel agencies, couriers, informal financial institutions, etc. MTOs owned and run by immigrants (or naturalized citizens of the same ethnic or national group) are denominated as 'ethnic stores'. Commercial banks are also in the remittances business, but are generally not important players (see Table 9.5). These financial intermediaries often charge fees for money transfers well above their marginal costs (see Orozco 2003). The most important MTO at the global level is Western Union with branches in many countries, followed by MoneyGram and Thomas Cook. The less competitive, more concentrated and more segmented the market for remittances, the higher the costs of the remittances. There are a number of reasons why the international market for remittances tends to be a thin and poorly competitive (only few players dominate the market and costs of intermediation are high). First, the legal status of the migrant sending the remittance is not always regularized. Some migrants have resident (working) visas, others are waiting for their visas to be processed and others are simply 'illegal'. Commercial banks are reluctant to enter the financial services market for low-income migrants whose immigration status often is not regularized.[15] The result is a less competitive market, where furthermore migrants are not well integrated as customers in the formal banking circuits. Second, it is important to note that worker remittances are small-scale transactions. In Latin America, the typical remittance per migrant is in the range of US$200–300 per month.[16] As individual transactions (remittances) are small, service standardization is needed for the remittances market to become a profitable activity at competitive fees. In this context, high fees may compensate for the cost of small transactions.[17] Finally, other factors that affect the market for remittances include exchange rate risk, government regulations for foreign exchange transactions in the receiving country and regulations in the sending country such as licensing costs.

Costs of remittances

Let us turn now to the efficiency of the market for remittances to the Andean region. If the costs of remittances are above the marginal cost (including a normal return to capital) of sending money, then the amount of the remittances is below the socially optimal level. As a consequence, consumption, investment, and output opportunities foregone in the receiving country cannot be realized.

---

[15] In the United States, banks request people (migrants) to provide a tax identification number, TIN, as a requisite for opening a bank account. In addition, some banks have recently accepted consular identification cards for opening bank accounts. Many migrants are totally compliant with tax returns even if their immigration status is not regular.   [16] See Orozco (2002) and Solimano (2003).

[17] In the aggregate, however, this is a sector that mobilizes a large volume of resources: aggregate remittances for Latin America were on the order of US$32 billion in 2002 for the main twelve recipient countries in Latin America (see IMF 2003).

The work by Orozco (2001, 2002) highlights two main cost components of sending remittances:

Total charges for remittances = explicit fee + exchange rate spread.

Companies charge a (explicit) fee that can be a percentage of the amount remitted or a fixed amount (often in dollars). The fee usually depends on the services offered (speed and type of delivery, etc.). The exchange rate spread is the difference between the exchange rate applied by the MTO to convert dollars into local currency and the market (e.g. interbank) exchange rate. MTOs usually offer the sender a less favourable exchange rate than the market rate. This is an additional source of profits for companies transmitting money and an additional cost component for the user.

The average cost of sending a remittance of US$200 through a commercial bank to selected non–Latin American countries is 7 per cent compared to the 12 per cent charged by such MTOs as Western Union and MoneyGram (Table 9.6).[18] Clearly, sending money through the bank is less expensive than sending it through the MTOs. Banks also offer a variety of money transfer services and charges decline substantially when the remittance is deposited with the same bank at both source and destination

Table 9.5. *Sources of remittances: countries and transfer agents*

Receiving country	Remittances sent from	Number of companies reviewed			All businesses
		Banks	MTOs[a]	Other	
Philippines	United States	5	14	5	24
Egypt	United States		2		2
Greece	Germany and USA	4	2		6
India	Saudi Arabia, USA, UK	7	11		18
Pakistan	Saudi Arabia, USA, UK	7	1		8
Portugal	France, USA	3	2		5
Turkey	Germany, USA	3	2		5
Mozambique	South Africa, USA	1			1
Zimbabwe	South Africa, USA		7		7
Bangladesh	UK	1	3		4
Ghana	UK		7		7

Notes: [a] Money transfer operators.

Source: Orozco (2003).

[18] Table 9.5 reports the countries and companies studied to determine the costs of remittances according to major source/destination countries and type of financial operator.

Table 9.6. *Average costs of sending money to selected non-Latin American countries*

Type	For a remittance of US$200		
	FX %	Fee %	Total %
Bank	1.0	6.5	7.0
Major MTO	1.7	10.9	12.0

Source: Orozco (2003).

Table 9.7. *Charges by types of operators for sending a remittance of US$200 to selected countries (%)*

Country	Type of business		
	Bank	Ethnic store/ exchange house	Major MTO
Egypt	—	—	13.8
Philippines	8.0	10.1	10.3
India	6.0	2.5	13.8
Greece	6.8	—	9.5
Pakistan	0.4	3.0	13.0
Portugal	3.4	—	12.3
Turkey	3.1	—	9.5
Mozambique	1.0	—	
Mean	7.0	6.0	12.0

Source: Orozco (2003).

countries. Foreign exchange spreads represent around 14 per cent of the total costs of remittances to non-Latin American countries. However, the country averages mask significant cross-country differences in the costs of sending remittances. For example, according to Table 9.7 drawn from Orozco (2003), the cost of sending money through banks is the lowest for Pakistan and the highest for the Philippines. These costs are much more uniform but also higher when money is sent through the major MTOs (in the range of 9.5–13.8 per cent).

The cost of sending money from the United States to Latin America is in the range of 8–9 per cent (see Table 9.8). Interestingly, as a share of total costs, the component of exchange rate spreads is twice as high for remittances to Latin American than to non-Latin American destinations. In fact, the exchange rate spread component for the latter is around 14 per cent of total costs of sending a remittance while it is nearly 28 per cent for Latin American recipients. Finally, let us look at the costs of remittances for the Andean region. Table 9.9 provides the average cost or charge of sending remittances of US$200, 250, and 300 to Bolivia, Colombia, Ecuador, Peru, and Venezuela. The

Table 9.8. *Average charges for sending a remittance of US$200 from the United States to Latin America (in US$ dollars, and as %)*

Charges	November 2001		November 2002	
	US$	%	US$	%
Total charge	20.06	10.10	17.02	8.50
FX charge	4.73	2.44	2.97	1.48
Fee charge	15.33	7.66	14.05	7.02

Source: Orozco (2003).

Table 9.9. *Cost of remittances from the United States to the Andean Countries (in local currency versus US$, averages per country)*

Amount	Country	Currency	Exchange		Fee charge		Total charge	
			Level	%	Level	%	Level	%
US$200	Colombia	Local	9.30	4.65	10.67	5.33	19.96	9.98
		Dollar	0.00	0.00	12.33	6.17	12.33	6.17
	Ecuador	Dollar	0.00	0.00	11.23	5.62	11.23	5.62
	Bolivia	Local	6.50	3.25	21.00	10.50	27.50	13.75
		Dollar	0.00	0.00	16.80	8.40	16.80	8.40
	Peru	Local	−3.54	−1.77	18.50	9.25	14.96	7.48
		Dollar	0.00	0.00	13.00	6.50	13.00	6.50
	Venezuela	Local	12.04	6.02	15.00	7.50	27.04	13.52
		Dollar	0.00	0.00	21.00	10.50	21.00	10.50
US$250	Colombia	Local	11.62	4.65	13.25	5.30	24.87	9.95
		Dollar	0.00	0.00	15.39	6.16	15.39	6.16
	Ecuador	Dollar	0.00	0.00	13.96	5.58	13.96	5.58
	Bolivia	Local	8.12	3.25	27.00	10.80	35.12	14.05
		Dollar	0.00	0.00	20.80	8.32	20.80	8.32
	Peru	Local	−4.42	−1.77	22.50	9.00	18.08	7.23
		Dollar	0.00	0.00	16.25	6.50	16.25	6.50
	Venezuela	Local	15.05	6.02	18.75	7.50	33.80	13.52
		Dollar	0.00	0.00	25.00	10.00	25.00	10.00
US$300	Colombia	Local	13.95	4.65	14.88	4.96	28.82	9.61
		Dollar	0.00	0.00	17.22	5.74	17.22	5.74
	Ecuador	Dollar	0.00	0.00	15.38	5.13	15.38	5.13
	Bolivia	Local	9.75	3.25	27.00	9.00	36.75	12.25
		Dollar	0.00	0.00	22.40	7.47	22.40	7.47
	Peru	Local	−5.31	−1.77	24.00	8.00	18.69	6.23
		Dollar	0.00	0.00	17.83	5.94	17.83	5.94
	Venezuela	Local	18.05	6.02	20.00	6.67	38.05	12.68
		Dollar	0.00	0.00	29.00	9.67	29.00	9.67

Source: Solimano (2003).

data are based on a survey conducted in January 2003 of MTOs and ethnic stores in the United States that are engaged in the remittances industry with these countries.[19] Table 9.9 gives the costs of a money transfer to be delivered in dollars and in local currency. The percentage charges are systematically lower across countries for dollar remittances than local currency remittances, ranging from 3 to 5 percentage points. For remittances of US\$200–250, the costs vary from 5.6 to 13.8 per cent, and for amounts of US\$300, between 5.1 and 12.7 per cent. In general, charges decline with the amount remitted, but there are significant differences in individual countries. Ecuador has the lowest charges and Venezuela the highest. An important factor explaining the lower charges for money remitted to Ecuador is that the exchange rate spread component of total costs (for the sender) is eliminated because the country's official currency is the US dollar. This is an important result: Ecuador, the Andean economy to have adopted the US dollar, enjoys lower costs for remittances than an economy with a national currency.[20]

9.6. POLICIES TO REDUCE COSTS OF REMITTANCES AND ENHANCE THEIR DEVELOPMENT IMPACT

As we have documented in this chapter, the cost of sending money transfers to developing countries is high, and this leads to an inefficient level of transfers. How to reduce the costs of sending money abroad? How to increase competition in the international market for transfers? How to enhance the development impact of remittances in the receiving countries? Measures are needed on both the sending side as well as the recipient side.

9.6.1. *The Sending-Country Perspective*

'Formalization' of the legal status of the migrant would certainly promote greater access by the migrant to a variety of bank services, including remittances services. This should lower the costs of remittances. For example, the use of ATM cards for making transfers rather than the current, more costly methods can be an effective mechanism for reducing the costs of remittances.

Another factor that apparently prevents a competitive atmosphere in the remittances business in the United States is the cost of procuring a license for becoming an MTO, which is about US\$100,000 per each state where operations are to be conducted. Prospective money operators find this cost high.

It is important also to avoid increases in transaction costs, or to add to the regulations governing worker remittances to reflect the mounting controls on financial intermediaries for preventing money laundering or the financing of terrorism.

---

[19] See Solimano (2003).

[20] See Beckerman and Solimano (2002) for an analysis of the macroeconomic and social impact of official dollarization in Ecuador.

In sum, we believe that increasing the efficiency of the market for remittances requires:

(i) The costs of licensing for new operators to be contained or reduced so as to make the process of certification of new financial intermediaries in the remittances business less costly and more expedite.

(ii) The process of granting residence visas and/or citizenship to be expedited so as to avoid long visa processing periods for migrants (which currently can take up to several years, at least in the United States). This would help to regularize the immigrant sector, inviting commercial banks to target the financial needs of the migrants.

(iii) Domestic banks (particularly those with an international scope) to be encouraged to develop new product lines for migrants such as chequeing or savings account, remittances services, etc. The creation of 'banks for migrants' is an idea worth exploring.

The remittance-receiving nations would benefit from a more efficient and less costly market for remittances. Currently, a significant slice of remittances goes to operators as profits rather than to families of migrants in developing countries. This has adverse efficiency effects and is socially regressive.

9.6.2. *The Recipient-Country Perspective*

From the viewpoint of recipient countries, leveraging remittances and enhancing their productive use for development are two important issues. There are various mechanisms for leveraging remittances in the receiving countries: governments and local financial institutions can issue bonds targeted for emigrants, who would thus earn interest, and it would create a more attractive instrument for channelling remittances.

In addition, housing and education accounts can be created to channel remittances to various productive uses in the home country, such as investment in durables (housing) and education (investment in human capital).

The development of alliances between domestic banks in the receiving countries and banks, credit unions and MTOs in the sending nations can help to increase efficiency and reduce costs in the remittances market. Mechanisms to ensure a productive use of remittances include the mobilization of HTAs similar to those that have evolved in the United States in recent years (Mexican migrants have been very active in creating HTAs and are being helped by their government in this effort).

Finally, taxing remittances (mainly worker remittances) in the sending countries or in the receiving economies does not seem to be a good idea.[21] These are transfers, sent in general by and to low-income groups. So, it is doubly inequitable that such flows, based on income that has already subject to the income tax system of the sending country, should be taxed. In receiving countries, remittances are a source of foreign exchange, a complement of national savings and a transfer to low- to medium-income

---

[21] Another possibility is to make remittances tax deductible.

groups. It is unclear what the social gain would be if governments were to interfere directly with these income flows in any way to diminish them.

9.7. CONCLUDING REMARKS

This chapter examines the developmental and financial dimensions of remittances from international migrants. Remittances are currently the second most important source of development finance at the global level after FDI. Also, they are more stable than private capital flows such as portfolio investment and bank credit. The sustainability over time of remittances as a source of income for developing countries depends also on the cycle of migration (recent versus older migration) and the expected flows of migration. Remittances have become a very significant source of development finance for several developing countries. They are a source of foreign exchange; they support the consumption levels of low-to-middle-income families and constitute a direct source for funding small, community–oriented investment projects through the migrants' associations that send donations home in support of these projects (the so-called 'community remittances'). From a social point of view, remittances can have a positive poverty-reducing effect, as families receiving remittances from migrants are often low-income people. However, the recipient syndrome of relying on remittances for income should be avoided. Properly mobilized remittances can contribute to increased investment in basic infrastructure such as water, roads, low-income housing, school-buildings, investment in human capital (education), and help to finance micro and small-scale firms. For remittance-sending countries, remittances represent a market-based international transfer to developing countries that indirectly reduces the demand for ODA.

Still, we have to recognize that earning foreign exchange through remittances entails an implicit tradeoff in the form of an outflow of skilled manpower from the sending countries.

Currently, the potential development impact of remittances is impaired, in part, by the existence of a costly, concentrated and poorly competitive international market for remittances. Empirical evidence shows that the costs of remittances are above what the marginal costs of (electronically) transferring funds provided that electronic transfers are possible. Although the involvement of commercial banks in the remittances market is still small, evidence shows that the costs of sending remittances tend to be lower when transferred through banks rather than through international MTOs. In addition, there are differences in the costs of sending remittances to non–Latin American countries compared to Latin American countries: the exchange rate spread component is higher for remittances sent to Latin American countries than to non–Latin American countries. Our empirical analysis, based on a detailed survey of MTOs in the United States who operate within the Andean region, shows that the total cost of remittances for these countries vary from 5 to 12 per cent of the value remitted depending on the type of currency to be delivered, destination country, type of financial operator involved, and other factors. Reducing the costs of sending remittances by, say, 5 percentage points could increase the amount of remittances received by developing countries by a few billion.

What can be done to increase competition and reduce costs in the remittances market? In the sending countries, facilitating the process of opening bank accounts for immigrants could be an important step for integrating the migrant community into the financial system of the host country. This would increase competition and reduce the costs of remittances. On the other hand, the costs of licensing for new operators and other regulations on the part of banks and non-bank intermediaries wishing to provide services for migrants should be minimal to as to avoid creating entry barriers into the this market. Also, efforts for controlling money laundering or the financing of terrorism should not unnecessarily increase the costs to emigrants of sending home remittances. On the recipient side, the issuance of remittance bonds, the opening of foreign currency accounts for migrant workers in the home country, the creation of facilities for voluntary donations to projects are all measures to leverage remittances for development. In turn, the creation of education and housing accounts at home for migrants could help to enhance the productive and social use of remittances proceeds. Also encouraging the return of emigrants—bringing fresh capital, new ideas, and international contacts—can be a promising way to attract remittances for growth and development in receiving countries.

REFERENCES

Barham, B. and S. Boucher (1998). 'Migration, Remittances and Inequality: Estimating the Net Effects of Migration on Income Distribution'. *Journal of Development Economics*, 55: 307–31.

Beckerman, P. and A. Solimano (eds) (2002). *Crisis and Dollarization in Ecuador: Stability, Growth, and Social Equity (Directions in Development)*. Washington, DC: World Bank.

Bendixen and Associates (2003). 'Receptores de Remesas en Ecuador. Una Investigacion del Mercado'. Presentation at Multilateral Investment Fund—Pew Hispanic Center conference on Remittances and Development, Quito, Ecuador, May.

Brown, R. (1997). 'Estimating Remittances Functions for Pacific Island Migrants'. *World Development*, 25(4): 613–26.

Ellerman, D. (2003). 'Policy Research on Migration and Development'. *WB Policy Research Working Paper* 3117. Washington, DC: World Bank.

Gammeltoft, P. (2002). 'Remittances and other Financial Flows to Developing Countries'. *Working Paper* 02.11. Copenhagen: Centre for Development Research.

International Monetary Fund (IMF) (2003). *Balance of Payments Statistics Yearbook 2003*. Washington, DC: IMF.

Orozco, M. (2001). 'Globalization and Migration: The Impact of Family Remittances in Latin America'. Washington, DC: Multilateral Investment Fund-IADB.

—— (2002). 'Attracting Remittances: Markets, Money and Reduced Costs'. Washington, DC: Multilateral Investment Fund-IADB.

—— (2003). 'Workers Remittances: The Human Face of Globalization'. Washington, DC: Multilateral Investment Fund-IADB.

Poirine, B. (1997). 'A Theory of Remittances as an Implicit Family Loan Arrangement'. *World Development*, 25(4): 589–611.

Ratha, D. (2003). 'Workers' Remittances: An Important and Stable Source of External Development Finance', *Global Development Finance, 2003*. Washington, DC: World Bank, chapter 7.

Smith, A. (2003). 'Leveraging "Mobile" Human Capital for Development. Migration and Development Finance'. Mimeo, UN-DESA.

Solimano, A. (2001). 'International Migration and the Global Economic Order: An Overview'. *WB Policy Research Working Paper* 2720. Washington, DC: World Bank.

—— (2002a). 'Globalizing Talent and Human Capital: Implications for Developing Countries'. *Series Macroeconomics of Development* No. 15. Santiago: UN-ECLAC.

—— (2002b). 'Development Cycles, Political Regimes and International Migration: Argentina in the 20th Century'. Paper presented at the UNU-WIDER Conference on Poverty, International Migration and Asylum, 27–28 September. Helsinki: UNU-WIDER.

—— (2003). 'Workers Remittances to the Andean Region: Mechanisms, Costs and Development Impact'. Santiago: UN-ECLAC. Mimeo.

Stark, O. (1991). *The Migration of Labor*. Oxford: Basil Blackwell.

World Bank (2002). 'Migrants Capital for Small-Scale Infrastructure and Small Enterprise Development in Mexico'. Project Report. Washington, DC: World Bank.

—— (2003). *Global Development Finance, 2003*. Washington, DC: World Bank.

10

Global Public Economics

JAMES A. MIRRLEES

10.1. GLOBAL TAXATION

Transfers by governments to low-income countries, whether to their governments or their citizens, through agencies such as the UN, or directly, are part of the global fiscal system of taxes and subsidies. We can think about optimal global taxes and subsidies, as they might be instituted by a world government. There is no possibility that such a system will be implemented, but it might provide a reference point to illuminate or suggest more realistic policy options; or a moral challenge that will merely leave us deeply uncomfortable.

Here is a specific, too simple model, of a kind many of us have used to think about optimal national tax systems. It is a timeless model, where income and consumption are the same, and people's labour is the only input into production of goods that will be used for private or government consumption. People have utility $u(c, \ell)$, where c is income, net of taxes and subsidies, and ℓ is labour supplied. u is, as we usually assume, concave, increasing in the first argument, decreasing in the second. The difference between people is that they have different productivities w. Assuming competitive conditions, a person's income before taxes and subsidies is $w\ell$. This income is the base for determining transfers, whether to or from the individual.

If an optimal system of transfers is one that maximizes the sum of individual utilities, it is to be expected that it would involve substantial positive taxes on almost everyone in the richer countries and substantial transfers to the majority of households in lower-income countries. There would also be transfers to governments in low-income countries to pay for public consumption. One would imagine that the optimal provision of public facilities like police and security, water supply, roads, schools, and health care would be rather similar in real (PPP, purchasing power parity) per capita terms among countries, and indeed that might be the most dramatic difference between an optimal world economy and a system of optimal national economies with only small transfers between nations.

Because of incentive considerations, marginal tax rates would not necessarily be any higher in an optimal world than in optimal nations, even if average tax rates would

Paper prepared for the UNU-WIDER Conference on Sharing Global Prosperity, September 2003, Helsinki, Finland.

be higher in rich countries, and lower (even sometimes negative) in poorer ones. It is interesting to consider this further. Unfortunately, there is a terrible lack of good general propositions in optimal tax theory: we must rely on qualitative differences that can be seen in numerical examples, or differences that are clear between extreme cases, and are likely to apply to most intermediate cases in a similar way.

It seems that world inequality in relative incomes is somewhat greater than inequality within most (but certainly not all) countries. We may take it that something similar is true of inequality in wage rates, though that is not easy to observe directly. Differences between countries in lifetime hours of work, though certainly quite marked, are clearly not at all as large as differences of income, and therefore inequality of wage rates should be somewhat similar to inequality of incomes. The question then is how inequality of wage rates affects optimal tax rates, most particularly marginal tax rates. The answer we expect is that greater inequality will be associated with higher marginal tax rates.

At the extreme of perfect equality, taxation can be lumpsum, with everyone paying the same amount of tax, and a marginal tax rate of zero. Thus, at least at small degrees of inequality, marginal tax rates should increase with inequality. (At the same time, we should remember that two-class models have been constructed in which the optimal marginal tax rates are negative (Allen 1982), though they are probably not too close to reality.) At the opposite extreme, when there are only very high-productivity people and very low-productivity people, the optimal schedule $c = x(w\ell)$ must be close to one of the high-w people's indifference curves. According to a familiar argument, we would want the high-w person to choose a point on that schedule where the slope was equal to the wage. Her marginal tax rate would be zero (just as in the no-inequality case), but she would still pay a substantial total tax, to be compared with the subsidy received by low-w individuals. The zero marginal tax rate feature is an artefact of the unrealistic assumption that it is perfectly known what the highest w (though the w of any particular individual is unknown to the taxing authority); but we can still derive instruction from this crude model.

One measure of progressivity in the tax system (though not one that has been used to my knowledge) is the difference in tax paid by richest and poorest divided by the difference in incomes. Call this the incremental tax rate. It is an average of marginal tax rates across the whole income range. As a particularly simple case, take a two-class economy with pure redistribution, that is to say, no public consumption. Compare across models with the same average product per person, but low and high wages diverging. When the divergence is large, all the work is done by those with high w. In a wide range of cases (with utility additively separable in the two arguments) it is found that the incremental tax rate converges to one as the high wage tends to infinity. There is a sense, therefore, in which as inequality increases, the progressivity of the system increases, and indeed with this measure becomes as great as possible, despite the fact that the marginal tax rate at the highest income levels is zero.

We do not have to rely on extreme examples of this kind for evidence that, on average, marginal tax rates increase as inequality increases. Numerical calculations have supported this conjecture. But, particularly at higher income levels, the rate at which marginal tax rates increase as inequality increases turns out to be quite slow.

The simplest tax system is a linear one, creating a universal budget constraint

$$c = (1 - t)w\ell + b$$

with constant marginal tax rate t applying at all income levels and a fixed lumpsum payment b. b is roughly equivalent to personal allowances in the income tax, along with welfare benefits and education and publicly provided health expenditures. Considering that greater inequality seems to imply greater marginal tax rates, but that world inequality is, in proportional terms, not much greater than inequality within most countries, we would expect a world optimal system to have a slightly larger level of t than is optimal for single nations without significant international transfers, whereas b would be much smaller than is appropriate for high-income countries, and larger, no doubt considerably larger, than would be appropriate for low-income countries (if they were to implement such a safety net). The different level of b is primarily dictated by the different level of average product in the different countries and the world.

As a consequence, people whose productivity is high even within a rich country would have a budget constraint not very different from that they currently experience, since the lumpsum element of the tax system is (and should be) small relative to their after-tax labour income. Paradoxically, the introduction of a world optimal tax/subsidy system would have the greatest negative impact (in relative terms) on middle-income people, while the greatest positive impact would, of course, be for people with the lowest productivity. In a sense, an optimal tax system will go far to extract as much revenue as possible from the richest in society, so that any further revenue requirement, as a result of joining a redistributive world tax system (or, more moderately, for increased foreign aid) will have to be drawn, to a considerable extent, from those in the middle of the income distribution.

10.2. TAXATION FOR AID

It is natural, then, to consider nations whose governments choose some fixed level of development assistance, presumably not the level that would be implicit in a world-optimal tax and transfer system, but where, within each country, national welfare is maximized. The arguments already developed can be modified to address the question how taxes should change if there is to be an increase in the development assistance grant.

When doing calculations of optimal linear income taxation, Nicholas Stern noticed that an increase in the revenue requirement for public consumption had little effect on the marginal tax rate: additional expenditure was to be financed to a considerable extent by a reduction on the lumpsum subsidy which we have denoted by b. This observation corresponds closely to the argument developed in the previous section.

It is difficult to tell how general or relevant this result is. One way of throwing some light on the question is to look at the inverse problem and ask for what utility functions the result would be exactly true in the simple model we are using. The answer is that the optimal marginal tax rate is independent of the government expenditure requirement when (and, in a certain sense, only when)

$$u(c, \ell) = -(k - c)^m - \ell^m, \quad k > 0, \quad m > 0.$$

It is shown in an appendix that this utility function implies the stated result: the necessity theorem is more involved and less interesting and is omitted. This is certainly a somewhat peculiar utility function, with a maximum level of desirable consumption, and no upper bound to the labour that a person can supply. Yet it may not be a bad approximation to people's consumption/labour preferences. It shows that in acceptable models, it is optimal to finance increased government consumption entirely by reduction of the uniform subsidy. Indeed it shows, implicitly, that there must be acceptable models in which the marginal tax rate would actually fall when the government expenditure requirement increased.

The conclusion is that, broadly, increased aid should come from everyone. That is to say, if it is generally recognized that development assistance does more good than had previously been appreciated, it is implied that the tax structure should be modified in such a way as to generate more revenue in an optimal manner, and that may involve only small increases in taxes on labour (and commodities).

A dual question to this is whether, when it is recognized that new revenue raising taxes are desirable, for example, to reduce smoking, or consumption of cholesterol, or environmentally damaging goods, it follows that more should be spent on foreign aid (and desirable public goods). No, it does not follow.

The simplest example uses the same model as before. Suppose it is newly recognized that production brings about global warming. In the model, we cannot allow for some kinds of production doing that and others not, nor for the damage occurring at a later date than the production. These would just complicate the analysis and lead to broadly the same conclusions. For simplicity, suppose that the damaging effect of global warming is just a reduction in production (actually at a different time, but all periods are combined together here). In the model, everyone's productivity is reduced from w to kw, where k is a positive number less than one. Since individual producers do not recognize the external impact of production, the competitive level of wages is still w. One further simplification gives a neat, clean result: it will be assumed that utility is a homogeneous function of consumption c.

The optimal budget constraint, with a given level of foreign aid, is then

$$c = (1 - t)kw\ell + bk,$$

where the optimal levels of t and b are independent of k.

This conclusion follows from the fact that one feasible tax system is preferred to another in the economy with $k = 1$, then both these tax systems remain feasible for the economy with externality, if modified by the introduction of the factor k as above. And, furthermore, everyone's utility is multiplied by a factor that is a power of k. Thus the order of preference between the two tax systems remains the same. Consequently, the optimal tax system is deduced from the original optimal system simply by introducing the factor k.

The actual marginal tax rate is changed, of course. Denoting it by t', we have

$$t' = 1 - (1 - t)k = 1 - k + kt,$$

which is greater than t, and grows as k diminishes. It is true then that taxation (of labour or, equivalently, goods) should be increased because of the environmental externality; but the uniform subsidy b should be reduced to kb. People will be worse off than they would have been if there were no externality, and their marginal utility of income (of b) will be reduced. Consequently, the domestic welfare cost of giving foreign aid, or of any revenue for public spending, is reduced. It follows that the case for foreign aid is less strong.

It may be argued that it is a different matter if new taxes are introduced because of a previously existing externality that had not been recognized. For this to modify the conclusion, one must accept the idea that people recognized the reduced marginal utility of income implied by environmental effects, but did not recognize the need for and desirability of controlling policies. Then the optimal-tax account is not really appropriate to the issue. In effect, I have argued that people's apparently simple-minded intuition that increased (environmental) taxes make them worse off is essentially correct, and that governments should not be told that they are in some sense better off and can afford to be more generous when they find that they ought to introduce these new taxes.

10.3. INTERNATIONAL IMPACT AND FACTOR MOBILITY

In the previous section, it was taken for granted that there was well-defined membership of the welfare function, which is to say that there is no doubt as to whose utility counts in determining the optimal tax system. In fact, there is considerable movement of people, both long term and short term. In reality, tax laws are applied in a bewildering mixture to residents, migrants, absentees, and nationals. It would be hard to construct a rationale for the way they are applied. Some few countries apply income taxation to nationals (or those with rights to reside and work) even when they have been resident abroad for some time. Surprisingly, it is unusual for the tax law to discriminate substantially against visitors or residents who are not entitled to vote.

The citizens of low-income countries often receive substantial remittances from nationals or relatives abroad. It is a major source of foreign assistance. It is an attractive proposal, then, that countries should tax their nationals (Bhagwati and Wilson 1989). Nationals of low-income countries abroad are generally much more prosperous than the average domestic resident. Such a move would surely benefit residents. The proposal envisaged double taxation, with nationals abroad paying taxes both to country of residence and country of nationality. It would be tidier and more natural to have an international agreement whereby income taxation applied to nationals, not to residents, with countries reporting people's income to their country of nationality.

The practical difficulties are considerable. Price levels vary considerably among countries. While there is no way of measuring PPP 'correctly'—it is impossible to give a rigorous definition of the concept—clearly some adjustment would have to be made.

A much more serious difficulty is that different countries use commodity taxation and factor-income taxation in different proportions. It is hard, too, to see how dual nationality (which is often a desirable status) should be handled, and how family taxation (dependent allowances and joint taxation) should operate when different members of the household have different nationalities. Probably the most serious objection is that many people would be sufficiently unaltruistic or unpatriotic that they would adopt a national flag of convenience. It is a matter of regret, but the idea of reconstructing the international allocation of tax bases is not worth pursuing.

10.4. SUPRANATIONAL TAXATION

A world agency might be given some taxation power, but probably not simply for development assistance. There are many cases where countries should negotiate to ensure that taxation on some commodity is at more or less the same rate in different countries. The European Union has been trying to achieve 'harmonization' of many taxes, without committing itself to anything like an equal tax-rate principle. It has not created any supranational taxes. On the other hand, the Common Agricultural Policy constitutes a system of supranational subsidies. Also there are rules for transfers of parts of tax revenues to central funds, which come close to creating supranational taxes.

There are cases where efficient and reliable administration seems to suggest a supranational agency. Taxes on the combustion of hydrocarbons might well have been done that way (except that we know it would not be accepted by many governments). At least a tax on aircraft fuel, which is much to be desired, could be administered supranationally. The Tobin tax, on foreign exchange transactions, could also be done that way. The main point is to ensure common tax rates for tax rates in different locations.

If there were such supranational taxes, should the revenue be used for aid? There is no particular reason why the international nature of the revenue flow constitutes an argument for using the revenue for an international cause. Presumably, international causes would include financing UN administration, refugees, and UN military operations as well as development aid. But the connection is merely terminological. The existence of international revenue, if any, does not strengthen the claims of development assistance (and these other international expenditures), and it is hard to see why governments or voters would think it. The best one can say is that it might be politically possible for a novel revenue source to be used for purposes that international civil servants and members of NGOs find attractive, because its novelty might mean that other claimants, such as national governments, would not be quick to secure it for themselves.

It is also possible for a supranational agency to undertake profit-making activities, the proceeds from which could be available for aid. In effect, the World Bank is such an agency, using borrowing and lending as its instruments. It is hard to think of other opportunities. Production should require little skill, and yet the operation should be profitable. The proposal of a global lottery is an interesting and promising one, since lotteries appear to constitute an industry where entrants can still make substantial profits, presumably because of national regulation. It is only socially optimal to have a high cost of gambling (which is what these profitable lotteries provide), if gambling ought to be discouraged. It is then rather dubious to try to increase supply. It is a bit like increasing the production of tobacco or other drugs as a way of getting revenue.

10.5. SUBSIDIES AND TRANSFERS

Subsidies are as much a part of public finance as taxes. We should, therefore, look at the expenditure side of development assistance as well as at the generation of revenue for it.

The general tax model we started with does not at first sight appear to describe very well the way that development assistance operates. Provision of schools and health care is rather close to the idea of a general uniform subsidy, if everyone is entitled to the same facilities, or at least does not pay or have entitlement related to income. The distribution of food aid can locally be of similar character. Grants to governments seem rather different. But where the recipient government is efficient and not corrupt, these grants do also fit the model fairly well, with the government using the funds as part of its revenues, influencing the level of subsidies to individual households as well as taxes. When aid is given in the form of finance for public projects, whether as pure aid or loans with concessional terms, that should mean that part of government expenditure is being paid for by aid, so that required tax revenue within the recipient country is reduced.

It is clear that the form of the tax/subsidy system within the recipient countries is of great importance. Generally, in the lower-income countries, these systems are not very progressive as tax systems. It is supposed to be difficult to redistribute in poor, particularly in agricultural, countries. No doubt, the leakages from a general system of subsidies to farming households, both through administrative costs and corruption, are great. That reduces the marginal social value of subsidies (represented by b in the model), and means that the optimal tax system should be less progressive than would otherwise have been desirable. There are also leakages in the collection of taxes and in the disbursement of funds for public or private investment. The latter makes public spending (g) less desirable than otherwise. The former consideration has ambiguous implications: the adverse incentive effects of higher marginal tax rates may be less when there is considerable evasion. Though one must allow for unfair variation in effective (as opposed to legislated) tax rates, higher legislated rates may be needed to raise the actual tax revenue.

The main issue is what form the tax system should take when there are substantial errors in the observation of income, or, equivalently, in the transfers (whether taxes or subsidies). Little work has been done on the problem. A preliminary conclusion, from a model with no explicit incentive effects, is that the formal (i.e. legislated) progressivity of the system should not necessarily be less because of measurement errors.

On balance, subsidy leakages probably imply that the tax system should be somewhat less progressive than in high-income countries. But there is nevertheless a strong case for bringing pressure on recipient countries to make their systems more redistributive, pressure that might well take the form of aid conditionality. Certain forms of aid are much less at the mercy of corruption and ineffiency than others, particularly aid programmes that are directly administered by international agencies, or at least that is what one hopes. One should perhaps question the common assumption that aid is always best given in the form of capital investment, rather than for consumption. Perhaps gifts of money (like the model) are best?

10.6. VOLUNTARY CONTRIBUTIONS AND TAXATION

Private voluntary contributions to development assistance are not negligible. When one remembers that much official aid has been in the form of concessionary loans, and the official figures have included many expenditures that are really only aid to manufacturers in the donor country and of little net benefit (after loan repayments) to the recipient, one realizes that private aid has been a quite substantial proportion of total aid to developing countries. It is worth modelling, so that we can consider whether and how it is to be increased.

Suppose people make voluntary contributions to aid because the income that recipients get contributes to their utility. (This assumption is not consistent with experimental evidence that people would not give more to larger groups.) Denote contributions by x_i. According to the hypothesis,

$$x_i \text{ maximizes} \quad u(y_i - x_i) + a_i v\left(\sum_j x_j\right).$$

This way of modelling has different people with different income y_i, and places different weight on the value of aid receipts. The amount people give provides some information about the value placed on aid, but of course is also influenced by their income.

Consider what would maximize the sum of utilities. Maximizing

$$\sum_i \left[u(y_i - x_i) + a_i v\left(\sum_j x_j\right) \right]$$

yields a very different outcome: much larger values of contributions to aid are implied. A similar result is obtained if we seek to maximize the median voter's utility. To do this calculation, of course we need to know incomes and the value placed on recipient utility. Income we may observe directly. a_i should be deduced from the amount an individual would choose to give. We can arrange for the value placed on aid to be revealed by individual choice if we introduce matching grants, so that a voluntary contribution x is expanded to Mx. (A more general function could be used.) The matching element comes from compulsory contributions, that is, taxation. We can let it be a proportional tax on income.

This will not in equilibrium bring about the welfare maximum, but a second-best. The second-best would be the welfare maximum if everyone were identical. In that case the optimal value of M is the number of people. More generally, we get a moderately complicated expression approximately equal to the number of people. When people all have the same income, and quadratic utility, optimal M is $(\sum a)^2 / (\sum a^2)$.

This is an absurdly large number, of course, and would mean people made extremely small individual contributions that get multiplied up to aid that would be a substantial part of total incomes. People could not calculate correctly. One cannot really take the result seriously, and yet it suggests a case for much more generous matching than is provided by tax systems in which voluntary contributions to charitable causes are simply tax exempt.

10.7. DEVELOPMENT ASSISTANCE EXPANSION

On the whole a public finance approach to development assistance is not sympathetic to some of the main proposals for expansion, using revenue from environmental taxes or a Tobin tax. Yet it acknowledges a strong case for increasing aid by government and by individuals. Two proposals that are rather utopian suggest themselves from a public finance perspective:

1. Introduce a voluntary additional income tax to be used for development assistance, this tax to be matched by a substantial multiplier from general revenues. The individual would choose what percentage rate should be applied to income. Matching by a double contribution from general revenues would not be unjustified.
2. High-income countries with particularly low tax systems, which are to a considerable extent tax havens, might be induced by international pressure to institute a supplementary income tax on income arising in their territories, the income from which should be used for development aid.

APPENDIX: CONDITIONS FOR MARGINAL TAX RATES TO BE INDEPENDENT OF THE REVENUE REQUIREMENT

It will be verified that when the sum of utilities is maximized, utility functions take the form

$$u(c, \ell) = -(k - c)^m - \ell^m, \quad k > 0, \quad m > 0,$$

the budget constraint is

$$c = (1 - t)w\ell + b$$

and the overall resource constraint is

$$E[c - w\ell] = g$$

(where we use the operator E for averaging over the population), then, regardless of the distribution of marginal products w, optimal t is independent of g.

Utility maximization by the consumer implies that for someone with wage w, ℓ maximizes $-[k - (1 - t)w\ell - b]^m - \ell^m$, so that

$$(1 - t)w[k - (1 - t)w\ell - b]^{m-1} = \ell^{m-1}.$$

Solving this equation for ℓ, and introducing the temporary notation $v = (1 - t)w$, we have

$$\ell = (v^{1/(1-m)} + v)^{-1}(k - b)$$

and from this we deduce that

$$c = k - (v^{-m/(1-m)} + 1)^{-1}(k - b)$$

Substituting these expressions into the utility function, we find that a w-person's utility is

$$-(v^{-m/(1-m)} + 1)^{1-m}(k - b)^m.$$

We want to maximize the average value of utility,

$$-E\left[(v^{-m/(1-m)} + 1)^{1-m}\right](k - b)^m$$

subject to the resource constraint, which we can now calculate: it is

$$\frac{t}{1-t}E\left[v(v + v^{1/(1-m)})^{-1}\right](k - b) = b + g,$$

which can be rewritten to give a formula for $k - b$:

$$k - b = \left\{1 + \frac{t}{1-t}E\left[v(v + v^{1/(1-m)})^{-1}\right]\right\}^{-1}(g + k).$$

Substituting this into our expression for average utility, we get

$$E[u] = -E\left[(v^{-m/(1-m)} + 1)^{1-m}\right]\left\{1 + \frac{t}{1-t}E\left[v(v + v^{1/(1-m)})^{-1}\right]\right\}^{-m}(g + k)^m.$$

This has to be maximized with respect to t (remember that $v = (1 - t)w$). g appears in the maximand only in the final factor, which does not involve t. Therefore the level of g does not affect the maximizing value of t. The result claimed is proved.

REFERENCES

Allen, F. (1982). 'Optimal Linear Income Taxation with General Equilibrium Effects on Wages'. *Journal of Public Economics*, 17: 135–43.

Bhagwati, J. N. and J. D. Wilson (1989). *Income Taxation and International Mobility*. Cambridge, MA: MIT Press.

11

National Taxation, Fiscal Federalism and Global Taxation

ROBIN BOADWAY

11.1. INTRODUCTION

This chapter draws on ideas from the fiscal federalism literature—where transfers from better-off to less well-off regions are the norm—for guidance in the search for innovative new approaches to development finance. While it may be fanciful—or utopian—at present to regard the world as a whole as a federation, thinking of it in this way is an interesting point of reference. A *global equalization scheme* mimicking the way in which redistributive finance occurs in a federation would lead to a pattern of official aid that differs considerably from what we observe in practice. Contemplating such a scheme and the principles behind it helps us understand how far problems with different proposals for development funding are the result of the fact that there is no counterpart of a central government, and how far they are the inevitable outcome of the cooperative interaction of political entities with different objectives and interests.

It is worth highlighting at the outset some similarities and differences between decisionmaking and institutions in federations and those that might be feasible in a global setting. We have in mind relatively decentralized federations in which sub-national governments have independent fiscal responsibilities. Organization for Economic Cooperation and Development (OECD) examples include Australia, Canada, Spain, Switzerland, and the United States, while Argentina, Brazil, India, and Malaysia are examples from the developing world.

The similarities arise from the fact that, in both instances, the population is divided among governing states that have more or less autonomous authority over their fiscal affairs. Subnational governments, like nation-states, raise revenues to provide goods, services, and transfers to their residents. Moreover, the decisions of individual subnational governments may be taken independently of those of others. This decentralization of authority gives rise to a number of relevant consequences.

Differences in average incomes. Residents of different states will inevitably have different average incomes, and the states themselves will also be endowed with different amounts

Prepared for the UNU-WIDER project on Innovative Sources of Development Finance. The many comments of project leader Tony Atkinson and members of the project team are gratefully acknowledged.

of natural wealth. As well, there will be different degrees of social and economic development. The disparities among subnations within nations may not be as great as those between nations. Nonetheless, qualitatively similar issues arise with respect to the desire to address these inequities through redistributive policies—the *vertical equity* issue.

Differences in fiscal capacity. Related to the previous point, the decentralization of fiscal responsibility will inevitably lead to states differing in their abilities to raise revenues and in their needs for public expenditures. This implies that different levels of public services can be provided at given tax rates across states. In the absence of corrective measures, this can compromise efficiency in the allocation of resources across states by giving rise to fiscally induced relocation. As originally observed by Buchanan (1950), it also precludes the equal treatment of equals—*horizontal equity*—across the group of states as a whole.

Spillover benefits and costs. Some policy issues transcend state borders and can only be addressed by coordinated policies. Thus, nationwide public goods (e.g. defence) provide benefits indiscriminately to residents of different subnational jurisdictions. Spillover benefits or costs may occur from public goods and services that are delivered at the subnational level (transportation facilities, cross-border pollution). And, goals of redistributive equity (income redistribution, poverty alleviation, equality of opportunity, social insurance) may be viewed as national goals, analogous to national public goods. Decentralization can cause inefficiencies to the extent that cross-border spillovers of these sorts occur.

Fiscal externalities. Related to the above, fiscal decisions taken by one government have indirect consequences for other governments because of the interdependency of markets for products and factors of production. Tax or expenditure changes in one jurisdiction may influence the allocation of factors or products across jurisdictions (fiscal competition). Alternatively, the burden of tax changes in one jurisdiction may be partly borne by agents in other jurisdictions, either at the same or a different level (tax exporting, vertical fiscal externalities). These fiscal externalities give rise to inefficiencies in the allocation of resources both within and across jurisdictions (Dahlby 1996).

Of course, offsetting these adverse consequences of decentralization are the benefits (Oates 1999). Subnational levels of government can design their government programmes with the needs, preferences, and values of local residents in mind. Moreover, they might be able to deliver public services and target transfers to their citizens more efficiently than a centralized government. The latter may be less informed and less accountable to local citizens. An important dimension of the case for decentralization is that it applies particularly to public services and targeted transfers that are important instruments for addressing economic and social development goals and redistributive equity more generally. Intergovernmental fiscal arrangements in federations are in large part devoted to ensuring that subnational governments have the capacity, the incentives and the discretion for delivering these programmes in a way that fosters equity and efficiency in the nation as a whole (Boadway 2001).

Parallel to these similarities, there are some critical differences between the situation faced by a federation comprised of autonomous subnational governments and the world economy comprised of independent nation-states. For one, the degree of mobility across state borders is typically much higher in federations than internationally. Citizens can move freely across borders; a common currency and a common set of legal and property rights institutions apply; and policies are better coordinated. While these differences in mobility lead to greater efficiency in the allocation of resources in the internal economic union, they also result in greater opportunities for inter-state externalities and spillovers, and therefore the need for coordinated or harmonized policies.

Another important difference is that there is likely to be much more consensus within federations than across nations for addressing the consequences of inequality of resources, incomes, and opportunities across states. The fact of common nationhood may imply that, despite the possibly lower degree of inequality across subnational jurisdictions, the will to redistribute—the sense of national solidarity—may be higher than exists between nation-states. And, the concern for horizontal equity may be more of a policy issue across subnational governments in a federation than across nations in the world economy.

The most important difference is that a federation has a national government with substantive powers to address the adverse consequences of decentralized decision-making. These powers typically include some degree of influence or even coercion over subnational governments. An important dimension of decisionmaking in a federation is the assignment of responsibilities between the national and subnational governments. Ideally, this is done in a way that represents the most reasonable compromise between achieving the benefits of decentralization while facilitating national equity and efficiency objectives. This is typically fostered by an asymmetric division of revenue-raising and expenditure responsibilities—a *vertical fiscal gap*—with the national government retaining the lion's share of revenue-raising, and transferring revenues in excess of its own requirements to the subnational governments. Federal government presence in the most important tax fields along with its ability to design appropriate transfers to subnational governments provides it with the instruments for addressing issues of redistributive equity, and avoiding to the greatest possible extent the adverse consequences of fiscal externalities and differences in fiscal capacity. Moreover, the fiscal dominance of the national government enables it to play an influential role in harmonizing taxation and expenditure policies of the subnational governments to enhance the functioning of the federation.

The presence of a central government that attends to issues of nationwide interest and has the coercive powers of taxation and spending distinguishes a federation from a community of nations, whether that is the entire world or regional groupings like the European Union. Since these latter groups have no strong central government, the ability to raise revenues and to address matters of internation redistribution and efficiency are considerably compromised. These tasks must necessarily be based on voluntary agreement, perhaps facilitated by the delegation of administrative authority to a central institution. Nonetheless, the manner in which federal governments raise revenues for the purposes of development-type objectives might be instructive as a benchmark against which to evaluate possible new revenue sources to finance worldwide development.

A natural starting point is to contemplate the case in which there is a national government overseeing a fairly decentralized federal system consisting of several autonomous subnational governments with independent fiscal authority. Both the accepted principles and the practice of fiscal federalism should be instructive in this regard. Using this as a benchmark, we can then consider financing arrangements in the more realistic situation in which a world government does not exist or does not have the coercive financial authority required to achieve the benchmark outcome. As a step towards that, we contemplate the hypothetical case of a federation without a central government after having discussed fiscal arrangements in a representative federation.

11.2. REVENUE-RAISING IN A FEDERAL SETTING

In a federation, the national and subnational levels of government typically share the responsibilities for redistributive equity, poverty alleviation, and development. Many of the nation's public services, targeted transfers, and development investments are provided under the authority of subnational governments. As well, the latter typically apply redistributive tax-transfer systems alongside the national government, although the degree varies from federation to federation. The national government assumes overriding authority for ensuring that minimum standards of redistributive equity and opportunities apply nationwide. Even where subnational governments are responsible for delivering important programmes for economic development, opportunity, and poverty alleviation, the federal government ordinarily assumes a significant share of the financial costs. In keeping with the project objectives, our concern is with the revenue sources used to fund these programmes rather than the design of the programmes themselves.

We focus on an idealized federation, one that draws on best practices around the world. In such a federation, expenditure responsibility will be more decentralized than revenue decisions: there will be a vertical fiscal gap. The delivery of important public goods and services—including those in the health, education, and welfare areas that serve important redistributive purposes—will be assigned to subnational governments. The national government's dominance in raising revenue flows partly from the desire to maintain an efficient and fair national tax system, and partly from a need to finance transfers to the subnational level. As discussed below, these transfers enable federal government to achieve horizontal balance in the federation. They also enable federal government to exert influence over subnational programme design to insure that national objectives are met. Both the assignment of taxes and the design of the intergovernmental transfer system are relevant for our discussion of global revenue sources, and we consider them in turn. Before doing so, it is worth highlighting the nature of economic objectives in a federation and how responsibility for them is shared between levels of government.

In a unitary state, economic objectives can be conceptualized by a national 'social welfare function' which encompasses efficiency and equity objectives. Equity can be further disaggregated into vertical and horizontal equity dimensions in which comparable persons are treated comparably by the public sector (horizontal equity), and a common degree of redistribution (vertical equity) applies nationwide: all citizens have equal weight regardless of where they reside. In a federation, equity becomes blurred since persons are simultaneously citizens of two jurisdictions, national and subnational. Vertical equity becomes a shared objective with the two levels of government both implementing policies that redistribute. The extent to which vertical equity is regarded as a national or a subnational concern depends upon the extent to which social citizenship is viewed as being at the national versus the subnational level, and that varies from federation to federation. Generally, there is a compromise in which subnational standards of vertical equity interact with national ones. In these circumstances, horizontal equity can be violated for two reasons. First, if subnations adopt differing degrees of redistribution, there cannot be horizontal equity nationwide, and this can be regarded as a tolerable cost of achieving the diversity that federalism brings. Second, decentralization itself implies that different subnations will have different abilities to deliver comparable average levels of public programmes at comparable tax rates. Even if it is desirable that subnations have some responsibility for determining the extent of redistribution among their own residents, it might still be desirable to ensure that they have the opportunities to provide comparable services at tax rates that are comparable in other subnations if they so wish. This objective of enabling all subnations to have the potential to implement comparable programmes at comparable tax rates—potential horizontal equity—is referred to below as fiscal equity. It is a main objective of intergovernmental transfers.

11.2.1. *Assignment of Revenue-Raising Authority*

The principles of assigning revenue-raising responsibility in federations have been widely documented, and the practice has been informed by the principles (McLure 1983). Since the tax-transfer system serves both a redistributive and a revenue-raising objective, issues of fairness, efficiency, and administrative simplicity all have a bearing. At the same time, specific forms of taxation may be used as a device for correcting inefficiencies in the allocation of resources that might arise because of externalities. Taxes may also serve as user fees or earmarking devices where one wants to abide by benefit taxation in limited areas or to create entitlements. It is generally agreed that the national government assumes major responsibility for nationwide efficiency—efficiency in the 'internal economic union'—as well as sharing responsibility for redistributive equity. Moreover, the assignment of taxes should take account of the consequences of decentralization mentioned above: induced differences in per capita incomes and in fiscal capacity, spillovers, and fiscal externalities.

These principles suggest that the national government should be assigned tax-bases that are important for redistributive purposes, those that are mobile across subnational boundaries, those that are unevenly distributed across jurisdictions, and those that might be difficult to administer at the subnational level. By the same token, subnational governments might be given access to taxbases that are not critical for redistribution, taxbases that are immobile, taxbases that do not induce large differences in fiscal capacity, and taxbases that are relatively easy to administer. With respect to the use of taxes as corrective devices or as sources of earmarked funds, their use depends on the jurisdictional scope of the activity to which they are directed.

By these criteria, the national government might have prior access to direct taxes on individuals, businesses, and major natural resources. Subnational governments might rely on property taxes, payroll taxes, and various forms of consumption tax. This presumes that while businesses and capital might be highly mobile across subnational boundaries, labour is not likely to be as mobile. Indeed, in what follows, we shall basically ignore issues associated with labour migration. Specific taxes used to price externalities might be applied nationally if the externality is national in scope (environmental externalities that cross subnational borders) or at the subnational level for externalities that are more local in nature (local congestion or pollution). This is necessary to ensure that the responsible level of government has an incentive to take account of all of the externalities: if externalities are nationwide, subnational governments will have no incentive to respond to those that spill over into neighbouring jurisdictions and will therefore tend to set the tax rate too low.

These considerations are not cut and dried. There may be conflicts among the criteria, and in some instances there are mechanisms for resolving such conflicts. Natural resources are both immobile and unevenly distributed among regions, and that leads to conflicting arguments about assignment. If it is important for subnational governments to have control over the development and taxation of natural resources, the immobility argument might hold sway. In this case, their unequal distribution will give rise to differences in subnational fiscal capacities that can be addressed by a system of equalizing intergovernmental transfers. Consumption taxes (such as a value-added tax) might be difficult to administer at the subnational level. Some taxbases can readily be used at both levels of government through harmonization agreements, so subnational governments can piggyback on personal taxes set by the national government. This provides both levels with access to a broad-based revenue source, while at the same time allowing the national government to dominate the choice of base and rate structure. As well, many of the administrative problems of subnational taxes can be resolved through the use of a single revenue-collection agency that serves both levels of government. The relevant point is that in a modern decentralized federation, it is desirable that both levels of government have discretionary access to broad-based revenue sources. This can be accomplished in ways that do not compromise either the optimal design of such taxes or the costs of administering them by suitable institutions of tax harmonization and coordination.

While broad-based taxes are ideal for revenue-raising and have suitable equity and efficiency properties, there are a number of narrow-based revenue sources that are used with other objectives in mind. In some cases, the fact that they raise revenues is a bonus, or a 'double dividend'. It is worth considering these individually since in some cases they are related to taxes that might be considered suitable as worldwide revenue sources.

Trade taxes

Taxes on international trade are used in OECD countries as instruments of industrial policy rather than for raising revenue, and are typically national government policy instruments. On normative grounds, economists might regard the case for them to be weak, at least in countries that have ready access to broader sources of revenue. The motive for using trade taxes may be political, or it may be strategic (to exploit terms of trade advantages). In either case, by protecting local producers, they lead to worldwide production inefficiency, and one would not be tempted to view them as a model for raising revenues at the world level. This is particularly the case if trade taxes protect producers from imports of LDCs.

Specific excise taxes

Although the bulk of tax revenues in federations comes from broad-based taxes, taxes on specific commodities are often used as well. Common bases include tobacco, alcohol, and petroleum products, luxury items, and some services such as hotels and communications. Specific excises may be viewed as efficient revenue sources to the extent that demands are inelastic, despite the fact that this very inelasticity also renders them highly inequitable. In the case of luxuries, they may serve redistributive objectives. They may be used for tax exporting purposes. Subnational governments often use them for revenue-raising purposes in federations where tax powers are otherwise highly centralized. Perhaps the most important motive is as deviced for addressing externalities arising from the consumption of particular goods, such as health, or policing costs due to tobacco and alcohol consumption or congestion from petroleum products. To the extent that this is a justifiable motive, they provide a free source of revenue as a side benefit to the government that levies them, which typically includes subnational governments. It seems equally likely that the motive for these taxes is paternalistic—to discourage persons from consuming the goods in question (hence, the term 'sin taxes').

Environmental taxes and levies

Related to the externality argument is the more general use of taxes as devices for coping with environmental pollution (Sandmo 2000). In fact, despite the economic arguments for using taxes for this purpose, the extent of their use is limited. More often than not, regulatory remedies or subsidies are used and the potential double dividend is not exploited. Although there may be political economy reasons for this, there may also be serious monitoring and administrative costs associated with environmental taxes.

Gambling

Revenues from gambling of various sorts can be important, especially for subnational governments. In fact, gambling revenues are effectively equivalent to excise taxes, and as such are every bit as inequitable as taxes on tobacco and alcohol. However, one feature of them worth noting is that their revenues are often at least partly earmarked for charitable purposes. This may make them a candidate for development financing, despite their adverse distributive properties (Addison and Chowdhury, Chapter 8, this volume). It seems likely that earmarked gambling revenues partly displace revenues that would otherwise be summoned for redistributive purposes.

Capital transaction taxes

Subnational governments often also impose taxes on various types of transactions, such as land sales, financial transactions, and charges on financial intermediaries. These may be regarded as revenue sources that are easily administered, or as taxes that can be exported to non-residents. Otherwise, the economic case for them is not at all clear.

User fees

Lower-level governments are often encouraged to use user fees to help finance public services. These can range from prices charged for local services (water, electricity, garbage) to school fees and user charges for health services. Since user charges are paid by those whom the services benefit, they have no potential as sources of finance for redistributive purposes except to the extent that the prices themselves are income-tested. The case for them as subnational revenue sources is sometimes based on the argument that redistribution should be a national responsibility.

Seigniorage

National governments obtain small amounts of financing from changes in the money supply. This can be a relatively costless source of revenue unless inflationary finance is used. In that case, inflation will impose its own tax on the economy.

While the revenue raised by these narrow taxes is relatively small, some of them can be important for subnational governments whose own revenue-raising capabilities are limited. Indeed, it can be argued that in some federations, subnational governments tend to rely too heavily on narrow taxbases with the result that the efficiency of the tax system is compromised. Unless narrow taxes have their own efficiency advantages, it is much fairer and more efficient to use broad-based taxes at both national and subnational levels of government. Moreover, the simultaneous use of broad taxbases can be achieved by agreements that retain a harmonized taxbase across the nation while at the same time allowing both levels of government to have the discretion to set their own rates.

There is a further complication in federations that is relevant for the case of world development financing. In a decentralized federation, subnational governments typically engage in redistributive policies alongside those of the national government. National redistributive policies can crowd out subnational redistributive policies. This is compounded by the fact that fiscal competition among subnations can induce a so-called 'race-for-the-bottom' in redistributive policies. In order to attract businesses and highly skilled persons, subnational redistribution is competed down. This leads to an important role for intergovernmental transfers to which we now turn.

11.2.2. *Intergovernmental Transfers*

In a federation, resources are transferred from the better-off to the less well-off via both the interpersonal tax-transfer system and intergovernmental transfers. The relative roles ascribed to these two mechanisms reflect the redistributive responsibilities that the national government assumes. One can roughly think of the former as addressing vertical equity objectives and the latter horizontal equity (or fiscal equity) objectives. The reasoning is as follows.

Redistributive objectives are achieved by a number of instruments, including the income tax-transfer system, social insurance, in-kind transfers to the needy, and the provision of public services like health care and education. These diverse instruments reflect both the multiple facets of redistribution policy and the usefulness of certain types of policies as effective targeting devices. In federations, it is common for many of these policies to be delivered by subnational governments, which finance part of the costs from their own sources. The national government typically retains sufficient influence over the structure of the income tax-transfer system, even if it is co-occupied by subnational governments. But it also has an interest in influencing subnational governments to design their programmes so that national norms of redistributive equity are satisfied. This is sometimes written into the nation's constitution. The national government relies on its system of intergovernmental transfers to pursue the national interest in a decentralized federation. (The same transfers also aim at enhancing efficiency in the internal economic union.) It is partly because of the need for transfers from the national to the subnational governments that a vertical fiscal gap is required.

Transfers take two broad forms. First, they may be used as an instrument for influencing programme design of subnational governments. Broad conditions can be attached setting out minimum standards that programmes in areas like health, education, and welfare must satisfy to be eligible for the transfers. The extent of intrusiveness of such conditions varies from nation to nation, and is a source of concern in many federations. Conditional transfers are directed at vertical equity objectives, such as ensuring that adequate levels of equality of opportunity and public services for the needy are being provided at the subnational level. Such conditionality has its parallel in development financing, despite the absence of the analogue of a national government.

Second, and more relevant for our purposes, transfers fulfil an equalization role. When the provision and partial financing of public services are decentralized to subnational governments, different subnations will have different abilities to provide common levels of public services, resulting in horizontal inequities across the federation. The argument is best illustrated, following Buchanan (1950), using a simple example as a benchmark. Consider a federation in which subnations differ in per capita incomes. Suppose subnational governments levy a proportional income tax and use the proceeds to provide equal per capita public services to all residents. (These are of the nature of private services rather than public goods, along the lines of important public services actually decentralized in federations.) If all subnational governments levied the same rate of tax, the level of public services provided per capita would differ systematically with per capita subnational incomes. Put differently, the *net fiscal benefit* (NFB) received per person of a given income level in a given subnation—the difference between the value of the public service provided and the tax payment—would differ across subnations, and the difference would be the same for all income levels. Nationwide horizontal equity would be violated. To correct for this horizontal inequity, a system of equalization transfers could be instituted which effectively compensated different subnations for differences in the amount of tax revenue they could raise by applying the common tax rate to the incomes of their residents.

With such an equalization system in place, the level of public services provided in each subnation would be the same, and horizontal equity would be satisfied. In fact, the outcome of the unitary state would be replicated. Interestingly, economic efficiency would be served as well. The same NFB differentials that give rise to horizontal inequity also provide a fiscal incentive for households and businesses to be misallocated among subnational jurisdictions (Buchanan 1952). This is a rare instance in economics in which equity and efficiency arguments are mutually reinforcing.

This simple example is a caricature of reality, but it does serve to illustrate the main point. Equalizing transfers enable different subnational governments to provide comparable levels of public services at comparable levels of taxation. In the real world, things are more complicated than in the simple benchmark example, and these complications affect the form of equalization transfers. Some of the complications are as follows:

Subnational budgets may have differing degrees of progressivity than assumed in the benchmark case, where proportional taxes are used to finance equal per capita benefits. If subnational budgets are more progressive than that, a greater degree of equalization will be needed to eliminate NFB differentials (and replicate the financial features of the unitary state). By the same token, if they are less progressive, less equalization is called for. In the limit, if the benefit principle is applied at the subnational level, no NFBs would arise and no equalization would be called for on horizontal equity grounds.

There are other sources of NFB differentials besides differences in per capita incomes. For one, public services may not be made available equally to all persons, but may be targeted to certain groups in the society—school age children, the elderly, the disabled, the ill, the needy, and so on. Different subnations with different population mixes will have different needs for public expenditures if they are to provide comparable levels of these kinds of services to their populations. For another, subnational governments may have access to source-based tax revenues such as those on natural resources, and this may give rise to significant differences in revenue-raising capacity. An equalization scheme should compensate for differences in needs and in capacities to obtain revenues generated at source.

In the benchmark case it was presumed that all subnational jurisdictions would behave alike, so that with full equalization, the outcome of a unitary state would be replicated. In fact, the essence of federalism is that different states have different needs and preferences for public goods and services, and exercise their discretion in very different ways. In these circumstances, there is a conflict between the desire to achieve horizontal equity and the desire to have subnational governments exercise their own discretion. The compromise typically made is to arrange the equalization system so that subnations have the *potential* to provide comparable levels of public services at comparable levels of taxation without being compelled to conform. *Fiscal equity* is fulfilled when this potential is achieved.

Some public expenditure takes the form of public goods rather than public services that are private in nature. In this case, the appropriate amount of equalization for horizontal or fiscal equity purposes becomes much more complicated, since there are economies of scale in the consumption of public goods. In fact, it seems more likely that the expenditure responsibilities decentralized to subnational governments are dominated by those that take the form of public services of a private nature.

Equalization according to these principles is employed in most federations (the major exception being the United States), as well as in many unitary states with respect to local governments. The nature of the schemes depends upon the extent of fiscal decentralization. In cases where expenditures are much more decentralized than taxes, equalization can be based largely on differences in need. Expenditure needs can be measured as crudely as total population, or they can be based on estimates of the standard costs of providing services of various sorts to particular segments of the population. In federations with more decentralized revenue-raising, equalization can also be based on the ability to raise revenues, and this can also take varying degrees of sophistication. In some cases, the ability to raise revenues from a representative tax system can be used. Alternatively, some more crude macro-based measure such as per capita incomes might suffice. Moreover, equalization can be based on 'gross' as opposed to 'net' systems. Net equalization refers to a purely redistributive system whereby revenues to transfer to the subnational governments with below-average fiscal capacity come from levies imposed on those above the average. However, equalization more often takes the gross form whereby the national government makes transfers to some or all subnational governments and finances them out of national general revenues. In this case, the allocation of transfers is based on relative fiscal capacities among subnations. The two cases differ mainly in the extent of vertical fiscal gap used to finance the system.

In either case, the important point is that the financing of public services provided by less well-off subnational jurisdictions comes partly from transfers from better-off jurisdictions. These public services are a very important element in the arsenal of instruments used to address issues of redistributive equity and economic and social development. They are arguably more important than the redistribution that takes place as part of the national interpersonal tax-transfer system. The use of intergovernmental transfers for horizontal or fiscal equity purposes is therefore of great importance from a national equity point of view.

11.2.3. *Cooperative Behaviour by Subnational Governments*

Despite the reliance on the national government as an institution for fostering national equity and efficiency objectives in a federation, it is useful to consider the possibility that subnational governments might also take initiatives voluntarily to achieve or to thwart these same objectives. Here and in Section 11.2.4, we take up these possibilities, with special emphasis on the revenue-raising function of subnational governments. In decentralized federations, subnational governments can have significant discretion in designing their programmes and in choosing their revenue structures. While this discretion enables them to serve their local residents more effectively, it also has the potential to induce inefficiencies and inequities in the national economic union. Some of these inefficiencies and inequities could be ameliorated by the harmonization of policies either undertaken voluntarily or negotiated collectively.

With respect to voluntary policy harmonization, the record is mixed. In the decentralized federations of Canada and the United States, opportunities do exist for subnational governments to harmonize their broad-based revenue sources. Canada has a formal mechanism for harmonizing personal and corporate income taxes, and provinces may choose to participate. The harmonization is limited to harmonizing taxbases and allowing for a single tax collection agency: provinces are allowed full discretion over tax rates. While most provinces participate in the personal income tax harmonization agreements, the largest provinces accounting for three-quarters of taxable income do not participate in the case of the corporate tax. On the other hand, for those that do not participate, their tax systems do not deviate significantly from those of the participating provinces. No doubt this is partly for historical reasons, since the current system evolved from one in which the national government was the sole income tax user. The record with respect to other taxes is more dismal. There is relatively little harmonization of provincial sales taxes with the national sales tax system, despite the possibility offered to them. And, for taxes that are mainly in provincial jurisdiction (resource taxes, property taxes), there is virtually no harmonization, much to the detriment of national efficiency. In the United States, there is even less harmonization, of either income taxes or state sales taxes. This may reflect in part the much larger number of US states than Canadian provinces. With respect to public services and transfers delivered by the provinces and states, there is again no voluntary harmonization (apart from that induced by national conditional transfers). On the contrary, there is some evidence that such programmes are used in a strategic way, such as to attract only the most desirable households to the jurisdiction.

Negotiated intergovernmental agreements that exist tend to involve both the national and subnational governments. As well, they are somewhat difficult to negotiate and turn out to be ineffective. A prime example of this is the Agreement on Internal Trade in Canada, whose purpose and features are much like trade liberalization agreements among groups of nations (NAFTA, EU, WTO). While the articles of the agreement are potentially far-reaching, in practice the agreement is ineffective because it relies on voluntary compliance for enforcement. This is a consequence of the need to have unanimous agreement and of the fact that the fallback position is for the national government to assume responsibility for efficiency in the internal economic union. There are many examples of bilateral agreements between the national government and individual subnational governments. But virtually all such agreements concern the interest of the residents of the subnational government involved. There are almost no agreements involving inter-jurisdictional redistribution.

This mixed record of the effectiveness of intergovernmental agreements is again a reflection of the primary role that a national government plays in a federation. This tempers the lessons that can be learned for situations in which there is no effective central authority to mediate, influence, and coerce state behaviour.

11.2.4. *Freeriding by Subnational Governments*

Not only might it be difficult to rely on subnational government to behave harmoniously, their behaviour might be overtly non-cooperative. This possibility exists because, as mentioned, a subnational government's policies can have an impact on residents or government budgets in other jurisdictions. We have mentioned fiscal competition that arises between subnational governments as a result of these fiscal externality effects. However, there can also be forms of vertical interaction between subnational and national governments—so-called vertical fiscal externalities—that can be detrimental to national efficiency and equity. These can take various forms (Keen 1998).

First, the fact that the two levels of government are taxing the same agents implies that policy changes at one level affect the budget at another. For example, if a subnational government increases its income tax rate, and if income is variable, the induced reduction in the base will also reduce national tax revenues. Technically speaking, the marginal social cost of revenues will be perceived by the subnational government to be too low. It can effectively spread part of the burden of raising its revenues to other jurisdictions.

Second, national government redistribution can crowd out redistribution at the subnational level. Potentially subnational governments can exploit this by limiting their own redistribution on the expectation that the national government will compensate.

Third, interdependence will arise if taxes paid at one level of government are deductible from taxable income at another level. A subnational tax that is progressive could become regressive if it can be deducted before levying a progressive federal tax.

Finally, subnational governments can sometimes manipulate the amount of transfers they receive from the national government through their fiscal policies. In the extreme case, they can exploit any soft budget constraint that might apply between the national and subnational governments. The existence of these opportunities depends on the design of the transfer system and on the ability of the national government to commit itself to a given level of transfers regardless of the fiscal choices taken by subnational governments.

11.2.5. *Summary*

In a well-functioning federation, subnational governments are assigned responsibility not only for local public goods but also for policies that are crucial to the efficient and equitable functioning of the national economic union. These include important public services like health, education, and social services, as well as some targeted transfers. Although this decentralization is motivated by concerns with efficiency and catering to local preferences and needs, the national government has a clear interest in the standards with which subnational programmes might conform. To ensure that national norms of efficiency, equity, and development are addressed, the national government typically retains a dominant position in the interpersonal tax-transfer system, which is one instrument for vertical equity. It also makes substantial transfers to subnational governments to equalize the capacity of subnations to provide comparable levels of public services at comparable levels of tax rates, and to ensure that they have the incentive to provide programmes in conformity with the national interest. This implies a vertical fiscal gap, with the national government collecting more revenue than it needs for its own purpose and transferring the remainder to the subnational governments. The latter are assigned sufficient revenue sources of their own, especially broad-based ones, to ensure that they are accountable to their constituents for the programmes they deliver. Ideally, their taxes are harmonized with those of the national government, and they are fully responsible for raising marginal revenues for determining the sizes of their budgets. The object of the national/subnational fiscal arrangements is to obtain the benefits of decentralized decisionmaking while at the same time avoiding its costs. The oversight role of the national government is critical to this objective.

11.3. A FEDERATION WITH NO CENTRAL GOVERNMENT

In a federation, the national government plays a critical role in pursuit of redistributive equity alongside subnational governments that deliver important public services. The balance between the two levels has shifted over the past several decades. Subnational governments have become more important as the role of public services like health, education, and social services as major redistributive devices has grown, and the virtues of decentralization have been realized. In some federations (Canada), the national government's expenditures are predominantly transfers, while those of the provinces are mainly on goods and services. This decentralization has put some stress on the ability of the national government to impose its redistributive objectives.

In the limit, decentralization would result in a federation with a weak national government. In this section, we pose the hypothetical question of how redistributive goals might be achieved in the limiting case where there is no effective national government. This serves as a useful benchmark against which to address similar issues globally.

It is worth first pausing to reflect on the nature of redistributive objectives in a federal setting, loose or otherwise. Redistribution is a key role of governments in any OECD nation. A cursory look at government budgets will confirm that a high proportion of spending is devoted to programmes with redistributive intent, not just those involving income redistribution but also public goods and services. For example, public spending on education, health, and social services would be hard to justify on purely efficiency grounds. While it might be possible to conceive of sizeable redistribution being the consequence of a political process that reflects purely the self-interest of the voting population, these considerations alone seem inadequate to account for the scale of redistribution one actually observes. It seems more likely that there is some more fundamental social consensus or solidarity underlying the phenomenon. Some observers have equated this solidarity with a notion of social citizenship: one's membership in a nation entitles one not just to the legal and political rights that come with citizenship, but also with social and economic rights (Purdy 2001). In other words, the political community is also a sharing community, as if reflecting some social contract. These rights of social citizenship may be written into the national constitution, or they may simply reflect an ongoing social consensus. The extent of the social consensus will vary from nation to nation, and will vary within nations from time to time as political outcomes change.

In a federation, social citizenship is blurred by the fact that one is a citizen both of the country as a whole and of a subnation. There are two simultaneous concepts of solidarity, one nationwide and one subnational. The balance between these two levels of solidarity can be the source of considerable tension within federations: to what extent should national solidarity trump subnational solidarity? That is, to what extent should redistribution be the role of the national as opposed to the subnational governments? The compromise will vary from federation to federation: national solidarity may be relatively more important in, say, Germany than in Belgium, where subnational solidarity in the linguistic communities is also important.

But even in highly decentralized federations, the relevance of social citizenship at the national level remains strong. The Canadian case represents a good example of this, given that it is one of the most decentralized federations in the world (although even here subnational solidarity in certain regions can be important). The provinces deliver all the important public services and raise a substantial proportion of their own revenues through broad-based taxes. A great deal of redistribution occurs at the subnational level of government. The national government also engages in redistribution, largely through the tax-transfer system. But, much of its redistributive activity involves intergovernmental transfers, and much of this is directed at achieving fiscal equity among provinces. Social citizenship is thus a compromise: the national government provides transfers to the provinces out of national general revenues to ensure that provinces have the potential for providing reasonably comparable public services at reasonably comparable levels of taxation. The provinces then choose their own fiscal policies more or less unfettered by national constraint. Even in this highly decentralized fiscal system, a high degree of consensus seems to exist for national social citizenship. Nonetheless, that consensus is perceptibly weakening as the nation gradually becomes more decentralized, although the direction of causation is unclear. Moreover, many of the instruments used to achieve social citizenship are the legislative responsibility of the provinces.

In contemplating a federation without a national government, two key differences with a standard federation must then be recognized. The first is that government-to-government transfers will be relevant for redistribution among regions since there is no national government that can collect revenues nationwide to transfer to subnational governments or their citizens. Second, the issue must be faced as to the degree of social consensus that exists for ensuring that citizens of different jurisdictions have comparable capacities for providing public services and engaging in redistribution of all forms. One presumes that national social citizenship becomes much weaker in this context, and the extent of intergovernmental transfers that citizens might wish their subnational governments to engage in will be less than in a full-fledged federation with a purposeful national government.

Let us presume that there is at least some degree of social consensus for redistribution from citizens of better-off subnations to those of less well-off subnations. Moreover, the principle of subsidiarity can be taken for granted: subnational governments are accepted as being those most capable of implementing redistributive policies within their own jurisdictions. Thus, the relevant form of redistribution is subnation to subnation. We consider some features that such redistribution might take, treating separately the cases in which subnational governments do and do not coordinate their activities.

11.3.1. *Non-Cooperative Subnational Redistribution*

To the extent that a consensus exists for some degree of solidarity among all citizens in the nation, individual subnational governments in better-off regions acting on behalf of their own citizens will want to make transfers to less well-off jurisdictions. The situation is analogous to nations voluntarily contributing to an international public good: here the public good is the total amount of the transfer, from which all nations simultaneously benefit. The economics literature has developed the characteristics of the outcomes that might be expected in a setting in which several nations make independent (non-cooperative) contributions to an international public good (Sandler 1992; Boadway and Hayashi 1999). Although the models are simplistic and the assumptions strong, the message of that literature is stark, even if it has only an element of truth. In fact, no matter how far the degree of solidarity or social citizenship extends across subnational borders, the outcomes that are predicted when subnational governments behave non-cooperatively differ considerably from those that could be expected to occur if a national government were overseeing interregional redistribution. The following summarizes some of the relevant results.

The total level of transfers—the sum of the transfers of all better-off jurisdictions—is less than the optimal level. There is a free-riding problem associated with each nation's contributions, implying that each subnation contributes less than it would in a coordinated approach, such as with a national government.

Subnations that have the highest per capita incomes will contribute proportionately more of their incomes to international public goods than they would in the coordinated setting. This is the phenomenon of disproportionate burden sharing, and is a consequence of the Shibata–Warr neutrality theorem whereby income redistributions among contributors are fully offset by changes in contributions in equilibrium.[1] In

---

[1] This theorem says that when a public good is financed by voluntary donations, the equilibrium level of public good is independent of the distribution of income. Any redistribution of income among contributors will be completely offset in equilibrium by equal changes in contributions, at least as long as contributions are not driven to zero. Thus, contributions by higher-income contributors will exceed those by lower-income contributors precisely by the difference in incomes. Moreover, any incremental contribution by the government will crowd out private donations on a one-for-one basis. See Shibata (1971) and Warr (1983). These results are based on models in which contributions finance pure public goods, and preferences are identical among contributors.

the context of these models of voluntary contributions to public goods, if contributing nations differ only in per capita incomes (but have the same populations), differences in per capita incomes will result in differences in per capita contributions of the same amount in equilibrium.

Subnations with the highest populations will contribute disproportionately more of their incomes to international public goods than those with lower populations. This reflects the fact that, the larger the population, the higher proportion of benefits of the contribution that are internalized. As a result, persons in more populous donor nations will tend to be worse off, all else equal. Combined with the previous result, we might expect to see countries with higher incomes and populations contributing disproportionately more to international public goods, while countries with high per capita incomes and low populations may contribute more or less as a proportion of their incomes than those with low per capita incomes and high populations.

Increased contributions to the less well-off subnations from some outside source will crowd out voluntary transfers. Indeed, if increased contributions were financed by taxes imposed on the contributing subnations, the crowding-out would be full.

These predictions are somewhat surprising, but they are also cautionary. They point out the inefficiency and inequity of a system of voluntary transfers—inefficiency because the amount transferred is less than all contributing jurisdictions would agree to, and inequity because the contributions in equilibrium may bear no close relation to a jurisdiction's well-being or ability to pay. The predictions also indicate that introducing small increments of transfers into a world in which subnations are making voluntary contributions can be effectively pointless. Thus, additional sources of revenues made available by, say, a new global tax source could largely crowd out voluntary subnational transfers. Equivalently, if the subnations collectively agreed to provide additional financing for transfers, this additional contribution would crowd out their voluntary transfers on a one-for-one basis, at least until the latter were fully crowded out.

The literature also suggests that the freerider effects of a voluntary contribution equilibrium could be undone by a system of incentives. If subsidies are provided for voluntary transfers—analogous to the tax incentives that are provided for individual contributions to charity—efficiency could be restored. Such a scheme would require either some national authority or coordinated action by the subnational governments, as well as some source of revenue to finance the subsidies. All of these are ruled out in the non-cooperative case.

11.3.2. *Cooperative Subnational Redistribution*

Given that non-cooperative subnational outcomes are likely to lead to inadequate levels of interstate redistribution and inequitable distributions of burdens, it is natural to consider the possibility of cooperative behaviour among subnational governments. Cooperative outcomes should be possible since all jurisdictions can potentially gain relative to the non-cooperative case. Moreover, cooperative solutions should in principle lead to a fully efficient outcome in the sense that, as in the case with standard public goods, the sum of the marginal benefits to all donor subnations from redistribution equals the sum of the marginal costs.

In contemplating such cooperative solutions, we immediately confront the problems that arise in arranging the terms of the cooperative bargain when the gains from the bargain must somehow be divided among the various subnations. A cooperative outcome must achieve unanimous agreement, and this is notoriously difficult, especially where many governments are party to the negotiations. This is particularly the case when all subnations are involved, both net donors and net recipients of the transfers. As well, some dispute settlement mechanism is required to ensure that all subnational governments abide by the agreement. In the absence of a central authority, this is difficult to achieve. As mentioned above, the record of achieving unanimous agreement among subnational governments in a federal setting is not encouraging.

On the other hand, among nation-states progress has been made with respect to such agreements, although success has been much more pronounced where pure efficiency gains are at stake than those involving redistribution. The European Union is a case in point, where agreements exist in a variety of areas including agriculture, competition policy, science and technology, regional policy, trade, and even social policy (Artis and Nixson 2001). In some cases, agreement was a long time coming and many compromises were involved. Moreover, sometimes the agreements were asymmetric in the sense that different countries participated to differing extents. Perhaps this illustrates that with enough persistence, agreements can be reached among nations even where redistributive policies are involved.

We proceed by setting aside the difficulty of bargaining to obtain some insight into the kinds of agreements that should be possible among subnational governments acting in the absence of a national government. In principle, these ought to be able to mimic what a benevolent central government acting on the basis of a national consensus would implement. Taking that as a reference point, we can imagine two sorts of institutional mechanisms being negotiated among subnational governments to finance redistribution from better-off to less well-off subnations—taxes on the better-off states or taxes on agents or their transactions. Since our focus is on the financing of development assistance rather than its use, we concentrate on the source of funds.

Taxes on subnational governments

Subnational governments might agree to tax themselves, that is, to make equalization transfers for the purpose of redistributing to the less well-off subnations. The question then is how the transfers ought to be distributed among the contributing subnations. The answer depends upon a judgement as to what constitutes a fair allocation of the burdens of the transfers. Following the above discussion of intergovernmental transfers in a federation, the concept of fairness applied to subnational jurisdictions is different from that applied to individuals in the case of a personal tax system. This is because the subnation consists of a distribution of households of different incomes. Presumably, in our hypothetical federation without a national government, subnational governments would assume full responsibility for vertical equity within their borders. They may choose differing degrees of progressivity because of different subnational consensuses about the desirable amount of redistribution. Fiscal competition pressures may also affect their policies of redistribution. In either case, there is little that a system of transfers from jurisdictions can, or should, do to rectify this. To the extent that different jurisdictions have different preferences for redistribution, there is no good reason to override those differences. And, dealing with the adverse effects of fiscal competition for intra-jurisdictional redistribution is something with which a system of intergovernmental transfers cannot cope. Addressing that problem is, after all, one of the roles of a national government in a federation.

Given this, a suitable basis for fairness in a federation with only subnational governments is fiscal equity. Full fiscal equity is equivalent to taking the normative position that citizenship in the nation carries with it some obligation of equal treatment nationwide, tempered only by the fact that subnational governments should have the discretion for designing programmes for vertical equity within their jurisdictions. Equivalently, full fiscal equity involves ensuring that each subnational government has the potential to be able to provide comparable public programmes at comparable tax rates to the residents of their respective jurisdictions.

In the context of a highly decentralized federation without a national government, the rights of social citizenship in this full sense may not reflect a societal consensus. Instead, the consensus might be that full fiscal equity is too extreme, and that some partial notion of fiscal equity is acceptable. In this case, the objective of the transfer system would still be to redress differences in the ability of subnational governments to provide programmes to their citizens at given tax rates, but now only partially, so fiscal equity is imperfectly achieved. There is still no particular reason to override the redistribution subnational governments undertake in their own jurisdictions.

Whatever degree of fiscal equity is deemed appropriate, the base that is suitable for determining the fair set of transfers is the same: only the rate of equalization applied to that base needs to differ. We have discussed in broad terms the principles of equalization in a federal setting. Those same design principles would apply here, although the degree to which equalization is pursued might differ. If full fiscal equity were the criterion—and this is a useful benchmark to use—transfers would equalize the ability of all subnational governments to provide comparable levels of public services at comparable tax rates. The precise equalization formula would include elements reflecting both revenue-raising capacity and expenditure needs, and would depend on the policies implemented by the representative subnational government, including both their tax structures and their expenditure programmes. A conventional standard case that informs the revenue equalization system in some federations is as follows. Suppose subnational taxes are roughly proportional to income when taken as a whole. And suppose that public services provided roughly equal per capita benefits to all households. Then an ideal equalization system for full fiscal equity purposes would be designed as follows:

1. Representative taxbases would be constructed for all taxes used by subnational governments. From this would be calculated the per capita base for each tax source in each subnation (b_{ij} for taxbase i in subnation j), and the average per capita taxbase nationwide for taxbase i (B_i).
2. Nationwide average tax rates (t_i) would be calculated as the ratio of total subnational tax revenue from the base to the nationwide size of the base.
3. The per capita equalization entitlement for a subnation j from a taxbase i would be calculated as $t_i(B_i - b_{ij})$.
4. The above calculation would be done for each subnation and each tax type. A subnation's total equalization entitlement would be the sum of all per capita entitlements (positive and negative) from all tax sources multiplied by its population: $\sum_I t_i(B_i - b_{ij})N_j$.
5. The sum of entitlements over all subnations would be zero. Those with superior revenue-raising ability would be positive, and those with deficient revenue-raising ability would be negative.

In the above calculation—referred to as the *representative tax system* approach—the use of national average subnational government tax rates ensures full revenue equalization. This rough and ready approach to equalization would be appropriate if subnational fiscal structures roughly corresponded to those of the standard case.

Since spending programmes are targeted to particular groups in the population rather than being of equal per capita benefit to all, equalization entitlements can be adjusted to account for the fact that different subnations have different expenditure needs arising from their differing population mixes. A representative expenditure-needs approach, analogous to the above, could be used. Differences among subnations in the per capita cost of providing a given level of a particular type of public service would be equalized. The procedure would be to estimate a national average cost of providing a unit of service to a person of a given demographic group. This cost would be combined with the number of persons of that group in each subnation to determine expenditure need for that service. Deviations from the average would then be equalized.

If the consensus is for less than full fiscal equity (or if the sum total of transfers is set exogenously), the above procedure could be revised accordingly. We can concentrate on the implications of partial fiscal equity for donor subnations. The simplest procedure would be to reduce each subnation's assessed equalization entitlement proportionately from the full equalization case. This would be equivalent to equalizing differences in per capita taxbases by less than national average tax rates, in the case of revenue equalization, and reducing the unit cost used for equalizing needs differences. Applying this procedure to the donor subnations would imply that proportionately less than full fiscal equity was implemented not only between donor and recipient subnations, but also among all donors.[2]

The above procedures, though not unlike what is done in various federations on either the revenue or the expenditure-needs sides, appear to be complicated. Some observers have argued for a simpler procedure, such as basing equalization on a single macro measure, such as per capita subnational income or consumption. This is the approach used by the European Union, whose budget is financed by a proportionate levy on member states' GDP. Though this leads to a simpler calculation, it is conceptually problematic. Macro indicators are unlikely to be an accurate reflection of either the revenue-raising capacity of subnational governments or their needs for expenditures. For example, they do not take account of the fact that different taxbases (e.g. resources versus capital income versus consumption) have different revenue-raising potential and typically are taxed at very different rates. Those who propose macro formulas typically have objectives other than simplicity in mind. Some treat inter-jurisdictional redistribution as being analogous to interpersonal redistribution and view the base as comparable to the ability to pay of the representative household (Barro 2002). However, as we have argued, there is a fundamental difference between interpersonal redistribution and inter-jurisdictional redistribution, the former being directed at vertical equity and the latter at horizontal equity. Nonetheless, if subnational tax structures are sufficiently different, the representative tax system approach to equalization becomes difficult to implement, and one may be forced back to a simple macro measure.

While agreement on the set of subnational transfers is primarily a matter of fiscal equity, subnational agreement may go beyond that to include some provisions for harmonizing vertical equity within subnational governments. This could be a way of dealing with the tendency for subnational governments to compete down their redistribution programmes. It might also reflect a national consensus for norms of vertical equity or social citizenship, analogous to the harmonization of social protection in the European Union. However, the existence of harmonized systems of social protection does not detract from the principles outlined above for the design of a system of equalization transfers.

Taxes on agents

An alternative means of raising revenues to transfer to less well-off regions is for subnational governments to agree to tax agents directly. This is natural to consider since it has the potential to mimic what a national government would do. The manner in which tax revenues might be raised cooperatively depends on the structure of the tax systems employed by subnational governments, as well as on the normative objectives of the national tax, including especially whether there should be common standards of equity applying nationwide (despite the absence of a national government). Some considerations are as follows.

---

[2] Note that this procedure would leave the list of donor nations unchanged: all those with per capita taxbases above the world average would be included. One could also adapt to a lower level of transfers by removing less well-off middle-income countries from the list of donors.

A key factor in contemplating a new national tax in an otherwise fully decentralized system of subnational governments is the perceived nature of nationwide equity. If the view is taken that vertical equity is the responsibility of subnational governments, the most that might be expected from a national tax is that some degree of fiscal equity is achieved. Then, the ideal tax would be one that mimics the equalization scheme outlined above. A single tax at a common rate on a broad base would not be perfect since the revenues raised from each jurisdiction would not reflect its tax capacity or its own expenditure needs. If a separate tax rate could be applied in each jurisdiction, any pattern of subnational incidence could be achieved, but one presumes that differential tax rates across subnations would not be an easy thing to negotiate.

Nonetheless, a broad-based tax at uniform rates would be an approximation of a fiscally equitable outcome. It would correspond with the macro approach to equalization. Suitable taxbases might include consumption or income. Indeed, if the tax were a direct one, it could be progressive. That would be appropriate if the vertical equity were the responsibility of the national government.

Even if there is agreement for a broad taxbase, there would be problems with administering the tax. In an ideal situation—such as exists in some federations—the taxbase would be harmonized among subnational governments. A national tax could be piggybacked onto those levied by subnational governments. There are different forms this could take, depending on the taxbase used. In the case of personal income taxes, a national surtax could be imposed on each agent's subnational income tax liabilities (in which case subnational progressivity is retained) or on subnational taxbases. In the case of sales taxation, if a multi-stage tax is used subnationally, the national surcharge could be limited to the final stage. This would, however, require a significant degree of harmonization among subnational sales tax systems. In the absence of such harmonization, piggybacking would be problematic since the amount of revenue raised in each subnational jurisdiction would vary arbitrarily with the definition of the taxbase. If piggybacking is not feasible, the national tax would have to be collected on its own, but with significant administrative costs.

Suppose, however, that a broad-based national tax is implemented. A further problem concerns the crowding-out of subnational government voluntary transfers. In the hypothetical context we are imagining of a nation without a national government, it is likely that better-off subnational governments would make voluntary transfers to less well-off ones as long as there were significant disparities in well-being among subnations. The parallel is with voluntary intergovernmental transfers among nations in the real world. In the case of subnations, the case for voluntary transfers would be stronger because of the presumed solidarity among national citizens residing in different subnational jurisdictions. To the extent that voluntary inter-jurisdictional transfers were undertaken—albeit inefficiently as discussed earlier—theoretical reasoning would suggest that they would be crowded out, perhaps on a close to one-for-one basis (the Shibata–Warr theorem). While that is not necessarily bad, given that the pattern of voluntary transfers is likely to be unrelated to a reasonable national equitable criterion, it does imply that more of a burden would be placed on raising revenues than would otherwise be the case. One way out of this dilemma would be for subnational cooperation to include elements of both taxes on states and taxes on agents.

An alternative to a new national tax imposed on a broad base would be one imposed on a narrower base. This might be attractive for three reasons. First, a narrow-based tax, such as one on a readily identifiable class of transactions, might be easy to administer in the absence of a national government. But, there are serious problems with a narrow-based tax whose only attraction is ease of administration. To the extent that the demand for the taxed item were elastic, inefficiencies would result. On the other hand, for less elastic bases, the tax would likely have adverse equity properties in the sense that their incidence would fall disproportionately on lower income persons. Moreover, the incidence of the tax by subnational jurisdiction would bear no close relation to fiscal equity.

Second, the inefficiencies of a narrow tax will be avoided to the extent that the transaction involved emits adverse national externalities. (If the externalities are localized, presumably they will be taken care of by subnational tax systems.) In this case, the revenues raised are seemingly costless from an economic point of view: the double-dividend argument (Sandmo, Chapter 3, this volume). However, relying solely on double-dividend taxation to raise revenues for the benefit of less well-off jurisdictions is not without problems. These tax revenues will have a strong tendency to crowd out voluntary transfers made by subnational jurisdictions or their residents. Also, the implicit incidence of these revenues on donor subnations will not correspond with what might be considered fair on fiscal equity grounds. However, this problem of the fairness of donor burden-sharing may be regarded as less pressing given that fiscal equity between donor subnations as a whole and recipient subnations has been improved. If the revenues raised from such seemingly costless means are insufficient, they could be supplemented by inter-jurisdictional transfers that took account of fiscal equity considerations.

Third, another efficiency-improving revenue source that might be collected on a coordinated basis is capital income taxation in one of its forms. Standard tax competition principles suggest that subnational jurisdictions would compete down the tax rate on capital income relative to the optimal level. (There are considerations that temper this effect, such as the so-called hold-up problem that leads capital tax rates to be excessive.) To the extent that this is the case, a coordinated agreement to impose a national capital tax would yield a 'free' source of revenue along the lines of the double dividend from externality taxes. Similar considerations as to the usefulness of this source of finance apply.

11.4. IMPLICATIONS FOR GLOBAL REVENUE SOURCES

There are both parallels and differences between a hypothetical federation of subnations with no national government and the global economy consisting of many national governments. In both cases, a number of states exercise independent authority with no oversight from an upper-level government. Some states will be better off than others in one or more of the following senses: their average incomes are higher, they have greater endowments of resources, their level of economic and social development is higher, and the needs for public services and infrastructure are easier to meet. They exercise their fiscal authority not only to provide public goods that would not otherwise be provided by the private sector, but more important, to promote redistributive equity through the tax-transfer system and the provision of important public services. And, since the states interact with one another in a broader economy, there will be various forms of fiscal spillover and fiscal competition that can lead to inefficiencies in resource allocation. There will presumably be some consensus by the citizens of better-off states to redistribute to those of less well-off states, whether out of altruistic motives or as a matter of ethical conviction. Taken together, the inefficiency of state fiscal interaction and the consensus to make it possible for citizens in less well-off states to advance imply that there is some collective gain to be had from coordinated decisionmaking. Uncoordinated state decisionmaking will lead to the same sort of inefficiencies and inequities in the global economy of nations as in the national economy of subnations.

Despite these similarities, the differences among nations are likely to be more pronounced than among subnations. Income and development disparities across nations are likely to be more pronounced. Cultural, linguistic, religious, and ethnic differences will be greater. Institutional differences will be sharper. National political decision-making will give rise to greater variations in national policy choices than is the case across subnations within a given country.

These differences will be reflected in the international policy imperatives that will arise. National economies are likely to be more highly integrated than the world economy, although this distinction is becoming blurred with globalization. Labour is less mobile internationally, interdependencies in markets for goods and services are less, and the importance of spillovers crossing national borders might also be less. At the same time, because of the distinct sovereign nature of nations, certain types of transactions between them might be much harder to monitor, regulate, and tax in an international setting than within nations. Good examples of this are financial capital and certain types of e-commerce. Nations are not able to tax these types of transactions at rates as high as they might prefer. With respect to world equity, it may be the case that the level of solidarity or social citizenship is less at the global level than the national level, so there may be more tolerance for fiscal inequity among nations than among subnations within a country.

The conceptual basis for addressing the inefficiencies and inequities in a world of nations—particularly the manner of raising revenues for international redistributive purposes—is similar to that in a highly decentralized federation in some fundamental respects. The sovereignty of nations implies that vertical equity among their citizens is primarily their responsibility. This is an issue of some importance from the point of view of considering new sources of global revenue, and the use to which it will be put. If one accepts the view that vertical equity is best 'assigned' to national governments, the main purpose of state-to-state redistribution is to achieve inter-state fiscal equity at least to some degree, that is, to reduce the gaps among nations in their ability to provide comparable public services and transfers at comparable levels of taxation.

This argument that pursuing fiscal equity is the appropriate basis for designing a system of development assistance is not innocuous. If instead one takes the view that the objective should be to further some notion of world vertical equity, the nature of optimal development assistance financing would be different. The criterion for financing development assistance would be vertical equity among individuals in the world rather than fiscal equity among nations. Financial instruments would then be judged and designed according to the incidence on persons of different income groups regardless of where they reside rather than their incidence on nations according to their abilities to finance public services. In other words, the ideal would be a system of progressive inter-personal taxes and transfers—a world income tax system—as opposed to a system of inter-state equalization transfers. On the other hand, the clearest message that comes out of the fiscal federalism literature seems to be: *it should be fiscal equity among states rather than vertical equity among individuals that informs the design of a financing development financing system.*

This point of view presumes that nations are best placed to assume responsibility for vertical equity within their jurisdictions. That involves a serious value judgement and is also subject to some important caveats. For one, donor countries may not accept the view that recipient countries should be (or can be) responsible for redistributive equity within their own borders. Donors may be 'paternalistic' about national preferences for redistribution, just like altruistic donors within a country may prefer their charitable donations or the transfers of their governments to be tied to certain uses by recipients rather than having no strings attached. Second, even if donor countries are willing to accept recipient nations' responsibility for vertical equity, there is still the possibility that fiscal competition entails inadequate levels of redistribution because of the race-to-the-bottom. These caveats need not be of primary concern to us to the extent that we focus on the raising of revenues from donor countries rather than their use by recipients.

What do these principles suggest about suitable sources of new revenues for financing development? Three separate classes of fiscal revenue sources can be distinguished: taxes on nations, taxes on global externalities, and taxes on transactions for which national tax rates have been competed down because of international mobility.[3]

11.4.1. *Taxes on Nations: A Global Equalization Scheme*

A system of taxes on the better-off nations to finance new development assistance for less well-off nations—effectively, a global equalization system—represents a purely redistributive source of revenue. It is the preferred form of redistributive taxation to the extent that one accepts the argument that vertical redistribution among households is the responsibility of nations themselves. An appropriate criterion for determining the allocation of tax burdens among nations is fiscal equity: a nation's contribution should be related to its ability to provide some international standard of public services and

---

[3] Other sources of revenue that are less related to our topic are discussed elsewhere in this volume, such as a global lottery, SDRs, private donations, and emigrants' remittances.

redistributive transfers to its citizens at comparable levels of taxation.[4] The principle of fiscal equity and how it could be made operational by a system of equalizing taxes and transfers has been discussed above. Here we point out the special problems that arise in an international setting.

Since there is no world government, donor nations must agree cooperatively on the system of taxes to impose on themselves. This is a serious issue both because achieving unanimous agreement is difficult when the sharing of burdens is at stake and because there may be disagreement about the principles that should be used. One advantage of the fiscal equity criterion is that it is a principle that can be defended on normative grounds, and that is used in a federal context.

Even if fiscal equity is a suitable objective, the global societal consensus may not be for full fiscal equity, that is, full social citizenship. Agreement must then be reached on the degree of partial fiscal equity to be pursued.

Consensus may differ among donor countries. It may then be sensible to begin with agreement among a subset of countries, what is referred to as flexible fiscal architecture and discussed in Atkinson (Chapter 2, this volume).

Putting fiscal equity into operation is more difficult in a global setting than in a federal setting. In the latter, subnational government tax-expenditure policies are likely to be much less diverse than is the case among nations. That means devising a representative standard level and mix of public services, transfers, and taxes against which to measure each nation's capacity is much more difficult internationally than among subnations in a federation.

A system of national contributions should take account of contributions that nations would otherwise be making voluntarily. There are two dimensions to this. First, fiscal equity would suggest that a nation's assigned contribution or tax take account of all voluntary contributions that the nation might make. Second, the possibility of crowding-out discussed earlier must be addressed. The system could give not only credit for such transfers but perhaps also an additional incentive, much as national tax systems give additional incentives for household voluntary contributions. If the agreement were only among a subset of nations, the additional problem must be recognized that voluntary contributions of non–participants could be crowded out.

Given these difficulties, especially that of devising a suitable measure of a nation's capacity to pay, it may be necessary to fall back on a macro indicator of fiscal equity. It would have to be one that can be measured on a consistent basis across nations and that also is a rough index of fiscal equity. The one that comes to mind is the nation's GDP.

11.4.2. *Taxes on International Externalities*

To the extent that certain types of activities give rise to externalities that transcend borders, taxes on these transactions would be potentially efficient sources of financing

---

[4] One could argue that a similar criterion should determine the allocation of development finance among less well-off nations, but the use of the funds is not our concern.

for global use. This is fully considered in Sandmo (Chapter 3), so there is little need to dwell on it here. However, some issues can be raised.

International agreement is obviously needed here as well in order to establish the authority to implement such a tax. The tax may be implemented by an international tax-collecting administration, or individual nations could be entrusted with collecting the tax and turning the proceeds over to an international authority.

The global externality tax (or taxes) will at least partly displace national taxes that are already in place. This implies that some revenues that are currently going to national governments will be diverted to a world authority. Some account would have to be taken of this at least for some period of transition. That might be easiest to do to if nations also have a tax against which credit can be given.

There will undoubtedly be design and compliance problems associated with externalities taxation to the extent that a given type of externality can come from diverse sources, some of which are difficult to monitor.

A global externality tax system will do little to address the fiscal equity objective, at least among donor nations. However, it will serve to reduce fiscal inequities between donor and recipient nations.

The problem of crowding-out of voluntary national contributions will apply with respect to revenues generated from this source as well.

Despite these problems, it is difficult to argue against 'free' revenues that can be obtained from a tax on global externalities. Presumably the same principle would apply to obtaining revenues from the use of world resources that are not owned by any nation. Thus, valuable resources from international waters (fish, minerals, etc.) and the use of the atmosphere or outer space, such as by satellites, might be regarded as legitimate common property resources of the world community.

11.4.3. *Taxes on Internationally Mobile Taxbases*

A third main source of finance for development use might be global taxation of taxbases that nations are liable to compete away because of international mobility, or that they underutilize because of monitoring problems. Examples include capital, especially financial capital, income (Grabel 2003), currency transactions (Nissanke, Chapter 4, this volume) and the taxation of internet transactions involving services that are difficult to monitor when they cross borders. In principle, international agreement should be possible for a harmonized increase in taxes of these types, given that non-cooperative tax competition is responsible for their low equilibrium tax rates. However, there are significant problems with relying on such taxes for financing new development assistance.

The incidence of these taxes will not bear a close relationship with fiscal equity considerations, so they may not be regarded as 'fair' taxes. In the absence of a need for development assistance, cooperative agreements on taxing mobile taxbases would likely lead to the taxes collected being returned to the nation of origin.

There will be significant administrative and compliance problems associated with taxing these transactions unless an international tax administration is instituted with significant powers of audit and information gathering.

Crowding-out of national voluntary contributions will be an issue.

These considerations would also apply to global taxes levied on specific transactions simply because they are good revenue sources. Narrow-based taxes will either be distortionary or inequitable, and their incidence among nations would bear little resemblance to a fair allocation based on fiscal equity.

REFERENCES

Artis, M. and F. Nixson (eds) (2001). *The Economics of the European Union*, 3rd edition. Oxford: Oxford University Press.

Barro, S. M. (2002). 'Macroeconomic Versus RTS Measures of Fiscal Capacity: Theoretical Foundations and Implication for Canada'. *Working Paper* 2002 No. 7. Kingston, Canada: Institute of Intergovernmental Relations. Available at: www.iigr.ca/publication_detail.php?publication=131.

Boadway, R. (2001). 'Inter-Governmental Fiscal Relations: The Facilitator of Fiscal Decentralization'. *Constitutional Political Economy*, 12: 93–121.

—— and M. Hayashi (1999). 'Country Size and the Voluntary Provision of International Public Goods'. *European Journal of Political Economy*, 15: 619–98.

Buchanan, J. M. (1950). 'Federalism and Fiscal Equity'. *American Economic Review*, 40: 583-99.

—— (1952). 'Federal Grants and Resource Allocation'. *Journal of Political Economy*, 60: 208–17.

Dahlby, B. (1996). 'Fiscal Externalities and the Design of Intergovernmental Grants'. *International Tax and Public Finance*, 3: 397–411.

Grabel, I. (2003). 'The Revenue and Double Dividend Potential of Taxes on International Private Capital Flows and Securities Transactions'. *WIDER Discussion Paper* No 2003/83. Helsinki: UNU-WIDER.

Keen, M. J. (1998). 'Vertical Fiscal Externalities in the Theory of Fiscal Federalism'. IMF Staff Papers, 45: 454–84.

McLure, C. E., Jr. (ed.) (1983). *Tax Assignment in Federal Countries*. Canberra: Centre for Research on Federal Financial Relations, ANU.

Oates, W. (1999). 'An Essay on Fiscal Federalism'. *Journal of Economic Literature*, 37: 1120–49.

Purdy, D. (2001). 'Social Policy', in M. Artis and F. Nixson (eds), *The Economics of the European Union*, 3rd edition. Oxford: Oxford University Press, 240–70.

Sandler, T. (1992). *Collective Action: Theory and Application*. Ann Arbor: University of Michigan Press.

Sandmo, A. (2000). *The Public Economics of the Environment*. Oxford: Oxford University Press.

Shibata, H. (1971). 'A Bargaining Model of a Pure Theory of Public Expenditures'. *Journal of Political Economy*, 79: 1–28.

Warr, P. G. (1983). 'The Private Provision of a Public Good is Independent of the Distribution of Income'. *Economic Letters*, 13: 207–11.

12

The Way Forward

ANTHONY B. ATKINSON

The aim of this project has been to advance thinking about new sources of finance for development. This final chapter draws together the main conclusions and considers how we can move forward towards concrete action.

12.1. THE CHALLENGE

Our starting point has been the widely recognized need for additional development funding if the Millennium Development Goals (MDGs) are to be achieved by 2015. All figures are estimates, and involve matters of judgement, but there is broad agreement about the magnitude. It seems reasonable to take a figure of additional US$50 billion, about the present total of official development assistance (ODA), as being required annually to achieve the international development goals. This means that we have *either* to double existing official development assistance *or* to find alternative sources of comparable magnitude *or* to abandon the MDGs. Here, we do not accept the third answer. The choice in raising additional funds is, therefore, between ODA and alternative sources—or a balance of the two.

This sharp presentation of the problem serves to focus our treatment of new and alternative sources of funding. *First, we are primarily concerned with the contribution of these sources to the finance of development.* Many of the proposals have multiple objectives. The creation of Special Drawing Rights (SDRs) was first proposed to ease problems of international liquidity, but here (Chapter 5) we are concerned with their potential role for development purposes. The Tobin tax was first proposed as a means of coping with financial volatility. Here (Chapter 4) we are primarily concerned with its potential as a generator of revenue to be used to finance development. Remittances from emigrants are used for many purposes, notably the financing of consumption by their families who have stayed. This consumption is important, but our concern here (Chapter 9) is with the contribution of remittances to funding investment for the future.

Our focus means secondly that we are *principally concerned with comparing different ways of funding the MDGs.* If a particular proposal is found to have shortcomings, this is not the end of the matter. We have to ask—what is the alternative? In the course of the book, we have made use of the insights of public economics, applied at a global plane. One of these insights is that one needs to specify the comparison. If the proposal were not to be adopted, what would come in its place? Here, in considering proposals for new sources, we ask how they would differ from an increase in ODA. How would their economic and social impact differ from that of an ODA increase? Or, more cynically, how far are different proposals simply different ways of dressing up an increased transfer from rich to poor countries?

In comparison with ODA, the closest are the proposal for the International Finance Facility (IFF) (Chapter 6), involving a forward commitment by donors of development funding, and for a development-focused allocation of SDRs (Chapter 5), which again involves the sovereign actions of governments. The other proposals are distinctly different, involving either global taxation or a global lottery or increased private transfers.

12.1.1. *What's New?*

Some of the proposals discussed in the book have been the subject of a large literature: the Tobin tax, for example. There have been a number of valuable overviews of the field, to which we have referred in Chapter 1. But our book is not without novelty. Even in the case of the Tobin tax, the fact that we are concentrating primarily on its revenue potential gives a different emphasis to Chapter 4, reflected in its title. In other cases, the field is less well tilled. In the case of the IFF, Chapter 6 provides, to our knowledge, the first external analysis of this proposal. There is relatively little economic literature on private donations for international development and the reasons why people give for one cause rather than another (Chapter 7). By applying approaches from public economics, we can derive new insights. This applies to the lessons from fiscal federalism (Chapter 11) that can be applied to multi-level policymaking with global concerns and national governments. It applies to the equivalence of taxes and the auctioning of quotas (Chapter 3).

The book contains some new ideas. Attention has been paid recently to the global lottery, but the authors of Chapter 8 have come up with a totally new mechanism—the global premium bond. The analysis of fiscal architecture in Chapters 2 and 11 has suggested the novel idea that national and individual taxbases can be divorced. By applying a method of subsidiarity, the national liability can be determined according to one formula, but national governments can choose to raise the revenue by other means. There is the application of the ideas of stochastic dominance to competition between the prize structures of different lotteries (Chapter 8).

12.2. CONCLUSIONS: NEW SOURCES OF FINANCE

Table 12.1 summarizes the main conclusions with regard to the seven proposals for new sources of development finance considered here. In each case, there is a brief description, and a summary of the potential contribution to the funding of development. The *first conclusion* is that the two global taxes considered could yield revenue of the magnitude required (tax on carbon use) or at least half of the requirement (CTT at a wholesale rate of 2 basis points). Moreover, the tax rates required for this purpose are an order of magnitude smaller than the tax rates proposed by those advocating these

Table 12.1. *New sources of development funding: summary of conclusions*

Source	Brief description	Potential to fund development?	Double dividend and cost?	Disadvantages	Main obstacles
Global environmental taxes	Tax on goods generating environmental externalities, with specific reference to a tax on use of hydrocarbon fuels according to their carbon content	Tax on high-income countries alone could raise revenue of US$50 billion. Tax rates required are order of magnitude smaller than those considered in proposals to halt global warming	Environmental gain as well as revenue. Tax borne according to final energy use	Distributional effect on households within high-income countries needs to be offset. Administrative cost of operating global tax	Requires general agreement of high-income countries. Account has to be taken of existing national taxes
Currency transactions tax (Tobin tax)	Tax on foreign currency transactions, covering a range of transactions (spot, forward, future, swaps and other derivatives)	Tax could generate US$15–28 billion for global public use. Tax rate considerably smaller than those considered in proposals to reduce exchange rate volatility	Reduces foreign exchange speculation. Tax passed on to final users	Final distributional effect and impact on real transactions hard to predict. Administrative cost of operating global tax	Requires general agreement
Creation of new Special Drawing Rights (SDRs)	Creation of SDRs for development purposes, with donor countries making their SDR allocation available to fund development	Allocation of US$25–30 billion could make significant contribution, but depends on frequency	Could have positive effect on the global macroeconomy	Impact on world economy not clear	Has to be ratified by 100 members with 85% of voting power
International Finance Facility (IFF)	Long-term, but conditional, funding guaranteed to the poorest countries by the donor countries. Long-term pledges of a flow of annual payments to the IFF would leverage additional money from the international capital markets	If introduced as planned could achieve flow of US$50 billion for 2010–15, building up from 2006 and falling to zero by 2020. Provides predictable and stable flows with agreed disbursement mechanism	Could have positive effect on the global macroeconomy	Cost of negotiation and administration of new organization. Difficult to ensure additionality. Administrative cost of establishing new institution. Problem of what happens after 2020	Requires sufficient donor countries to sign up, and to continue to make commitments. Involvement of all rich countries not required. Requires agreement on conditions to be attached to outflows

Increased private donations for development	Charitable donations by private individuals and firms. Measures to encourage private funding of development: tax incentives, global funds, corporate giving, and the Internet	Present flows marginal but important for psychological reasons. No sign of crowding out. Total charitable giving sizeable and potential for development to attract larger share	Giving benefits both donors and recipients	To the extent that total giving increased, through shifting consumer preferences, no direct cost; to extent that achieved at expense of other recipients, there is opportunity cost	Primarily individual action, but national governments can stimulate by income tax deduction. Link with use of funds important
Increased remittances from emigrants	Logistics (reducing cost of remittances), financial institutions (encouraging repatriation) and legal (regularising the status of migrants)	Remittances are a large, growing and relatively stable flow of funds. They can contribute to infrastructure projects. A reduction in transfer costs could significantly increase remittances	Transfer benefits both donors and recipients	Link to development uncertain	May run into money laundering and counter-terrorism legislation
Global lottery	Global lottery operated through national state-operated and state-licensed lotteries, with proceeds shared between national participants and an independent foundation established in conjunction with UN	Difficult to estimate but could reach US$6 billion a year	—	Ethical issues. Distributional burden borne by lower income groups, including low-income countries	Competition with national lotteries
Global premium bond	Global premium bond, parallel to national bonds with lottery prizes in place of interest; capital value preserved	Provides loan finance, volume hard to estimate	—	Crowding out of other government debt. Administrative cost	Competition with other borrowing

A.B. Atkinson

taxes on allocational grounds. The Tobin taxes proposed to 'put sand in the wheels of international finance' have been of the order of 10 or 20 basis points—ten times that considered here. The energy tax considered in Chapter 3 has a rate per metric ton of a tenth or a twentieth of those typically considered in the literature on global warming. The taxes are not, therefore, guaranteed to have the major behavioural impact, discouraging pollution and speculation, which has been sought. This conclusion has both negative and positive aspects. On the minus side, it means that the double dividend—of revenue plus improved functioning of the economy—may fall short on the second dimension. But it is revenue that is our concern here. The second aspect is positive, which is that the much more modest tax rates envisaged here are more acceptable and less likely to have disruptive economic consequences.

The *second conclusion* is that there are alternatives to global taxation. The IFF proposed by the UK government could, if it attracts sufficient support from other major donors, yield flows over the crucial period up to 2015 of the magnitude required. It is, of course, open to question how far this differs at heart from a commitment to expand ODA. The creation of SDRs for development purposes has been envisaged as raising some US$25–30 billion. This means that it could contribute a significant part of the total, but would need to be combined with other measures, particularly if such allocations were only to be made less frequently than annually. One such additional source is the global lottery, which is potentially the source of significant revenues, if agreement can be reached with national lotteries. A global premium bond could provide a flow of loan funding that would not be otherwise be available. Supporting roles could be played by increased remittances from emigrants, and, on a more modest scale, increased private donations.

In each case, however, we have to consider the extent of additionality. The *third conclusion* is that there is a distinct risk of crowding-out. A country signing up to the IFF may implicitly offset this commitment against its regular ODA. The same may apply to countries that transfer any new SDR allocation. Agreement to the introduction of a global tax may mean that governments feel less pressure to increase their ODA, or that firms are less likely to contribute to charitable funding of development. Measures to stimulate private donations may adversely affect other forms of giving. Issuing a global premium bond may crowd out other borrowing for development purposes, although this is less likely if it is targeted at the individual investor.

The next column in Table 12.1 summarizes the contribution to generating a double dividend. In other words, how far do the proposals have other advantages apart from the revenue raised? As already noted, the proposed tax rates are much lower than those advocated for other purposes, but both energy use and currency transactions taxes have potential to act as corrective taxes. There is an allocational benefit rather than a deadweight loss. In the same way, tax incentives to private donations and remittances by emigrants may act to encourage an activity that is undersupplied, a gift benefiting the recipient as well as the sender. The *fourth conclusion* is that there are possible double dividends, but they are a by-product but not the primary rationale of the proposals. The double dividend argument should not be over-sold.

The existence of a double dividend does not mean that there is no cost. With an ordinary tax, the burden of a tax generating $x billion can be said to consist of two parts: the $x billion that taxpayers hand over, and the additional deadweight cost (excess burden) due to the distortion of economic decisions. Where there is a double dividend, the second element becomes a benefit: decisions are improved by the corrective tax. But revenue is still raised. There are good reasons to expect that the taxes will be passed on to final users. This applies to energy taxes, where we have to follow through the full input-output implications. People tend to think immediately of the impact of a carbon tax on the fuel and transport costs of households, but energy costs enter also as inputs in other sectors. The operating costs of the financial sector, for example, will be increased, so that part may appear as higher prices for apparently unrelated products. In the case of the Tobin tax, we can regard it as an excise tax on all purchases according to their foreign exchange content. One disadvantage of the tax is that the final incidence is not easily determined. Part of the burden may well fall on developing countries: for instance, if the tax reduces the effective flow of remittances from emigrants. The other measures, too, may have costs. The increase in ODA that is effectively envisaged under the IFF has to be financed, and the future commitments may affect the budgetary position of donor countries. Tax relief for remittances by emigrants has a cost to the host countries. The *fifth conclusion* is that it is illusory to suppose that simply adopting an alternative funding route avoids all cost.

In considering both double dividends and cost burdens, one important consideration is the impact on the macroeconomy. It is the specific purpose of some measures, such as the creation of SDRs, to stimulate the world economy. Given that there is significant unemployment, and under-use of productive capacity, it may be possible to generate new resources at little or no real cost. Donor countries may, via the IFF, be able to engage in borrowing in a way that acts as a macroeconomic stimulus. In the opposite direction, a significant increase in funding for development may run into the absorption, or transfer, problems considered in Chapters 2 and 6. We have not attempted here to assess these macroeconomic arguments, but they are potentially important. A *sixth conclusion* is that the policy towards funding the MDGs has to be seen in conjunction with stimulating the global economy and with an eye to the absorption issue.

The fourth column in Table 12.1 identifies the main disadvantages of the different proposals. One common element is, *seventh conclusion*, the fact that we have only limited understanding of the economic impact of the different proposals, which is, of course, highly relevant to judging their final cost, as noted above. The final incidence of a global tax, such as the carbon tax, depends on the responses of firms and households that determine the ultimate general equilibrium. We can only guess that the impact of a currency transactions tax will be larger in countries more engaged in international trade. Views about the macroeconomic impact of SDR creation depend on how one believes that the world economy operates. We know relatively little about the impact of remittances from migrant workers. We know little about what influences the destination of private giving.

In considering the disadvantages, we need to bear in mind that we are comparing alternative ways of increasing development funding. Take, for example, the argument that the burden of a global lottery falls on low-income groups (discussed in Chapters 2 and 8). If the choice is a global lottery or nothing, then it seems likely that the recipients of the benefits from global lottery funding have lower incomes than the poor in rich countries who play the lottery. If, however, the alternative is increased ODA financed by higher income taxation, then the distributional argument does not favour the lottery.

The final column in Table 12.1 lists the main obstacles to the proposals. This naturally leads one to ask how they can be overcome. This is in part a question of design. How can they be made more compelling? In this book, we have identified a number of routes by which the design can be refined. In the case of the global lottery, the prize structure can be constructed in a way that helps differentiate the product from that of national lotteries and to avoid the possibly negative effects of astronomical prizes. We have described ways of increasing the efficiency of the market for remittances.

Overcoming the obstacles is in part a matter for political action. In the next section, we consider the possible role of different actors.

12.3. THE WAY FORWARD

How can we achieve the target level of an annual increase of US$50 billion in resources for development? The first point to be made is that the increase could quite realistically be achieved via ODA. Viewed in relation to previous aid achievements and aspirations, the US$50 billion increase seems quite feasible. If donors were to raise their ODA to 0.5 per cent of GNP, then the US$50 billion additional ODA would have been realized. Nor is an increase of ODA by existing donors the only route by which ODA could be increased. The world distribution of income is changing. The growth of middle-income countries means that they can be expected to come into the equation.

The funding of the MDGs could be achieved solely by increasing ODA. At the same time, it would require a step change from the present, going considerably beyond what has so far been promised. This is not going to be achieved overnight. The widening of the circle of aid donors is equally going to take time. Time is, however, of the essence. For this reason alone, it may be necessary to consider new sources. It may indeed be that consideration of negative aspects of alternatives may lead donor countries to be more willing to make the step change in ODA. In this book, we have considered seven such sources. While a carbon tax on its own might be sufficient to raise the required funds, this is not true of the other proposals and it is likely that any programme will consist of a *package of measures*. Such a package could be constructed by the UN and other international agencies, which would monitor its introduction. The enactment of the package would, however, involve a large cast of actors. Indeed, it is important from the standpoint of democratic accountability that there should be the widest possible engagement.

To begin with, there is an essential role for the *individual citizen*. Individuals can contribute significantly both by their private support and by their influence on governments. Individuals make generous donations to charity, but relatively little goes to development purposes. We have seen how there is considerable scope for the globalization of charitable giving. Increased support for development charities serves both the direct purpose of helping poor countries and the indirect purpose of demonstrating to governments of rich countries the concerns of their voters.

National governments are indeed the key actors. First, they have considerable independent impact. Acting alone, the government of a rich country can take steps to increase the flows of finance for development. A single country could, for example, allow income tax deductions for taxpayers making contributions to hometown associations (Chapter 9) that are funding community projects in the home country. A single country could launch a premium bond dedicated to development funding. A single country could decide to allocate to development purposes part of the proceeds from its national lottery. A single country could match out of public funds the amounts donated by its citizens to development charities.

Matching also applies at the national level, and governments may be more willing to provide funding where other countries are also participating. The logic of the International Finance Facility is that a number of countries join together in making the commitment. This brings us to the class of proposals where common action is required but it is sufficient for a significant subset of countries to agree. This includes the IFF and the global lottery. Finally, there are those proposals where the involvement of all donor countries is effectively necessary. This includes the creation of new SDRs and (probably) the carbon tax.

Our focus has been on the role of high-income countries, but, as stressed at the outset, we do not believe that this is the only important aspect. Within the context of the proposals considered here, there is much that developing countries can do to facilitate their effective enactment and to take forward the necessary dialogue.

Index

AAA credit ratings 117, 118, 119
absorptive-capacity issue 111, 122, 123–4, 129
Action Aid 151
Agreement on Internal Trade (Canada) 221
Ahtisaari, Martti 156
'aid fatigue' 9, 173
air travel tax 22
Asian crisis 90
asset markets, model of 62

Bank for International Settlement (BIS) 70
Barnado's 136
basket, band, and crawl (BBC) rule 67
Bill and Melinda Gates Foundation 138, 140
Brandt Commission report 90
Budd, Sir Alan 174
burden sharing, disproportionate 225–6, 232

Camdessus, Michel 91
Canada
    revenue generation 221
cancer 140
capital transaction tax 217
carbon tax 11, 21, 23, 24, 25, 26, 29–30, 31, 42,
        50, 239, 243
    revenue potential 47–9
Caritas Internationalis 137
'cash-substitute' instruments 69
Catholic Agency for International
        Development 137
'cause-related marketing' 148, 149, 151
Change for Good scheme 20, 149
charitable donations
    see donations, private
charities
    children's 13, 136, 137, 138, 139, 141, 145,
        146, 151
    children's contribution to 143, 152
    UK 136
'Chartist technical analysis' 63
Child Health Site 151
child labour 149
'click for good' websites 151
Clunies-Ross, A. 10, 48, 49, 71, 72, 83, 102
co-insurance strategy 187
common agricultural policy (CAP) 205
consumption efficiency 34

contagious diseases
    see infectious diseases
Continuous Linked Settlement (CLS) Bank 70–1
'corporate social responsibility' 148–9, 150
corporation tax 22
Crisis Management Initiative (CMI) proposal
        14, 157, 158, 165
currency transaction tax (CTT)
    see Tobin tax

debt instrument 171
debt relief 7, 105
decentralization 211, 223
development education 150, 160
    lottery's role in 168–9, 173, 174
development finance 11–12, 14
    new sources 4–6, 85–6, 208, 238–9, 240–1
        and ODA expansion 18–9
        economic impact 12, 87
        political cost 9–10
        requirements 1, 3
development goals, international 1
'differential tax incidence' 19, 25
donations, corporate 134, 148
    for international development 149
donations, online 150–1
donations, private 6, 13, 132–3, 152–3, 244–5
    for international development 134–5
        impact of income-level on 137, 140, 141
    for UNICEF 143–5
    for United Nations agencies 143, 146
    taxation 207–8
    United Kingdom 136
    United States 132, 138
    see also donors, individual
donor education 151–2
'donor fatigue'
    see 'aid fatigue'
donors, individual
    development funding 7, 13
    motives 138–41, 142
    super-rich 141–2, 147–8
    tax incentives to 146–7
    see also donations, private
'double dividend' 8, 11, 25–7, 38–9, 67, 242–3
drinking water 1, 2
Dutch disease effect 28, 123, 124, 189

education 12, 99, 103, 133, 134, 186–7, 190, 196,
        213, 218, 222, 223
   donations to 140, 141, 147
   gender equality in 1, 2
   primary 1, 2, 169
   role of MNCs 147
'education for development' 152
'elite donors' 137
emergency relief 134
environmental externalities 34–5, 40–1
   quota system 36–7, 37–8
environmental pollution
   in developing countries 41
environmental taxation 13, 25, 33, 35, 36
   distributional effects 39–40
   double dividend 38–9, 45
   models
      single country 50–2
      two-country 52–5
   theoretical principles 35–6
environmental taxation, global 6, 8, 49–50,
        216, 242, 243
   collecting 47
   design of 44–6
   imposition of 41–3
Equality and Efficiency 23
European Union (EU) 10, 20, 212, 221
   funding of ODA 3
exchange rate mechanism (ERM) crisis 64, 66, 76
exchange rate volatility 62, 65, 87
   see also foreign exchange (FXE) system; foreign
        exchange transactions
excise tax 216
externalities
   taxation on 13, 235–6

federation 223–4
   revenue generation in 213–16
fiscal equity 228, 229, 234, 234–5
fiscal federalism 23, 26, 210, 212–13
'fiscal response' 124–5
Fitch/IBCA 118
'flexible geometry' 7, 20–1
Food and Agricultural Organization (FAO) 142
Ford Foundation 138
foreign currency exchange (FXE) system 71
foreign direct investment (FDI) 180, 197
foreign exchange transactions 73–5, 77
   currency distribution 76
   geographical distribution 78
   taxation 68–9, 81–2, 205
fossil fuels 45, 47
free rider problem 10, 44–5, 50, 226
fuel tax protests, 2000 (Europe) 23

G7 countries 4, 70, 103, 128, 171
gambling 173–4
   taxation 216–17
gambling industry, global 164
gambling, online 162–4
Gaming Board for Great Britain 162
Gap 149
Gates, Bill 133, 147, 148
George Soros on Globalisation 99
Global Alliance for Improved Nutrition
        (GAIN) 150
'global altruists' 160
Global Fund to Fight Aids, Tuberculosis,
        and Malaria 148
'global funds' 147–8
'global greenbacks'
   see Special Drawing Rights (SDRs)
Global Health Fund 113
global lottery
   see lottery, global
*Global New Deal: A Modern Marshall Plan for the
        Developing World* 110
global public goods
   see public goods
'green' taxation
   see environmental taxation

'halo' effect 159
Hawking, Stephen 18
Her Majesty's Treasury 3, 110, 111
HIPC Initiative 105, 171
HIV/AIDS 1, 2, 138, 140, 169
HM Treasury-DFID
   development estimates 3
HM Treasury-DFID proposals
   on International Finance Facility 110–11, 112
hometown associations (HTAs)
   remittances by 188–9
Hunger Site 151

IDA-13 117–18, 122
ILO World Commission on the Social Dimensions
        of Globalization 6, 10
'implicit tax' 166
income disparity 210–11
income distribution 166, 202
   impact of remittances 178, 188, 189, 190
   impact on donor behaviour 137, 140, 141
income tax 19, 22, 23, 24, 25, 29, 143, 146,
        166, 196, 202, 204, 208, 218, 221, 231,
        234, 244, 245
'inconsistent trinity' thesis 58
incremental tax rate 201
infectious diseases 2, 103, 140

intergovernmental transfers 218–20, 225–6
International Aids Vaccine Initiative (IAVI) 148
International Air Transport Association (IATA) 22
International Bank for Reconstruction and
    Development (IBRD) 127, 147
International Development Association (IDA)
    112, 117, 122, 127, 147, 171
International Finance Facility (IFF) 4, 5, 6, 8, 9,
    21, 30, 121–2, 127–30, 242, 243
  disbursement of funds 114, 115, 117, 120–1
  donor commitment 114, 115, 118, 125
  features 110–11, 112–14
  governance structure 118–19
  in national accounts 126–7
  organizational costs 127
  revenue potential 120
International Monetary Fund (IMF) 20, 90,
    92, 95–6
  and development focused SDRs 105–6
IMF's Articles of Agreement 93, 94, 96, 97, 98,
    99, 103–4, 106
  SDRs allocation 6, 96, 103–4
  SDRs voluntary transfers 98
International Tax and Public Finance 17
Internet gambling
  see gambling, online

Kenen, P. B. 68, 69, 70
Keynes, John Maynard 27, 28, 99
Kohler, Horst 129
Kyoto Agreement 8

'logrolling' model 11
Lotteries (Regulation) Act, 1998 (India) 168
lottery gambling
  addiction 167–8
  ethical issues 167–8
  religious issues 167
lottery market 159–60
lottery operators 158–9
lottery, global 7, 14, 156–8, 159, 160–2, 244
  cross-country equity 165–6
  distributional effects 166–7
  revenue potential 164–5
  role in development education 168–9
  vs premium bond, global 173
lottery, national 158, 160–2
  India 162, 168
lottery, online 162
Lotto (game) 158, 159

'macroeconomic policy trilemma for open
    economies'
  see 'inconsistency trinity' thesis
malaria 2, 138, 140, 148

market speculation 65
Marshall, Alfred 34
Mendez, R. P. 71
Millennium Challenge Account (MCA) 4, 121
Millennium Development Goals (MDGs) 1, 2, 8,
    10, 19, 125, 140
  Africa 1
  domestic charities 146–7
  financial requirements 1, 11, 48, 108
  funding for 4–6, 11–12, 50, 90, 91, 105, 110,
    111, 112, 120, 121, 123, 128, 129, 152–3,
    168, 238–9, 243, 244
Millennium Summit, 2000 1
Money Transfer Organizations (MTOs) 191, 192
MoneyGram 191, 192
Monterrey Conference on Financing for
    Development, 2002 3, 6, 99, 111
Moody's 118
mortality, child 1, 2, 3
mortality, maternal 1, 2, 3
Multilateral Development Banks 127

natcoms 143–6, 151
national committees
  see natcoms
national governments
  development funding 20, 245
  taxation 20–1, 22
    environmental 47
National Trust (UK) 139
Natural History of the Rich 141
NetAid 151
New Partnership for African Development
    (NEPAD) 103
Nike 149
'noise traders' 61–2, 63
non-governmental organizations (NGOs)
  development funding 7
North American Free Trade Agreement
    (NAFTA) 221

Official Development Assistance (ODA) 1, 3, 4,
    13, 239, 244
  alternatives to 8–9
  funding of 3
  sources 18–9
Okun, Arthur 23
'online volunteering' 151
  see also voluntary work
Organization for Economic Cooperation and
    Development (OECD) 9, 25, 48, 59, 85,
    132, 133, 134, 139, 140, 152, 216, 223

Organization for Economic Cooperation and
    Development-Development Assistance
    Committee (OECD-DAC) countries
    funding for ODA 3, 4, 9, 25
Oxfam 6, 134, 151

Pareto optimality 34
payment vs payment (PVP) settlement 70
'payroll-giving' 147
peace 2, 103, 138
philanthropy
    see donations, private
Pigou, Arthur C. 34
Piguovian tax 35, 37
Pocantico Conference on Feasible Additional
    Sources of Finance for Development,
    2003 129
Pocantico Report 102
politically feasible Tobin tax (PFTT) 72
Poterba, James 44
poverty 41, 165, 168
    impact of remittances 188, 189–90, 197
    reduction 1, 2, 3, 8, 12, 105, 110, 112, 113, 147,
        166, 167, 211, 213
Poverty Eradication Action Fund 123
premium bond, global 4, 30
    modalities 171–2
    vs lottery, global 173
premium bond, national 169, 169–70
    United Kingdom scheme 169
principle of targeting 35
'prize bond scheme' 169
'problem gamblers' 167
production efficiency 34
public economics 17
public finance, global 14
public goods 1–3, 35, 43, 50, 59, 173, 225–6,
    227, 233
    lottery proceeds to 157, 160
    national 203, 211, 213, 219, 220, 222, 223
    SDRs for 91, 99–100, 101–2, 103, 104, 106, 108

real time gross settlement system (RTGS) 70, 71
Red Cross 136–7
redistribution 12, 19, 39, 40, 43, 44, 46, 52, 177,
    201, 211, 212, 214–5, 217, 220, 222, 223,
    224–5, 226–32, 233, 234
'regulatory capture' 159
remittances by migrants 6, 14, 177–8, 185,
    197, 238
    costs 191–5, 197–8
        reduction of 195–6, 198
    development impact 188–90, 196, 197
    international markets 191
    motives 186–7

regional trends in 178–80
stability 187–8
taxation 196
to developing countries 181–3
reserve system, global 94–5, 99
'reverse aid' 95
Rich and the Super-Rich, The 141

Save the Children 136, 137, 145, 151
Schimdt, R. 70, 71
'scratch cards' 158, 167
security transaction tax (STT) 85
seigniorage 217
Shibata-Warr neutrality theorem 225, 231
social citizenship 224
'social lotteries' 167
Soros Foundation 138
Soros proposal
    for SDRs 99, 101–2, 103, 104
Soros, George 91
Spahn, P. B. 66
Special Drawing Rights (SDRs) 6, 13, 28, 93, 238
    allocation 93–4, 96–7
    definition 90
    development focused 99–100, 102–3, 105, 107–8
        creation of 103–4
        issue and management of 108–9
    features 90–1, 92
    voluntary transfers 98
speculative bubbles 61–2, 63, 65
Stability and Growth Pact 9
Standard & Poor's 118
Stern, Nicholas 202
Stiglitz, J. 95
subnational governments 222–3
    cooperative redistribution 226–7
    revenue generation 220–1, 230–2
    taxes on 227–230
subsidies 206
supranational taxation 205–6

'tax/expenditure incidence' 19
taxation, global 6, 7, 21–2, 200–2, 233, 236–7
    for international development 202–4
tax authority, global 12, 22
T-bills 69
'terms of trade' 27
Theory of Public Finance 19
Thomas Cook 191
Tobin, James 8, 59, 60, 70, 79
Tobin tax 6, 8, 11, 13, 21, 24, 59–61, 62–3, 72, 83,
    205, 238, 239, 242, 243
    and market efficiency 61–2, 63
    collection 70–1

criticism 61, 65
enforcement 70, 86
political feasibility 72
revenue potential 64, 79–83, 84
Tobin Tax, The 8
tourist tax 24
trade tax 216
'tragedy of commons' 34, 45
'transfer problem' 27–8, 243
Triffin's dilemma 90
'two birds' test 10, 11
two-tier tax system 66–7, 85
tuberculosis 138, 140, 148
Turner, Ted 20, 133, 138, 141, 143, 147, 148

UN Foundation 138, 140, 142–3
United Nations (UN) 1, 10, 18, 70, 71, 156, 157, 159, 200, 205, 244
United Nations (UN) agencies 13, 138, 148
funding 142, 156
private donations 133, 142, 146
United Nations (UN) Volunteers 141, 151
United Nations Children's Fund (UNICEF) 13, 137, 138, 142, 146, 149, 151, 152, 153
private donations 6, 13, 20, 133, 136, 143–5
corporate donations 149
natcom contributions 143–6
United Nations Conference on Trade and Development (UNCTAD) 1
United Nations Development Programme (UNDP) 142, 165
United Nations High Commissioner for Refugees (UNHCR) 146
United Nations Population Fund (UNFPA) 142
United States

funding for ODA 3
funds for MCA 3–4
United States (US) Congress 96
United States (US) Peace Corps 141
UNU-WIDER and UN-DESA Project on Innovative Sources for Development Finance 110, 153, 156
user fees 217

Vaccine Fund/Global Alliance for Vaccines and Immunization (GAVI) 148
vaccines 2, 13, 138, 148
value added tax (VAT) 22, 23
video lottery terminals (VLTs) 158
Voluntary Service Overseas (UK) 141
voluntary work 133, 141, 151

Western Union 191, 192
World Bank 4, 48, 70, 101, 127, 147, 205
delivery channel 113
global public goods 103, 108
World Commission on the Social Dimensions of Globalization 6, 10
World Development Report 1999/2000 48
World Food Programme (WFP) 142, 150, 151
World Health Organization (WHO) 142
World Lottery Association (WLA) 159
World Trade Organization (WTO) 221
Worldwide Fund for Nature 7

Zacatecas
development projects 188–9
Zedillo, Ernesto 1
Zedillo Report 1, 2, 3
on SDR allocation 91, 95, 97, 98, 105